Retrieving Women's History

BERG / UNESCO COMPARATIVE STUDIES

Women and Economic Development: Local, Regional and National Planning
Strategies, edited by Kate Young

Contents

Contents

Preface

The study of the role of women in history has only recently received the attention it deserves. The aim of this book is to investigate the role played by women in ancient, more recent, and contemporary history and to identify theoretical and methodological approaches to research. One significant contribution of women's studies to the discipline of history has been to challenge the form and emphasis of traditional history by the use of gender as a category of historical analysis. Incorporating women's activities alters the topics studied, the methodologies employed and the conclusions reached by historians.

The book has its origins in the International Meeting of Experts on 'Theoretical frameworks and methodological approaches to studies on the role of women in history as actors in economic, social, political and ideological processes' convened by Unesco in Paris in November 1984 as part of the Unesco sub-programme on 'Research, training and international cooperation concerning the status of women'. Several of the chapters in this book are based on papers read at the International Meeting; others were commissioned by Unesco to round out the international coverage.

The themes treated here represent distinct but closely inter-related topics. First, consideration is given to the conceptual and methodological issues raised by advances in the study of women in history. Alternative approaches have been proposed towards a redefinition of historical concepts resulting from a new perception of women as active agents of change. The omission of women from the historical record distorted the perception of past events; their inclusion broadens the topics examined and leads to a reconceptualisation of such issues as work and politics. A second area of inquiry addresses perspectives on women, work and the family, notably the geographic variations and historical evaluation of the sexual division of labour both within and outside the household. Women's history has expanded the scope of labour history by noting women's economic role, the connections between the family and the economy, and between waged and unwaged labour over time. Exploring the relationship between production and reproduction heightens the historical understanding of the complexities of work and family life as influenced by differing modes of production and politics. Thirdly, state policies towards women and the links between women and the political sphere are analysed. A broader consideration of the relationship between women, the state, and politics encompasses not only exceptional women but also women's political rights and their representation in political affairs. The final section of the book provides an overview of women's roles and the historiography of women in various geo-cultural regions of the world. These chapters examine the materials available to researchers in these areas, the treatment of women by scholars, and religious writings on women.

This collection of studies provides valuable synthetic and up-to-date research on women's history, which is aimed both at those who study specifically the condition of women and at historians interested in furthering the field of their inquiry. It also provides reference materials for researchers and academic curricula.

The contributors are responsible for the choice and presentation of the material in their chapters; their opinions are not necessarily those of Unesco and do not commit the Organisation.

Introduction

S. JAY KLEINBERG

Historians searching for evidence about women's history have encountered the phenomenon of women's invisibility; women have been systematically omitted from accounts of the past. This has distorted the way we view the past; indeed it warps history by making it seem as though only men have participated in events thought worthy of preservation and by misrepresenting what actually happened. As historians of women have addressed themselves to the question of invisibility they have focused on four primary areas of investigation. The first of these is *work*, which is defined not merely as work for wages but includes all productive endeavours whether directly recompensed or not. The second is *family*, which includes patterns of household organisation and their relation to economic and political structures. The third area is *politics* including both formal and informal political movements and activities and the fourth is *ideology/culture/religion*: their impact upon women, women's participation in them and the ways in which they shape male-female interactions and men's and women's roles in society.

Reinstating women in historiography can lead us to change our basic understanding of what history itself is. Do we, for example, need to adopt different chronologies if we write women into the historical record instead of ignoring them? In other words how relevant are the traditional historical time schemes for women? The late Joan Kelly opened this area of inquiry in an essay asking, 'Did women have a Renaissance?' in which she put forward four criteria for gauging the relative expansion or contraction of women's power and determining the quality of their historical experience during the Renaissance. These criteria were: the regulation of female as compared with male sexuality; women's and men's relative economic and political roles, including women's access to property, political power, and the education or training necessary to that work, property, and political power; women's cultural roles, including ability to shape the outlook of their society, and their access or otherwise to the education and/or institutions to do this; and lastly, the prevailing ideology about women.[1]

These same criteria, or variations on them, could be used to evaluate the status of women in any society and the impact of events upon them and their place in their community. Historians at the Unesco Meeting of Experts touched on similar areas of inquiry when they asked whether the national events traditionally used to organise historical data have the same relevance for women as they do for men. For example, does the periodisation dividing Latin American history into pre-conquest, colonial, and national eras hide more about women's experience than it reveals? Are these political demarcations the most pertinent way to divide history into significant time spans? Should they still be used if they mask more than they reveal about the majority of the population? If we were to consider alternative chronologies, what would they be?

To what extent is the history of women the same as feminist history? To what extent does writing about women's past imply an ideological unity or common set of references among those who undertake it? Certainly the study of women can lead to the rethinking of institutions, of modes of production, of ideological, religious, political, and social systems. Several of the chapters which follow suggest that power in a society may reside in informal as well as formal institutions. By examining female political participation we may uncover informal but nonetheless real areas of power and expand our understanding of the relationship between the private and public sectors. This, in turn, may lead to a re-evaluation of what politics is. It might also lead to a critical appraisal of decision-making bodies and processes at any level which legislate for or about women, but in which there are few or no female representatives.

To what extent does writing women back into history lead us to re-examine the institutions and events which have been the traditional objects of historical inquiry? Occasional women have had power in the traditional sense, have been queens or otherwise 'great'

1. Joan Kelly, 'Did Women have a Renaissance?', in *Women, History and Theory: The Essays of Joan Kelly*, Chicago, University of Chicago Press 1984.

women. But emphasis on individual greatness ignores the vast majority – of women as well as men. As historical understanding has branched out from political and military history into economic, social, demographic and labour history it has become easier to see women as active participants in the lives of their families, their economies and their societies, and to attend to the particularities of sex, class, race, religion, and region in such as way as to make useful comparisons across those categories possible. Historians of Africa, for example, have demonstrated that a feminist perspective on African history leads to a different understanding of the economies of different areas once women's agricultural labour is included as work, rather than ignored as though it did not exist. Previous historians had simplified the complexity of African society by completely omitting women's economic contribution. Analysing the sexual division of labour in societies with different modes of production heightens our historical understanding of the impact that capitalist or other external penetration had on those societies. Including women in the economic history of an area provides a much fuller picture of what economic change actually entails. Africa is just one example; it could be replicated for virtually any nation or community. Close examination of economic change has led historians to query the extent to which complementary roles for women and men in traditional societies imply women's subordination or their equality, instead of making assumptions based upon incomplete information or cultural biases. The impact that the colonial experience had on the writing of history, the perception and reality of gender roles, and the ways in which colonialism itself affected gender relationships are also important.

Writing the history of women broadens the entire field of historical research. It does this by generating new questions and expanding the sources we use to answer them. History has traditionally relied upon written records: diaries, memoirs, account books, compilations of laws, censuses, tax lists, and the like. These sources present problems for historians of women. In the first place, women are less likely to be the authors of written documents. In many parts of the world female illiteracy is significantly higher than that of males and less affluent women are much less likely to leave written accounts of their daily activities, thoughts, or feelings. Secondly, many of the official records either omit women through prejudice or neglect or write about them in a biased way. Occupational censuses, for example, frequently ignore women's work. This provides historians with an opportunity to expand the sources upon which they rely. Oral history, artefact interpretation, iconography, and folklore can be added to the historians' repertoire, increasing our data sources about the past. Traditional sources can also be used in new ways and re-examined to fill in the gaps in our knowledge. History will be a more accurate reflection of human experience for our endeavours. We shall all be richer for the increased understanding we gain about the development of economic, social, ideological, and political relations.

Part I

Theoretical and Methodological Issues in the Study of Women in History

Introduction to Part I

The chapters presented in Part I document the extent to which women have been omitted from the historical record. It is suggested that historians' own understanding of what is important forms the basis for the history they write and the topics they select. In so far as this is the case, each generation rewrites history based upon its current concerns and reinterprets documents and other materials in the light of those concerns. The inclusion of women in the historical record and the rewriting of history to take account of women's activities therefore depended, at least to some extent, upon social pressure.

Joan Scott places the awakening of interest in the history of women in the context of the women's liberation movement of the 1970s. The growth in women's studies courses in that decade reflected the political awareness of university students and faculties and their desire to know more about women in history, in literature, in the arts, sciences, and social sciences. The emergence of interdisciplinary women's studies programmes and of journals devoted to the scholarly study of women mirrored that awareness and, at the same time, legitimised it by providing outlets and a market for the products of that scholarship. From a handful of courses and a few women's studies programmes in 1970 to thousands of courses and hundreds of programmes today, women's studies has grown enormously in numerical and intellectual importance.

All five chapters in Part I analyse the types of history which have been most amenable to the incorporation of women. It has been suggested that part of the reason for the growing number of studies has been the reawakened interest in social history pioneered by the French Annales school, the use of computers to analyse large quantities of data, and the general trend towards the incorporation of the supposedly inarticulate into the historical record. Women were not the focus of historical discourse as long as history was primarily an analysis of wars which women did not fight (though that itself

3

*reflects a battlefield rather than a social or economic analysis of war),
of parliaments in which they did not sit, or of empires that they did
not conquer. But even where history itself is broadened beyond a
study of power and might, as both Davin and Imam discuss, women
may still be omitted because of the way the questions are asked or
the way that historians themselves see the world. In this way labour
history became the study of (male) trades' unionists and work was
defined as paid wage labour. Similarly, histories of agriculture
concentrate on cash crop farming to the neglect of women's agricultural activities. Ethnographers and historians either ignored or
downgraded this work, negating the significance of women's economic activities.*

*Where women are made invisible by historians, as Imam points
out, reality is distorted and we are left with an inadequate representation of the past. Both Davin and Perrot discuss the literary,
iconographic, oral and material sources which can be used to reincor-
porate women's experience into the historical record. Kader calls
particularly for the use of hitherto under-utilised sources such as
folklore, folk traditions, and popular religious practices. Scott considers the wealth of documentary material collected if not catalouged
in European and American libraries, and Imam documents the way in
which male bias and western ethnocentricity can distort the reading
of the evidence. Kader criticises the 'static, idealised caricature' of
Muslim women and argues for detailed local studies that can adequately represent the diversity of their experience.*

*All five contributors to Part I believe that 'invisibility' results from
the ways in which historians have hitherto disregarded women and
the fact that the sources that document women's activities have been
underused or neglected. These chapters show how they might be
used for the writing of more significant and comprehensive historical
accounts which would rewrite women back into the historical record.*

1

The Problem of Invisibility

JOAN WALLACH SCOTT

Since the early 1970s and the rebirth of political movements for
women's rights, national and international attention has focused on
women. The declaration of the United Nations Decade for Women
brought not only statements from government representatives and
feminist leaders about the importance of women in every aspect of
social life, but determined efforts on the part of advocacy groups to
achieve improvement in women's education, economic situation,
social status and political participation. As a result, discussions by
and about women play an important role in contemporary political
debate. Indeed, what the nineteenth century dubbed 'the woman
question', is a visible and central issue. It would be hard to imagine a
history of this age written that did not include mention of the
emergence of women as agents of historical change and as the object
of policy considerations.

Yet historians searching the past for evidence about women have
confronted again and again the phenomenon of women's invisibility. Recent research has shown not that women were inactive or
absent from events that made history, but that they have been
systematically left out of the official record. In the evaluation of
what is important, of what matters to the present in the past,
women as individuals or as a definable group rarely receive mention. The story of the development of human society has been told
largely through male agency; and the identification of men with
'humanity' has resulted for the most part in the disappearance of
women from the record of the past. In a way this is the most
troubling and difficult of the findings of historians of women in
recent years. For if we discount the notion of deliberate misogyny
or of a male conspiracy to deprive women of social value, how can
we explain the fact that women were there, but forgotten or ig-

nored, 'hidden from history' in the phrase Sheila Rowbotham used? And what can we do to assure that today's efforts, too, will not somehow disappear from the history books our children and grand-children will read?

The answers to these questions must be tied to analyses of history itself, and to an understanding of the relationship of official histories to the politics of any age. Beyond this, we have to figure out how sexual difference (the understanding of the meaning of differences between men and women) figured in politics and the writing of history. This is a large task and one that, for purposes of this paper, puts the cart before the horse. It takes us to the end point of a complex and interesting movements among historians, the attempt to conceptualise and to write a history of women. Nonetheless it is worth mentioning, for in one way or another the problem of invisibility is central to the women's history that has been produced during the past fifteen years.

In this chapter, I attempt to summarise the major developments in the field of women's history. My major focus is on Western Europe and North America from the eighteenth century to the present, since that is my own area of expertise. My approach is not so much to review all the substantive findings of a diverse and rich literature, for I and others have done that and our essays are available in print,[1] but to look at how the field developed, its discovery of sources, its development of methods and its formula-tion of analytic categories, its theoretical explorations, and its attempts to address the increasingly complex problem of invisibil-ity. The problem of invisibility is at the heart of theoretical and methodological approaches that have emerged in the past ten or fifteen years.

---

1. See, for example, my review article and that of Olwen Hufton in *Past and Present* 101 (1983); Barbara Kanner's essays in *Suffer and be Still*, ed. Martha Vicinus, London, Methuen, 1980 and *A Widening Sphere*, Bloomington, Ind., Indiana University Press, 1977 and her book *Women of England from Anglo-Saxon Times to the Present*, Hamden, Conn., Archon Books, 1979; also the survey compiled by Barbara Sicherman, William Monter, Joan Scott and Kathryn Sklar, *Recent United States Scholarship on the History of Women*, Washington, DC, American Historical Association, 1981.

The Generation and Diffusion of Women's History: Institutions

The practice of women's history was nurtured in university settings in the United States much earlier and with greater success than anywhere else. (The reasons for this have yet to be fully studied. There is no question that the civil rights movement of the 1960s spurred demands for women's equality, as the anti-slavery movement of the 1840s and '50s had also produced demands for female rights. But the women's movement also developed with official encouragement, as the American government sought ways to promote affirmative action, encourage women's entry into various professions, and organise local committees on the status of women. There is important work to be done on the connections in the American experience between economic expansion, government policy, movements for social justice and feminist movements.) As feminist students turned their attention to the university curriculum, seeing it as a bastion of male power, they demanded courses that would let them address their current political concerns. Courses on women in the past – what was referred to as 'herstory' – would provide exemplary role models for students, documentation of their claims that women had long been oppressed, and evidence about women's political movements that might offer ideas for contemporary strategy. The student demand was willingly met by a small number of historians – most of them women – who improvised syllabuses and courses, often teaching these in addition to their regular course load. Many of these historians were themselves active in the women's caucuses of the professional historical associations, seeking to increase the numbers and improve the status of women historians.[2]

In the US courses in women's history developed in the larger context of the 'women's studies' movement, an attempt to rectify the absence of attention to women in the curriculum as a whole. At some universities, earliest, in fact, at the state universities, interdisciplinary programs quickly came into being. At others, no formal structure linked individual courses, but those who taught them met to discuss methods, approaches, sources. Locally, the women's

2. For an important account of the ties between the civil rights movement of the 1960s and the feminist movement see Sarah Evans, *Personal Politics: The Roots of Women's Liberation in the Civil Rights Movement and the New Left*, New York, Knoff, 1978.

studies programs provided faculty, who were otherwise isolated in their departments, with networks of intellectual exchange and political support. The National Women's Studies Association provided a forum for intense debate about the future of scholarship and its implications for women's politics. Several journals were founded to publish new scholarship and promote debate, among them *Signs*, *Feminist Studies* and the *Women's Studies Quarterly*.

As centres for both political advocacy and academic inquiry, women's studies' programmes faced a difficult problem of scholarly legitimacy. They had to prove their academic integrity to dubious colleagues – those who disapproved of any interdisciplinary programmes and those who found the explicit connection between politics and scholarship a violation of the academy's commitment to impartiality or objectivity.[3] In addition, there was debate among women scholars themselves about the advisability of locating studies of women in separate enclaves; the danger of 'ghettoisation' was a real one, for it could result in the continued marginalisation of women in the university and in the curriculum. In fact, a kind of dialectical relationship developed. The separate existence of women's studies courses permitted intense focus on women and furthered important and innovative interdisciplinary research. Furthermore, the programmes developed a certain visibility and, in some institutions, the ability to establish ties with traditional departments. As professors published and students wrote theses of high quality, the legitimacy of the women's studies enterprise gained ground. Funding from the National Endowment for the Humanities and from private foundations, especially in the 1970s from the Ford Foundation, additionally enhanced the standing of women's studies in the academy and permitted the creation of some 35 university-based research institutes, now coordinated by the National Council for Research on Women.[4] The interest of publishers in promoting women's studies research and the apparently positive response of the 'market' (a market created in part by women's studies courses) added to the visibility and respectability of the field. Indeed, one measure of growing academic legitimacy seems to have been the

3. Indeed the choice of 'women's studies' represented a retreat from the more overtly political title 'feminist studies'. The program at Stanford University, established in 1980, was the first to identify itself as feminist in its title.

4. The NCRW is located in New York and is headed by Mariam Chamberlain who as a programme officer at the Ford Foundation helped to fund the individual research institutes.

very recent willingness of the private universities, especially the prestigious institutions such as Yale, Princeton and, now, Harvard, to accept women's studies programmes in their midsts. Another indication is the increasing evidence in traditional university courses of material on women and the incorporation in doctoral and faculty research of questions about women and gender.

Women's history scholars found additional encouragement in the decision of the Berkshire Conference of Women Historians[5] to sponsor major conferences annually or bi-annually. These conferences became the meeting ground for individuals working on similar topics and they were the place at which ideas were exchanged and major conceptual advances promulgated. With national and international participation, the Berkshire Conference exemplifies the strength and diversity of approaches to women's history. It is one of the institutional bases on which the field's visibility and influence has been built.

Taken together, the institutional influences have been vital for women's history in the United States. Despite continuing questions about whether the subject is really serious, and despite the need for continual attention to the status of women's history courses and the participation of women in meetings of professional associations, the impact of the new field is hard to deny. Historians seem to have learned to pay attention to women's history; they are familiar with some of its best exponents, if not with all its internal interpretive debates. In comparison with the situation of women's history in other western European countries – where it seems still marginal to 'mainstream' historical production – women's history in the United States has achieved a measure of recognition. This must be attributed at least in part to the fact that the field has been able to establish a secure foothold in the academy. That foothold has been extremely important for the size, quality and success of the movement. One question for comparative discussion ought to be the extent to which the US experience is unique, or to which its elements can be adopted elsewhere. In countries where academic institutions are not well-financed or central to the production of information, where ought women's history to be located? Who

5. The Berkshire Conference was founded in 1929 by women historians looking for support and some influence in the male-dominated American Historical Association. It was a purely professional group until its decision in 1973 to promote scholarly research on the history of women.

ought to write and publish women's history? These questions of institutional location and diffusion of information are political as well as practical and they must be addressed by feminist scholars as they pursue their research and writing.

Sources

Source material for historians of women has not been difficult to find. Traditional archival and published sources turned out to be rich in materials about women, once the search for them began. Indeed, the question of invisibility is most apparent in relation to source materials. Historians interested, for example, in major wars and revolutions have simply gone back to the usual repositories and uncovered valuable descriptions and information that were collected, but never used explicitly to write about women.[6] Collections of family papers and letters have revealed information about the texture of women's lives and family relationships. Trade union congresses and political party publications contain important information on women's membership and economic situation, and on the policies and debates of those organisations about questions relating to women. And government documents, ranging from census and civil records to social investigators' reports on urban poverty, turn out to have vast quantities of information about the economic and political experiences of women. It is clearly not the absence of information about women, but the sense that such information was not relevant to the concerns of 'history' that led to the invisibility of women in the formal accounts of the past.

The discovery of sources for women's history was stimulated by the parallel development in the 1970s of the field of social history. Influenced variously by the development of quantitative methods of analysis (and particularly by refinements of historical demography), by the French *Annales* school's interest in the details of ordinary life, and by English humanist Marxist scholars (such as E.P. Thompson, Eric Hobsbawm and Raymond Williams), social his-

6. For example we now have collections such as Darlene Levy and Harriet Applewhite's *Women in Revolutionary Paris 1789–1795*, Urbana, Ill. and London, University of Illinois Press, 1979; articles such as Keith Thomas's, 'Women and the Civil War Sects', in *Crisis in Europe 1560–1660*, ed. T. Aston, 1965; and books such as Richard Sites's, *The Women's Liberation Movement in Russia 1860–1917*, Princeton, NJ, Princeton University Press, 1979.

tory insisted on the importance of the experience of various groups of people (peasants, workers, teachers, businessmen, women) as a focus for historical investigation. The point was to gauge the impact of large-scale processes of change (demographic expansion, secular-isation, industrial capitalism, the growth of nation-state) on the lives of members of a society, to understand these processes in terms of the diversity of human experience. Not only was it necessary to look at formal political organisation or at labour force participation, as conventional historians had done at least since the nineteenth century, but information was needed as well as 'private' experience, family relationships and informal community practices and ties. Social history insisted that history was not only a narrative of statesmanship, diplomacy and war (what Jane Austen had dismissed as 'the quarrels of popes and kings, with wars and pestilence in every page; the men so good for nothing and hardly any women at all.') Instead, history covered a broader terrain which included all aspects of society and social organisation. In the course of this turn to the details of all kinds of human experience and to consideration of family and community, as well as of economy and politics, information about women inevitably entered the picture.[7]

In addition to the sources opened up by social history, those searching for information on women encountered libraries built by earlier generations of feminists to house the 'proof' of women's capabilities and accomplishments. These libraries, often in the form of personal collections, contained published writings by and about women from every historical period and country, journals devoted to women's causes, private papers written by feminist political activists, letters and diaries. Dating most often from the moments of major feminist activity in the past (the 1840s and 50s and then the 1890s through the 1920s in the United States, the 1860s onward in Britain, the 1880s, and 90s through the 1930s in France), these collections are arsenals of intellectual weaponry, assembled to push forward the struggle for women's rights.[8] Those who compiled them understood the value of historical documentation for the

7. Austen, cited in Bonnie G. Smith, 'The Contribution of Women to Modern Historiography', *American Historical Review* 89 (1984), p. 721.
8. Examples of such collections are: the Bibliothèque Marguerite Durand, the Archives Marie-Louise Bouglé at the Bibliothèque Historique de la Ville de Paris, and the Fonds Gabrielle Duchêne at the Université de Paris (Nanterre), the Arletta Jacobs-Gerritsen collection at the University of Kansas, the Holden collection at Princeton University and the Schlessinger Library at Radcliffe College.

political fight they waged and they were determined to leave to posterity the evidence that would bolster the cause. Interestingly, the materials in these archives remained largely invisible for many years, uncatalogued and unused.[9] Only in the context of a reemerging feminist movement did their contents come to light.

Methods and Theories

On first appearance there has been no definable methodology associated with women's history. Some historians have employed straightforward political narrative to tell the story of women's suffrage movements; others have taken a more analytic stance in attempting to locate that story in a broader social context or to use it to shed light on unexplored aspects of politics. Similarly, biographers have detailed the lives of famous and not-so-famous women in much the same way historians have always written biography. Those interested in economic activities have collected data on jobs and wages and union membership; those interested in the family have, like any historical demographer, culled numbers from civil records and censuses and measured changes in the size of households over time.

Much of this work, moreover, has remained within the interpretive framework of its approach, stressing the causality of immediate political issues, or individual influences on a life, or the effects of capitalism, or the determining impact of age of marriage on family size. As long as women's history has addressed itself to making women visible in existing historiographical frameworks, it has contributed new information, but not a distinctive methodology. In a sense, it could be said that the task of making women visible serves a compensatory purpose: it insists that women were actors in the past and provides information to prove that. Its effect is to supplement the picture we have traditionally had; sometimes even to change that picture. One historian, for example, has shown that the Renaissance was not a renaissance for women.[10] Others have argued that technology did not emancipate women either at work or at

9. For an interesting history of the 'discovery' of the Fonds Marie-Louise Bouglé see Maîte Albistur's introduction to the inventory of the collection, which she prepared.

10. Joan Kelly-Gadol, 'Did Women Have a Renaissance?', in *Becoming Visible*, ed. R. Bridenthal and C. Koontz, Boston, Mass., Houghton Mifflin, 1977.

home;[11] others that the 'Age of Democratic Revolutions' excluded women from politics;[12] still others that the rise of the 'affective nuclear family' constrained women's individual development.[13] Yet another group of historians has argued that advances in medical science, while lengthening women's lives, deprived them of knowledge, autonomy and a sense of feminine community.[14] And Margaret Rossiter has eloquently demonstrated how the great breakthroughs for women into scientific careers were accompanied by greater invisibility for them in their chosen professions.[15] These findings advance interpretation, but they do not address directly certain more fundamental theoretical and methodological problems. These have begun to be addressed as historians ask *why* and *how* women become invisible to history when, in fact, they were social and political actors in the past.

The search for answers to these questions has resulted in an important discussion about the usefulness of gender as a category of analysis. How can we understand the operations of ideas about sexual difference (the different meanings attributed to masculine and feminine in societies of the past) in society and culture? How is the sexual division of labour (the different roles attributed to women and men) reproduced? What is the relationship between ideas of sexual difference, social organisation, and political ideologies? These questions require the elaboration of new methodologies and new analytic perspectives for historians.

Some historians have turned to various theories as a way of developing these new perspectives. The most influential of these theoretical formulations seem to have been provided by (*a*) Marxists; (*b*) the writings of Jacques Lacan, and (*c*) the writings of Michel Foucault. Marxist scholars have addressed themselves especially to the sexual division of labour and its relationship to capitalist development. Arguing that the ideology of separate spheres (male –

11. See my summary of this material in the *Scientific American*, Sept. 1982.

12. See for example Linda Kerber, *Women of the Republic*, 1980, Chapel Hill, NC, University of North Carolina Press, 1980; Mary Beth Norton, *Liberty's Daughters: The Revolutionary Experience of American Women*, Boston, Mass., Little, Brown & Co., 1980; and Susan Miller Orkin, *Women in Western Political Thought*, Princeton, NJ, Princeton University Press, 1979.

13. B. Ehrenreich and D. English, *For Her Own Good: 150 Years of the Experts' Advice to Women*, Garden City, NY, Anchor Press, 1978.

14. See the special issue of *Penelope* on 'Les Femmes Soignantes', 1981.

15. Margaret Rossiter, *Women Scientists in America: Struggles and Strategies to 1940*, Baltimore, Md, Johns Hopkins University Press, 1982.

production, public activity in the workplace and the polity; female – reproduction, domestic activity in the 'private' sphere, namely the home) fulfills capitalism's need always to lower labour costs and to have uncompensated reproductive labour, they find the gender system an important component of the capitalist system. Their analyses have also been extended by scholars interested in 'development' in the Third World; the imperatives of capital accumulation there, it is argued, have often introduced new forms of the sexual division of labour and seriously altered family structures and social relationships.[16] Women's invisibility, in this account, follows from the ideology of separate spheres which defined women as exclusively 'private' creatures and thus denied their ability to participate in public, political life. The power of the ideology was such that even when women did work or act politically, their activities were defined as 'extraordinary' or 'abnormal' and so outside the realm of 'real' or serious politics. The devaluation of women's activities (as a source of cheap labour in the market and of free labour at home) also devalued a vision of them as historical subjects, as agents of change.

The work of Lacan has been used by some feminist historians because of its emphasis on the importance of language, of symbolic representations, in the construction of sexual identity and subjectivity. Since symbolic representations are collectively developed and used, they offer access to the unconscious processes by which individuals identify with social groups and construct social relationships. In the analysis of how gender figures in political language, for example, historians have found ways to account for the greater participation of women in Owenite socialist movements, or for their exclusion from nineteenth century British trade unions. Drawing on the implications for feminists of Lacanian theory (as developed by Juliet Mitchell and Jacqueline Rose), these historians have begun to analyse material from the past as a way of understanding how the terms of sexual difference are articulated, adapted, transformed and, sometimes unwittingly, reproduced.[17] From this

16. See for example A. Kuhn and A. Wolpe, *Feminism and Materialism*, London, Routledge & Kegan Paul, 1978; S. Rowbotham, *Hidden from History*, London, Pluto Press, 1973; R. Coward, *Patriarchal Precedents*, London, Routledge, 1983; also the following special issues of *Signs*: Women and National Development, 1977; The Labour of Women: Work and Family, 1979; Development and the Sexual Division of Labour, 1981. See also Maria Patricia Fernandes, *Women in the Maquiladoras*, 1984.

17. Juliet Mitchell, *Psychoanalysis and Feminism*, London, Allen Lane, 1974; Juliet

perspective it might be argued that woman's historical invisibility follows from her symbolic association with lack and loss, with the threat posed by femininity to unified male subjectivity, with the status of the female as 'other' in relation to the central, powerful, privileged male.

For those who have used the writings of Foucault language is also an important focus. For Foucault relationships of power are constructed through 'discourse', a term that means not only particular discussions, but the entire organisational and ideological technology associated with the implementation of ideas. In *The History of Sexuality*, Foucault suggests that relationships of power were constituted through the discourse of sexuality as it emerged in the nineteenth century; expert knowledge (protected in the scientific disciplines) of medical and psychological functions defined normal and abnormal behavior, elaborating the 'meanings' of sexuality and constructing human sexual identities. For historians of women, this has led to explorations of the relationship of (male) doctors and female patients, to attempts to understand how certain female behaviour resisted or appropriated medical definitions, to attempts to understand how other relationships of power – those of class for example – were formulated in terms of gender.[18]

Indeed, with the Foucaultian approach, the question of women's invisibility in history becomes a question of power. Although women have contested their powerlessness at various points in history, they have usually lost the battle for equality (even if they have gained political, legal or economic rights). As a continuation of their subordinate position they are denied status as historical actors. Instead, the rights they have won are recorded for history as rights they have been granted by benevolent rulers, employers, politicians. The historical discourse that denies women visibility also perpetuates their subordination and their image as passive recipients of others' acts. History, in this interpretation, is part of the politics of the gender system. And writing the history of women assumes status as political strategy.

At this point in the writing of women's history, no single theory

Mitchell and Jaqueline Rose, *Feminine Sexuality: Jaques Lacan and the Ecole Freudienne*, London, Macmillan, 1982; Barbara Taylor, *Eve and the New Jerusalem*, London, Virago, 1983; Sally Alexander, 'Women, Class and Sexual Differences in the 1830s and 1840s', *History Workshop* 17 (1984).
18. See Jeffrey Weeks, *Sex, Politics and Society*, London, Longman, 1981; Biddy Martin, 'Feminism, Criticism and Foucault', *New German Critique* 27 (1982).

or method prevails. Indeed, the field is characterised by a healthy eclecticism which has, over the years, yielded innovative and important insight. The trend, if there has been one, has been away from simple documentation of women's historical agency to a preoccupation with gender as a category of analysis. Borrowing from social, linguistic, and psychoanalytic theory, historians of women have begun to articulate the need for a method and theory that is definably feminist, historical in its uses and conceptions, and applicable not only to Western experience, but to the rest of the world. Only comparative work will test the possibility of such a unified methodology; for the immediate future, it is more likely that diversity and variety in method and theory will continue to characterise this field of study.

Topics, Themes and Conceptualisations

Women's history has treated almost every area of female experience in the past, but certain topics have emerged more prominently than others. These, in one way or another, speak to the preoccupations of the contemporary women's movement. The topics are Work, Family, Politics and the State, and Ideology, including religious teachings. Cutting across these topics are a set of themes that touch on the issues of class and ethnicity, sexuality, and symbolic representation. In addition, there is a question about how to assess women's status; by what measures can improvement or deterioration be judged? And perhaps the most difficult question of all is whether we can speak historically of a single category of woman.

Work

Much of the history of women's work turns on the attempt to assess the impact of industrial capitalism on western societies (beginning in the eighteenth century). Although there is divided opinion about whether women's situation improved with the coming of factories, machinery, and, later, white collar jobs, there is agreement about certain patterns. First, as early as anyone can ascertain, jobs were divided along sexual lines. Men did one kind of work, women another, even if sex-typing varied from place to place; even if men's work in one region was women's in another. The coming of the industrial revolution did not end sex-segregation. It did, however, make clearer distinctions between work and home, by removing most productive activity from the household. In the early industrial period among working class families women were wage-earners. Single girls were, as they had been for centuries, farm hands and domestic servants. They also worked in the garment trades and in textile factories. Cities which offered female employment (commercial centers with demand for domestic servants, textile towns, centers of the garment trades and of casual, service jobs) tended to attract women to them. The population of these cities often had far higher percentages of females than of males. Married women, too, took textile factory jobs when their families needed income; but they were more likely to be found in various kinds of casual labour and in jobs that could be done at home. As far as it can be determined, married women's work seems to have followed an episodic pattern, of entries into the labour force to provided needed family income (when a husband was sick or unemployed, for example) or to coincide with the departure of children to school or marriage.

Second, the wages paid women tended to be lower than those paid to men and their work required less training. Employers seem to have anticipated turn-over in female labour forces; that was part of the reason women could be hired so cheaply. Low wages also, seem to have been tied to an economic calculation that considered women always to be 'natural dependents' of men – a father, husband, or brother. It was unnecessary, argued political economists of the nineteenth century, to pay women subsistence wages because theirs were always a supplement to the primary wage-earner's income.[19] In fact, this calculation created dependency for women, who could not afford to maintain themselves on their individual wages. The economic system of early industrial capitalism thus helped reproduce the 'gender system' as it was embodied in family organisation.[20]

Third, the issues faced by middle and working class women during the nineteenth (and twentieth) centuries were very different. They can be expressed as a contrast between exclusion and exploi-

19. Louise Tilly and Joan Scott, *Women, Work, and Family*, New York, Holt, Rinehart & Winston 1978; London, Methuen, 1987.
20. In the United States the situation was even more difficult for black women, both during and after slavery. On this see Herbert Gutman, *The Black Family in Slavery and Freedom, 1750–1925*, Oxford, Blackwell, 1976; and Eugene Genovese, *Roll, Jordan, Roll: The World the Slaves Made*, New York, Pantheon, 1974.

tation. Middle class women sought education and entry into professional jobs (as teachers, nurses, doctors, social workers, etc.); they attempted to end their exclusion from meaningful work and wage-earning and to dispute the ideology which consigned them exclusively to motherhood and home. Working class women, on the other hand, were a source of cheap labour and their family conditions sent them into the labour market. If married, they carried the 'double burden' of home and work; if single they faced unsteady employment and the difficulty of supporting themselves. As the trade union movement developed during the nineteenth century, its position was at best ambivalent on women. And the issue of protective legislation for women workers divided many political groups along both class and gender lines. Still, organisations like the Women's Trade Union League or the Women's Cooperative Guild in England drew an important following; and the various strikes by women workers (especially in textile factories and garment shops) indicate their sense of what the issues were: wages, working conditions, fairness in employment practices. At the turn of the century state protection in the form of legislation limiting hours of women's employment, or maternity insurance, or family allowances became the focus of efforts to end women's oppression.[21]

Considerations about unpaid labour at home are also included in inquiries into women's work. For the most part historians have disputed the argument that the mechanisation of the household at the beginning of the twentieth century freed women from domestic tasks. Important class differences must be introduced into this analysis and when they are, it becomes apparent that labour-saving appliances were developed to replace servants in middle class homes. Poor women, who most often went into the labour force, benefited little from these inventions. Moreover, even women who could afford them ended up spending more time at home cleaning and washing than they had before. The 'Industrial Revolution' in the household ended up increasing middle class women's attachment to the home.[22]

21. On middle-class work see Lee Holcombe, *Victorian Ladies at Work*, Hamden, Conn., Archon Books 1978; on work in France see the important bibliographic essay by M. Guilbert, N. Lowit and M-H. Zylberg-Hocquart, *Travail et condition féminine*, Paris, Editions de la Courtille, 1977; for the US see Alice Kessler-Harris, *Out to Work: A History of Wage-earning Women in the United States*, Oxford, Oxford University Press, 1982. Various interpretations are presented in A. Amsden, *The Economics of Women and Work*, Harmondsworth, Penguin, 1980.
22. Ruth Schwartz Cowan, *More Work for Mother*, New York, Basic Books, 1983;

Family

Studies of the family cover a broad range, extending from the 'family economy' of working people to the household organisation of the middle class. Topics such as reproduction, fertility, contraception, childrearing, and sexuality are included. Indeed, in some work the family is treated as synonymous with the 'private sphere', the area of activity and relationships that is somehow outside market and political activity.[23] But this work is representative of only one approach to the study of women and the family. Another approach refuses the 'private' designation, arguing instead that the family is a social and public institution, integrally connected to economic and political life. From this second perspective, the treatment of the family as somehow apart from other kinds of social relationships simply perpetuates the 'ideology of domesticity' that came into being in its western form with the rise of industrial capitalism. Moreover, it promotes the invisibility of women as workers, for it tends to study them only in their domestic locations. And it ignores the existence and experience of single women who, at any moment, have formed a significant portion of the female population.[24]

It is probably no accident that most studies of the working class family take the second approach, insisting on the relationship between available work and family roles. In working-class families before and after the Industrial Revolution women earned wages and adjusted their work patterns to childbearing and family monetary needs. The 'family economy' was a clear demonstration of the interconnections between wage work and household structure; indeed the wage (earned by however many members of the family were needed) seems to have been the link between work and family. And it is difficult to account for what happened in the so-called 'private' sphere without invoking the influences of the economy – available jobs, periods of unemployment, wage rates, etc.

The first approach tends to be associated with historians writing

---

and Susan Strasser, *Never Done: A History of American Housework*, New York, Pantheon, 1982.

23. An example is Bonnie Smith, *Ladies of the Leisure Class: The Bourgeoises of Northern France in the Nineteenth Century*, Princeton, NJ, Princeton University Press, 1981.

24. A. Farge and C. Klapisch-Zuber, *Madame ou Mademoiselle? Itineraires de la solitude feminine, 18–20e siècles*, Paris, Montalba, 1984.

about the middle class family, whose organisation and role division more closely approximated the prescriptive standards. Where financial pressures were less immediate, women and children did not engage in wage-earning. Instead women's roles as household managers and mothers received primary emphasis. Historians who study this subject have developed very different interpretations of its significance. Some suggest that the emphasis on maternity represented a devaluation of women's status, a restrictive definition of women's possibilities. This was surely the critique offered by some nineteenth-century feminists.[25] Recently, historians have also suggested that emphasis on women's domestic roles enhanced their status by giving them a claim to a specialised, sex-typed expertise. Certainly this expert knowledge was invoked by feminists in the nineteenth century women's movements when they argued that women must have a role in government.[26] But in this debate, as in other areas of women's history, the question of what is meant by status is inadequately defined.

By studying middle-class women only in the context of the family, the terms of the ideology of separate spheres are perpetuated rather than questioned. Furthermore, it is difficult to decide whether theirs were truly influential roles (having influence over whom? children and servants surely, husbands on domestic matters, but elsewhere?) and what the ultimate source of the influence was (in dealing with the lower classes, how did female expertise weigh against wealth and class standing?) It might be more fruitful to apply some of the notions of Pierre Bourdieu about cultural reproduction to the role of women in nineteenth century middle class western European families. Bourdieu's analyses (of institutions other than the family) suggest that socialisation, and informal education – the reproduction of middle class values, standards and styles of life – might have been the result of women's domestic activities. From this viewpoint, social and cultural reproduction is the woman's role; her family position then must be analysed in terms of the dynamics of middle class formation – a subject emi-

25. Barbara Welter, 'The Cult of True Womanhood', *American Quarterly* 18 (1966).
26. L. Stone, *The Family, Sex and Marriage*, London, Weidenfeld & Nicolson, 1977; E.C. DuBois, *Feminism and Suffrage: The Emergence of an Independent Women's Movement in America, 1848–69*, Ithaca, NY, Cornell University Press, 1978; M. Albistur and D. Armogathe, *Histoire de feminisme français*, Paris, Editions des Femmes, 1977.

nently public and political, although denied that status in ideological terms.

Under the rubric of the history of the family, reproduction has received a great deal of attention. Family size differed by class in the eighteenth and nineteenth centuries. Compared to earlier periods when the rich had more children and the poor fewer, the coming of industrialisation reversed that pattern. Birth control seems to have appeared first among families aspiring to wealth (if not already wealthy);[27] the birth rates of the (urban and wage-labouring) poor that had so alarmed Malthus continued high through most of the nineteenth century. Most of the work done in historical demography focuses on the 'demographic transition' and its causes and not on the effect of high fertility on the lives of working class women. (Some studies do suggest lower birth rates in textile towns, implying or deducing a link between women's wage-earning and their sexual autonomy and some studies have discussed the opposition of organised (male) workers to the suggestion that birth control would eliminate poverty.) Most women's history that deals with fertility and contraception focuses on the middle class. Here there is general agreement among US scholars at least that the use of contraception signalled a determination by women to control their bodies. In contrast to the English sociologists James and Olive Banks, who argue that economic motivations for using birth control (by middle class families after 1876 in England) imply male decisions, feminists insist that contraception implies female autonomy. The feminist debates about contraception in the nineteenth century seem to have been very heated; some arguing that its use would lead to further male exploitation of women, others (by the early twentieth century) insisting that sexual enjoyment would become a possibility for women if they no longer had to worry about pregnancy. How these debates figured in women's rights movements on the one hand, and in the texture of family experience, on the other, has not yet received the historical attention it needs.[28]

The focus on women in the 'private' sphere has led to interesting

27. For a summary of this literature see E.A. Wrigley, *Population and History*, New York, McGraw Hill, 1976. See also Philippe Aries, *Histoire des populations françaises et de leurs attitudes devant la vie depuis le 18 siècle*, Paris, Éditions du Seuil, 1971.

28. J. and O. Banks, *Feminism and Family Planning in Victorian England*, New York, Schocken, 1972; Linda Gordon, *Women's Body, Women's Right: A Social History of Birth Control in America*, New York, Penguin, 1977.

discoveries about social bonds among women. Formed around shared activities, these bonds became the basis for some collective movements of women,[29] and for what one historian, referring to middle class women in the nineteenth century US, has termed 'homosocial' ties or networks.[30]

Among middle-class women such networks developed from shared interests, and from time spent together caring for children, nursing the sick, preparing ritual social occasions. Similarly, among poor rural and urban women, shared concerns and activities – marketing, childbirth, care of the sick, laundering clothes in communal washhouses – developed networks of information and mutual support. The documentation of the existence of these networks suggests that women did indeed share common identities and that they acted on them to reinforce one another's influence or to support one another's choices. On the personal and political levels, such support permitted women an agency they were otherwise denied. To the extent, however, that these networks and the actions that followed from them did not challenge prevailing views of women, their existence might continue to be ignored – by contemporaries and historians alike.

Politics and the State

Under this heading at least three different issues have been studied by historians of women: (i) the participation of women in general political movements (revolutions, war, political movements and parties); (ii) the formation of specifically women's political groups, devoted to advancing some perceived common agenda for all women or of a particular group of women; and (iii) the relationship between the political and legal status of women and the form, organisation, or announced purposes of the state.

Women in General Political Movements

Those who have documented the participation of women in such events as the French Revolution are, of course, involved in making

29. Temma Kaplan, 'Female Consciousness and Collective Action: The Case of Barcelona, 1910–18', *Signs 7* (1982).

30. Carroll Smith-Rosenberg, 'The Female World of Love and Ritual', *Signs* 1 (1975).

women's public past visible. Simply to demonstrate that women were there is an important task. In addition, these histories have turned up information that reveals something about patterns of participation, moments of intense and widespread female participation and moments of their diminishing involvement. Women's involvement in political movements – bread riots, *sans-culottes* militance in Paris in 1789, counter-revolution in France in the 1790s, Owenism, St. Simonianism, Chartism, socialism – seems to be tied both to the community-based nature of the activity and to ideas expressed in 'feminine' terms. Thus, Barbara Taylor links the emphasis by certain Owenites on affective, harmonious ties, on complementarity expressed as the union of opposites – male and female – to the greater presence of women in those movements. And Dorothy Thompson ties the decrease in the numbers of women in Chartism to the increasingly centralised and nationally-based form of its organisation. In contrast, among early Chartists who developed a community-based locally-run movement, there was extensive female participation. During the French Revolutions of 1789 and of 1848, women were to be found on the barricades, in rioting crowds, and in formal political organisations. Then, as in the later English examples, community issues, local organisation and democratic rhetoric about the need to represent all interests, drew impressive female response. In these revolutions, however, women's participation eventually was formally forbidden by government edicts (in October 1793; and in July 1848). In both instances, the crackdown on women in politics was associated with a more general tightening of political authority – in 1793, the Jacobins sought to eliminate opposition to their increasingly centralised rule; in 1848, an emergency government was intent on restoring order in the wake of the insurrection of June. It may be that these women's activities were lost to view because of subsequent developments which ended their participation in politics. Chartism's last phase may have defined retrospectively for its leaders (and historians) its earlier phase. In the case of the French Revolution, the edict banning women's clubs was presented as a general endorsement of a sexual division of labour which, following Rousseau, argued that only men were suited for politics; women's place was at home. By legal definition, then women were not public actors; they were banished from contemporary politics and from history.[31]

31. Taylor, *Eve and the New Jerusalem*; D. Thompson, 'Women and 19th

Women participated in trade union and socialist movements during the nineteenth century, although not without difficulty. Although the situation differed from country to country (and was a function in part of specific historical contexts), similar patterns emerged. Trade unions were ambivalent, at best, when it came to organising women. Indeed, some of the most successful organising was done in all-female unions. Some examples of mixed unions do exist, but the more typical pattern was one which led to the marginalisation of women in leadership and membership. National union federations paid lip service to the need to win equal pay scales for women, but they also endorsed the goal of removing women from the labour market when possible.[32] This seems to me to have been tied not only to assessments made of the impact of women's wages on male pay scales, but also from the overwhelmingly male orientation of the organised labour movements.

Socialist parties at the end of the nineteenth century had a mixed record on women's participation, though all attempted to recruit female membership. Different organisational structures were more or less successful in maintaining women's participation: in Germany, separate groups within the SDP drew a large and active female constituency, while in France, the absorption of such groups into the general membership lost numbers and potential leaders.[33] As socialist parties became increasingly involved in electoral politics, their attention focused on voters – all of whom, in this pre-1914 period, were men.

Another kind of involvement for women in politics came with direct mobilisation by the state. During the First and Second World Wars, the US, French, and British governments appealed to women to work on the 'home front' in munitions industries and in other war-related work. Women were also enlisted in all kinds of government offices and services. Day nurseries were provided for some

---

Century Politics: A Lost Dimension', in *The Rights and Wrongs of Women*, ed. Juliet Mitchell and Ann Oakley, Harmondsworth, Penguin 1976; Levy and Applewhite, *Women in Revolutionary Paris*; Olwen Hufton, 'The Reconstruction of a Church 1796–1801', in *Beyond the Terror: Essays in French Regional and Social History 1794–1815*, ed. G. Lewis and C. Lucas, Cambridge, Cambridge University Press, 1983.

32. M. Guilbert, *Les Femmes et l'organisation syndicale avant 1914*, Paris, Centre Nationale de la Recherche Scientifique, 1966; Sheila Lewenhak, *Women and Trade Unions*, London, E. Benn, 1977.

33. C. Sowerwine, *Sisters or Citizens? Women and Socialism in France since 1876*, Cambridge, Cambridge Univesity Press, 1982.

working women, and other incentives were offered as well. Government mobilisation of women also occurred in Nazi Germany, as women's organisations were set up to support and implement policies designed to disenfranchise women, to encourage them to breed, and generally to fulfill 'traditional' women's roles. Whether in the service of democracy or of fascism, twentieth century governments successfully have enlisted women in public, political activities. Perhaps the final definitions of the nature of this activity – in the democracies it was 'for the duration' of the war only, for the Nazis it was an extension of women's traditional duty – has made it marginal to historical accounts of the period. Perhaps because women responded to the call of the state they are not seen as historical subjects, but as the objects of official policy and thus not central to history's major concerns.[34]

The Formation of Women's Political Groups

The formation of women's interest groups developed in the general context of interest group politics in the middle of the nineteenth century. Informed by ideas of individual rights or of the rights to expression and representation of definable groups, women sought to influence employers, educational institutions, professions, and politicians to implement policies favorable to the improvement and advancement of women.[35] Interestingly, there seems to have been a difference in some of these areas in the experience of women in Protestant and Catholic countries. In Protestant countries such as England and the United States, traditions of voluntarism and of individual action on behalf of moral issues moved women to organise to promote temperance, the abolition of slavery, an end to the double standard of sexual morality, and the vote.[36] In contrast, Catholicism provided institutional outlets and clerical supervision for moral or charitable impulses. Not only reform activities, but

34. L. Rupp, *Mobilizing Women for War*, Princeton, NJ, Princeton University Press, 1978; C. Koontz, 'Nazi Women before Emancipation', *Social Science Quarterly* 56 (1976); T. Mason, 'Women in Nazi Germany', *History Workshop* 1 and 2 (1976).
35. L. Tilly, 'Women and Collective Action', in *The Role of Women in Conflict and Peace*, ed. D. McGuigan, University of Michigan, Center for Continuing Education of Women, 1977.
36. R. Evans, *The Feminists*, London, Croom Helm, 1979; J. Walkowitz, *Prostitution and Victorian Society*, Cambridge, Cambridge University Press, 1980.

suffrage movements tended to be weaker in Catholic countries.[37]

In many instances there was a clear connection between those involved in moral reform movements and in the suffrage campaigns. The practical experience gained in England, for example, by the followers of Josephine Butler in the campaign to repeal the Contagious Diseases Acts (from the late 1860s through the 1880s) fed into suffrage movements. In addition women became convinced that the only way to prevent legislation that permitted a sexual double standard to prevail was to be in a position to vote and pass legislation themselves.

The organised suffrage movements drew large followings in England and the US, much smaller membership in France. Although leadership was largely middle class, significant working class participation developed as well. When suffrage leaders appealed to working women in England, for example, they won support in areas that had traditionally high female union membership and strong Labour Party representation.[38] The working women tended to define the movement in terms of the general interests of their class in securing greater political representation and they supported those who articulated this position. Other factions of the English suffrage movement opted for a separatist strategy and failed to win working-class women's support.

The interest in the vote by English working-class women coincided with other organised activity addressed to the state. In fact, other countries in this late nineteenth-century period also saw the growth of women's groups demanding protective legislation (an alternative, perhaps, to union pressure), maternity and health insurance and welfare allowances. It may be that heightened government attention to population and war and the provision of welfare services created the context within which women directed their demands to the state. It may be, too, that democratic ideology became increasingly statist in this period. In addition, of course, suffrage movements focused women's attention on the role of the state, directing activity to legislative ends. All of the reasons have yet to be explored, but the development is clear: by the end of the nineteenth century women sought redress for various of their grievances through government action.

37. S. Hause, *Women's Suffrage in France*, Princeton, NJ, Princeton University Press, 1984.
38. J. Liddington and J. Norris, *One Hand Tied Behind Us: The Rise of the Women's Suffrage Movement*, London, Virago, 1978.

Women and the State

The growth of nation states did not initially improve the position of women; in fact, there seems to be mounting evidence to show that the emergence of centralised and formal government structures diminished women's informal access to political power. Aristocratic and courtly societies seem to have permitted women of the elite greater influence than did republican city-states or representative forms of government. The 'democratic' revolutions of the eighteenth century closed the door to citizenship for women.[39] The socialist and social-democratic revolutions of the twentieth century, on the other hand, extended women full voting rights.[40]

Women's demands for political rights developed with ideas about natural rights and liberties. Indeed, the ideology of individual liberty – the notion that all 'men' were born equal in rights – informed women's political action as it did men's. In the insistence that despite physical differences, women were nonetheless equal, feminists posed a challenge to democratic ideologies of individual rights. The terms of resistance to this claim must be further studied. For it is in analysing why and how notions of sexual difference were used to refute feminist claims that we may begin to understand the relationship between democratic and gender ideologies.

Another aspect of women's relationship to the state has to do with state interest in women. In addition to laws regulating property and legal representation (laws which, for the most part protected family, not women's interest), there began to be legislation at the end of the nineteenth century and into the twentieth that protected women in the interests of society and the state. Thus, various pronatalist policies were based on the notion that the state had the right to regulate women since they produced future citizens. Many of these policies stressed women's reproductive role as their primary obligaton to society. At certain periods (after war, for example) state policy encouraged large families by rewarding those

39. J. McNamara and S. Wemple, 'The Power of Women through the Family in Medieval England', in *Clio's Consciousness Raised*, eds. M. Hartmann and L. Banner, New York, Harper & Row, 1974; C. Lougée, *Le Paradis des femmes*, Princeton, NJ, Princeton University Press, 1976; Levy and Applewhite, *Women in Revolutionary Paris*; Kerber, *Women of the Republic*.

40. Sites, *Women's Liberation in Russia*; J. Quataert, *Reluctant Feminists in German Social Democracy, 1885–1917*, Princeton, NJ, Princeton University Press, 1979.

women who had them and punishing those who used contraception or resorted to abortion. The role of the state in setting 'family' policy and thus in defining gender roles is an important area that needs further historical investigation.[41]

Ideology

The analysis of 'ideology' has undergone important development among historians of women. Beginning with a fairly simple notion that ideas 'reflected' reality, historians sought to document women's oppression by citing prescriptive literature about them.[42] Although this literature has changed over time, it seems typically to assign women lower status than men. The terms of female inferiority or subordination have differed, but those notions seem regularly to recur in western thought. What, however, do they mean?

In response to the initial emphasis on ideas about women, a number of historians insisted on looking at 'reality'. They suggested that when women could be found working or wielding power, that when women were not passive or dependent, that when women's actual experience seemed to contradict the idealised or prescriptive accounts, those accounts were clearly false. Among a number of social historians particularly, the attempt to document real as opposed to idealised experience involved examining the daily activities of various classes of women in the past.[43]

Recently, a more complicated analysis has been offered which suggests that ideas about sexual difference at once inform the definition and perception of 'experience' and are affected by such 'experience'. More general cultural notions of male and female are adapted to particular circumstances. There is variation by class, ethnic and religious affiliation in the way that terms of sexual difference are understood and, yet, there are also recognisable themes that seem to characterise western thought. These are then expressed usually in binary terms – man and woman are thus constructed through a series of oppositions that are rich in variety, symbolism and interpretive possibility.[44] Woman is to man as wet is to dry, weak is to strong, passion is to reason, superstition is to science, evil

41. D. Riley, *War in the Nursery*, London, Virago, 1983.
42. Welter, 'The Cult of True Womanhood'.
43. Among the many examples is P. Branca, 'The Myth of the Idle Victorian Woman', in *Clio*, ed. Hartmann and Banner.
44. N.Z. Davis, 'Women's History in Transition: The European Case', *Feminist*

is to good, good is to evil, passionlessness is to sexuality, nature is to culture, home is to work, passive is to active, reproduction is to production, spiritual is to material, domestic is to public, dependent is to independent, community is to individual, powerlessness is to powerful. These themes have appeared in different formulations in different periods and among different groups in societies. The scientific, secular thinking of the Enlightenment brought with it variations on and transformations of earlier religious themes (in which Eve and Mary offered the two poles of female behavior). But the religious imagery did not entirely disappear. Instead, modifications and transmutations occurred in symbolic representations and in the way people acted on their beliefs.

How and why ideas change; how ideologies are imposed; how such ideas set the limits of behavior and define the meaning of experience – these are the questions that confront historians of women. In their search for answers they are joined by others working on these questions from different perspectives. What historians of women add to the discussion is a preoccupation with gender; how the terms of sexual difference are defined discursively; how they differ for women and men; how they are changed or imposed; how, finally, they are reproduced. If the writing of history has, for the last two centuries, figured importantly in the construction of knowledge about sexual difference, then it is in the examination of history as part of the 'politics' of gender representation that we will perhaps find the answer to the question of women's invisibility in the written story of the past.

Studies 3 (1976), and 'Women on Top', in her *Society and Culture in Early Modern France*, London, Duckworth, 1975.

2

The Presentation of
African Women in
Historical Writing

AYESHA MEI-TJE IMAM

The presentation of African women in historical writing has been characterised by four main approaches. In the first (and most obvious) case women have simply not been present at all. In the second they have been seen as inferior and subordinate to men. The third trend has had a conception of women's roles as equal and complementary to those of men. Finally, there has been a movement towards seeing women as active agents in historical processes. This chapter briefly outlines these four approaches and then discusses some of the reasons for and consequences of these differing presentations.

That the presentation of African women through history can take so many forms demonstrates what by now should be a truism: that 'facts' are not neutral and immutable natural objects but part of theoretical and conceptual constructs. As Gloria Thomas Emeagwali points out, historical reconstruction is influenced not only by primary sources but also by the researcher's 'speculative philosophy of history, which is itself affected by his or her own value system and the intellectual and socio-economic environment'.[1] It will be argued later that the same may also be true of the primary sources themselves. A world view that relegates women to the background has obvious implications for the treatment of the role of women in historical reconstructions: women will be accorded scant and superficial attention and thereby rendered absent from history.

1. G.T. Emeagwali, 'Explanations in African history', *Journal of the Historical Society of Nigeria* 10.3 (1980), pp. 95–110.

In the examination of historical works on Africa it is clear that 'the specific role, contribution and general activities of women is a neglected theme, relatively speaking. We are in fact dealing with gross sins of omission in historical reconstruction'.[2] As the most cursory survey can establish, this absence is the longest established and most dominant trend in African historiography *vis-à-vis* women. In *The Revolutionary Years: West Africa since 1800*[3], for example, – a popular college textbook – there are but two references to women, a single line on female soldiers in Dahomey and a short paragraph on the Igbo 'Women's War' of 1929 (referred to here as the Aba Women's Riots).

The non-appearance of women can be most clearly highlighted by considering studies on issues in which women might be expected to play a role. Adam Kuper's study of bridewealth in Southern Africa,[4] for instance, implicitly discusses the role played by women in maintaining the corporate structure of various societies, but women as a group receive only superficial attention. As Margaret Strobel points out, Kuper 'only occasionally reflects upon the extent to which women exercised power or not in the context of bridewealth . . . how women fared as recipients, negotiators or objects of bridewealth is of little concern'.[5]

Similarly although Ester Boserup has pointed out that Africa is the region of women's farming par excellence,[6] Agboola's study of agricultural changes in Western Nigeria totally ignores the changes in the gender-based division of labour that resulted from the establishment of cocoa as a cash crop.[7] Another example is migration, which clearly affects the division of labour and so male-female relations. Yet despite this, neither Van Dantzy,[8] Meillassoux,[9] nor

2. G.T. Emeagwali, 'The woman question in the context of the precapitalist socio-economic formations in Nigeria', in *Women in Nigeria: Proceedings of the First National Seminars* (forthcoming).

3. J.B. Webster and A.A. Boahen, *The Revolutionary Years: West Africa since 1800*, London, Longman 1980.

4. A. Kuper, *Wives for Cattle: Bridewealth and marriage in South Africa*, London, Routledge & Kegan Paul 1982.

5. M. Strobel, Review of ibid. in *International Journal of African Historical Studies* 16.6 (1983), p. 38.

6. E. Boserup, *Women's Role in Economic Development*, New York, St Martin's Press 1983.

7. S.A. Agboola, 'Agricultural changes in Western Nigeria 1850–1910', in *Topics in Nigerian Economy and Social History*, eds. I.A. Akinjobin and S.O. Osoba. Nigeria, University of Ife Press 1980.

8. A. van Dantzy, 'Effects of the Atlantic slave trade on some West African

Alpers[10] in their studies of the impact of the slave trade make any reference to this aspect although, as Maria Rosa Cutrufelli points out, one of the effects of the depopulation of Africa that resulted from the slave trade was the increased importance and rigidity of the concept of motherhood, i.e. the ideology of women as reproducers.[11]

A final example of this is E. Njaka's study of the transition of Igbo political institutions during the colonial experience.[12] In discussing Igbo political institutions, Njaka mentions women's organisations on fewer than 20 pages of a 669-page thesis. While Kamene Okonjo refers to 'a dual-sex system' in Igboland,[13] and Judith Van Allen to 'a more or less stable balance of male and female power',[14] Njaka sees women's organisation merely as one of four minor counterbalancing agents. His attitude towards women can be seen from the following words: 'Despite this power, however, the Umuada are said to be like mothers – always lenient and not as fierce as it sounds,'[15] i.e. not to be taken seriously.

The second theme in the presentation of African women through history typifies them as oppressed and totally subordinated to men. The main works of this type are not historical texts as such but ethnographical and anthropological monographs such as the work of the Ottenburgs or that of Evans Pritchard. These studies assert that the African woman had 'a position and status that is in many ways definitely inferior to that of a man, and this is in spite of the fact that she does most of the hard work in supporting the family'[16] or that 'the greater number of indigenous societies (in Africa)

societies', in *Forced Migration*, ed. J.E. Inikori. London, Hutchinson 1982.

9. C. Meillassoux, 'The role of history in the economic and social history of Sahelo-Sudanic Africa', ibid., pp. 74–99.

10. E.A. Alpers, 'The impact of the slave trade on East Central Africa in the nineteenth century', ibid., pp. 242–73.

11. M.R. Cutrufelli, *Women of Africa: Roots of Oppression*, London, Zed Press, 1983.

12. E.E. Njaka, 'Igbo Political Institutions and Transition', PhD dissertation, University of California, 1975, p. 669.

13. K. Okonjo, 'The dural sex political system in operation: Igbo women and community politics', in *Women in Africa: Studies in Social and Economic Change*, Stanford, Calif., Stanford University Press 1976, p. 45.

14. Judith van Allen, '"Sitting on a man": colonialism and the lost political institutions of Igbo women', *Canadian Journal of African Studies* 6.2 (1972), pp. 165–81.

15. Njaka, 'Igbo political institutions', p. 260.

16. John Beattie, quoted by T. Awori in *La Civilisation de la femme dans la tradition africaine*, Paris 1972, p. 31.

reserve for women a place which is clearly inferior, approaching that of a domestic animal'.[17] They focused on such issues as childhood betrothal, polygyny, or the lack of divorce rights.

These views are influenced, as several commentators have pointed out, by two prejudices: male bias and western ethnocentricity. The influence of male bias may come both at the point of the primary source and at the point of the researchers themselves (usually himself). Evans Pritchard's *Man and Woman Among the Azande*, for example, might more accurately have been entitled *How Azande Men View Women*, since it consists of Azande men's comments on women, collected by other African men and compiled by a European man. Nowhere in the book do women present their own viewpoints.[18] The point is that very often 'data' on women and their roles are merely male informants' views of this – male versions of reality are accepted as the group's reality. Renée Pittin points out that there may often be 'selective remembering' in terms of historical documents. For instance, although myths of origin similar to those relating to those of Daura and Kano testify to her existence as the first ruler of Gobir, Tawa of Gobir's name is not found on any of the extant 'King-lists'. Pittin goes on to argue that there may be a deliberate downplaying of the importance of women's roles, in what came to serve as primary sources for historians. She suggests that this was the case, for example, in the Habe kingdoms in present day Niger and Nigeria where, with the spread of Islamic influence, women's political titles either fell into disuse or were adopted by men, such as the title of Iya in the Katsina emirate.[19]

The issue of ethnocentricity in anthropology has been the subject of criticism even among anthropologists themselves, but it is sufficient here to point out that many researchers came to their subject matter with pre-conceived assumptions about the superiority of European culture and were only too ready to dismiss customs that were different from their own as barbarous and degrading. Iris Andreski's introduction to *Old Wives' Tales*, for example, shows a totally negative view and lack of understanding of Ibibio society and culture.[20]

17. Georges Hardy, a French colonial administrator, quoted in *Women in Africa*, ed. Hafkin and Bay, p. 3.

18. See, among others, *Women in Africa*, ed. Hafkin and Bay.

19. R.I. Pittin, 'Marriage and alternative strategies: career patterns of Hausa women in Katsina City', PhD dissertation, University of London 1979, Appendix 1.

20. I. Andreski, *Old Wives Tales: The Life Stories of African Women*, New York, Schoken 1970.

In direct opposition to this presentation of African women's inferiority is the theme of women's complementarity to men, equal but different so to speak. According to this framework, while African men were dominant in some spheres of social life, African women were equally responsible for other areas of influence, that is, male and female roles were complementary and the issue of super- or subordination did not arise. Practices such as the levirate, polygyny, female seclusion or clitoridectomy are therefore simply cultural practices which have been misunderstood by ethnocentric westerners. This theme is exemplified by the articles in '*La civilisation de la Femme dans la Tradition Africaine*', particularly those by Thelma Awori, Colette Houeto, Delphine Yeyet and Sarah Kala-Lobe. Houeto states: 'Pour l'Afrique traditionelle, il n'importe pas de savoir si la femme est mineure, esclave ou secondaire. . . . Au regard de cette conception anthropologique de l'histoire, nous comprenons mieux la femme 'debout', inlassablement en action aux côtés de l'homme'.[21]

This trend is also evident in studies of the political roles of women in Africa. Annie Lebeuf states:

> In general, the profound philosophical ideas which underline the assignment of separate tasks to men and women stress the complementary, rather than the separate nature of these tasks. Neither the division of labour nor the nature of the tasks accomplished implies any superiority of one over the other, and there is almost always compensation in some other direction for the actual inequalities which arise from such a division.[22]

Similarly Nina Mba argues that in pre-colonial Southern Nigeria the 'women's world is not subordinate to that of the men but rather complementary'.[23]

This approach to African women's roles is part of what has been termed the concept of 'the Golden Age of Merrie Africa' in which pre-colonial Africa is seen as a land of peace and harmony free from conflict – something like the garden of Eden before the serpent. It owes its genesis to a number of factors. On the part of African researchers the impetus is very much that of the anti-colonial feeling

21. C. Houeto, 'The woman, source of life in traditional Africa', in *La Civilisation de la femme dans la tradition africaine*, ed. Awori, pp. 51–66.
22. A. Lebeuf, 'The role of women in the political organisation of African societies', in *Women of Tropical Africa*, ed. Denise Paulme, 1971.
23. N. Mba, *Nigerian Women Mobilised: Women's Political Activity in Southern Nigeria 1900–1965*, University of California Press 1982.

generated in nationalist struggles and the resurgence of interest and pride in African indigenous institutions that came with the philosophy of Negritude. This influence is particularly clear in the work of francophone writers such as Houeto, where the complementarity of men's and women's roles is based on their appropriateness to the complementary physical and psychic nature of each sex. Houeto states: 'Nous sommes alors loin de cette base conflictuelle qui oppose dans autres civilisations l'homme et la femme. . . . Aussi, si la femme est *mejito* (procreator), l'homme est *ga* (external, active). La *mejito*, genitrice, s'accomplit à travers la maternité. . . .'[24] For American and European researchers the influence of the Black civil rights movement led to interest in Africa's past glories, while the women's movement heightened interest in women's activities. However, as Hafkin and Bay put it: 'In this period some of the literature that emerged was romantic or historically inaccurate. In a search for great glories to counteract a past that had ignored and distorted the history of women and of Africa, writers described great queens, amazons and matriarchy'.[25]

These writers see the present subordination of women as caused by colonial policies, in particular the bourgeois male-chauvinist assumptions of European colonial administrators, which were reflected in colonial legal structures, formal western education and Christianity. Thus Awori states:

The effects of education and Christianity can be discussed together because the issues are similar. By education here is meant the process of cultural indoctrination accomplished through the teaching of history, literature and religious knowledge. It is necessary to note that much of what is taught to Africans as Christianity is more western European culture than the teachings of Christ.

It is from a combination of these two sources that ideas such as the following emanate:

1. Women should be dependent on men for support.
2. Women should marry men who are of superior social status, educational achievement and financial standing.
3. The place of women is in the home (kitchen).
4. Chastity, fidelity, monogamy etc. These ideas embedded in our minds by our colonial masters have created a very oppressive state of affairs for African women today.[26]

24. Houeto, 'The woman', pp. 54–5.
25. *Women in Africa*, ed. Hafkin and Bay, p. 4.
26. *La Civilisation*, ed. Awori, pp. 43–4.

The fourth and most recently developed trend in the presentation of African women's history explicitly sees women as actors in social processes rather than passive recipients of change. Here, however, there is a recognition of the social structures and mechanisms that constrain women and place them in subordinate positions, but the approach focuses on the ways in which women have been active in attempting to establish their autonomy and independence nonetheless. Within this approach two currents can be identified. The first tends to concentrate on the activities of women as leaders (of women's organisations in particular). These writers share with some of the writers of the 'Merrie Africa' tradition a conception of historical processes in terms of the leading personalities of social groups (and usually of the dominant social grouping). Personalities such as Queen Amina of Zazzau or Madam Yoko of the Kpa Mende are prominent but the analysis tends to be silent in terms of the generality of women. For example Cheryl Johnson considers the roles played by Madam Alimotu Pelewura in the Lagos Market Women's Association, Lady Oyinkan Abayomi in the Nigerian Women's Party, and Mrs Funmilayo Anikulapo-Kuti in the Abeokuta women's Union.[27] Agnes Akosua Aido looks at 'Asante Queen Mothers in Government and Politics in the Nineteenth Century' and concludes that these women had great personal strength and ability, that they were most effective where they were 'free from ritual constraints and there was no effective male leadership'. She also states that Asante queen mothers derived their power and support not from '"female power" but from all effective sections of Asante society'.[28] Kamene Okonjo, on the other hand, considers what she terms 'the dual-sex political system' in Igboland, where women had political spheres of authority that were parallel to those of men, although 'as elsewhere men rule and dominate'.[29] As with those who present pre-colonial African women as being complementary rather than subordinate to men, writers in this current attribute the decline in women's status to the patriarchal Victorian ideology of colonial administrators. Okonjo concludes that 'the absence of women from significant political representation in inde-

---

27. C. Johnson, 'Grassroots organising: women in anti-colonial activity in South Western Nigeria', *African Studies Review*, 25.213 (1982), 137–58.

28. A.A. Aido, 'Asante Queen Mothers in government and politics in the nineteenth century', in *The Black Woman Cross Culturally*, ed. F.C. Steady. New York, Schenkman 1981.

29. Okonjo, 'The dural sex political system', p. 45.

pendent Nigeria can be viewed as showing the strength of the legacy of single-sex politics that the British colonial masters left behind'.[30]

The second current within the approach to seeing women as active agents focuses not on individual women but on women as groups and the socio-economic and ideological conditions within which they have acted. For example, Richard Roberts's study of household social relations in Maraka in the nineteenth century argues that patterns of household relations (including gender relations) are directly influenced by changes in the larger political economy within which the household is embedded. He concludes that it was the combination of the increased influence of Islamic ideological practices and of market forces that heightened the tendency of Maraka households to be patriarchal.[31] *religion + economy*

Once again the position of African women is seen as having deteriorated through the colonial experience, but here it is attributed not simply to the ideologies of colonialists but also to the deterioration of women's economic positions resulting from the imposition of capitalist underdevelopment. Judith van Allen's analysis of Igbo women's political institutions, for instance, considers only political and administrative reforms based on Victorian male ideology.[32] In 1976, however, she also refers to women's loss of economic autonomy brought about by colonialism. Maud Shimwaayi Muntemba's analysis of women and agricultural change in Zambia traces the changing fortunes of peasant women. She argues that the transformations in agricultural production which were directed towards supplying the requirements of the British economy and the white settler population resulted in the deprivation of rural women as a group *vis-à-vis* rural men, despite women's efforts to fight against this.[33]

This fourth approach is what Emeagwali refers to as the materialist model in historiography which 'focuses on the totality of production relations, productive forces and superstructural forms'[34] and is, as I argue below, the most adequate of the four approaches to

---

30. Ibid., p. 58.

31. R. Roberts, 'Women's work and women's property: household social relations in the Maraka textile industry of the nineteenth century', *Comparative Studies in Social and Economic History* 26.2 (1984), pp. 229–50.

32. van Allen, 'Sitting on a Man'.

33. M.S. Muntemba, 'Women and agricultural change in the railway region of Zambia', in *Women and Work in Africa*, ed. E.G. Bay, 1982.

34. Emeagwali, 'The woman question', p. 8.

the representation of African women through history.

Having outlined these variations in the presentation of African women in history, and the factors which have influenced these approaches, I shall conclude with some brief comments on their adequacy.

The first approach, that of the invisibility of women in history, has an obvious inadequacy: it leaves out a whole sector of reality. It should be seen as an ideological representation of the past rather than as historical reconstruction. As such, it reinforces beliefs about women's passivity and lack of importance in societal processes. Since it remains the dominant trend in history courses generally and in school textbooks particularly, it is obviously a major impediment to the generation or dissemination of a view of women as social actors.

The presentation of African women as historically subordinate and inferior to men also has obvious insufficiencies in terms of accurate historical reconstruction. As argued above, this presentation is usually no more than the dominant male ideology in relation to women as recounted by male informants to male researchers. Seldom is there any analysis of actual women's roles and activities, much less an attempt at reconstructing women's views of social reality. Nor is there any recognition of the possibility that women not only do not subscribe to these representations of themselves but may, as Christine Obbo records, have struggled against oppressive practices of marriage and family life.[35] Furthermore van Allen shows that even when women have struggled overtly and collectively against their exploitation, as in the Igbo 'Women's War' against the imposition of colonial taxation, this has been interpreted in the light of preconceived assumptions about women's inferiority – hence, in this case, the colonial administration assumed that the Igbo women's collective and organised campaign was a riot organised and directed by men.[36] Renée Pittin also points out that there may be a discrepancy between ostensible acceptance of ideologies of superiority (including even verbal subscription to them) and actual female practice. She states that 'through the use of symbolic behaviour, and particularly through the resort to male ideology, women "mystify" the extent of their actual extensive options and indepen-

---

35. C. Obbo, *African Women: Their Struggle for Independence*, London: Zed Press 1980.
36. van Allen, 'Sitting on a Man', pp. 60–2, 73–5.

dence and thereby protect them from exposure and possible curtailment'.[37]

Just as the presentation of African women as submissive inferiors to men reflects male prescriptions of how women ought to be, so does the concept of pre-colonial Africa as a harmonious age of male-female complementarity reflect a romantic myth. Like the myth of a classless pre-colonial Africa, issues of control, power and exploitation are ignored – whether these are between groups distinguished by gender, lineage or classical Marxist production relations. It is, however, an amalgamation of these two myths, of submissive female inferiority and complementarity of male-female roles, that forms the basis of the most potent ideology aimed at controlling women in many contemporary African states. In this amalgamation, which also draws upon capitalist ideology of the male as the sole provider for the family, the ideal (and historically, traditionally sanctioned) role of the African woman is that of a mother and housekeeper firmly under the control of her husband and male relatives, acquiescing meekly to her husband's acquisition of co-wives, whose main duty is to reproduce and socialize children. Women who also work outside the home or are unmarried are characterised as prostitutes and/or neglectful mothers responsible for immorality, delinquency and social indiscipline generally.

The continuing presentation of African women through history as inferior and/or complementary to men is not only historically inaccurate but also poses a serious constraint on women as actors in social, political and economic processes in contemporary Africa.

The historiographic focus on women as leaders and dominant personalities is also problematic. Most of the leaders about whom there is documentation tend to come from the ruling class of the periods studied. The stress on individuals emphasises their exceptional qualities and ignores the conditions and roles of the generality of women. This type of analysis obscures the factors that divide women and glosses over the role of women, as members of dominant social groups, in the exploitation and oppression of women and men in subordinate groups.

In terms of its political use as an ideology the 'great women' thesis is contradictory. On the one hand it provides reassurance of women's active participation in historical processes. On the other hand the emphasis on the (implied or overt) exceptionality of the

37. Pittin, 'Marriage', p. 21.

individuals focused upon may deter 'ordinary women' from attempting to emulate their achievements.

The variations in the presentation of African women discussed above have all been shown to produce inadequate and ideologically damaging representations in terms of viewing women as actors in historical processes. The need for a development of the final trend in presenting women in history should therefore be clear. It is necessary to bring out both the specific social, political, economic and ideological constraints within which women have lived and the ways in which women have interacted in relation to them.

3

Making History: Women in France

MICHELLE PERROT

In the past ten years, the history of women has gained ground in many different countries. Now we may ask: How far have we come? What are the strengths and weaknesses of the process? What difficulties and obstacles have been encountered? How has the history of women changed the outlook for the writing of history in general? What, today, are our most urgent needs – the specific needs of women historians in different countries? And what are our next objectives? Where do we go from here?

What Stage Has the History of Women Reached in France?

To begin with, a few words on historiography. Ever since history has been recognised as a 'scientific' discipline – approximately since the nineteenth century – women's place in it has varied according to the point of view of historians, who until recently were all men. Romantic history – Michelet's for example – views the relation between the sexes as one of the motive forces in history; but in contrasting woman/nature with man/culture, Michelet reflects the ideologies of his time. Women are a benign force so long as they remain in the private sphere as wives and mothers – as, for example, when on 5 and 6 October 1789 they rose up to demand bread – but they are a force of evil and misfortune when they usurp public roles. When this happens, history breaks down, the times are out of joint[1] and women are witches.

Positivist history, which was of great importance in the develop-

---

1. Therese Moreau, *Le sang de l'histoire, Michelet, l'histoire et l'idée de la femme au 19e siècle*, Paris, Flammarion, 1982.

ment of history as a 'profession' and which had Seignobos as its *grand maître*, virtually banished women, along with daily life as a whole. There are many factual and epistemological reasons for this retrograde step. The 'profession' of the historian is a profession of men writing male history. The fields they cover – with political history in the forefront – are those of male action and power. If they turn to 'civilisation' or later to 'mentality', they talk about generic 'man', who has no sex. Moreover, the materials they use – diplomatic or administrative records, parliamentary documents or periodicals – are produced by men who monopolise the written word as well as public affairs. Women who have achieved fame – through piety or scandal – provide material for the chronicles of 'minor' history, the stuff of anecdotes, but nothing more.

With the *Annales* school (Lucien Febvre, Marc Bloch, and their colleagues and followers), whose influence began to spread in the 1930s, the prospects definitely improved, in the sense that the field covered by history expanded considerably. Economic and social aspects still predominated, however: priority was given to studies of circumstances and structure, social categories and the class struggle; the sexual dimension was virtually ignored. It is significant that a newly emergent branch such as historical demography had so little to say about women, who were regarded solely as a factor in reproduction. It is also significant that in 1979 this same discipline felt the need to organize a meeting on 'historical demography and women',[2] a sign that the approach was changing.

A whole series of factors are behind this change: the development of historical anthropology, concerned primarily with studies of the family; the emergence of what is sometimes wrongly referred to as the 'New History', which takes account of ideas and everyday practices, all this being subsumed under the somewhat vague term 'mentalités'.[3] The time is ripe for a history of women, although the attention paid to them in learned journals is still limited. Between 1970 and 1982, for example, the periodical *Annales (Economies, Sociétés, Civilisations)* published 71 issues and 751 articles; 139 are

2. Societé de démographie historique, *Annales de démographie historique*, 1981. *Démographie historique et condition féminine*, Paris, Edition de l'Ecole des hautes études en science sociales, 1981. (Numerous papers, especially on the influence of single women.)
3. On *mentalités*, see *Revue de synthèse*, July-December 1983 (111–12), 'Journée histoire des sciences et mentalités', Paris, Albin Michel, 1983. Very interesting studies.

written *by* women (18.5 per cent), and 34 articles (4.5 per cent) are *about* women, half of them by men and half by women.[4]

But the history of women, in France and elsewhere, actually owes its existence to the women's movement and to the spate of questioning that it has entailed. Who are we? Has there, down the ages, been a common identity of women as a group? Where have we come from? Where are we going? Apparently doomed to the silence of reproduction, the infinite repetition of daily tasks and a division of the world according to sex that would appear so immutable that its origins are sought in the mists of time – have women any history at all? What are its motive forces, events and lines of emphasis? Are there forms of expression and of culture that are peculiar to women?

These questions were raised in particularly forceful terms in the period 1970–1975, when the women's movement made its political breakthrough. A need for history came to be felt almost everywhere, including within universities, as soon as women teachers were available to meet the new demand on the part of women students (or even to arouse it). I do not propose to review the achievements of these ten years of 'primitive accumulation': this has been done elsewhere.[5] I shall merely point out some of the institutional and thematic landmarks.

The first courses were organized in 1973. At the University of Paris VII (Jussieu), we were so unsure of ourselves that we named the programme of studies 'Have Women a History?' (1973–1974), and as nobody was capable of taking responsibility for such a question we proceeded by means of a series of lectures by a number of different people. Research was begun at master's degree level and in dissertations, which are now bearing fruit. Study panels were set up: CEFUP (Feminist Study Centre of the University of Provence) in 1972, CLEF (Feminist Contact and Study Centre) in Lyon, GEF (Feminist Study Group) in Paris VII in 1975 and GRIEF in Toulouse in 1978. Symposia were held, in Aix-en-Provence in 1975 (where the role of Yvonne Knibiehler deserves special mention) on 'Women and Human Sciences' at Paris VIII (Vincennes) in 1978

4. Paper by Arlette Farge for the Saint-Maximin symposium (June 1983), 'Pratique et effets de l'histoire des femmes'. A comparable article, referred to below, was written for the journal *L'Histoire*. The records of the Saint-Maximin symposium, 'L'histoire des femmes, est-elle possible?' were published in 1985 by Rivages.

5. Main surveys: M. Perrot, 'Sur l'histoire des femmes en France', *Revue du Nord* lxiii, (1981); Arlette Farge 'Dix ans d'histoire des femmes en France', *Le Débat* 23 (January 1983); Joan Scott 'Survey Article: Women in History', *Past and Present* 101, (November 1983).

(Madeleine Rebérioux) on 'Women and the Working Class', and in Lyon in 1980 on 'Women and Work'. We may note in passing the persistent links with social history and also, perhaps, the difficulty of breaking away from it.

The first publications appeared: in 1977, *Questions féministes*, the first theoretical feminist journal in France was launched. In 1979, the *BIEF* of Aix-Marseille came out. *Pénélope: Cahiers pour l'histoire des femmes*, a biannual (first issue, autumn 1979, *Les femmes et la Presse*),[6] which is modest but indispensable, is still the leading French publication on the history of women.[7]

The political changes of May 1981 created a new situation which women turned to account, first, in the context of the CNRS (National Scientific Research Centre), by organizing a national interdisciplinary symposium in Toulouse in December 1982[8] and submitting a report, 'Research on Women and Feminist Studies' (M. Perrot) in the framework of the Mission Godelier.[9] An 'ATP' (Planned Thematic Action) was organised in the autumn of 1983; in response to an invitation to tender, over 100 research projects were received, 30 of which were selected; among the latter, some concerned the history of women, particularly the recent history of feminism.

In the universities, too, posts described as 'in women's studies' were established in the summer of 1984 by the Ministry of Education, principally at the request of the Ministry of Women's Rights. One of the four posts was in history (in Toulouse). These posts were to assist in establishing courses on women, not as a separate subject – most women are against this, as we shall see later – but as part of traditional disciplines.

This real assistance, which must be welcomed, carries the same risks as any other form of institutionalisation. It is a question that

6. Liliane Kandel's excellent study, 'L explosion de la presse feministe', was immediately reproduced in *Le Débat* 1 (May 1980).

7. Issues of *Pénélope* published to date: (1) *Les femmes et la presse*, Autumn 1979; (2) *Education des filles, enseignement des femmes*, Spring 1980; (3) *Les femmes et la création*, Autumn 1980; (4) *Les femmes et la science*, Spring 1981; (5) *La femme soignante*, Autumn 1981; (6) *Les femmes et la violence*, Spring 1982; (7) *Les femmes et la terre*, Autumn 1982; (8) *Femmes et folie*, Spring 1983; (9) *Femmes et techniques*, Autumn 1983; (10) *Femmes au bureau*, Spring 1984; (11) *Les femmes et les associations*, Autumn 1984.

8. The symposium was attended by more than 700 women. The papers are to be published.

9. Maurice Godelier, *Mission sur les sciences de l'homme et de la société*, Paris, Documentation française, Autumn 1982.

merits discussion, and I shall return to it.

The history of women has therefore won some recognition both within the institutional framework and outside it. Two further examples: in June 1983 a symposium was held in Saint-Maximin (Var) on the subject: 'Is a history of women possible?'; an occasion which was very useful in enabling us to review the situation and give thought to the status of the history of women, especially from the point of view of theory. The initiative for the symposium came from the cultural centre itself. The second case concerns the RATP (Independent Parisian Transport Corporation, responsible for the underground and bus services), which was preparing a future-oriented project 'Réseau 2000' (Network 2000) and in that connection wished to undertake research on the history of the RATP; it was relatively easy to propose a line of research on women and male/female relations since the founding of the RATP. This indicates a growing awareness of the significance of sex-divisions in history and in society.

But before basking in triumph we must analyse the responsibilities that such progress entails. It is still fragile and reversible, and the permanent infrastructure on which it rests is alarmingly weak.

From the point of view of subject-matter the history of women in France has also changed, both in its attitude and in its objectives. Initially intent on revealing the hidden foundations of domination and oppression and strongly drawn to the image of 'women as victims', it subsequently became more concerned to show women as agents of history, with their own forms of action and expression, their gestures and words, or even (a more questionable notion) their 'culture'. It focused on women as active and rebellious, and tended perhaps to veer to the other extreme.[10] Research objectives were at first bound up with bodily issues: pregnancy, childbirth, prostitution. This type of history was primarily one of the *body*.[11] It then shifted its emphasis towards women's 'work': paid work, housework, and the social functions of the 'leisured class';[12] and problems relating to 'women's jobs' and their requisite 'qualifications'. On the borderline between literature and history research has also been

10. *L'Histoire sans qualité*, Paris, Galilée, 1979, a collection of writings on the history of women, is very typical of this stage in historiography.
11. Catherine Fouquet, 'Le detour obligé ou l'histoire des femmes passe-t-elle par celle de leur corps?', Paper for the Saint-Maximin Symposium, June 1983.
12. Some examples: *Travaux de femmes dans la France du 19e siècle*, ed. M. Perrot. Special issue of *Mouvement social* 105 (October-December 1978); Katherine Blun-

conducted on the representation of women.[13] Attention has been focused on women's struggle, but much remains to be done, especially on the history of feminism.[14] Lastly, the history of women sees itself as the history of the relations between the sexes.

The purpose of this very rapid survey is simply to place the history of women in France in a comparative context. How are we to judge whether this kind of historiography is distinctive or not, representative or not? What influence have social, political or, indeed, sexual conditions in France had on this kind of history? To what extent does it faithfully reflect the relationship between the sexes in France? Which European, broadly western, or worldwide model comes closest to this kind of historiography? It should be possible, by comparing various national histories of women, to identify currents and patterns that are revealing in themselves. Our various limitations as well as our contributions should thus be brought to light.

Sources for Women's History

At the end of his book, *Le Chevalier, la femme et le prêtre* (Paris: Hachette, 1981), which re-examines the whole question of marriage in medieval times, Georges Duby notes reflectively: 'Among all these men loudly proclaiming what they had done or dreamt of doing, we must take care not to overlook the women. *A great deal is said about them, but how much do we really know?*' That indeed is the crux of the question.

The silence of the main sources of information is in itself an indication of the place allotted to women. It varies, moreover, from

den, *Le travail et le vertu. Femmes au foyer: une mystification de la Révolution industrielle*, Paris, 1982; Anne Martin-Fugier, *La bourgeoise. Femme au temps de Paul Bourget*, Paris, Grasset, 1983; Bonnie Smith, *The Ladies of the Leisure Class. The Bourgeoises of Northern France in the 19th Century*, Princeton, NJ, Princeton University Press, 1981. On housework, see the recent dissertation by Martine Martin, 'Les femmes et le travail ménager en France entre les deux guerres', University of Paris VII.

13. See in particular the work of Maurice Agulhon, *Marianne au combat. L'imagerie et la symbolique républicaines (1789–1880)*, Paris, Flammarion, which shows how the female image was used in Republican symbolism. Also Stéphane Michaud, *La Muse et la Madone. Visages de la femme rédemptrice en France et en Allemagne de Novalis à Baudelaire*, Paris, Seuil.

14. See Genevieve Fraisse's paper on 'L'histoire du féminisme' for the Saint-Maximin symposium.

one age and one form of society to another. It depends on prevailing ideas about the role of writing and the recording of facts (what an era considers worthy of note) as well as on the role of the sexes and the relations between them. Periods when there was a greater interest in private life tend to yield more information about women (for example, the eighteenth and nineteenth centuries in the United Kingdom or in France). Some eras are better disposed than others to the utterances or even the writings of women. In the nineteenth century, for example, Protestant or Catholic religious traditions urged girls to keep diaries as a means of self-discipline and edification, but the diaries often became outlets for self-expression. Very rarely were they intended for publication, and the historian's first task is to track them down. At all events the history of women involves looking at existing records from a new angle, with historians discovering their own sources and often bringing them to light. Several approaches are possible, of which I describe four:

1. Approaching traditional sources from a different angle is certainly the first step. It is well known that historical research is largely a matter of preconceived ideas brought to bear on the subject-matter, and that there are many different ways of consulting the texts. The historians of societies in Antiquity have shown us the way. Obviously, the amount of explicit information on women is very scanty, but the works of M.Z. Rosaldo, A. Weiner, N. Loraux and P. Schmitt-Pantel – to mention but a few – have introduced a radically new approach by raising the question of the difference between the sexes and the division in roles between male and female.[15] 'Every study on death, food, clothing, war, ritual, property, gifts, and production in general, sheds light on the division into male and female territory and roles. . . . One of the cornerstones of any study of this kind is a fresh interpretation of iconography. It is not enough to reconsider all the vase-paintings described as gynaeceum scenes. It is also necessary to juxtapose and study the simultaneous or alternating presence of men and women on occasions as important for the *polis* as the departure or return of warriors, funeral ceremonies, banquets, certain festivals', writes

15. A.B. Weiner, *Women of Value, Men of Renown. New Perspectives in Trobriand Exchange*, Austin and London, 1976; M.Z. Rosaldo, *Woman, Culture and Society* Stanford, Calif., 1974; 'The use and abuse of anthropology: reflections on feminism and cross-cultural understanding', *Signs* 5, (1980); N. Loraux, *Les enfants d'Athena*. Paris, 1981; MacCormack and M. Strathern, *Nature, Culture and Gender*, Cambridge, 1980.

Pauline Schmitt-Pantel.[16] This method may be extended to a vast quantity of data. It is the point of view in this case that constitutes the subject of the inquiry and even the information itself. In a sense, it is perhaps untrue to say that the records do not mention women: rather, nobody looked for traces of women in the texts. It is well known that records do not speak for themselves. There are no raw 'facts'; they are always 'processed'.

2. Making greater use of records dealing with commonplace events and private life, which tended to be neglected because of their insignificance: family correspondence, for example. Moreover, a major effort must be made to encourage the emergence from family secrecy of private records buried and sometimes forgotten as being of no interest. The writings of women, the scribes of the family, are generally very much in evidence. See how much can be learned from the fifteen volumes of Georges Sand's *Correspondance* currently in print.[17] But there are also unknown women who are no less interesting: Caroline Chotard-Lioret, for example, has made good use of a collection of 12,000 letters, the correspondence of a family covering the period 1860 to 1930.[18] There is an enormous amount of work to be done in bringing to light, exploring and communicating material from private archives. It is a field in which women historians can be pioneers. Some public records also yield information on these subjects. Legal records for instance, especially for the working class, which comes into conflict with the law more often than the wealthier classes. Women, of course, are much less often charged with offences or crimes than men, but they often appear as the victims of crime, for example crimes of passion, as shown in Joelle Guillais-Maury's illuminating study.[19] When they do come into conflict with the law,[20] the more specifically 'female' crimes – infanticide, abortion, fuel-stealing, shoplifting, etc. – say a great deal about women's relationship to society as a whole, including the way

16. Pauline Schmitt-Pantel, 'La différence des sexes. Histoire, anthropologie et cité greque'. Paper for the Saint-Maximin Symposium, June 1983.

17. This correspondence, now running to fifteen volumes, is edited by Georges Lubin and published by Les Belles Lettres, Paris.

18. Caroline Chotard-Lioret, 'La socialité familiale en province. Une correspondance privée entre 1870 et 1920', PhD thesis, University of Paris V, 1983. A study group on private correspondence in France is organising its second symposium.

19. Joelle Guillais-Maury, 'Recherches sur le crime passionnel à Paris au 19e siècle', PhD thesis, University of Paris VII, 1984. Using legal records (court of criminal appeal) the author analyses love and sexual relationships between working-class men and women: she concludes that female initiative and vitality was much greater than is generally believed.

they are viewed by that society. In general, miscellaneous news items – dealing with the drama of private life – are an interesting source of information, providing genuine case-studies for in-depth analysis.[21]

3. *Literary* sources, frequently discounted by traditional social history as being too disjointed and unreliable, are also very rich in material. What is the nineteenth or twentieth century novel if not the history of families and the adventures of individuals? In our own time, the novel has become heavily autobiographical, and this enhances its value as a first-hand testimony. Of course this type of source, no less than the others, must be used with caution. The more talent and imagination a writer has, the more the material will be filtered through his or her own personality. But the imaginary is part of reality, and the borderline between the two is often blurred. Novels cannot be taken at their face value, but neither can they be ignored, and there is often more individual truth in a literary text that tries to express something of the quality of life than in an administrative table that sets out to give exhaustive particulars. The resources of iconography are also vast, but even more caution is required in interpreting them. In painting, women have always been a favourite subject: symbolised, typecast and imagined rather than seen and described. For example, what do we learn from the portraits of nineteenth-century women painted by Flandrin or Bouguereau[22] if not the code of appearances governing the attitudes and deportment of women? In other words, a great deal. Postcards and photographs deserve very special attention, conveying as they do a variety of gestures, poses and family groupings to be decoded.

4. The recent development of oral history. To my mind, this term is a misnomer: there is no 'oral' history, consisting solely of oral evidence; there are, however, 'oral records' to be incorporated in history, and these are invaluable: the emergence of a word or a memory from forgotten depths; things seen from the angle of the participants, as they are experienced; Luisa Paserini (Turin) has used this new approach to portray fascism and its hold on daily

---

20. Cf. May Hartman, *Victorian Murderesses: A True History of Thirteen Respectable French and English Women accused of Unspeakable Crimes*, New York, Schocken, 1977.

21. *Annales*, July-September 1983. Special issue on *Le fait divers*.

22. William Bouguereau Exhibition in the Petit Palais, Paris, 1984; a major exhibition of the works of Hippolyte Flandrin, the 'painter of respectable women', Paris, Musée du Luxembourg, November 1984.

life.[23] For women, who have spoken a great deal more than they have written, and most of whose life is lived in a private sphere ignored by the written word, oral research is essential, hence most of the practitioners of this method are women.[24] Accounts by women of their experience of historical events, the part they have played in them, their private family life or their 'life story' in general, illustrating the distinctiveness of women's experience – are all contributions of considerable value, provided the user bears in mind the fact that memory is a selective construction, by no means spontaneous, and that tape recordings provide only raw data, to be sifted and compared like other information.

Experience on these practices has already been gathered in the form of analyses that make it possible to proceed in a more methodical[25] and no less confident way. The work of retrieving women's forgotten past is fascinating and necessary, and leads to a reassessment of history. One example is the work on Frenchwomen in the Résistance by Margaret Weitz and Paula Schwartz, describing the part played by women under the cover of the banalities of daily life: a message concealed in a shopping-bag, a tea party camouflaging a secret meeting, and so on. Women participated on a considerable scale, and were deported in comparable numbers, yet they won little official recognition (of 1,059 '*Compagnons de la Libération*', only six are women).[26]

In general, it should be stressed that this use of sources suggests a method that concentrates on quality rather than quantity, an approach that is micro-historical rather than sequential and statistical, an attention to words, gestures, images, places and objects that is derived both from literary analysis and from ethnography or even psychoanalysis, a multidisciplinary approach that should break down certain barriers without degenerating into empty talk.

23. Some of Luisa Paserini's mostly unpublished research has appeared in *History Workshop* and in various Italian journals.

24. As was the case at the Fourth International Symposium on Oral History, held at Aix-en-Provence in 1982.

25. S. Van de Casteele-Schweitzer and Danièle Voldman, 'Sources orales pour l'histoire des femmes. Bilan d'une expérience'. Paper for the Saint-Maximin symposium on *Histoire orale et histoire des femmes*, Institut d'histoire du temps present (80 bis rue Lecourbe, 75015, Paris), 1982. Mimeographed collection of papers, bibliography.

26. Symposium on Women and War organised at Harvard University in January 1984 by the *Center for European Studies*. See M. Perrot, 'Sur le front des sexes: un combat douteux', *Vingtième Siècle* 3 (July 1984). (Report on the symposium and its main conclusions.)

A number of activities might usefully be envisaged in the field of sources. First, drawing up an inventory of existing resources in different countries: in France, a 'Guide to Research on the History of Women' is being prepared with CNRS funds by two librarians, Colette Chambelland and Michel Dreyfus,[27] well known to social historians. It would be interesting to find out whether similar guides or inventories exist in other countries, and, if so, it would be useful to designate a place where these various tools of the trade might be kept together.

Second, the preparation of inventories of existing collections of records or documentation should be encouraged in order to make them better known and more accessible to the public. The story of the Fonds Bouglé, currently deposited with the Historical Library of the City of Paris (rue Pavée, near Saint-Paul underground station), is typical of the problems involved. The collection was set up by a feminist office worker, between 1910 and 1939. Through purchases or gifts she amassed, with the assistance of her husband, an impressive quantity of records. They include manuscripts (thousands of letters from feminists such as Hubertine Auclert, founder of the newspaper *La Citoyenne* and a committed feminist), printed material (leaflets, newspapers) and even objects (a belt as worn by the Vésuviennes of 1848, feminist badges, flags, etc.). Marie-Louise Bouglé's clearly stated intention was to set up women's archives; she bequeathed her collection to the Marguerite Durand Library, founded by another feminist under the aegis of the *Mairie* of the 5th *arrondissement* in Paris. Marie-Louise Bouglé died in 1938, just before war broke out. Her husband attempted to deposit the bequest with the Marguerite Durand Library, but was turned away. It was provisionally deposited with the National Library, whose staff found the crates long after the war and transferred them to the Paris Historical Library where, being unclassified, they were inaccessible for many years. The collection was finally classified by Maîté Albistur, as a PhD dissertation at the University of Paris VII. This is a painstaking inventory of the collection, yet the Fonds Bouglé is still difficult to consult. No way has yet been found of stamping the items so that they can be lent to the public. . . . It is a

27. Colette Chambelland is Director of the Musée Social and Michel Dreyfus a former librarian at the BDIC in Nanterre, where he helped to catalogue another feminist collection, that of Gabrielle Duchène, a very valuable source of information for peace movements. Both writers have also produced a guide to working-class history.

safe bet that if the collection had borne the name of a famous male writer or a statesman, it would have met with a happier fate. No doubt there are other 'Fonds Bouglé' elsewhere, and there would be many more if a campaign of persuasion and incitement were waged among women, both committed feminists and others, to make available any papers they possess.

The third type of activity should therefore be to set up women's archives in a number of centres where various series of records can be deposited.

Printed matter: newsletters, newspapers, journals and pamphlets written by women, which are often so difficult to trace; the originals, if not available, could be replaced by microfilm collections.

Private papers: correspondence, memoirs and diaries which are known to exist in families, though often neglected and in danger of destruction. If attention were drawn to records of this kind through appropriate publications or studies, the owners might be encouraged to donate them instead of throwing them away. Moreover, women's movements, which generally – and understandably – show little interest in record-keeping, should be requested to deposit their documentation. The matter of consultation rights could easily be settled: archives practice, at least in France, is well-established on this point.

Sound records: especially tape recordings of interviews and autobiographical narrative, that are all too frequently discarded after use. They provide a means of storing oral memories. Systematic programmes could, I think, be initiated to record certain personal testimonies, even without immediate historical research in view. A case in point is the *Fondation nationale des sciences politiques*, in France, which conducts regular lengthy interviews with politicians, providing records for future historians. Why should there not be a similar arrangement for women?

Iconographic records of all kinds, especially collections of photographs.

Women's archives of this kind exist throughout the world. Besides those already mentioned in France, there are outstanding examples in the United States, such as the Schlesinger Library at Harvard. This is another case where an inventory would be necessary, but assistance must be given for the development of such collections, which are indispensable to the writing of women's history. There can be no history without records.

The Future and Objectives of Women's History

As history is at least to some extent a combination of our particular world view, our present demands, and the past, it stands to reason that its objectives vary from one country or culture to another: the needs and aims of western women may very well seem self-indulgent or even superfluous to women in the Third World. Furthermore, in the past ten years, the aims, problems and procedures of women's history have already changed.

Hence the desirability of a systematic historiographical analysis covering an extended period of time. When and in what terms do historians talk about women? We have already noted that, in the nineteenth and twentieth centuries in France, this depended on the relationship between the public and private spheres, between society and the individual. Other examples could be given. For example, in the nineteenth century the great debate on matriarchy in which Morgan, Bachofen and Engels participated and which stirred the imagination of the European intelligentsia (and not only its female members), was part of a process of investigation of the concept of power at work in societies.[28]

An analysis of contemporary historical journals – for both specialists and the layperson – to discover how much space women occupy in them and in what terms they are referred to would prove highly illuminating. In France this has been done in the case of the *Annales* and *l'Histoire*. The latter, an admirable journal for the layperson founded in 1978, has devoted between 2 and 3 per cent of its space to in-depth articles on women, chiefly famous women or communities of women (convents, harems, etc.). There are only isolated instances of articles that address themselves to more complex subjects. Popularisation in this case is lagging behind research and has failed to reflect it faithfully. And yet women play an active role in the journal itself: between 1978 and 1982, one-seventh of the overall output was written by women, though, they were not writing specifically on the subject of women, but much more often on customs, society, ethnology and travel.

28. Françoise Picq, 'Sur la théorie du droit maternel. Discours anthropologique et discours socialiste', PhD thesis, University of Paris-Dauphine, 1979, has made an overall study of the matter. Martin Green's book, *The Von Richtofen Sisters* [*Les soeurs Von Richtofen. Deux ancêtres du féminisme dans l'Allemagne de Bismark face à Otto Gross, Max Weber et D.H. Lawrence*] French translation, Paris, Le Seuil, 1979, shows the scale of discussions in Germany on these subjects.

All this raises the more general questions of the place and function of women in the historian's profession. As history in France is a highly esteemed branch of knowledge, for reasons of intellectual prestige but also of professional practice (for example, its role in the training of journalists, politicians or senior civil servants), it has remained a male preserve. Since the mixing of the sexes in the competitive examination *(agrégation)* for history teachers in France, the proportion of successful women candidates has fallen sharply. This does not, of course, on any account mean that we should revert to separate examinations. But it leads one to wonder about the male/female ratio in the professions and various branches of intellectual activity. For example, the *'agrégation'* examinations in languages and especially in literature, which lead to teaching posts and nothing else, are dominated by women.

No discussion of history and research, especially in the scientific and academic field, can afford to ignore this characteristic of professional circles. How do matters stand in the other countries represented here?

Piecing together and reconstituting women's memories can be a prime objective of women's history, bringing to light what has been suppressed, held back or forgotten, filling in the 'blanks' in history. It can be done in many different ways, by taking, for example: the presence of women in 'historical events', from which they are too easily removed. How did they experience them? What role did they play? A symposium on Women and War organised at Harvard by the Center for European Studies sought to highlight and understand the various roles played by women in the two world wars, including their work in the Résistance, and to investigate the impact of the wars on male/female relations. It reached the somewhat pessimistic conclusion that war sometimes accentuates current trends but more frequently halts their progress, putting each sex in its place in a highly conservative way, although in the long run this leads in turn to a feminist backlash.

The presence of women in daily life should be recorded: their roles and life-styles, their status and their activities – facts so frequently obliterated – and an attempt made to identify the distinctive characteristics of each era and country: the history of childbearing and childbirth; types of female work, in particular housework; the history of female spheres of action, forms of power and expression, etc. Women's accounts of their everyday lives in recent times are of great interest, and a number of surveys, interviewing retired women, for example, have sought to break through the barrier of silence.[29]

A world history of women's movements and struggles for change is needed. This is especially the case for feminism, which is the form taken by the women's movement in democratic countries as a result of the contradictions arising in those same countries, since the proclamation of the 'natural rights' of individuals ultimately pre-supposes equal rights for the sexes, although this is not usually the case even in politics (women being deprived of the vote and more generally of political office). But the history of these movements tends to be played down. Feminism is regarded as a social, much more than a political, movement, and feminists are for the most part dicredited. Women themselves tend to forget the struggles of their predecessors. The sporadic development of the women's movement, pressing forward and then falling back, favours amnesia. Women themselves have a task of recollection and historiography that they must carry out, not in order to sing the praises of the pioneers, but to find the hidden thread that will string the successive movements together and give them unity.

With this end in view, a number of women in France, associated for the most part with the Marguerite Durand Library (and, in particular, its former librarian Madame Léautey) conceived the idea of compiling a *Dictionary of Feminism*, to build on the isolated projects undertaken in the past few years and to make their results accessible. It is a difficult proposition, beset with many epistemo-logical and practical problems. How are 'feminist' women to be defined? Who belongs to that category? A broad definition was adopted: by 'feminist' is meant any woman who, at any time in her life, has made some contribution to achieving equality of the sexes through a reversal of traditional roles. The project is still in abeyance for the time being, partly for financial reasons. But we must bear in mind the fact that all knowledge eventually finds its way into a dictionary, and that careful thought should therefore be given to definitions.

Although it is indispensable, the gathering of data is not enough. Besides, even data-gathering calls for a certain sense of history – epitomized in the dictionary.

29. In Paris, research carried out by Catherine Rhein and Françoise Cribier on the memories of retired Parisian women, Laboratoire de Géographie sociale, Institut de Géographie, rue Saint-Jacques, 75005 Paris.

As we have seen, the history of women has passed through various stages: the desire to show that women are oppressed and to understand why they are subjugated, followed by the determination to bring out their positive role at all levels, their presence and their active involvement. The burning questions nowadays have to do with 'power': although women may not have power, it is claimed, they have 'strength'; or alternatively, 'political' power is contrasted with women's 'social' power, the latter being suddenly considered more important. What does it all mean?

A further topic is women's 'culture': is it a separate, independent culture, if not linked to distinctive sexual characteristics then at least to the historical fact of 'gender'? Or is there simply a fluctuating division between the cultural practices of the sexes? This question has given rise to a major discussion, especially in Italy.[30]

At any rate, the question at issue is still that of the relations between the sexes, as was perhaps first pointed out by women historians of the ancient world, who were more experienced in handling anthropological subjects and studying myths and other forms of representation. 'What we need now is to compile a history of the tension between the male and female roles, and to trace the links between conflicts and harmony throughout the course of history', writes Arlette Farge.[31]

We are not setting out to constitute a new discipline, a closed field of knowledge entitled 'women's history', with all the risks of isolation and indifference that that would entail. Such a tendency is already discernible: a certain amused or annoyed condescension, an attitude of indulgence – sometimes mingled with a vague sense of guilt – towards this new female whim that one might as well be humoured while it lasts.

In placing the relations between the sexes at the centre of historical research the intention is to encourage a possible review of

---

30. A report on these important discussions among Italian feminists has been published in two CRIF (Centre de recherches, de réflexion et d'information féministes) *Bulletins* 4 (Winter 1983–4) and 5 (Spring 1984), with references to the principal texts, in particular those by Rossana Rossanda, her book *Le Altre*, 1979 and her article, 'Il modello Luisa e il modello Sidonia' in *Orsaminore* No. 6. The CRIF *Bulletin* is worth noting in general, as are the centre's activities aimed at gathering information on research in progress. Address: 1 rue de Fossés Saint-Jacques, 75005 Paris.

31. Paper already mentioned in connection with the Saint-Maximin symposium. On this symposium, pending publication of the records, see A. Farge's report published in CRIF *Bulletin*, No. 3, Autumn 1983.

history as a whole and to attain a better overall understanding. Some people have referred, unjustifiably in my opinion, to the 'epistemological break' that has occurred as a result of feminist research. But I do not think that the approaches and methods we have been discussing are radically different. What is different is the question being asked. How great is its operational value, its capacity to change the *status quo*? Can it make people see things from a different angle? Or is it only a projection of our fantasies? If there has indeed been an 'epistemological break', then it has occurred at the level of the questions asked.

The Question of Resources: Some Practical Proposals

Although unevenly developed in different countries, research on women's history has already produced a number of written works. Many of them, however, are rendered ineffective and unproductive by not being communicated. Establishing inventories and promoting circulation are top priorities. To inform, communicate and circulate material among existing groups and individuals would seem preferable to setting up any cumbersome institution that would require a great deal of energy merely to maintain itself. Minimum centralisation (there must after all be some kind of meeting-point) for maximum dissemination: that would be the ideal. Could not information technology come to our aid?

There might, for example, be a documentation centre whose main purpose would be to gather information at various levels:

1. Existing works:
    A bibliography of bibliographies, working aids and research centres.

    A file of printed works: books, and especially articles in journals, these being the medium for the latest advances in research. There are two kinds of journal: (i) those specifically for women (there are now, scattered across the world, several reviews or journals on women's history); (ii) the leading historical journals in which studies on women are showing a marginal increase. A computerised file would be a tremendous asset. Another possibility is to ask bodies that produce computerised bibliographies (e.g. the CNRS) to introduce new data under the headings 'women', 'feminism', etc.

An inventory of 'grey' literature, especially work produced in universities and in many cases unpublished. This represents a considerable and frequently ignored and wasted investment: dissertations for master's degrees, doctoral theses, especially for PhDs and equivalent qualifications, and papers prepared for symposia. All these provide a mine of information. If the original itself cannot be obtained, it should at least be possible to consult a file indicating where it may be found.

2. Teams, groups and research centres on women's history throughout the world.
3. Male and female researchers in the field.

Taking this as a starting-point, several forms of dissemination may be envisaged:

1. A data-bank system operating on a question-and-answer basis.
2. An awareness list providing information, if only in outline, on works existing in different countries.
3. Comparative thematic analyses designed to take stock of particular subjects. Contracts for this kind of work, no less important than new research and influencing it in some respects, could be given to qualified researchers. Secondary analysis, comparisons and criticism of existing works are being acknowledged more and more as ways of enhancing the value of isolated research findings.

A second field is that of education. As a rule, this pays scant attention to the role of women. Indeed, it is very often biased by a highly traditional or even decidedly anti-feminist depiction of roles. Critical analyses of history books in different countries from this point of view would certainly provide an insight into cultural images of the roles of the sexes.

How can things be changed? How can the findings of research be made to influence education? A number of uncomplicated and original approaches might be contemplated, such as the preparation of files summarizing information regarding a particular period, problem or issue (women in the French Revolution, women in the Commune, women's work during the industrial revolution; history of birth control, childbearing, etc.), pending the publication of an attractive book making research findings available to the general public.

The media could also be approached. A French television channel has currently prepared a series of programmes portraying feminist women. History in the form of apologia or hagiography, however, should be ruled out. Humour, on the contrary, should be a basic ingredient.

Nothing could be more daunting than the adoption of a dogmatic or censorious attitude. We certainly want women's history to be critical, but we also want it to be a source of freedom, releasing the powers of fantasy and imagination.

4

Redressing the Balance or Transforming the Art? The British Experience

ANNA DAVIN

Approaches to Women's History

It is essential, intellectually and politically, to try to understand the past if we are to understand the present and to work effectively for the future we want. Historical analysis enriches political understanding and counters today's emphasis on public personalities as opposed to historical and economic forces and processes. It can help people to see themselves as agents rather than victims and to discover common interests and solidarities. As women we need our history.

But in established historical writing and teaching women have received little or no attention. This is not surprising. The dominant version of history in any society will be one which bolsters an existing situation. Thus in a class society history has meant the history of rulers, in an imperialist society the history of empire, in a male-dominated society the history of men. Such history will also reflect the general assumptions and concerns of the dominant group. It will embody belief in their superiority – over women, the young, those of other race, religion or nationality, the poor, the landless, the illiterate. It will focus on the powerful and their doings – political leaders, the military, royalty, the great men of industry, finance, and landed property. Of course there are other histories, other assumptions, other concerns, but to let them be heard is not always easy. Those whose forebears were exploited and oppressed – the colonised and enslaved, sharecroppers or poor peasants, workers, victims of ethnic or religious persecution, women – nourish as best they can their

alternative traditions. Their memory of how things once were different, of what has been lost, of resistance and its champions may be
repressed and stifled, or it may be preserved only in myth, song or
ritual.[1] It may be an underground stream or it may emerge to flow
openly. These alternative currents carry with them a potential challenge to the present. For this reason history is always a site of struggle.

Women's history provides such a challenge, and not a new one.
Over many generations women who have questioned the restrictions placed upon their sex have turned to the past for ammunition
or for understanding. Some, like Mary Wollstonecraft in her *Vindication of the Rights of Woman* (1792), have fuelled their indignation
by 'considering the historic page', whose lesson – that 'the civilisation which has hitherto taken place has been very partial'[2] – they
have then used as an argument for reform or even revolution.
Others have sought to disprove the 'natural' character of woman's
subordination by pointing to societies with different customs. (This
approach, overlapping with the anthropological, was adopted by
Engels, by Olive Schreiner, by Margaret Mead, and by others after
them.) Others again have sought for outstanding women in the past.
Margaret Fuller, in New York in 1845, challenged women's alleged
inferiority both in contemporary ideology and in historical convention by cataloguing examples of strong and noble women from
classical times onwards, and contended that despite 'great disparity
betwixt the nations as betwixt individuals . . . yet the idea of
Woman has always cast some rays and has often been forcibly
represented'.[3] Similarly, tableaux and pageants mounted by English
campaigners for suffrage in the early twentieth century presented
women warriors, artists, scholars, monarchs and saints, so as to
show 'the physical, intellectual, creative and ethical strengths of
women'.[4] Today, in rather the same spirit, some women search the
historical record for matriarchies and goddess cults. History can
thus serve to provide inspiration, through examples of long injus-

1. An interesting fictional example of historical tradition embodied in Afro-
Caribbean ritual dance occurs in the novel *Praise Song for the Widow* by the black
American writer Paule Marshall, London, Virago, 1983. Irish mythology, song and
dance are other obvious examples.
2. Mary Wollstonecraft, *Vindication of the Rights of Woman*, London, Penguin
edn, 1985, p. 79.
3. Margaret Fuller, *Woman in the Nineteenth Century*, New York, Norton, 1971,
p. 61.
4. Julie Holledge, *Innocent Flowers: Women in the Edwardian Theatre*, London,
Virago, 1981, p. 70.

tice, or through evidence which counters stereotypes and assertions of inevitable female destiny, or through golden visions of erstwhile equality or even power.

There are weaknesses in this selective approach, however, and my preference is for the more exploratory approach taken by other pioneers of women's history: one which looks for explanation rather than inspiration, and which starts with questions ('Why is it like this now?' 'Has it always been this way?' 'What are the processes of change and can we control them?') rather than with expected answers. Olive Schreiner, in *Woman and Labour* (1911), compared primitive and modern societies (with a touch of 'golden-age-ism', it is true) and traced connections between accumulation of wealth and the subjugated 'parasitism' of women.[5] Alice Clark explored the lives of seventeenth-century women in meticulously researched detail so as to examine the influence of capitalism on women's productive capacity and their position in society. Clark also justified her enterprise in historiographical terms. She pointed out that historians had 'paid little attention to the circumstances of women's lives' because they had mistakenly regarded women as unchanging, 'a static factor in social developments'. Moreover, she argued, since men and women were indissolubly linked, this neglect made a full understanding of society impossible.[6] This insight continued to be ignored by mainstream historians. In the middle decades of the twentieth century women's history remained a tenuous and little regarded minority tradition, largely conducted by women, and rarely integrated into university teaching, although important and interesting work was being produced. Frances Collier's thesis of 1921 on the family economy of early cotton workers, for instance, provided important information and analysis on the relation of men's and women's, adult and child labour, and on family earnings and expenditure, but had to wait until 1964 for full publication and appreciation.[7] Ivy Pinchbeck's rich book on women workers in the industrial revolution was published in 1930 but remained outside the canon and hard to find until (and indeed beyond) a new hardback edition in 1969.[8] Wanda Neff's historical

5. Olive Schreiner, *Woman and Labour*, London, Virago, 1978.
6. Alice Clark, *Working Life of Women in the Seventeenth Century*, London, Routledge & Kegan Paul, 1982. The 1982 edition has a useful introduction by Miranda Chaytor and Jane Lewis.
7. Frances Collier, *The Family Economy of the Working Classes in the Cotton Industry, 1784–1833*, Manchester University Press, 1964.

and literary study of Victorian working women (1929) resurfaced only in 1966.[9] Dorothy Gardiner's *English Girlhood at School* (1929) is still out of print; so is Rosamond Bayne-Powell's *The English Child in the Eighteenth Century* (1939).[10] Some women historians within this tradition produced books for a wider audience, whose impact lasted longer. Eileen Power, for instance, besides more monographic work such as her book on *Mediaeval English Nunneries* (1922), wrote *Mediaeval English People* (1924), which was an early paperback (1937) and has maintained consistent popularity since.

The rise of labour history in the last thirty years should have made more space and allowed more recognition for women's history. It was developed as a challenge to dominant history, asserting instead the importance of the working class – their labour, their struggles and their organisations. Women, too, were workers and members of the working class, engaged in and affected by its struggles, if sometimes excluded from its organisations. Working-class women have been even more neglected in conventional history than have their menfolk. Unfortunately, much labour history has continued this neglect. It arises in part from the nature of the sources – information about men is easier to come by. But the inherent bias of the sources is often matched by the unconscious bias of the usually male historian. The values and attitudes of the skilled male workers of the nineteenth century – the backbone of so much labour history – seem to creep in from the memoirs and minute books of the early labour movement. So, for example, the sexual division of labour has been taken as constant and 'natural', rather than recognised or – better still – studied as being continually constructed, contested and modified. New work is rectifying this. 'Work' has meant waged work, and preferably work done in mine or workshop or building site or steelworks – not outwork or laundry or service, let alone unpaid domestic labour. And 'struggle' has also been defined in a partial way, which has concentrated on issues relating to wage and employment, and excluded those relating

8. Ivy Pinchbeck, *Women Workers in the Industrial Revolution, 1750–1850*, London, Virago, 1981.

9. Wanda Neff, *Victorian Working Women: a Historical and Literary Study of Women in British Industries and Professions, 1832–50*, London, Frank Cass, 1966.

10. Dorothy Gardiner, *English Girlhood at School: a Study of Women's Education through Twelve Centuries*, Oxford, Oxford University Press, 1929; Rosamund Bayne-Powell, *The English Child in the Eighteenth Century*, London, John Murray, 1939.

to the quality of life, or taking place away from the point of production. (E.P. Thompson is of course a major exception here.)[11] The family is left to demographers and social historians, or is dealt with by cursory references to general works whose confident generalisations appear to fill the gap but are based on thin research and anachronistic assumptions.

Women's history has benefited substantially, however, from the growing importance since the 1960s of social history, both as an academic discipline influenced by sociology and anthropology, and as a post-'68 political project influenced by feminism and other political developments. (In Britain the complementary wings are represented by the journal *Social History* on the one hand, and by publications and activities connected with the History Workshop on the other.) Social history gives academic sanction to the study of many questions which are important to women's history – sex roles and socialisation, family and daily life, health, culture and leisure, and so on. A rapidly expanding body of secondary literature is being produced; social history courses are increasingly available; school teaching is being influenced; and students starting research on women are less likely to be discouraged with assertions that they will find no relevant information in the sources. But the 'respectability' of even social history, let alone women's history, must not be overestimated. Other specialisms, such as military or narrowly 'political' history, or demography (the 'hard' and more respectable version of family history) still rank higher, and in times of financial cutback, as the present, jobs and funds go elsewhere. Women's studies programmes in Britain, where they exist (e.g. in the universities of Bradford Essex, Kent, and York), have been established against resistance, and are not invulnerable.

The academically marginal position of women's history has been beneficial, however, as well as irksome. Links with beleaguered feminists in other disciplines, such as anthropology, psychology, literature, or art history have produced exciting cross-fertilization.[12] Feminist historians work in museums, libraries and archives, in

11. Classically in E.P. Thompson, *The Making of the English Working Class*, Harmondsworth, Penguin/Allen Lane, 1963 but also in later work.

12. Among other examples, see Ellen Ross and Rayna Rapp, 'Sex and Society: a research note from social history and anthropology', *Comparative Studies in Society and History* 23:1 (Jan 1981); Rayna Rapp, Ellen Ross, and Renate Bridenthal, 'Examining Family History', *Feminist Studies* 5:1 (Spring 1979) reprinted in Judith L. Newton, Mary P. Ryan, and Judith R. Walkowitz, (eds.), *Sex and Class in Women's History*. London, Routledge & Kegan Paul, 1983; Carolyn Steedman, *The*

theatre and radio, TV and film, in community history projects and schools, and above all in adult education. University extra-mural programmes, along with other adult education institutions and the Workers' Education Association – all alas now under threat – employ a number of us as part-time teachers, and the classroom interaction with eager and often knowledgeable students of all ages and backgrounds has helped many of us to clarify and organise our ideas, as well as providing rather more stimulus and encouragement than is always available in academic circles.[13] Informal feminist history groups such as those in London, Bristol or Manchester, provide support and criticism for women researchers and the chance for others to share their findings.[14] Autonomous resource centres such as the Feminist Library (previously the Women's Research and Resources Centre in London) the Feminist Archive in Bath, and the Lesbian Archive in Manchester have grown up to compensate for shortcomings in conventional collections.[15] The appetite for women's history is widespread, and catered for in many different ways. Besides the proliferating evening classes there are tape-slide shows and videos, exhibitions, plays, radio and TV productions (documentary and fiction), novels, schoolbooks, do-it-yourself guides, and other publications.[16] The success of the Virago publish-

---

Tidy House: Little Girls Writing, London, Virago, 1982; Denise Riley, 'The Free Mothers: pronatalism and working mothers in industry at the end of the last war in Britain', *History Workshop Journal* 11 (Spring 1981), and *War in the Nursery: Theories of the Child and Mother*. London, Virago, 1983; Ellen Ross, 'Fierce questions and taunts: married life in working-class London 1870–1914', *Feminist Studies* 8:3 (Fall 1982); 'Surival networks: Women's neighbourhood sharing in London before WW1', *History Workshop Journal* 15 (Spring 1983); 'Not the sort that would sit on the doorstep: respectability in pre-WW1 London neighbour-hoods', *International Labour and Working-Class History* 27 (Spring 1985).

13. Since this paper was presented at the Meeting of Experts on 'Theoretical Frameworks and Methodological Approaches to Studies on the Role of Women in History . . .', Unesco, Paris, 13–16 November 1984, the abolition of the Greater London Council and similar authorities, along with increasingly tight education budgets, have considerably diminished financial support for such activities.

14. See Anna Davin, 'The London Feminist History Group', *History Workshop Journal* 8 (Autumn 1979). Similar groups are currently active in Bristol, Brighton, Manchester and elsewhere. They can be contacted through 'A Woman's Place', Hungerford House, Victoria Embankment, London WC2.

15. The Feminist Library is at Hungerford House (see previous note); the Feminist Archive is c/o University of Bath, Claverton Down, Bath, Avon BA2 7AY; the London Lesbian History Group is c/o A Woman's Place, Hungerford House, as above; and the Manchester Lesbian Archive is c/o Lesbian Link, 62 Bloom Street, Manchester.

16. Novels include Buchi Emecheta's *Second Class Citizens*, *The Bride Price* and

ing house's reprints of classic fiction and history by women, as well as the popularity of new work in history such as Sheila Rowbotham's, testify to women's eager interest in their past. Nor is the demand only from the counter culture of the women's movement: women (and men) of a wider political, cultural and academic range are also involved. The support for 'people's history' (see below) and for History Workshop meetings and publications is part of the same development – both incentive and response to the attempt to democratise access to history, its production, and its content.

Working With Women's History – Some Problems

This enthusiastic appetite for women's history is of course a stimulus for those who are working to uncover women's past and to transform our understanding of society, past and present. But the commitment to 'redressing the balance' by disseminating new historical findings and analysis as widely as possible, along with the commitment to support other women in their research and writing, often drain time and energy. It is hard to get on with research and writing while also teaching, lecturing, participating in support groups, helping to organise conferences (or to correct imbalances in other organisers' planning by 'injecting' women), advising isolated and struggling students, reading and commenting on other people's work in draft, making sure new work by women is noticed and reviewed, answering enquiries about women's history, and so on. Of course all these activities are worthwhile; some, like reading draft work and taking part in support groups, involve reciprocity; and to be active in a lively network is invigorating and enriching. But the problem of time remains, and it is compounded by the particular demands of research on women, especially if the whole

---

The Slave Girl, London, Allison & Busby, 1974, 1976, 1977; Zoe Fairbairn's *Stand We at Last*. London, Virago, 1983; Meredith Tax, *Rivington Street*, New York, Morrow, 1981; London, Heinemann, 1982. Schoolbooks include Carol Adams, *Ordinary Lives a Hundred Years Ago*, London, Virago, 1982, and the Cambridge University Press Women in History series edited by Carol Adams, Paula Bartley, Judy Lown and Cathy Loxton, 1983. Elyse Dodgson describes historical drama work with school children in 'From oral history to drama', *Oral History* 12:2 (1984) and *Motherland*, London, Heinemann Educational, 1983. Deirdre Beddoes's *Discovering Women's History*, London, Routledge & Kegan Paul/Pandora, 1983, is an excellent guide to research and Janet Horowitz Murray has assembled very useful extracts from nineteenth-century documentary material in *Strong Minded Women*, New York, Pantheon, 1982.

context of their lives is to be understood.

All historical research is of course laborious and slow. When the quarry is women it takes even longer. The evidence is scattered and often problematic: the historian pans much mud and sand for the occasional nugget. Then its worth has to be assessed. The questions which must continually be asked are, for instance, Who wrote this, in what context, and why?, 'Does it reflect direct experience, or hearsay, or prejudice?' Even apparently straightforward data such as census returns raise many problems. Definitions of work as occupation are too blunt to explore women's shifting balance between different kinds of casual and domestic labour; the age groups are a coarse measure for changes in the age and incidence of marriage or in the patterns of employment at different stages of the life cycle; and comparison across the decades is almost impossible because the basis on which work and occupation were defined kept changing, especially in relation to married women's contribution to family enterprises such as farms, workshops and shops.[17] Inconsistent recording of married women's work by local enumerators also undermines confidence in the value of the aggregate tables. This illustrates the importance of studying the ideological context in order to read and evaluate the sources. The enumerators' class position or identification means that they did not expect married women to do anything but their housework, especially if the household seemed 'respectable', and might not even ask whether they did. Some husbands might prefer for status reasons not to mention that their wives were in paid employment, and not to count work they did in a domestic enterprise. Wives and husbands alike might not see the wife's work as amounting to an occupation. The historian has therefore to be continually alert for the influence of ideological prescription and class on what purports to be description or fact. Jennie Kitteringham has argued that middle-class codes of 'proper' behaviour led to the denunciation of field work for women as immoral because it could involve a rolling up of the skirts, or a removal of top layers of clothes, or their relieving themselves behind hedges (or with long skirts, even not behind

17. Desley Deacon, 'Political arithmetic: the nineteenth-century Australian census and the construction of the dependent woman', *Signs* 11 (Autumn 1985); Catherine Hakim, 'Census reports as documentary evidence: the census commentaries 1801–1951', *Sociological Review* 28 (1980). For a useful general discussion of women's employment, see Jane Lewis, *Women in England, 1870–1950*, Brighton, Wheatsheaf Books and Bloomington, Indiana University Press, 1984.

67

hedges), and that this class gulf affects much of the 'evidence' given to parliamentary enquiries into women's work in agriculture.[18] Not only class, but also regional, cultural, ethnic, religious and other variables would influence the exact content of prescriptions for femininity. And the extent to which ideological prescription and actual behaviour matched up has to be continually questioned, never assumed. Women did not always accept constraints, though resistance did not always involve open defiance.

Another difficulty (at least so far as Britain and North America are concerned) is that they are everywhere and nowhere – where do you start? Secondary works and bibliographies are no longer as scarce as they used to be, and libraries have sections on 'women', though many more works of relevance will be scattered throughout economics, sociology, psychology, literature, education, anthropology and other categories. Fifteen years ago there were fewer preliminary guides. We searched catalogues for titles containing words like 'woman', 'female', 'lady', 'girl', 'domestic', 'home', 'everday life', and for women's organisations and their publications. We read everything that might be useful.

So for my own work on the childhood of working-class girls in late nineteenth-century London I have ranged through anything that might throw light on London working-class life in general and on children and women in particular. I read memoirs by clergymen and other middle-class observers; newspaper reports and magazine articles depicting the strange ways of the poor; discussions in Parliament and elsewhere about elementary education for the masses; administrative records from the schools and the bodies that ran them; folklorists' investigations into popular – especially child – traditions; the publications of the Child Study movement; reports by innumerable officials; evidence and reports of various official and unofficial inquiries; novels and other fiction purporting to portray working-class life or aimed at a working-class audience; the textbooks used in school and the fiction bestowed as prizes; and finally all the autobiographical material I could find, printed, manuscript, or recorded on tape. I also tried to acquire a sense of the physical environment 'my' children inhabited, by looking for photographs and other kinds of visual representation from the time, studying

18. Jennie Kitteringham, 'Country Girls in Nineteenth-Century England', in Raphael Samuel, (ed.) *Village Life and Labour*. London, Routledge & Kegan Paul, 1975.

maps, and exploring London for survivals of what the children would have known. Schools are the most inevitable remnants, along with churches and chapels (not always still in use). Here and there, pockets of the old streets and neighbourhoods can still be found. Older houses still sometimes have features allowing a glimpse of children's everyday life in the past – the fireplace-cum-oven, the wooden floors and furniture, the doorsteps, the washhouse perhaps still containing copper and mangle, the backyard. And other reminders may be found in museums and exhibitions, or in junk shops: school textbooks and prizes, clothes and toys (though multiple ownership and hard wear make these rare survivors), treasured knick-knacks from the overmantel, kitchen equipment or furniture.

Evidence of this kind does not figure in my footnotes, but it has contributed to my understanding, just as the spatial relations of an upper-class house can be used to illumine the class and gender relations of its various inhabitants.[19] A comprehension of the proportions and characteristics of the material environment is not only an aid to the imagination, it also helps us to understand, for instance, what was involved in the domestic labour done by children and women, or what demands on their energy were made by the journey to school or to shop or market, or how far play and responsibility were dovetailed. In the same way, to walk along old streets of terraced houses, or to look at the long, shared balconies of 'model dwellings', or to see the size of the single rooms which held whole families, prompts questions about how people handled what seems to us such dense proximity – what strains there might have been (on the mother especially, perhaps, or is that an anachronistic question?), and what compensations lay in the shared public spaces which allowed women to meet and talk.

This wide-ranging approach to sources results in part from the attempt to examine a large subject (childhood and women) across thematic boundaries such as work, education, health, socialisation or play, and to understand the full context of women's lives. It is also an attempt to counter the problems of bias which are inherent in all historical data but which acquire special significance when the

19. Leonore Davidoff, 'Class and Gender in Victorian England', *Feminist Studies* 5:1 (Spring 1979) and reprinted in Newton, Ryan, and Walkowitz, *Sex and Class in Women's History*; also Leonore Davidoff and Catherine Hall, 'The Architecture of public and private life: English middle-class society in a provincial town, 1780–1850', in Anthony Sutcliffe, (ed.) *The Pursuit of Urban History*, London, Edward Arnold, 1983.

group or class being studied were not in a position to leave their own account of themselves.

Documentary evidence is overwhelmingly the record of those who were in a privileged position of some kind, most obviously, by class, but also by gender and by age. Levels of literacy (and perhaps too of self-consciousness and self-importance) were higher in the middle and upper classes. The views of such people, especially of the men, would be more likely to get into print, with correspond- ingly improved chance of survival. But even their private papers would be favoured in the process of conservation. Families in those classes would both value their papers and also have facilities to keep them, from a fully equipped library to an attic where trunks could remain forgotten and undisturbed. Later, perhaps, (although many such hoards remain in private hands), archivists would consider they had more 'historical value' because of their ruling-class origin. Letters, diaries, shopping lists or accounts from poor families had little chance of survival.

The printed record embodies similar bias. Working-class people, especially women, had little access to print unless they were in some way exceptional – by their education, their confidence and probably their politics. Few wrote memoirs: of women there are almost none. Some records do survive from organisations, but in the nineteenth century organisations were usually based in the élite with regular and well-paid work, which never included women. (Towards the end of the century there are records from women's own organisa- tions, but still their members were not typical.) Newspapers some- times wrote up strikes, but only if they were long dramatic ones. Long strikes needed union funds or outside support: women's strikes were most often spontaneous, brief, unsupported and scarce- ly reported. The one well-known exception is the match girls' strike of 1888, prolonged and won by outside support and pub- licity. Working-class domestic and family life was sometimes dis- cussed in the press and in parliament especially at times when anxiety about the dangerous classes or the health of the nation was translated into denunciation of married women's employment and the decay of the family.[20] Information was collected by parliamen- tary and other inquiries on employment, education, health, hous- ing, public order and so on, which means that official sources

20. Angela John, *By the Sweat of our Brow*, London, Croom Helm, 1980; Anna Davin, 'Imperialism and Motherhood', *History Workshop Journal* 5 (Spring 1978).

include a mass of evidence presented orally or in writing to countless committees and commissions, and printed and archive material compiled by bureaucrats in every field. But generally this material reflects the standpoint of men, most of them middle or upper-class as well. The questions were asked by men, addressed largely to men, and mostly concerned with men or with problems from a male point of view. So, for instance, women's low wages were undercutting men's, a threat to men, rather than inadequate wages for any person to live on. Ill-health and exhaustion from excessive hours of ill-paid factory work in terrible conditions was a problem in so far as it affected women's performance as wives and mothers, not because of its effect on them. Unofficial but comparable inquiries, like those conducted by the Women's Industrial Council or the Childhood Society in the 1890s and 1900s, or, most notably, Charles Booth's massive survey of life and labour in London in the 1880s and '90s, provide rather similar material: detailed, specific, well-organised, and relying at least partly on those like school attendance officers, teachers, clergymen or policemen whose official position gave them some familiarity with working-class life.

The dominant voice throughout is that of the adult, usually male, middle-class informant, administrator or investigator – a long way from the working-class woman or child. And in the perspective of authority individuals disappear into cases: the complex flexibility of the working-class household struggling for survival is seen in terms of problems (often 'moral' ones); and the information filed is restricted to what seems relevant to describing the problems and assessing what help is deserved. Even when cases are given in some detail they will often be couched in set terms, perhaps based on fixed questions and recorded on a form. Just occasionally there is a paraphrase of more than the bare facts, an echo of what the person might have said. More often there is a judgment – 'very deserving', 'respectable poor woman', 'sober and honest but cannot work much', 'a good character for sobriety and industry', and so on. The focus is on character, income, and formal resources, when most poor families survived by more informal means.

Unofficial writings by members of the propertied classes on working-class life are also handicapped by their 'outsider' perspective. Most well-off people with the confidence to write about poor homes must have owed any direct knowledge of them to their class position: it was their work (as clergyman or social worker or journalist) or their simple class position (like the diarist A.J.

Munby)[21] which gave them the right to enter and ask personal questions that their social equals would have found intolerably intrusive. Their accounts cannot escape or close the class gap: it is there in their assumptions of cultural superiority and in the implications for the relationship between observer and observed. Deference and hostility are obvious possible blocks on one side; ignorance and misunderstanding, desire to reform and sentimentalising, on the other. Conflicting assumptions about what was proper behaviour for women would be another obstacle to easy communication and to straightforward reporting.

'Transforming the Art'

The feminist search for women's history has generated new definitions of the historically significant, new questions and new practices. It requires a rereading of the existing sources so as to take account of gender (and class and age and race) bias. It also drives us to look for other sources – to find echoes of the 'voices from below' wherever they survive. The development of oral history since the early 1970s has been of service in this pursuit. A whole new body of material has been generated which is immensely useful for the study of childhood, family, daily life, work, socialization and sexual divisions over the last 100 years. Of course oral evidence is not without its bias. 'Survivors' as a sample exclude those whose lives were shortened from the first by extreme poverty and ill health. And an eighty-year-old is not the child of 70 years ago – adult experience, consciousness and reflections are all bound to interpose themselves, distorting or repressing recollection. As with written autobiography, there is a tendency to retrospective gloss, whether rosy or black, and some things are remembered more willingly than others. (There has been much useful discussion of these questions in the pages of three journals, *Oral History*, *History Workshop Journal*, and *International Journal of Oral History*.)[22] Nevertheless, the

21. The fascinating diaries of Arthur Munby and of Hannah Cullwick, the servant whom he married, are in the library of Trinity College Cambridge. See Derek Hudson, *Man of Two Worlds*, London, John Murray, 1972 and Abacus Paperback 1974; and, for feminist discussion, Leonore Davidoff, 'Class and Gender in Victorian England'; and Liz Stanley's introduction to *The Diaries of Hannah Cullwick*, London, Virago, 1984.
22. See especially Luisa Passerini, 'Work ideology and consensus under Italian

relationship between historian and source is dynamic, here as in no other case. Critical evaluation is easier than with documents, whose contexts can rarely be so thoroughly understood. Sensitive listening, responses and questions allow the historian to explore areas which are generally inaccessible: this can include the hidden experience of those whose sexual or political practice was not conventionally acceptable in their time, as well as the aspects of daily life which are not documented.[23] Used in conjunction with documentary sources, oral evidence illumines them and supplies their deficiencies. Sometimes, too, the people recorded produce their own texts – hoarded certificates or letters or diaries or photos – and augment the stock of documentary material.[24]

The 'ordinary' women willing to talk about their lives rarely have a strong sense of their own importance. On the contrary, it is sometimes hard to convince them that their memories have any interest. Because history has always been presented as concerned with the achievements of the great and well-known, they find it difficult to believe that the everyday can be historically significant. They regard their childhoods, families, neighbourhoods and lives as somehow typical, and therefore unimportant. The more of these 'typical' experience the historian recovers, of course, the more complexities are revealed, the more undercurrents within the main stream. But it is a very labour-intensive form of research, which, moreover, may lead into long-term friendships such as cannot be endlessly multiplied. Group work is one way round this: over the last twelve years, there has been a mushrooming of local groups which, through recording individual life histories and group discussions, combined sometimes with research in local newspapers and archives, have been constructing histories of their neighbourhoods, of shared experiences such as migration, or childbirth, or particular

Fascism', *History Workshop Journal* 8 (Autumn 1979); Allesandro Portelli, 'The peculiarities of oral history', ibid. 12 (Autumn 1981); Sally Alexander, 'Women, class and sexual difference', ibid. 17 (Spring 1984). A number of useful and stimulating articles are collected in Ron Grele, (ed.) *Envelopes of Sound*, 1975; new rev. edn Precedent Publishing, 1985, and in Paul Thompson, (ed.) *Our Common History: the Transformation of Europe*, London, Pluto Press, 1982.

23. For a recent example of such exploration, see Madeline Davis and Elizabeth Lapovsky Kennedy, 'Oral history and the study of sexuality in the lesbian community: Buffalo, New York, 1940–1960', *Feminist Studies* 12:1 (Spring 1986).

24. See Jill Liddington, 'Rediscovering suffrage history', *History Workshop Journal* 4 (Autumn 1977), and her biography *The Life and Times of a Respectable Rebel: Selina Cooper 1864–1946*, London, Virago, 1984.

employments, or local struggles. (They are usually called People's History Groups or History Workshops; their work overlaps to some extent with what is being done in adult literacy classes; some have been able to publish cheap booklets which are very successful locally, and some belong to the Federation of Worker Writers and Community Publishers.) Oral History Archives are beginning to be established, too, as at the London History Workshop Centre, to secure preservation of such material and give access to it.[25]

The range of sources has had to be extended and their use refined because of the initial question, 'where were the women and what were they doing?' But further questions have emerged with our findings. We are uncovering the diversity and specificity of women's experience, and we ask how other factors (class, race, age, religion, location, economy etc.) intersected with their identity as women. We are exploring the operation of sexual divisions and their changing character, and we ask how 'femininity' (and 'masculinity') have been historically constructed, and how women lived, modified, or resisted particular definitions of femininity. We are asking what was different and what was shared in women's and men's experience of work, sexuality, childhood, parenting, leisure, politics, migration, war etc. We are asking 'what is a woman?' and learning to separate out different aspects of that identity. Here I find the Australian feminist historian, Jill Matthews, particularly helpful.

> In European societies and their extensions during the past several cen-
> turies, (she says,) there seem to have been four levels to the question,
> what is a woman? Each level of meaning is historical, that is, it changes
> over time, over both the individual's life cycle and the society's history.
> These four levels of woman are the biological, the psychological, the
> systemic and the social. Or, to put it another way, there are four
> histories: of she, the female body; of me, the woman; of it, the gender
> system; and of us, the women.[26]

These questions and distinctions help the project of historical understanding; they also send us critical explorations of the methods and findings of other disciplines.

25. The Federation of Workers, Writers and Community Publishers publishes an occasional list of people's history groups and publications: c/o Janet Burley, 16 Cliffsend House, Cowley Estate, London SW9 6HE. The London History Workshop Centre is at Mary Ward Centre, 42 Queen Square, London WC1.

26. Jill Julius Matthews, *Good and Mad Women, The Historical Construction of Femininity in Twentieth-Century Australia*, Sydney and London, Allen & Unwin, 1984 and 1985, p. 10.

Feminist history has, in short, moved on from challenging the dominant male version of the past by spotlighting inspiring exceptions or filling in gaps. Research aimed at 'redressing the balance', at showing that 'we were there', is still needed, of course, and is still going on. But the challenge is becoming a wider one as the concerns and consciousness of today's feminists broaden. New areas continue to be staked out as demanding historical attention. To housework, birth control, motherhood and women's employment (our early preoccupations) have been added women's networks and associations, our loves and sexualities, our autonomous cultures, the implications of our various simultaneous identities – as Jewish or Irish or Black, for instance, or as spinster or lesbian, and specific forms of our common experience as women, such as sexual harassment or rape.[27] Old perspectives have been redrawn. As Joan Kelly suggested in 1977, in her talk on the 'doubled vision' of feminist theory, we have superimposed the separate spheres and can perceive woman's place as 'a position within social existence generally'.[28] This has allowed us to challenge established definitions – are those who by childbearing and domestic work reproduce and maintain the workforce really 'economically inactive'? New distinctions are made and remade. Ann Oakley drew a clear and useful line in 1972 between sex and gender: '"sex" is a word that refers to the biological differences between male and female: the visble difference in genitalia, the related difference in procreative function. "Gender" however is a matter of culture: it refers to the social classification into "masculine" and "feminine".'[29] This distinction is still useful, but it is seen as perhaps less clearcut. To quote Jill Matthews again: 'human biology is not unchanging; the human body is not an ahistorical entity. Both have changed over time and, more importantly, the significance or meaning given to both is social and hence historically created'.[30] New concepts from today's feminist thought

27. These new areas were first opened up in the United States by such historians as Mary Ryan, Carroll Smith Rosenberg and Joan Kelly. For work on Britain (often by North Americans, Australians or New Zealanders) see London Feminist History Group, *The Sexual Dynamics of History: Men's Power, Women's Resistance*, London, Pluto Press, 1983; Jan Lambertz, 'Sexual harrassment in the nineteenth-century English cotton industry', *History Workshop Journal* 19 (Spring 1985); Martha Vicinus, *Independent Women: Work and Community for Single Women*, London, Virago, 1985.
28. Joan Kelly, 'The Doubled Vision of Feminist Theory', in Newton, Ryan and Walkowitz (eds.) *Sex and Class in Women's History*.
29. Ann Oakley, *Sex, Gender and Society*, New York, Harper & Row, 1972, p. 16.
30. Matthews, *Good and Mad Women*, pp. 10–11.

are being brought to bear on historical work, sometimes with rash anachronism, sometimes bringing important insights: compulsory heterosexuality, for instance, or marriage resistance, or the all-encompassing (and so sometimes obscuring) 'patriarchy'.[31]

Accepted analyses based on masculine universals have to be rethought. Assertions of 'progress' and 'modernization', for instance, whether made for Europe and neo-European developed countries, or for countries in the Third World, may sound less convincing when assessed in terms of women's exclusion from new economic sectors and from training, their relegation to the most highly exploited employments, and their dispossession of former skills and status.[32] Studies of capital accumulation in early industrial Britain which ignore the role of dowries and sex-determined inheritance customs seem partial in the light of new work.[33] So does discussion of late-nineteenth-century living standards which leaves out women's manipulation of credit (and its costs), or their 'maternal altruism', or their mutual support systems.[34] Imperialism and colonialism will be better understood when the workings of the gender orders in the imperial nations and those they take over are included in the analysis,[35] just as feminist work benefits from

31. London Feminist History Group, *Sexual Dynamics of History*; Ann Snitow, Christine Stansell and Sharon Thompson (eds.) *Powers of Desire: the Politics of Sexuality*, New York, Monthly Review Press, 1983; *Desire*, London, Virago, 1984; Lal Coveney, Margaret Jackson, Sheila Jeffreys, Leslie Kay and Pat Mahony, *The Sexuality Papers: Male Sexuality and the Social Control of Women*, London, Hutchinson, 1984 (Explorations in Feminism Collective); Sheila Jeffreys, *The Spinster and Her Enemies: Feminism and Sexuality 1880–1930*, London, Pandora Press, 1985. For an important historical analysis of sexuality (especially of male homosexuality), see the work by Jeffrey Weeks, *Coming Out: Homosexual Politics in Britain from the Nineteenth Century to the Present*, London, Quartet, 1977; *Sex, Politics and Society: the Regulation of Sexuality since 1800*, London, Longman, 1981; and *Sexuality and its Discontents: Meanings, Myths and Modern Sexualities*, London, Routledge & Kegan Paul, 1985.

32. Barbara Rogers, *The Domestication of Women: Discrimination in Developing Societies* (1980), London, Tavistock Publications, 1981; Ester Boserup, *Women's Role in Economic Development*, London, Allen & Unwin, 1970.

33. Catherine Hall, 'Gender divisions and class formation in the Birmingham middle class, 1780–1850', in Raphael Samuel (ed.) *People's History and Socialist Theory*, London, Routledge & Kegan Paul, 1981.

34. Melanie Tebbutt, *Making Ends Meet: Pawnbroking and Working-class Credit* London, Methuen, 1984; Annie Whitehead, 'I'm hungry, Mum': the politics of domestic budgeting', in Kate Young, Carol Walkowitz, and Roslyn McCullagh (eds.). *Of Marriage and the Market*, London, Routledge & Kegan Paul, 1981; Ross, 'Survival Networks'.

35. Anna Davin, 'Imperialism and motherhood', *History Workshop Journal* 5

integrating an understanding of race and class. Even conventional political and economic periodisation of history may need to be reworked when sexual divisions are taken as central, and women's experience is no longer seen as subsumed by or deviant from men's norm.[36]

The implication of looking at women's history as well as men's are far-reaching. Besides piecing together the various aspects of women's lives and locating them within their larger context, we are seeing past and present – of men as well as women – with new eyes. We have learnt that one cannot simply add 'new' women's history to 'old' men's history. Neither is adequate without the other – they are 'indissolubly linked'. They interact to transform historical understanding.[37]

Because this project has implications for the status of women, many of us see it as urgent in a way that academic research often is not. To take women's experience seriously is to strengthen their confidence and their collective consciousness, to give them power. This means also that dissemination is a priority: we have to find ways of making the work that we do as widely available as possible, so that school teaching is transformed along with every other official and unofficial representation of the past – museum displays, documentaries, photograph collections, tourist guides, historical quizzes, exhibitions and their catalogues, radio, theatre and TV productions and so on. It also means that wherever possible we should be treating our work as a collective enterprise and involving other women in the process of gathering, interpreting and presenting historical evidence. The urgency and the aim of collective work will each, perhaps, be in tension with the trained historian's slow, cautious and often individualist approach, but it is a creative ten-

---

(Spring 1978); Matthews, *Good and Mad Women*; Ann McGrath, 'Spinifex Fairies: Aboriginal workers in the Northern Territory, 1911–1939', in Elizabeth Windschuttle (ed.) *Women, Class and History: Feminist Perspectives on Australia 1788–1978*, Australia, Fontana/Collins,1980; Amirah Inglis, *The White Women's Protection Ordinance: Sexual Anxiety and Politics in Papua*, London, Chatto & Windus for Sussex University Press, 1975; Amrit Wilson, *Finding a Voice: Asian Women in Britain*, London, Virago, 1978.

36. Jill Matthews's discussion of the domestic service economy and the consumption economy is a good example of such rethinking. *Good and Mad Women*, London, Allen and Unwin, 1985. pp. 65–73.

37. Barbara Taylor's *Eve and the New Jerusalem*, London, Virago, 1983, is an example of how new questions and new research transform understanding, in this case of early socialism in Britain.

sion. It is important to get facts as accurate as possible, and to make the end analysis fit all that is known. But it is also rewarding and a spur to know that the work is needed, and to realise that others are engaged in it.

By recovering and analysing social structures and processes in the past we are working towards a more complete understanding of the past, encompassing the complementary and sometimes conflictual diversities of both women's and men's experience. This certainly has involved and will involve transforming the practice of history. My hope is that in the long run we will also be contributing to a transformation of society.

5

The Role of Women in the History of the Arab States

Soha Abdel Kader

Introduction

This chapter takes a critical look at the treatment in the literature of the Arab woman's role in the economic, social, political and ideological history of the Arab states. It is generally believed that the Arab states, or countries of the Middle East, share much in common. Islam, the Arabic language, local customs, traditions and geographical proximity are repeatedly cited as unifying factors and women in the area are often treated as a unified whole.

Islam in particular has been singled out as an important factor in determining the status of Arab women and images of Arab women, especially in the West, have consequently tended to conform to one or two stereotypes. On the one hand is the exotic odalisque of the harem who is dedicated to the service and sensuous pleasure of her man. On the other hand is the beast of burden, born and reared for childbearing and arduous chores inside and outside the home and subject to all forms of physical and mental exploitation. Orientalist explorers and missionaries, who were mostly foreign men with little opportunity to converse with or get to know Arab women in any real way, did much to reinforce these images of them.

And yet each country in the region has been shaped by different historical developments and has its own local economic, political and social characteristics. Social change, sometimes taken to mean modernisation, or more specifically Westernisation, has occurred at different rates in different countries and among different social strata within these countries. As a cultural unit the Arab world has been described as 'complex and mosaic-like', as 'intricately structured both vertically and horizontally'. It has even been argued that a lack of communication favoured the emergence of local differences beneath 'the overall, but rather thinly-spread, veneer of Islam'.

The Arab region constantly poses conundrums to its researchers. So do its women. My attempts in this chapter to analyse former studies on the historical role and status of women in the Arab states and to delineate future theoretical and methodological areas of research need, therefore, to be set within the context of these complexities.

The Present State of Historical Research

The study of women in the Middle East has, until recently, suffered from benign neglect. Middle East historians consigned women, along with many other social groups and classes, to a minor, if not totally insignificant, place in the histories of these societies. Their concentration on visible political institutions, diplomatic events and intellectual currents of high (as opposed to popular) culture effectively meant that all but upper-class males were left out of the historical process.[1] The neglect of women can partly be explained by the state of Middle East history itself, which retained its rather narrow approach long after historians in Europe and other parts of the world had started writing social and economic histories. But this neglect is also due to the male bias of Arab and Western researchers alike who tend to base their views on the assumption that what is important and of value in the study of a culture is limited to the norms, formal prescriptions, rights and obligations of the men who hold authority, control resources and act as power brokers: in sum, the formal domains of politics and economy. Women who have few rights and duties in the political sphere are thus assumed to be marginal and unimportant to the social system. From this perspective, studies that concentrate on women or women's issues are considered secondary, if not peripheral, to the understanding of society and culture.[2]

1. Judith Tucker, 'Problems in the Historiography of Women in the Middle East: the Case of Nineteenth Century Egypt', *International Journal of Middle Eastern Studies* 15, 1983, p. 321.

2. Amal Rassam, 'Towards a Theoretical Framework for the Study of Women in the Arab World', paper presented at the Meeting of Arab Women Researchers on the Development of Research in Social Sciences on Women in the Arab World, Tunis, Tunisia, May 1982, p. 1; Mohamed Talal, 'Images of Women in Arab Mass Media',

The accessibility of sources on literate, powerful and influential historical actors encouraged scholars to study women as and when they participated in the élite politics of a male-defined culture and there are quite a few biographical sketches of the great women of the ancient Middle East. Joanna McKenna offers us a brief glimpse at 17 Middle Eastern women who not only 'accomplished great feats' but also represented a significant juncture in history. These women include Hagar, the second wife of Ibrahim, Hatsepsut and Nefertiti from ancient Egypt, the Queen of Sheba from Yemen, Khadija, the wife of Muhammad, and Fatima, his sole surviving child. Fernea and Bezirgan provide similar examples through the translations of the literary works and writings of some early Muslim women. A number of historical studies in Arabic follow the same line and offer biographical sketches of famous Arab women. F. Abdel Megeed's *Women in Struggle* is an anthology of extracts of the works of such history makers as Khadija, Fatma Al Zahra, Rabai El Adamiva and others.[3]

The underlying assumption, sometimes implicit and sometimes explicit, in these and other writings, is that 'great women' of the past should serve as worthy examples for modern women. All accounts of the lives of women in pre- and early Islamic times agree that they actively participated in all community activities of the desert Arabs. There was free interaction between the sexes and, in fact, very few restrictions on marriage and divorce. Ilse Lichtenstadter says that 'Women in that remote age were an integral part of communal life' and that 'segregation and seclusion, which impoverished and narrowed the life of Muslim women for centuries, were instituted much later'.[4]

The seclusion and confinement of Arab women in modern times are thus arbitrary and extra-Islamic measures which deprive them of

---

report (in Arabic) prepared for the Arab League Commission on Arab Women, 1983, p. 4.

3. A.L. Marsot, 'The Revolutionary Gentlewoman of Egypt', in Lois Beck and Nikki Keddie (eds), *Women in the Muslim World*, Cambridge, Mass., Harvard University Press, 1978, pp. 261–76; and Thomas Phillip, 'Feminism and Nationalist Politics in Egypt', also in Beck and Keddie, pp. 277–94; Joanna McKenna, *Great Women of the Ancient Middle East*. Cleveland, Ohio, Greater Cleveland Association of Arab Americans, 1975; Elizabeth Fernea and Bezirgan, *Muslim Middle Eastern Women Speak*, Austin and London, University of Texas Press, 1977; Faiza Abdel Mageed, *Al-Mara Fi Miadeen Al Kifah* [Women in Struggle] (in Arabic), Cairo, Ministry of Culture, 1967.

4. Ilse Lichtenstadter, *Islam in the Modern Age*, New York, Bookman Associates, 1967, p. 43.

self-confidence. A look at the famous Arab women of the past contradicts the view that men alone were created for leadership in politics, war and the building of civilisations. Women in the East, like women in the West, have creatively contributed to the development of mankind. 'In my review of the lives of these immortal feminine characters,' writes F. Abdel Megeed, 'I only offer an example for modern Arab women to follow'.[5]

Middle Eastern history bears the imprint of 'orientalism', which has tended to tie students of the Middle East, both historians and others, to the written word. This has resulted in a specifically 'Islamic' definition of history affecting both the sources and the methodology used. Most historians shied away from exploring the wider social, economic and political realities and limited themselves to the confines of the text, specifically the Koran and the Prophet's Hadiths. The bulk of the literature on women in the Arab world, in both Arabic and other languages, centres on the eternally controversial issue of whether Islam raised or lowered the status of women in the region. A review of this literature reveals that it is divided into two broad categories: studies that adopt a *defensive posture*, that is which maintain that Islam sustains rather than undermines women's rights, and those that adopt a *critical posture*, that is blaming Islam for the 'low' status of women and the inequality of the sexes prevalent in the Muslim world.[6] There is little concern in these studies with how Islam in reality and in everyday life affected and continues to affect the lives of Muslim women.

The defenders of the position of women in Islam argue that while the Koran and the Prophet's original teachings may at the present time seem subjugative to women, an examination of the style of life prevalent during Muhammad's time indicates loose family ties, predominant polygamy, easy divorce and remarriage and an obsession with sexual pleasure. Pre-Islamic institutions, particularly female infanticide and marriage by kidnapping, were highly unfavourable to women. In this respect the Prophet's rulings were directed towards improving the 'moral' quality of life for both men and women. Islamic institutions, particularly of the 'Utopian Age of Islam', the seventh century, elevated the status of women by banning female infanticide, limiting to four, the number of women a

5. Abdel Mageed, *Women in Struggle*, p. 8.
6. See bibliography in Soha Abdel Kader, *The Status of Research on Women in the Arab Region 1960–1978*, Paris, Unesco, 1979.

man could marry, and imposing adequate provision by the husband for his wife and children within marriage and even after divorce.[7]

The critics of the status of women in Islam argue that in essence the Koran offers no real ethical codes or moral values regarding male/female relations. The enjoyment of carnal pleasure, particularly for men, is accepted and provided for. Women, on the other hand, are primarily sexual objects to be protected from their own immoral qualities and to be hidden behind veils and curtains. Muslim marriage is based on the premise that social order can only be maintained if the woman's dangerous potential for chaos is restrained. Women are thus held as prize pieces of property, not as persons. Islamic law, particularly when dealing with divorce and polygamy, is a major cause of the suffering of Muslim women. A new sexual order and new legislation is needed to remove all dehumanising limitations of women's potential.[8]

Within the last two decades or so, interest in social and economic history has risen dramatically in the Middle East. Several pioneering works utilising theories and approaches developed in other disciplines have made their appearance. There is little unity in the conceptual frameworks or theoretical approaches to this history. The empiricism of modern social science and both orthodox and neo-Marxism have left their imprint on the different authors. Yet even in these works women, regardless of class, are largely ignored and receive only cursory treatment. At best, some of the authors lament the dearth of information on women, but on the whole the social history of the Middle East, at least in its early stages, is being written without women.[9]

Studies focused specifically on the lives and history of women in the Middle East started to appear in the early 1970s. These were inspired either by the example of women's history in other regions or by the growing interest in social history in general. The predominant focus of these studies was the lives, attitudes and institutions of the nineteenth and twentieth centuries, specifically

---

7. Saneya Saleh, 'Women in Islam: their Role in Religious and Traditional Culture', *International Journal of Sociology of the Family*, 2 (September 1972), pp. 35–42; S.H. Yusef, 'In Defense of the Veil', in Rivlin and J. Szyliowicy (eds), *The Contemporary Middle East*, New York, Random House, 1965, pp. 355–9.

8. G.H. Bousquet, L'éthique sexuelle de l'Islam. Paris, Maison Neuve et Larose, 1966; V.L. Bullough, 'Sex is not enough: Women in Islam', in *The Subordinate Sex: a History of Attitudes towards Women*, Urbana, Illinois, University of Illinois Press, 1973, pp. 134–52.

9. Tucker, 'Problems in the Historiography of Women', pp. 322.

highlighting the contrast between the 'traditional' and changing or 'modern' worlds of Arab women.[10] Anthropological research has provided an important impetus to the emergence of these studies because this discipline, at least in the Middle East, has led the way in exploring the world of non-élite women. The works of Lois Beck, Elizabeth Fernea, Vanessa Maher, Emrys Peters and others interjected the issues of class, productive activity, family structure and social participation into the analysis of women's position in the contemporary Middle East.

Beck has studied the physical and symbolic boundaries or limitations upon interactions (codes of social distances) among nomadic societies of the Middle East. She demonstrates that the limitations are flexible, often varying with the status of the group and the status of individuals (especially women) within the group. Fernea discusses how Shiah women in villages in southern Iraq use religious rituals as a legitimate arena of activity outside the home. Maher examines female networks, cooperative labour exchange among female relatives and clients, and the effects of these non-monetarised exchanges upon the status of women and their conjugal relationships in several rural settlements in the Middle Atlas of Morocco.[11]

Up to the early 1970s, studies that dealt with women in the Arab region tended to treat Arab women as one cohesive whole, homogenous in all needs and resources. Individual differences, social and economic differences or rural–urban differences were not significantly taken into account. Researchers often used imported models and imported methodology which undermined the understanding of indigeneous cultures. These models and methodology ignored the structural and dynamic aspects of the societies in question. The wide spectrum of multi-regional studies only answered questions that transcended cultural boundaries as well as rural–urban differences. They were useful only for a general understanding of the situation of women.

In her analysis of the emerging area of study in the 1970s, Roxanne Van Dusen wrote that:

10. Margot Badran, 'Middle East and North African Women', *Trends in History: a Review of Current Periodical Literature in History* 1: 1 (1979), pp. 123–9.

11. Lois Beck, 'Women among the Dashga'i Nomadic Pastoralists in Iran', in Beck and Keddi (eds), *Women in the Muslim World*; Elizabeth Fernea, *Guests of the Sheikh*, New York, Doubleday & Co. Inc., 1965; Vanessa Maher, *Women and Property in Morocco*, New York and London, Cambridge University Press, 1975.

What the new wave of studies is attempting to do is to fathom how the various (poorly understood) roles that Middle Eastern women play can be integrated to provide a realistic and believable picture of women's life and life styles. In a sense, then, today's students of the Middle Eastern woman are attempting to breathe life into a static, idealized caricature.[12]

One aspect of this 'static, idealised caricature' that was challenged through the accumulation of more realistic and specific information on the life styles of Arab women was the public/private dichotomy, for long a leitmotif of the literature on Middle Eastern women. Ethnographic studies of Middle Eastern societies usually refer to the existence of two separate and sharply differentiated social worlds: men are said to inhabit the public world of politics, religion and the market, while women are confined to the private sphere of the home. Implicit in this dichotomy of public/male, private/female is the assumption that power, viewed as belonging in the public–political domain, is a monopoly of men and that women, being confined to the domestic sphere, are therefore powerless. Cynthia Nelson argues that this misrepresentation of reality is largely because most ethnographers of the area have been North American or European males who, as foreigners and males, had little or no access to women and the household.[13]

In an examination of the concepts of power, authority, status and communication systems in nomadic and pastoral societies, she questions the assumption that women, because they lack authority and visibility in the public domain, are actually without power. Advocating a redefinition of power to encompass how men and women are involved in 'negotiating their social order' she suggests that ethnographers should raise a different set of questions, questions designed to examine the role and position of women in Middle Eastern society from the standpoint of women themselves: 'From the ethnographic literature, we know precious little about how women in those societies view their situation, whether they feel they have power or whether they wield it.'[14]

Viewed from this new perspective, men's power and women's

12. Roxanne Van Dusen, 'The Study of Women in the Middle East: Some Thoughts', *Middle East Studies Association Bulletin* 10, (1976), pp. 1–20.
13. Cynthia Nelson, 'Public and Private Politics: Women in the Middle Eastern World', in Saad Ibrahim and Nicholas Hopkins (eds), *Arab Society in Transition*, Cairo, American University in Cairo Press, 1977, pp. 121–49.
14. Ibid., p. 135.

power can be understood only in terms of the reciprocity of influence that prevails in interactive situations; and the segregation of men and women in the Middle East need not necessarily imply the restriction of women or their subordination. The recent work of women ethnographers on women in Muslim societies has therefore been most invaluable in correcting the all too rigid and formalistic conceptions of earlier scholars. Carla Makhlouf, for example, in a study of North Yemeni women, shows how the conventional veil, rather than restricting women's manipulative powers, is in fact a means they adeptly use to express themselves and their desires. Soraya Al-Torki found that Saudi Arabian women among élite families exercise their power by influencing and in fact determining marriage alliances, the major form of the creation of new links within and between families.[15]

In the field of history proper, progress has been somewhat slower; but the number of studies on the roles of women is growing, and the scope of inquiry is gradually expanding to include the study of ordinary women and their significance for the history of the region. While the field is slowly liberating itself from the idealist and empiricist epistemologies which dominated the study of the Middle East in general, new approaches, better suited to address the question of women's role in society, are still to be found.

An all too familiar line of thought in some of these historical studies is one that shares the idealist bent of Middle East history as a whole. According to this line of thought, Arab women's status and roles in society are perceived as the product of a set of ideas, whether indigenous or imported. Women's history is perceived as part of the history of the region, that is, as a derivative of the history of the West and of Western penetration in the region. The link is not between the effects of the area's integration into a European market or the organisation of economic and social activities, but rather a

15. Carla Makhlouf, *Changing Veils: Women and Modernization in North Yemen*, Austin, University of Texas Press,1979; Soraya Al-Torki, 'Family Organi-zation and Women's Power in Urban Saudi Arabian Society', *Journal of Anthropological Research* 33 (1977), pp. 277–87. For other examples of studies that argue that Arab women are more powerful than they seem, see Ursula M. Sharma, 'Women and their Affines: the Veil as a Symbol of Separation', *Man: Journal of the Royal Anthropological Institute* (London), new series 13 (1978), pp. 218–33; Sue Wright, 'Prattle and Politics: the Position of Women in Doshman – Ziari', *Journal of the Anthropological Society of Oxford* 9 (1978), pp. 98–112; Fatima Mernissi, 'Women, Saints and Sanctuaries', *Signs* 3, (1977), pp. 101–12; Maher, *Women and Property in Morocco*.

result of the transfer of Western ideas about women's roles. Implicit in this analysis is the idea that women's history was shaped predominantly by intellectual currents which began in the nineteenth century within the context of the Islamic reform movement. Implicit also is the assumption that Arab women were doomed to unchanging oppression, dictated by Islam, the Koran and Hadith. It was only after the coming of Western thought that this oppression began to lift.[16] Other writers, however, absolve Islam and the Hadith of primary responsibility for the condition of women and consider the history of women in the Arab region as a reflective product of social rules, traditions and customs. The roots of these traditions are explained by male insecurity and the drive to dominate women, which lie at the heart of the social system which has physically and psychologically suffocated them.[17]

In contrast to the studies that exhibit this idealist bias, there are a number of others that present primarily empirical material. The history of women's movements in the region and particularly of women's activities in the political sphere is subjected to a highly empirical approach. Most of the studies in this area concentrate on the participation of women in the sphere of visible political institutions, but some of them examine the history of women who stood outside the realm of élite politics. Underlying these studies is the assumption that women's role in social production is the key to their past and future and that their roles can only be understood within a particular political context.[18]

The rise of Arab socialism in the 1950s and its fuller growth and expansion in the 1960s generated a number of studies on the history of women's labour. The authors of these studies were inspired by the official statist goal of equality for women and imbued with the conviction that Arab socialism could achieve this goal through programmes of training and employment. The *a priori* assumption underlying many of these studies is that female participation in wage labour serves as the index of, as well as the catalyst for, their liberation. According to Tucker, these studies are based on ideas extrinsic to Arab society and neglect the specificity of Arab history,

---

16. See, for example, Gabriel Baer, *Studies on the Social History of Modern Egypt*, Chicago, University of Chicago Press, 1969; and most works on the modern history of Egypt in both Arabic and English.

17. Youssef Al-Masry, *Le Drame Sexuel*, Paris, 1962; Germain Tillion, *Le Harem et les Cousins*, Paris, 1966.

18. Iglal Khalifa, *Al-Harakah Al-Nasaiyah Al-Hadithah*, Cairo, 1973.

social organisation and culture. Official state policy is given central importance, while the indigenous forces which acted and may still act to encourage or impede female participation in social production are neglected.[19]

In her pioneering and now classic study of the participation of women in the labour force in the Middle East and Latin America, Nadia Haggag Youssef[20] redresses the balance somewhat. She argues that female participation, or rather lack of participation, in the labour force in Middle Eastern countries is primarily a result of Islam, which she defines as a 'total institution' rather than an abstract ideology. Islamic customs, concepts and sexual mores, as mediated by a monogamous family system, dictate women's role in society. Youssef attempts to situate empirical findings within a wider framework, but the idea that Islam dominates all institutional structures and upholds a common normative order neglects historical and regional specificity in Islamic societies.

More recently researchers have been interested in studying the 'hidden labour' of women. Time budget studies have revealed that Arab women contribute in significant ways to family economies through their work in agriculture and the 'informal sector' of the economy. Because their work is unremunerated, however, it goes for the most part uncounted in labour force census data. In another pioneering work on women's economic participation in the Middle East, Huda Zurayk developed new statistical techniques for the measurement of women's work and for its accurate inclusion in population censuses in the region.[21]

Additions to our limited store of knowledge on the history and present situation of women in the Arab states remains a vital task for empirical research. As I pointed out above, some work on well-defined aspects of women's role in this history has already been undertaken. There have even been attempts to cover the wide range of Arab women's history, with attention to differences of class, epoch, city and countryside, as well as ideological and ma-

19. A. Al-Marah Ahmad Taha, *Kifahha Wa Amalha* (in Arabic), Cairo, 1964; Tucker, 'Problems in the Historiography of Women'.

20. Nadia H. Youssef, *Women and Work in Developing Societies*, Berkeley, Calif., University of California Institute of International Studies, Population Monograph Series 15, 1974.

21. Huda Zurayk, 'Women's Economic Participation', in Frederick C. Shorter and Huda Zurayk (eds), *Population Factors in Development Planning in the Middle East*, New York and Cairo, Population Council, 1985.

terial factors. An example of such ambitious attempts is Nawal Sadawy's *The Hidden Face of Eve*.[22] In the absence of sufficient information, however, the value of such studies lies in their provocative challenge to accepted views on women's history in the Arab states.

In conclusion, as Van Dusen expresses it, what the status of research on women in the Middle East amounts to is that we have some knowledge about some aspects of women's lives in some parts of the Middle East and for some strata. What is needed is a theoretical framework within which information can be accumulated, the unevenness of the data assessed and the gaps in knowledge filled.

Methodologies for Future Research

The methodology cannot be separated either from the means selected for data collection or from the epistemology or theory in which it is grounded. In other words, the research is shaped by a particular ideology or vision of the world. In seeking to develop a new approach towards generating data on women and women's history, numerous important questions have to be confronted throughout the process.[23] Without a theoretical framework that recognises the intricate relationship of women's roles and status to the economic, political and social organisation of society, the simple accumulation of more data may be both haphazard and futile.

A new approach to women's studies is now needed, an approach in which there is a shift of emphasis away from treating women as marginal (or at best complementary to an understanding of society) and towards seeing women and their activities as integral constituents. To dispel misconceptions about the place and role of women in history we need to expand our field of inquiry to include the numerous and often subtle ways in which women's activities and status reflect and affect the organisation of production and social interaction in any given society. In other words, the study of women requires an awareness of the multitude of institutions and

22. Nawal Sadawy, *The Hidden Face of Eve*, Zed Press, London, 1979.
23. Marie Aimee Lucas, 'An African Science – a Feminist Science: Epistemological and Technical Problems', paper presented at the Seminar on Methodology organised by the Association of African Women for Research and Development, Dakar, Senegal, December 1983, p. 1.

activities that elude analysis at the level of official political institutions, mainstream intellectual movements and economic overviews.
The world of informal networks, popular culture and the basic
organisation of production and reproduction demands our attention.

In developing this new approach, it is important to avoid the
pitfalls of female chauvinism; namely, of regarding women and their
activities as the motors of society while ignoring or neglecting to
study male roles and statuses. A preferable approach would be one
that views men and women as equally integral to the functioning of
the system. The beliefs and activities of both men and women and
their interrelationships have to be taken into account if any true
understanding of any cultural system, Arabo–Islamic or otherwise,
is to be achieved. As Sheila Rowbotham puts it:

> Within . . . channels of the new feminist history there are the implicit
> assumptions that women's history will be done by women and be about
> women. I think that these assumptions are disorienting and can actually
> restrict the radical assumptions of a feminist approach. . . . There is a
> chance, if we interpret feminist history in this way, that we pursue an
> abstract category called 'women' through history and isolate women
> from social relations in the family and at work.[24]

Understanding the general position of women in Arabo – Islamic
cultures is not a problem *sui generis*. It partakes of the same
problems of understanding women in any society. Yet, given the
low status of research on women in the region, we are still far from
being able to formulate a grand theory with which to interpret and
explain women's statuses across time and place. There is too little
comparable data on Arab women to formulate a theory broad
enough to explain, for example, the various statuses of Bedouin
women, peasant women and the urban élite. This is especially true
of societies as large as complex and with as long and rich a history as
those of the Arab world. As Amal Rassam points out, 'we are still
exploring the tip of the iceberg: much remains hidden'.[25]

None the less, given what we know, we can begin to order our
data and prepare our research agenda in terms of a number of
questions and organisational concepts that will hopefully yield the

24. Sheila Rowbotham, *Hidden from History*, New York, Pantheon Books, 1973,
pp. xxi.
25. Rassam, 'Towards a Theoretical Framework', p. 1.

insights that would permit us to undertake such theoretical formulations in the future.

To understand the status and position of women in Arab history and society, it is necessary to focus the research on three main areas: the position of women within the Arab family, the participation of women in social production and reproduction, and the ideological definitions of women's roles in the Arab world.

The Family

In the Arab world the family (whether extended – patrilocal – patrilineal or nuclear) is the basic socio-economic unit. It is where sex roles are defined and cross-sexual relationships delineated. But until there has been some historical and comparative investigation into the structure and function of the Arab family, it is impossible to assess the significance of the observed variations in women's statuses or to evaluate the implications of changes in sex roles.

The position of women in the Arab family can be studied from a number of perspectives. Sex role expectations and patterns of cross-sexual relations have at their base the differential access of men and women to the major sources of power and prestige in society. To unravel the status of women, we must take into consideration the formal and informal sources of power that are available to women in the household. The power and prestige assigned to a woman differs according to the position she occupies in the family. A new wife, for example, occupies the lowest status and power position within her husband's household until she begets male children. The mother-in-law, on the other hand, is both active and powerful. Her power derives from her close relationship to her adult son, a relationship she closely guards from his wife, whose own sources of power derive from her active sexuality and her procreative functions. Women sometimes acquire power through resorting to witchcraft or through feigning illness.[26]

The position of women in the Arab family is also closely linked to their access to property. Two questions need to be raised in this respect: first, questions concerning women's formal rights to property as embodied in Islamic law and accepted customs and secondly

26. Ibid.; Sohair Morsy, 'Sex Differences and Folk Illnesses in an Egyptian Village', in Beck and Keddie (eds), *Women in the Muslim World*, pp. 599–617.

questions about the ability of women to use these rights to attain economic independence and status. Access to property might strengthen a woman's position within the family power structure; on the other hand, family control of her person may negate any meaningful exercise of her property right. Vanessa Maher and Judith Tucker have already undertaken research in this area, demonstrating a relationship between property rights and the status of women.[27]

By comparing the statuses of urban and rural women in Morocco, Maher shows that a relationship exists between property, divorce rates and the status of women. Berber women in the villages, where the main property is in the form of land, do not inherit their legal share, but retain important service obligations with their matrilineal kin. This reduces their economic and social dependence on their husbands and contributes to a high rate of divorce. In the town, where property is in the form of movable goods, women inherit their legal share but sever their ties with their kin. The resultant increased dependence on their husbands leads to greater submissiveness and, ironically, contributes to the stability of marriages. Tucker uses court records to show how male bias among court judges often worked to deprive peasant women of their legal land inheritance rights (and hence of their status) in nineteenth century Egypt.

Participation in Production and Reproduction

Looking at the patriarchal family household in terms of the interaction between the relations of production and the relations of reproduction would probably yield some valuable insights into the women's position and its historical dynamics. Despite its vagueness and abstraction at present, this approach does provide a sound starting point for conceptualising the position of women within the dual framework of ideology and economy.

According to this approach the family household unit should be examined in its reciprocal relationship with society. It should be viewed as the product of the requirements of material production, or alternately, as an institution which both reflects and structures

27. Maher, 'Women and Social Change in Morocco', in Beck and Keddie (eds), *Women in the Muslim World*, pp. 100–23; Tucker, 'Problems in the Historiography of Women'.

material production and social life. Factors such as the availability of land, the intensity of cultivation and the prevalence of wage labour, all affect the division of labour and, thus, the numbers, roles, and power of various family members. At the same time, the wider functions of reproduction, including the care of children, the elderly and the infirm, also affect the distribution of power. Women's position in the family is conditioned by the need for reproduction, in the broad sense, and the assignment of particular roles, especially the nurturing of children, to women.

To understand the position of women in the Arab family, we therefore need to study the Arab family not only as a unit of production, but also as a unit of reproduction in which constraints on women's rights and power arise as much from her role in reproduction as from her role in production.

Further, the position of women within the Arab family has undoubtedly been affected by their participation in the public sphere. The increased monetisation of the economy and the accelerated rate of urbanisation in the region are already placing severe constraints on the family's ability to meet its traditional obligation to support its womenfolk. More and more women are forced to go outside the home to earn an income, a factor that will no doubt lead to a restructuring of relations within the household. With the exception of urban middle-class women, the majority of women who join the labour force tend to be concentrated in the urban informal sector where they work as domestic servants, laundresses and small traders. As attested by the ongoing discussion in seminars on methodology, measuring the 'hidden labour' of Arab women, whether within the household or in the informal sector, remains a research problem without a feasible solution.

The recent increase in migration to the oil-rich Gulf states is surely having a profound effect on the traditional division of labour and responsibility within the household. While a number of studies are currently addressing this issue,[28] we still know very little about the impact of male migration on the labour-exporting countries such as Egypt, Algeria, Jordan and North Yemen. The increase in the number of female-headed households, whether through male migration or through a more profound transformation of the struc-

28. Fatima Khafaga, 'The Impact of Immigration on the Status of Urban Women in Egypt', paper presented at the Meeting of Euro–Arab Research Group, Amman, Jordan, 1983.

ture of the Arab family, has introduced concepts such as the 'feminisation' of the Arab family. Yet, we are still far from being able to ascertain whether these changes have resulted in the increased autonomy and 'emancipation' of Arab women or have just piled more responsibilities on their shoulders.

Ideological Images

While the position of women in the Arab family unit and their participation in production and reproduction are important determinants of their status, the ideological definitions of their roles cannot be overlooked. While, as mentioned earlier, the bulk of the literature on women in the Arab world addresses the issue of the status of women in Islam, Islamic Sharia, the Koran and the Prophet's Hadiths, what is important is how these views and ideological definitions are expounded in any specific community. Since sexuality in the Middle East, as elsewhere, is the basic component of self-identity and since past studies have indicated the presence of a coherent and dominant ideology concerning female sexuality in Islamic thought, it would be most valuable to know how Arab women view themselves and their sexuality in the light of this dominant ideology. Do they passively accept their received image and pass it on unquestioningly to their daughters? Or do they construct their own self-images? Do men accept these dominant images or do men and women negotiate different images of one another? In other words, how does Islam and Islamic ideology affect the daily lives of Arab men and women? In an attempt to answer some of these questions, Abdel Kader uses the private diary of a middle-class Egyptian woman who lived at the turn of the century to reconstruct the daily lives of women of her class and to discern their attitudes towards themselves and their status in society. She reaches the rather disappointing conclusion that women of this time and class were even stronger upholders of the prevailing morality and social order than men. Indications of suppressed dissatisfaction are, however, evident in the frequent references to 'zar' exorcist parties in which 'possessed' women rid themselves of 'evil spirits'.[29]

29. Soha Abdel Kader, 'The Consciousness of Middle Class Egyptian Women in the First Quarter of the 20th Century', paper presented at the Seminar on Method-

There has also been a tendency in the literature to analyse the ideology of sex and sexuality in official Islamic scriptures and legal codes. The various images of women in myths, folktales and proverbs of popular culture are often very different from the images expounded by official political or religious pronouncements. A study of Egyptian cultural images of women throughout history and in the mass media, revealed not one, not two, but several images.[30] The image of women as mothers, highly venerated and respected, is in direct conflict with their image as females, fickle, weak beings who are feared and despised. Both images also conflict with the more recent portrayal of women as equal to and like men, officially espoused by the government as part of its national strategy to integrate women into the processes of socio-economic development. Still other images of Egyptian women are disseminated by the all-powerful mass media. It is possible that the richness and variety of these images gives them an elusive character that is probably responsible for the tendency to ignore them in speaking of the ideology of sex in Arabo–Islamic countries. Popular perceptions defining the roles and statuses of women, although undoubtedly coloured by official Islamic pronouncements, may, in certain historical periods, appear relatively autonomous and play a real part in determining the position of women.

The various ways in which Arab women (and men) acquire their gender identities at different periods of time and the manner in which they interact with the dominant ideology, may offer some valuable insights into the implications of the modern-day Islamic revival and the resurgence of Islamic fundamentalism. Why are Arab women overtly and in such large numbers rejecting modern or liberated images of themselves? Why are they freely opting to advocate a much more conservative and conformist image? Why have they decided to veil and retreat into their homes? Why have they decided to segregate themselves from men and from the public domain? According to Fadwa El-Guindy, Arab women are seeking freedom behind their veil. Theirs is a veiled activism – it frees them from the restrictions of being treated primarily as sex objects and

---

ology organised by the Association of African Women for Research and Development, Dakar, Senegal, December 1983.

30. Soha Abdel Kader, 'The Four Faces of Eve: Images of Women in Egyptian Cultural Heritage and the Mass Media', paper presented at the Seminar on Third World Women organised by the University of Los Andes, Bogota, Colombia, August 1984.

allows them to assert their identity first and foremost as human beings. Others see this movement as a political reaction to Western ideology, which they perceive as having failed to bring their countries and peoples the promised prosperity and affluence. Still others explain it as a psychological reaction, much like Erich Fromm's fear of freedom. The multitude of choices and alternatives available to women bewilder and confuse them. They find salvation in Islam, with its well-defined rules of conduct and correct behaviour. The explanations are as many and as diverse as the movement itself is mysterious and complex. This dimension of the lives of Arab women certainly deserves closer scrutiny and further research.[31]

Sources

The historical study of women in the Middle East calls for attention to sources that have hitherto been underused. Anthropological and archaeological evidence, records of court cases and folklore could be used to fill the gaps in our knowledge of the lives of ordinary women in the history of the area. Historical sources should be expanded to include material that sheds light on the relatively obscure world of women. However, all sources have to be scrutinised for bias, class bias as well as male bias.[32] Tucker, for example, in her study of Egyptian women in the nineteenth century, overcame the problem of using official documents that over-represent the views of upper class male culture by drawing primarily on the minutes of religious court proceedings. 'The religious courts, the *mahkamah al-Shar'iyyah*, constituted the single institution with extant records to which women of all classes had access, and where they could tell their stories and lodge their complaints.'[33]

The problem of uncovering the hidden experiences of women in more recent periods may be approached simply by speaking to older people. It is true that there is always the problem that the

31. Fadwa El-Guindy, 'Veiled Activism', *Femmes de la Méditerranée: peuples méditerranéens* 22–23 (January–June 1983); Joan A. Williams, 'Veiling in Egypt as a Political and Social Phenomenon', in John Esposito (ed.), *Islam and Development*, New York, Syracuse Press, 1980, pp. 71–85.

32. Nikki Keddie, 'Problems in the Study of Middle Eastern Women', *International Journal of Middle East Studies* 10 (April 1979), pp. 225–40.

33. Tucker, *Women in the Nineteenth Century in Egypt*, New York and London, Cambridge University Press, 1985, p. 10.

passage of time will affect the way they remember, but this is also a disadvantage with written sources, such as eye-witness evidence or biographies. Oral history could be an important means of discovering what women thought and felt in the immediate past.

The problems of methodology, theoretical formulation and sources in the study of women in history loom large , but many of these issues have already begun to receive some attention.

Part II

Women, Work and Family

Introduction to Part II

Considerations of women's work frequently begin by defining or redefining work to go beyond a description of it as paid wage labour. This permits an examination of the varieties of tasks and occupations performed by women, although not always documented by historians or economists. Our understanding of what constitutes work has changed over time with industrialisation and the development of commercial, cash crop agriculture. The location of work has also shifted as has the description of tasks performed by women. As production has moved from a subsistence to a commercial basis, the possibilities of women combining production and reproduction, characteristic of subsistence modes of production, have decreased. Where work has been defined as paid wage labour and where married women do not undertake employment outside the home, the result has been to neglect or understate their economic contributions.

The five chapters in Part II document the development of work and the relationship between production and reproduction in economically and geographically distinct regions: the Caribbean, the Netherlands, Nigeria, the United States, and Great Britain. The papers on the Caribbean and Nigeria analyse the sexual division of labour in agricultural economies while those on the Netherlands, Britain, and the United States focus on the same topic but primarily in industrialising settings. One common theme in all five chapters is the emphasis on the allocation or definition of work based upon gender, with the reservation of 'skilled' work to men in cash crop agriculture and in most industrial occupations. Even where the jobs performed by women and men overlapped, as they did on the cotton plantations of the American South or the sugar plantations of the Caribbean, certain jobs were reserved for men, giving them greater access to skills and rewards.

The study of Caribbean slavery shows the extent to which planters manipulated women's productive and reproductive capacities in accordance with their need for workers or the replication of the

101

labour force. Reddock also explores women and marriage in slave society, the extent to which planters attempted to manipulate slave fertility and family structures, and the uses to which historians have put data on family relationships. She warns that we should take a historical rather than ahistorical approach in order to discern the changing nature of the relationships between women and men and thus identify the factors which influenced those relationships.

The complexity of the interaction between custom, economic structure, and the gender based allocation of work is also discussed by Afonja, who analyses the complexities of women's and men's work among Nigerian regional and ethnic groups. By looking at the broad sweep of Nigerian history, this paper traces the way different modes of production have created changes in the sexual division of labour, the continuities and discontinuities which emerge, and the importance of non-economic factors (including religion and kinship ideology) in determining women's labour contributions to their communities.

A similar approach is taken by Kleinberg who follows the development of women's economic contributions from small scale agriculture to industrial production and isolates certain non-economic factors (race and ethnicity) as explanations for the sorts of work undertaken by some women. This chapter surveys female labour force participation, but also examines the extent to which women undertook productive activity within their homes. Kleinberg emphasises the development of a gender segregated labour market and the difficulties women had in breaking down barriers of race and class.

The chapter by Jane Lewis begins with a theoretical consideration of the relationship between gender and work and discusses the growing importance of the family wage ideology from the point of view of both female and male members of the working class. Lewis also analyses the ways in which labouring families used paid and unpaid work and how policy makers integrated prevailing ideologies about women's productive and reproductive roles into legislation.

Leydesdorff explores some of the same territory in her examination of women's role in industrialisation in the Netherlands which focuses on the industrial work that married women did in their own homes. She notes the extent to which women's labour force participation has been masked by official documentary sources, but can be gauged from other data. She is concerned about the extent to which religious and political groups opposed women's employment for ideological reasons, and notes that laws designed to regulate wo-

men's employment could simply displace it from the public sphere (the factory) to the private (the home.) This compares with Kleinberg's findings that in the United States, protective labour legislation could decrease women's employment or preclude their working in certain well-paid jobs.

Despite their distinct settings and time periods these chapter all point to three factors: the vital contributions women have made to the economic production in their societies, the difficulties of combining family responsibilities and employment in modern settings, and the extent to which all societies allocate work on the basis of gender. By examining women's work and family relationships across time and place the pervasive nature of the sexual division of labour becomes clear, although the precise type of work varies between societies and over time.

6

Women and
the Slave Plantation Economy
in the Caribbean

RHODA REDDOCK

Introduction

Studies of women's labour in various forced labour systems and in the different Caribbean plantation societies all point to the manipulative way in which women's labour was and is utilised. This is because, apart from being the potential producers of labour-power and the reproducers of the labour force, at a given point in time women are also, in themselves, a potential source of labour-power. And, because of their historical positioning within the sexual division of labour, they can also at the same time be used as the reproducers of daily expended labour-power, as well as the stabilisers of a skilled and experienced male labour force. The study of women's labour in slave plantation production in the Caribbean presents an interesting case for the analysis of this phenomenon.

Such analysis is important in that it strengthens our understanding of the fact that women's labour, as presently positioned within the capitalist sexual division of labour, provides an extremely manipulative variable which is far more flexible and adaptable than male labour to the changing needs of capital. In other words, although capitalism did not create the subordinate position of women, its maintenance in the long term is in its interests. This viewpoint, if explored further, would go some way towards explaining why capital at one and the same time preserves the male dominance of the labour market while profiting considerably from women's definition outside it.

The other issue cogently raised by this data is the need to

combine different production relations within individual units of production (such as the plantation) within single countries and internationally. Of relevance to this discussion is the variable inter-relationship of subsistence and petty-commodity production to these forced labour systems, the periods during which they were introduced, their connection with the emergence of nuclear family units as a base for production and the transfer, or shift, of the responsibility for reproduction from the plantocracy onto the women of these units.

This leads to another important issue – periodisation in women's history. Joan Kelly-Gadol's essay was a warning to feminist historians that the traditionally-accepted great steps forward for humanity in history often meant different things for woman than they did for men. In this respect she agreed with Engels's statement in *The Origin of the Family, Private Property and the State* that 'every advance is likewise a relative regression in which the well-being and development of the one group are attained by the misery and repression of the other'. In Caribbean history, the introduction of subsistence and petty-commodity production often meant greater economic independence for the women and men involved. As introduced, however, they usually brought with them the economic and social bases for the imposition of greater degrees of male dominance over individual women and later the withdrawal of some women from wage labour. The material gains of women as members of 'a family unit' therefore have to be measured against their losses as individuals. The eventual ideological conjuncture between these two (namely women's interests being defined as those of the family) has tended to cloud the issue. This is particularly important in that it brings out the contradictions among various types of historical reclamation.[1]

One example, which is relevant to this chapter, is that of the black family in the Americas. The Caribbean family, sometimes described by euro-centric and andro-centric social scientists as 'matrifocal', 'incomplete', 'denuded', 'matricentred', 'matrilocal', and 'matriarchal', has been the focus of attention since the 1930s.[2] In the 1970s,

1. J. Kelly-Gadol, 'The Social Relation of the Sexes: Methodological Implications for Women's History', *Signs*, vol. 1, no. 4, Summer, 1976; Frederick Engels, *The Origin of the Family, Private Property and the State*, Moscow, Progress Publishers, 1972, p. 66.
2. Franklin Frazier, *The Negro Family in the United States*, Chicago, University of Chicago Press, 1939; Melville J. Herskovits, *The Myth of the Negro Past*, New York, Alfred A. Knopf, 1941; Basil Matthews, *Crisis in the West Indian Family*, Port

the publication of the Moynihan Report on the negro family in the United States resurrected what has since become known as the Frazier/Moynihan thesis. Since then, a barrage of publications seeking to refute this have emerged, testifying to the preponderance of male-dominated families over female-headed households.[3]

This thesis is now being re-examined by black women historians using new sources of data and critically examining traditional ones. More importantly, however, they challenge the euro- and androcentric biases and assumptions from which the discussion emerged in the first place by challenging the moral superiority of the Western conjugal family with its dominant male and subordinate, dependent female. From this standpoint, therefore, female-headed households (already deviantly defined) would be, when found, seen as a fact of life and not as a source of shame.

Similarly, although of less international significance, recent attempts by Indo-Caribbean historians to improve the content of the Indian experience in Caribbean history and present 'an Indian view of history' have usually been marked by the invisibility of Indian women. In the absence of a history of Indo–Caribbean women, myths as to their 'natural' docility and subservience have flourished and many Indian women have been trapped by their nationalist male's ideal of Indian womanhood. Again the contradictions of Indian women as members of a Caribbean minority, as well as of an oppressed sex, become apparent. In the work of feminist historians the complexities of these two relationships (oppression as a sex and by race and class) have to be brought out rather than one being sacrificed at the altar of the other.

The Sexual Division of Labour

It is important to point out that female slaves, like their male counterparts, were brought to the Caribbean as labourers. Their

---

of Spain, 1953; Nancy Solein, 'Household and Family in the Caribbean: Some Definitions and Concepts', *Social and Economic Studies* 9: 1 (1960).

3. Daniel Moynihan, 'The Negro Family: the Case for National Action', in L. Rainwater and W.L. Yancey (eds), *The Moynihan Report and the Politics of Controversy*, Massachusetts and London, MIT Press, 1967; examples include Elizabeth H. Pleck, 'The Two-Parent Household: Black Family Structure in late Nineteenth-Century Boston', *Journal of Social History* 4 (1972); Herbert G. Gutman, *The Negro Family in Slavery and Freedom: 1750–1925*, Oxford, Blackwell; New York, Pantheon 1976.

contribution to the accumulation process was, therefore, as important. The evidence seems to suggest that for most of the nineteenth century, women predominated in the back-breaking work of field labour and not as domestics, as some believe. According to Lucille Mathurin, 'by the eve of emancipation, not only were the majority of Jamaican black women labourers in the field, but the majority of Jamaica's labourers in the field were black women'. In his study of the pre-emancipation slave population, Barry Higman also found that women worked much longer in the fields. But what was the character of this field labour? Mathurin quotes Elsa Gouveia as saying that 'no other group of slaves was so completely subject to the harsh realities of slavery as an industrial system', that the gangs of field slaves were worked for long hours under the discipline of the whip' and that in these final years of slavery, when the workforce was being worked harder, it was the women who provided most of this labour.[4]

It is important to note that, despite this exacting labour, by the end of slavery female slaves in all British slave-holding territories reflected a higher survived rate than male slaves. Whereas in 1815–17 the registration of slaves showed a slight excess of male slaves, by 1825 there were 112 women to every 100 men in the Leeward Islands, 119 in Barbados and 120 in St Lucia. Similarly, Craton found that by the 1820s, on Worthy Park Estate in Jamaica, the percentage of males had fallen to 45 per cent and by 1838 to just under 40 per cent.[5]

The stamina of slave women was not only evident in field labour. Patterson found that during the period of 'seasoning', when slaves were acclimatised to the rigours of plantation life and labour, the mortality rate was much higher for men than for women. One overseer was known to have remarked that during the seasoning period (at least between 1776 and 1786) 'three men died to one woman'. This was only grudgingly accepted by Patterson, who put forward his own explanation:

This difference in mortality rate between the sexes began from the middle

4. Lucille Mathurin, 'Reluctant Matriarchs', *Savacou*, vol. 13, p. 4; Barry Higman, 'The Slave Family and Household in the British West Indies, 1800–1834', *Journal of Interdisciplinary History*, 6: 2 (1975).
5. Winifred Cousins, 'Slave Family Life in the British Colonies, 1800–1834', *Sociological Review* 27 (1935), pp. 36–7; Michael Craton, *Searching for the Invisible Man: Slaves and Plantation Life in Jamaica*, Cambridge, Mass., Harvard University Press, 1978, p. 74.

passage when the ratio could be as great as 2 to 1. Apart from recovering their spirits earlier the women's chances of survival were improved by their more spacious accommodation in the hull of ships, by the fact that they were not chained and also by the fact that since they were sexually exploited by the seamen, these latter *probably* ensured the better treatment of whatever woman or women had taken their fancy'. (emphasis added)[6]

In a similar manner, Craton tried to play down the apparent strength and stamina of the slave women by seeing this predominance of women in field labour as 'unbalanced' and probably 'unnatural'.

> Clearly women were normally expected to perform the arduous tasks of digging and cuttting, as well as the lesser jobs of weeding and carrying, that books of slave husbandry advised for their limited strength. It was significant that easily the best results recorded at Worthy Park during the eighteenth century – a production equivalent to 2.51 hogsheads of sugar per field hand – occurred in a year (1789) when 24 male canecutters were hired to augment a dangerously unbalanced field force, of which three-quarters were women.[7]

In his study of Cuba, however, Moreno Fraginals examined the similar situation of the increasing number of women on plantations by the mid-nineteenth century. He noted that, although planters initially bought women slaves primarily as a means of improving the sex ratio and with the economic rationalisation that although they yielded less they also cost less, 'experience soon showed that the low yield of females was a myth; they worked the sixteen to eighteen hour day alongside the men. We have seen that La Ninfa's 1827 harvest was cut by women who met their daily 400 arroba quota'.[8]

Although women proved their capability in hard labour under difficult conditions, men monopolised the specialised and prestigious occupations of the factory, such as those of the boilers and distillers and also those outside the factory, such as drivers (foremen) and watchmen. Few specialised tasks were allocated to women. These were mainly as domestics or in the hospital as

6. Orlando Patterson, *The Sociology of Slavery*, London, McGibbon & Kee, 1967, p. 99.
7. Craton, *Searcing for the Invisible Man*, p. 143.
8. Manuel Moreno Fraginals, *The Sugarmill: the Socio-Economic Complex of Sugar in Cuba, 1769–1860*, New York and London, Monthly Review Press, 1976, p. 142.

'nurses' or 'midwives' which, according to Mathurin, were in many instances euphemisms for a 'superannuated field worker'.[9] While at least in this case Craton expressed some concern over the situation, Patterson, in a more recent review, finds all this quite natural. He rejects any suggestion that this division of labour reflected the internalised partriarchal prejudices of the planters, and instead argued that:

> The mystery of why so few women were in his so-called élite categories vanishes when the nature of the jobs involved is examined. The job of boiler may have been a skilled one, but it was also very hard, gruelling work. Men monopolized it, not because the masters were sensitive to masculine pride, but simply because they were stronger than women. . . . The positions of stockmen and wainmen also called for unusual strength. Whatever skills are involved, both of these are men's work for the simple reason that they require frequent and periodic bursts of extraordinary strength.[10]

One can only assume that this was also why women were not usually drivers or watchmen. As we shall see later, notions of 'women's work' and 'men's work' change from time to time. Even agricultural field labour, which at that time employed so many women under the difficult conditions of slavery, eventually became 'too difficult' for them under conditions of 'free' wage labour in the twentieth century.

Reproduction

In Jamaica, according to Patterson, changes in the approach to female slaves can be divided into different periods: in the first, 1655 to the beginning of the eighteenth century, most estates were small landholdings with few slaves and dependent on natural reproduction to maintain the slave population; the second, beginning in the early eighteenth century, saw the introduction of large-scale mono-crop production of sugar known later as the 'sugar revolution'. This period marked the incorporation of Jamaica into the emerging world capitalist system and the use of extreme capitalist cost–benefit analysis in the organisation of production.[11]

9. Mathurin, 'Reluctant Matriarchs', p. 4.
10. Orlando Patterson, 'Recent Studies on Caribbean Slavery and the Atlantic Slave Trade', *Latin American Research Review* (1982), p. 256.
11. Patterson *Sociology of Slavery*.

The low fertility of slave women, especially during the eighteenth century, is recognised by most historians, but the reason for it is still, however, open to analysis. What is even more mysterious is that the low rate of fertility among slave women continued even in the years shortly before emancipation when incentives were given to have more children and the number of women of childbearing age on the plantations had increased.[12]

In his demographic study of Worthy Park Estate in Jamaica Michael Craton found that slave women exhibited a low fertility rate in the eighteenth century. In 1795, slaveowner, Rose Price, had calculated that more than 50 per cent of the women had never given birth at all. This was true for all ages and continued for sometime even after the ameliorating measures aimed specifically at reversing this trend had come into effect at the end of the eighteenth century. Similar observations had been made earlier for other parts of the Caribbean, but Craton challenged the reasons given for this development. The low fertility levels, Craton suggested, were the result of physiological factors, similar to those experienced in Nazi concentration camps during the Second World War, in conjunction with a prolonged lactation period during which sexual intercourse was taboo.[13]

Poor health caused by overwork, disease and malnutrition was of course a major factor in the low fertility of slave women. As Patterson pointed out in 1967, slave women often suffered from gynaecological complaints such as amenorrhea, menorrhagia, injury to the ovaries, or problems in the endocrinal glandular system due to excessive beatings; all resulting in early menopause.[14] These complaints were not, however, inevitable and, given the control the planters exercised over slaves' lives, they could have been removed, as they later were, if they conflicted with the planters' interests. The question therefore is *why* did this low fertility among slave women suit the interests of the planters during the eighteenth century?

During that time a similar rejection of natural reproduction of labour was evident in the Spanish and French colonies. This, however, was manifested in slightly different ways. In Cuba, for example, very few women slaves were purchased, an initial prejudice

12. Patterson, 'Recent Studies on Caribbean Slavery', p. 254.
13. Craton, *Searching for the Invisible Man*, pp. 66–7; Noel Deere, *A History of Sugar*, 2 vols, London, Chapman & Hall, 1950; Gwendolyn M. Hall, *Social Control in Slave Plantation Societies*, Baltimore, Johns Hopkins University Studies in Historical & Political Science, 1971.
14. Patterson, *Sociology of Slavery*, pp. 106–7.

producer of cash-crops and minerals. The 1807 abolition of the slave trade put a virtual stop to imports of slaves directly from Africa to the British colonies. But is also meant increased difficulties for those colonies where the slave trade was still legal. The new policy now had to focus on the introduction of strategies aimed at increasing local natural reproduction of labour. These included the increased importation of female slaves and changes in the slave law regarding against women's capabilities as labourers was combined with the planter's aversion to the natural reproduction of labour. Some planters, according to Moreno Fraginals, 'imported only males; very few mills had any females, using the excuse that they wanted to avoid the sin of sexual contact between unmarried persons.[15] Craton on the other hand, refused to attribute this situation to the economic preferences of the planters, but a great deal of evidence exists to suggest that this was the case in almost all Caribbean sugar colonies at this time.

As early as 1926 F.W. Pitman remarked that 'the opposition of the planters to breeding was a primary cause of the low birth rate among slaves was the opinion of many contemporary observers'. In this context he quoted Sir George Younge who, on his visit to the islands in 1768, found that 'the planters did not seem desirous to encourage the breeding of slaves, but thought it cheaper to purchase'. Pitman also referred to the Revd J. Ramsay who, during the years 1762 to 1791 in St Kitts, had seen 'wretches who were upbraided, cursed and ill-treated . . . for being found in a condition to become mothers'. Even on one of Sir Edward Long's estates, which between 1766 and 1768 had 123 males and 140 females, the 77 women of childbearing age produced an average of only six births a year. In later works on this subject the reasons for the planters' attitudes became clear. In the case of Cuba, G.M. Hall found that planters had calculated the financial losses incurred during the pregnancy and nursing period of female slaves as well as the 'lengthy care of the new born' to be considerable.[16]

Similarly, in the French colony of Ste Domingue (later Haiti), Hall found that Masters had calculated the eighteen-month period (pregnancy and breast-feeding) to be worth 600 lives during a time when the woman could perform only half her normal work. For

15. Moreno Fraginals, *Sugarmill*, p. 142.
16. F.W. Pitman, 'Slavery on the British West Indian Plantations in the Eighteenth Century', *Journal of Negro History* 9: 4 (1926), pp. 639–40; Hall, *Social Control*, p. 24.

them, a fifteen-month old slave was not worth this sum.[17]

By the last quarter of the eighteenth century, however, the realisation that the free flow of slaves would not always be forth-coming affected a change in policy and ushered in the third phase. This decline in the position of Africa as a supplier of labour coincided with its incorporation into the world economy as a abortion, infanticide, child care and women's work during the late eighteenth and early nineteenth centuries.

Despite these pro-natalist incentives, most slave women still failed to bear children for the slave system. This was seen by Patterson as a form of protest and resistance against the planters, what others have called a birth strike. Even where births did take place, infanticide and abortion continued despite laws making them illegal. Another important factor was the anti-motherhood feelings internalised by slave women. Patterson suggests that the pain and suffering of childbearing, combined with the alienated character of motherhood under slavery, supported the creation of an ideology against motherhood which initially, in the eighteenth century, was in the interest of the planters. This can also be seen as an example of the way in which the ideology of ruling classes could, for different though connected material reasons, become the accepted ideology of the oppressed. This view is supported by Moreno Fraginals who reported that in Cuba in the mid-nineteenth century two slave doctors had reported that 'female slaves so detested pregnancy that they used bitter herbs to produce abortions'. In addition, where children were born, many were allowed to die out of the women's 'natural dislike for bearing them to see them become slaves, destined to toil all their lives for their master's enrichment'.[18]

As a result of the continued failure of slave women to reproduce the labour force 'naturally', as late as 1830–31, a number of planters from Jamaica, Trinidad, Barbados, Demerara (Guyana) and Antigua submitted evidence to the Board of Trade on the comparative costs of rearing slaves as opposed to buying them. This, if anything, is a clear indication that these considerations (to buy or to breed) were definitely in the minds of the planters. Douglas Hall, however, has suggested that at that time the problem was not simply a matter of the costs of production, but rather that the planters would have little control over production. Moreno Fraginals argues that, in

17. Hall, *Social Control*, p. 24.
18. Patterson, *Sociology of Slavery*, pp. 107, 106; Moreno Fraginals, *Sugarmill*, p. 143.

Cuba, it was in response to this intrasigence on the part of the slave women that 'stud farms' were established and slave-breeding became a business.[19]

The developments described above illustrate one of the clearest examples of the manipulation of women's productive capabilities by capitalist interests. In addition, it shows how the use of ideological and material factors shape oppressed people's experience of 'normal' behaviour. So as long as Africa was incorporated in the capitalist world economy only as a producer of human labour there was no need to produce labour locally. Through the use of cost/benefit analysis the planters had taken the most profitable line of action. When this was no longer profitable for them, they were surprised by the resistance shown by the slave women who, as we shall see in the following section, recognised clearly their position as the property of the plantation owners. The fact is that, for more than 100 years, the majority of slave women in the Caribbean were neither wives nor mothers and by exercising control over their reproductive capabilities were able to affect the plantation economy significantly.

Women's Labour

Slave girls began work on the plantations at the early age of four. Together with boys of their own age they were usually part of the small 'vine gang' (known today as the chip-chip gang) doing little jobs, such as collecting vines for the sheep, under the supervision of an older woman slave driver. This kind of work continued until the age of eight or nine, after which they would begin hoeing and weeding the young canes. Most of this information comes from an account by Mrs A.C. Carmichael, the wife of a planter who owned Laurel Hill Estate in Tacarigua in the early nineteenth century. Hers is one of the few contemporary accounts of the experience of slavery in St Vincent and Trinidad in the nineteenth century, but it was written from the very obvious stance of an apologist for the plantocracy against the efforts of the anti-slavery lobby in England. Her statement that very young slaves continued with these tasks until the age of sixteen when they were considered fit for adult

19. Douglas Hall, 'Slaves and Slavery in the British West Indies', *Social and Economic Studies* 11: 4 (1962), p. 307; Moreno Fraginals, *Sugarmill*, p. 143.

work, has therefore to be taken with a pinch of salt.[20]

It is interesting to note however, that Mrs Carmichael's explanations of the planters practices had somehow to fit into the British bourgeois idea of what was proper and normal. She explains, for example, that in addition to hoeing and weeding, young boys were also given tasks such as driving the mules. Attempts at instituting the West European sexual division of labour among the girls, however, proved more difficult. As Mrs Carmichael put it, she 'found nothing more difficult than to get the little girls to sew – they disliked it extremely. They learnt well enough but they did not like sitting'. Over and above these tasks, she states, girls and boys worked on their parents' provision grounds cultivating produce for sale. In addition to crops, pigs and poultry were reared. If nothing else, this discussion shows the very short period of childhood enjoyed by slave children of both sexes.[21]

Among adult slaves the sexual division of labour was similar to that described for the other territories. The labour force of a typical estate could be divided into three main groups: the domestic slaves – butlers, cooks, storekeepers, maids, cleaners, washerwomen, seamstresses, coachmen and the stable crew; artisans – head carpenters, coopers, blacksmiths, masons, potters, boilermen, distillers and their assistants and apprentices; and field labourers, drivers and field hands. Among the field hands there may be further subdivisions into 'gangs', usually three or four according to strength, the lowest being the children's gang which would be the only one with a female driver.[22]

As described earlier, there were more women in field labour than in the domestic occupations. The breakdown of positions within the 'domestic' range reveals that many of the tasks normally regarded as female were carried out by males. For example, young boys were often household servants and cooks were often men. According to Mrs Carmichael, 'the cook is frequently a male, and is also a person of consequence; if the family be large either a boy or a woman assists him'. It is interesting to note that not even in the 'domestic' domain did women hold positions of prestige. The head servant was

20. Mrs A.C. Carmichael, *Domestic Manners and Social Condition of the White, Coloured and Negro Population of the West Indies*, 2 vols, Negro University Press, 1969 (originally published in 1898).

21. Ibid., vol. 2, p. 151.

22. W.E. Green, *British Slave Emancipation, the Sugar Colonies and the Great Experiment 1830–1865*, Oxford, 1976, p. 23; L.J. Ragatz, *The Fall of the Planter Class in the British Caribbean*, New York, Century Publishers, 1928, pp. 25–6.

often male and he usually controlled the houseboys. In some families a head female servant was employed, but her main task was to assist the lady of the house in dressing, to do needlework and to prepare pastries and puddings. She usually had a young girl under her to look after the bed-chamber. The other main domestic occupations of slave women were therefore the skilled ones, such as washerwomen, seamstresses, nurses (to the planters' children), cleaners and general maids. It was estimated that a 'moderate' family of five would require about 15 or 16 domestics, of which about ten were adults.[23]

There are no records of women being employed as skilled artisans. These trades were, however, the most prestigious and offered a far wider range of occupations. In addition, they presented an opportunity during the later years of slavery of earning a cash income.

Despite the predominance of women in field labour, the drivers, as noted before, were always men. The work in the field was organised in such a manner that men and women could be used at every stage of their lives. According to a simple breakdown into gangs by Ragatz, the first or 'big' gang comprised the most able-bodied women and men. During the crop season they cut and ground the canes and boiled down the cane juice. Out of season they cleared and hoed the land and planted the cane. In Trinidad, where the soil was relatively fertile, the system of continuous ratooning was used. The second gang, according to Ragatz, usually comprised boys and girls, convalescents and pregnant women. These were supposed to weed the canes and do 'light' tasks. The third or 'small' gang, referred to earlier, was made up of small children who hoed the garden and cut grass and vines for the animals.[24]

With both women and men fully occupied in field labour it would be interesting to find out what happened to small children before the age of four. According to Patterson, during the earlier days of slavery in the older colonies estate supervisors considered small children a nuisance. At the same time he describes the attitude of Creole slave mothers to their children as one of ambivalence. One Jamaican planter said that 'many mothers who are fond of their

23. Carmichael, *Domestic Manners and Social Condition*, vol. 1, pp. 114, 116–17, 120.
24. Ratooning refers to the process whereby the ends of the canes are left in the ground to spring up again in a new crop; Ragatz, *Fall of the Planter Class*, p. 26.

children when once they have brought them into the world, would yet very gladly avoid having them'.[25] During the later years of slavery, when childbearing was actively encouraged, there was an increase in the use of material incentives and reductions in the workload of pregnant and nursing women. This change in overall approach was evidenced in the new slave laws but the slaveowners themselves, with their short-term horizons, often had difficulties in implementing them.

In Trinidad, where large-scale plantation production started later, there were many similarities with the older colonies. Especially during the earlier period, children were taken from their mothers from a young age and placed with a 'nurse'. It is clear that, at least for a certain period, the need for children did not overrule the need for women's field labour. It is important here to differentiate between the 'nurse' (the old woman who took care of young children) and the 'wet nurse'. Obviously these could not always have been the same person. Article 7 of Picton's 1800 Slave Code stated that 'Nurses having children at the breast shall be permitted to leave the field at noon and night, half an hour before the others and are exempted of throwing grass', which suggests that wet nurses were often involved in field labour or that the 'nurses' in this instance were the mothers.[26] The wet nurse must be differentiated from the 'nurse' at the estate hospital, of whom more will be said later. The laws of 1800 and 1824 exempting women from all field labour after having seven and six children respectively living on her master's estate, were seldom put into effect. The conditions of slave labour, as well as the women's own ambivalence to childbearing, made this an extremely rare occurrence.

In addition to the laws, individual planters put forward their own incentives to childbearing. Mrs Carmichael says that her husband offered a reward of two 'joes' to any women who could produce her child at two years old. Similarly, in Tobago in 1792, Sir William Young reported that he had offered five yards of fine printed cotton to every women who had reared a child.[27]

Michael Craton found that in Jamaica between 1787 and 1838 women with six living children comprised 0.90 per cent of the total slave work force òn Worthy Park Estate, while Barry Higman, writing on Trinidad, found that according to the 1813 registration

25. Patterson, *Sociology of Slavery*, p. 154.
26. Carmichael, *Domestic Manners and Social Condition*, p. 381.
27. Ibid., vol. 2, p. 200; Deere, *History of Sugar*, p. 350.

returns most women had fewer than two living children.[28]

It is very important to analyse this situation as it presents an excellent example of how motherhood was manipulated to suit the economic requirements of the ruling class. This is exposed extremely clearly in Mrs Carmichael's apologetic to nineteenth-century bourgeois British society, where the 'housewifisation' of women was taking place. On the one hand, she was quite eager to show that despite the existence of domestic servants European women took personal care of their own children. As she put it, 'all West India ladies are patterns in this respect; their solicitude and personal activity in attending to their young children, being beyond praise. Therefore a nurse has little work, comparatively with the duties attached to that office in Britain'. On the other hand, by defining the African woman as outside normal 'humanity', she was able to justify an apparently contradictory approach to the children of the slaves in saying that: 'Negro children are brought up altogether differently from European infants; and however strange the mode may appear, I have seen such fine healthy robust infants treated in the way I am about to describe, that I feel no hesitation in believing it to be perfectly adapted to the climate'. She went on to describe how mothers handed their children over to the nurse during the day and reclaimed them at night. The justification offered to the British public for this assumed aberration was that, unlike European women, African women were mercilessly cruel to their children and (surprisingly) preferred to work rather than to take care of them all day. She wrote: 'Negro mothers, with only one exception, I have found cruelly harsh to their children; they beat them unmercifully for perfect trifles'. The nurses, she went on 'are far kinder to the children than I ever knew any of the negro mothers to be, and the infant invariably shows more affection for the nurse than for its parent' and, in any case, 'negro women like the gossip and the fun of the field; . . . to stay at home and nurse their child is too monotonous and dull a life for them'.[29]

The difference between the European 'housewife' with her servants and the African slave woman engaged in full-time labour on the plantation was, in many respects, a reflection in microcosm of

28. Craton, *Searching for the Invisible Man*, p. 141; Higman, 'African and Creole Slave Family Patterns in Trinidad', in Margaret E. Craham and Franklin W. Knight (eds), *Africa and the Caribbean: Legacies of a Link*, Baltimore, Johns Hopkins Press, 1979, p. 52.
29. Quotations taken from Carmichael, *Domestic Manners and Social Condition*, vol. 1, p. 121; vol. 2, p. 189; vol. 1, p. 269; vol. 2, p. 188, vol. 2, pp. 200–1.

the contradictions among women in the existing international division of labour. The withdrawal of middle-strata and some working-class women from wage-work outside the home in Europe was largely made possible by the enslavement and forced labour of men and women in the colonies. The one depended on the other. Thus, during the later days of slavery, only selective aspects of European domestic ideology could be applied to slave women, creating the double standard Mrs Carmichael sought to explain. By maintaining this dichotomy within the plantation structure, slave women may have equated the position of white women as full-time wives and mothers with higher social and economic status in the society. This could have led them to devalue the importance of their own relative independence from these structures.

Non-Plantation Slavery

In addition to plantation slavery, slaves were also owned by people who owned no land. The population structure of Trinidad, for example, in which 67 per cent of the population were slaves in 1819, differed greatly from those of older British slave colonies, in which at least 90 per cent were slaves. In addition, slaves were much more often owned by free black or coloured slaveowners in Trinidad than in other colonies. Another characteristic was their concentration into small units, with the effect that, in 1813, 60 per cent belonged to units of fewer than 50 slaves and only 8 per cent lived in units of over 150 slaves. As late as 1834, according to Brereton, 'the average owner had only seven slaves, 80 per cent owned less than ten, while only 1 per cent had over 100 slaves.[30]

The slaves of landless owners were usually hired out to plantations or to other enterprises to perform specific skilled tasks, in a form of subcontracting in which a fixed portion of their weekly income was given to the owner who usually lived in the urban areas. These 'jobbing slaves', as they came to be known, were mainly skilled artisans or field workers and their tasks were usually closed to women. The women tended to be hired out as domestic slaves, field labourers, or concubines for temporary male European settlers, or were made to work as petty traders or prostitutes, handing

30. Bridget Brereton, *A History of Modern Trinidad 1783–1962*, London, Heinemann, 1981, pp. 54, 54–5. In Jamaica only 24 per cent of the slaves were in units of fewer than 50.

over most of their earnings to their masters. According to W. Green, 'jobbing' slaves were given the most difficult tasks on estates or in enterprises, but received none of the compensations of provision grounds, medical care, or a stable environment.[31]

During the later years of slavery, when the various ameliorative Orders in Council were coming into effect, possibilities for slaves to earn a cash income increased. This was the forerunner of the outburst of independent petty entrepreneurial activity which was to characterise the post-emancipation period. On the plantations, as would be expected, slaves were able to earn an income through the sale of produce at the Sunday markets. These were sold both to other slaves and to free citizens, including the planters themselves.

It is important to note that the provision grounds and other income-earning activities provided slave women with a certain degree of independence. Mrs Carmichael cites the example of 'C', who was supposed to be a difficult slave; 'she was the torment of everyone – she poured forth abuse upon her master, the overseers, the driver and her mother, in the stocks or at work'. On the other hand:

> C's grounds were indeed a source of riches to her: she kept a complete huckster's shop on the estate and many, both on Laurel Hill and the adjoining properties, bought thread, candle, soap and pins, etc. from her. She had always plenty of money. . . . She gave dances, and made a great deal of money by them: she paid for everything – supper, liquor and music, and each negro paid half a dollar for admission.

It is no wonder that by 1830 this slave was able to *manumit* (free) herself. Mrs Carmichael also described hucksters who went from estate to estate bartering bread, cakes and pastry for fruit, vegetables and eggs, which in turn they would sell at the St Joseph market; she did not, however, ascertain whether all of these were slaves or not. These examples suggest that slave women, predominantly field labourers, often participated in petty trading as a means of earning an income. It also suggests that during the later days of slavery, slave labour, even when combined with forms of subsistence production and petty trading, was for the planters still more profitable than 'free wage-labour', a possibility they fought to the very end.[32]

This economic independence of slave women was identified by

31. Green, *British Slave Emancipation*, pp. 22–7.
32. Carmichael, *Domestic Manners and Social Condition*, vol. 2, pp. 183, 184–5, 165–6.

Matthews as a causal factor of what he termed *the crisis in the West Indian family*. He argued that on slave plantations men and women each had a separate economic base, as each had an independent land grant (possibly provision ground). Women controlled their own money and, according to Matthews, 'tampering with the reputed wife's money or garden produce was a major crime, as disreputable as theft by a common stranger'.[33]

Both Green and Knight note that in most slave societies the number of freed women in the population was always greater than that of men. Franklin Knight shows that in Trinidad in 1811, for example, 56.7 per cent of the free non-white population was female while in Tobago there were 153 free adult women to 92 adult men. The common explanation for this is that manumission was conferred on slave women in return for sexual favours. The above data suggest, however, that at least some of these women could afford to pay their own manumission costs and did so, especially during the later years of slavery. Some support can be lent to this supposition by the frequency with which examples of prices for *female* as opposed to male slaves appear in the literature on manumission, suggesting that such manumissions were bought not given.[34]

Marriage

Throughout slave society, marriage remained the preserve of the upper classes, namely the plantocracy and the wealthy merchants. By the word 'marriage' is meant here a 'legal union sanctioning the cohabitation and sexual intercourse of man and women'.[35] Even for middle-class whites, the European nuclear family with its non wage-earning housewife and consumer oriented lifestyle was an impossibility on their meagre incomes and on some estates (as in the old European patriarchal family) marriage was actually forbidden.

33. Matthews, *Crisis in the West Indian Family*, p. 23.
34. Green, *British Slave Emancipation*; Franklin Knight, *The Caribbean: Genesis of a Fragmented Nationalism*, New York, Oxford University Press, 1978, p. 107; Brereton, *History of Modern Trinidad*, p. 60. This point is further illustrated by the following quotation from Richard Hart, *Slaves who Abolished Slavery, vol. 1, Blacks in Bondage*, Kingston, Jamaica, Institute of Social & Economic Research, 1980, p. 136: 'But a high price was paid for the freedom of some of the manumitted. The owner of Frances Phipps received £300 in 1817. Anne Hood's freedom cost £160 in 1821. Cecelia Cohen's manumission was purchased for £34.13.4d in 1826 and Anne Wright's cost £150 in the same year.'
35. *Penguin English Dictionary*, 2nd edn, 1977.

121

At the same time, in the British colonies marriage among slaves was forbidden for most of the eighteenth century. This situation resulted in a contradictory approach to marriage on the part of the slaves. According to Patterson, marriage became associated with high class and privilege, so much so that slaves who did marry during the nineteenth century were jeered at by other slaves partaking in 'high caste' activity.[36]

There were many reasons why marriage (and even long-term cohabitation) was initially discouraged. First of all the absence of marriage facilitated the exigencies of the 'sugar revolution'. It made the sale and purchase of slaves, relatively easy, as control over women and children was in the hands of the planter and not in those of individual men. Male–female ratios could be determined by production requirements and not by the desires of slaves. In addition, the 'risk of childbearing' among women was reduced as was desired by planters.[37]

From the 1780s, however, a change in attitude towards slave marriage could be perceived. The Slave Codes of this period all encouraged marriage, now seen as a means of increasing reproduction. Individual planters, however, found it difficult to give up their flexibility of control, organisation, sale and purchase, so that later laws became more pronounced and more specific in this regard. But whatever the changes in attitudes of the planters and colonial authorities, they had to come to terms with the strong rejection by slaves of the institution of marriage. This was often used by the planters as an excuse for their failure to encourage marriage, but it cannot be disputed that it was true.

Also, marriage was originally seen as part of the Christian religious tradition and, as such, not to be extended to slaves. According to A. Caldecott, a great contradiction existed between the concepts of Christianity and slavery. According to the laws of the Church of England, no Christian could be a slave, so to make a slave Christian would negate the existence of slavery. More important though was the fear among planters that religious instruction would lead to 'notions of equality'. To get around this problem, so Caldecott holds, the slave was defined as outside humanity and consequently 'the colonialists took very kindly to the suggestion of

36. Patterson, *Sociology of Slavery*, pp. 42, 164–5.
37. Demographers in the twentieth century have found that married women or women in permanent cohabitation relationships carry a higher 'risk of childbearing' because they have more opportunities for sexual intercourse.

ethnologists of that day that the Negro was not the same "species" as the European; they welcomed this convenient distinction between "genus" and "species".' This justification of the planters clearly supports Maria Mies's position that the 'exterritorialisation' of non-whites and women and their definition into nature was a rationalisation for their exploitation, often in non-wage forms.[38]

The argument has often been put forward, both for the slavery and post-emancipation periods, that the low number of marriages was more by default than design and that slaves appreciated marriage as an ideal but were unable to fulfil it for legal, social and economic reasons. The available evidence, however, does not support this thesis. In the St John's Parish Register in Jamaica, Craton found that whereas there were hundreds of baptisms between 1811 and 1835 (in response to amerliorative conditions and increased access to European middle-class status norms), not a single marriage was recorded. Similarly, Brereton found that in Trinidad, despite the 1824 laws encouraging marriage, only four slave marriages took place between 1824 and 1829. Mrs Carmichael found that at Laurel Hill, both female and male slaves refused to marry when they had lived together for many years. The explanations given by these slaves for their resistance to marriage show that they held particular ideas of what 'husbands' were and what 'wives' were which did not fit their situation. Mrs Carmichael saw these explanations as an appreciation on the part of the slaves of the moral superiority of the European way of life. For example, when asked why she had refused to marry, one woman answered, 'when nigger come good like white man, she might marry', while a man, when advised to marry the woman with whom he had lived for twelve years, said 'me know that me neber marry nigger wife: if Massa King George send out white wife to me from England, and den me marry as many as he like'. In expounding his reasons he went on to argue that 'white wife no run bout here, dere and everywhere like negroes; massa if you gie me your wife, me marry her today; but afore me marry any nigger wife, me go hang me sel in a Paradise wood'. From this Mrs Carmichael concluded that 'they come by very slow steps to perceive that their customs are inferior to ours. One grand step is already gained in favour of the civilisation of the negroes – it

38. Alfred Caldecott, *The Church in the West Indies*, London reprint by Frank Cass & Co. Ltd, 1970 (first published 1898), pp. 63–70, 67; Maria Mies, 'Towards a Methodology of Women's Studies', occasional paper, Institute of Social Studies, the Hague, 1980.

is that they universally admit that white man is wiser and better than they.'[39]

Perhaps this was the slaves' way of humouring the whites while resisting attempts to interfere in their domestic lives. Even so, at that time a full-time labouring black woman and an economically-deprived black man unable to support a non-earning 'housewife' or to own a house, were hardly the stuff of which marriages were made.

In response to the criticism by Methodist missionaries that planters were discouraging marriage, Mrs Carmichael suggested that men often wanted more than one wife, while the slave woman saw marriage as a tie, which forbade her from leaving her husband, put her under his control and subjected her to his punishment. Again, this can be seen as an apologetic for the plantocracy. But Alfred Caldecott, a church historian writing on the immediate post-emancipation period, found that movement towards marriage was slow despite the fact that 'the institution was pressed with unfailing insistence'. In the immediate post-emancipation period there was even a decline in the number of marriages. Caldecott's eventual conclusion shows that he realised that the slaves had a different approach to man–woman relationships than that of the Europeans. In other words, the slaves did not simply have an underdeveloped European middle-class mentality, but rather, based on their own material and historical experiences, they had come to their own understanding of what their relationships should be. In the following quotation Caldecott bemoans the power of the women in determining the nature of these relationships. He ascribes this to the Negro's inability to rise to the level of 'Christian character' required for marriage:

> Both men and women among them are aware of the difficulty of controlling fancy, and of the transitory character of most of their affections, and they shrink from the promise of constancy. With them it is the women as much as the men who are thus constituted; *there is in the Negro race a nearer approach to equality between the sexes than is found in European races.*[40] (emphasis added)

It was this relative equality which women had inadvertently gained

39. Craton, *Searching for the Invisible Man*, p. 166; Brereton, *History of Modern Trinidad*, p. 66; Carmichael, *Domestic Manners and Social Condition*, vol. 2, pp. 185, 178, 215–16.

40. Carmichael, *Domestic Manners and Social Condition*, vol. 2, p. 239; Caldecott, *Church in the West Indies*, pp. 107–8, 195.

during slavery which the Church and missionaries were now attempting to remove. Years later, in 1953, Dom Basil Matthews, a clergyman in Trinidad, blamed this 'dead level equality and uniformity of slave society' on the 'rudderless', 'restless' and 'unmanageable' character of the female slaves.[41] It was this character that the Church and colonial society sought to domesticate during the nineteenth and twentieth centuries.

The Slave Family

Attempts in the 1970s by scholars in the United States to refute the Frazier–Moynihan thesis have already been mentioned. Recent work has tried to rescue the Afro–American family from its image of a 'matriarchal', 'disorganised', 'promiscuous' institution in which the status of the man as the head of the household was drastically reduced and to establish, once and for all, that female-headed households were not the dominant form during and after slavery and that black men were in fact powerful and high in status. Perhaps the most famous example is that of Herbert Gutman, who argues that the slave and free black family household was predominantly a stable, male-headed unit, which was neither disorganised nor pathological and that the black matriarchy thesis is no more than a myth. These new interpretations were initially welcomed by some black women in the United States who were eager to shed the responsibility placed on them by white society for the oppression of their men. Recent scholarship by black women, however, has become more critical of this work as new material comes to light and as they challenge the assumptions on which these counter-arguments were developed in the first place.[42]

In the Caribbean, the Jamaican-based historian Barry W. Higman has sought to do the same. In a series of articles,[43] he has sought to do for the Caribbean what Gutman and others have done for the United States. In common with the majority of US studies, Higman's material is limited to the later years of slavery, especially after the abolition of the slave trade when planters were attempting to

41. Matthews, *Crisis in the West Indian Family*, p. 26.
42. Gutman, *The Black Family in Slavery and Freedom*.
43. These include Higman's, 'The Slave Family and Household in the British West Indies'; 'Household Structure and Fertility on Jamaican Slave Plantations', *Population Studies* 27 (1978); 'African and Creole Slave Family Patterns'.

shift the responsibilities of reproduction onto the slaves (mainly by encouraging them to have nuclear families) and when, according to Craton, the ameliorative proposals were coming into effect. Yet, like these researchers, he sought to extend its relevance as a 'constant model' to the entire period, including the previous 150 years.[44]

In recent years the use of a great deal of quantitative material and complex mathematical and statistical techniques to revise long-held historical theses has become fashionable. This in many ways is a welcome development as it often gives a necessary support to qualitative data. It would be a mistake, however, to be mesmerised by the sheer mass of figures into accepting unquestionably all the conclusions. Experience has shown that figures often reveal far less than they claim.

In his work on the slave family in the Caribbean, Higman has tried to show that the nuclear family, defined by him as 'consisting of a man, his wife and their children', was more common among slaves than was previously held and that, as a result, the slave family was not disorganised, matrifocal or disorderly.[45]

Using the 1813 slave registration returns, Higman attempted to analyse the slave family in Trinidad. He also sought to examine the extent to which the ethnic origin of African-born slaves (or the fact that there were born locally) affected the process of domestic organisation. In introducing this dimension, the author tried to confront the question of whether or not slavery of African retentions was the main determining factor in social organisation among slaves. Taking the latter point first Higman found that the majority of African-born slaves came from patrilineal groups with the exception of a relatively large contingent from the Gold Coast, Benin and Biafra. This therefore was not a determining factor in the creation of what he termed 'slave families'.

In his analysis of the entire slave population, he identified a number of different 'family types'. These were (1) man, wife, their children; (2) man, wife; (3) woman, her children; (4) woman, her children, her grandchildren; (5) man, wife, various children; (6) polygynists; and (7) extended siblings and their children.[46]

This diverse array of domestic arrangements accounted for 50.1 per cent of the slaves in 1813 leaving another 49.9 per cent who

44. Craton, *Searching for the Invisible Man*, p. 163; Higman, 'The Slave Family and Household in the British West Indies', pp. 285–7.
45. Higman, 'The Slave Family and Household in the British West Indies', p. 271.
46. Higman, 'African and Creole Slave Family Patterns', p. 53.

Table 6.1: Domestic organisation among slaves in Trinidad in 1813

| | | | | Slave in families | | % |
Family Type	Family units	Slaves	Mean size	% Units	% Slaves	of total slave population
Man, wife, their children	932	3670	3.9	22.3	28.5	14.3
Man, wife	518	1036	2.0	12.4	8.1	4.0
Woman, her children	2066	5690	2.8	49.4	44.2	22.2
Man, his children	138	357	2.6	3.3	2.8	1.4
Woman, her children, her grandchilren	48	227	4.7	1.1	1.8	0.9
Man, wife, various children	230	1005	4.4	5.5	7.8	3.9
Polygynists	7	31	4.4	0.2	0.2	0.1
Extended siblings, and their	49	218	4.4	1.2	1.7	0.8
children	197	547	2.8	4.7	4.2	2.1
Total in families	4185	12,781	3.1		50.1	49.7
Slaves not in families		12,892			49.9	50.2
TOTAL		25,673			100.0	99.9

Source: Barry Higman, 'African and Creole Slave Family Patterns in Trinidad, '*Africa and the Caribbean: Legacies of a Link*, ed. M.E. Craham and F.W. Knight, Baltimore, John Hopkins Press, 1979, p. 53 (last column added).

could not fit into any of these categories.[47] Of those 'in families', only 28.5 per cent were found in the real 'nuclear families' as defined by himself above. When taken as a percentage of the total slave population, however, the figure is reduced to 14.3 per cent. On the other hand, units of a woman and her children comprised 44.2 per cent of the slaves in 'family' units or 22.2 per cent of the total slave population.

Higman's thesis can thus be turned on its head by his own data. By excluding from his computation those 50.2 (or 49.9) per cent of slaves categorised as 'not in families' he performs the same statistical

47. Using Higman's figures, I get the percentage of slaves in 'families' as 49.7 per cent and of those not in families as 50.2 per cent. The difference is negligible; both categories are approximately equal. See Table 6.1.

trick that labour force statisticians after the Second World War used to exclude women's unemployment from the computation of unemployment rates (by placing the majority of women (defined as housewives) in the category 'not in the labour force'). This kind of approach has recently been referred to by Patterson as the 'its-half-full; no-its-half-empty problem', for by not analysing the particular phenomenon in its totality a great deal can be hidden in the categories.[48]

So far as the distribution of these household or domestic units is concerned, it was found that they were much more likely to occur on larger plantations. This was because of the greater possibilities for choice of partner, the lower possibility of separation through sale and the isolation from other plantations. Nuclear families for example, exceeded mother–child units on plantations of over 50 slaves while the only polygamous units were recorded on the country's largest plantation, *Paradise and Cane Farm* which had 250 slaves. In addition it was found that mother–child units greatly exceeded nuclear families in urban areas and on smaller plantations, both among African-born and Creole slaves. A slightly larger proportion (17.8 per cent) of the urban African-born population lived in nuclear families as opposed to 5.6 per cent urban Creoles and this was also true for the African-born on plantations.[49]

The establishment of nuclear families by Africans Higman saw not as a recreation of an African family form, as this was not characteristic of the majority of Trinidad Africans. He saw it rather as an initial attempt to build up an extended or polygynous family type.[50] What is interesting is that most of these units comprised two Africans. Only 10 per cent of African males had Creole mates, while 13 per cent of the African women had Creole mates. In general, it was found that the proportion of nuclear families decreased as the population became more Creolised.

One of the findings most indicative of the factors determining the establishment of nuclear families was the characteristics of the husbands. While only 60 per cent of the men were labourers, 90 per cent of the women were. At least one-third of the male heads therefore were skilled workers, tradesmen or drivers. Among the seven polygynists, four were skilled artisans, while all their wives were labourers. Higman suggests that these findings show that the

48. Patterson, 'Recent Studies on Caribbean Slavery', p. 261.
49. Higman, 'African and Creole Slave Family Patterns', pp. 50–2.
50. Ibid., p. 54.

values associated with family headship among Africans did not disappear entirely in the Caribbean. In an earlier paper, he heralds this as a sign that the male did not lose his 'status' under slavery. As he put it, 'This means that the husband/father very often had a greater social "status" than the wife/mother, and hence relatively greater economic power in terms of direct grants of rations, clothing and utensils from the master, and in access to superior housing and grounds.' On this basis therefore he suggests that, 'The supposed devaluation of the status and role of the male under the slave system thus needs to be reconsidered.'[51]

Again the extent of skilled male 'headship' is a bit dubious. One-third of the male heads possibly refers to one-third of the men of 'families', but they comprised only 23.6–24.4 per cent of the total slave population. The data also suggest (although he does not) that a higher male status was encouraged by the plantocracy far more than by African survivals. This was done through the allocation of skilled prestige jobs and the direct grants from the master of rations, clothing and utensils to men, as well as access to superior grounds and housing. Mathurin, quoting Elsa Gouveia, noted that the field slaves were usually the most dependent, having fewer opportunities to earn a cash income than others.[52] In this way, the plantation owners were able to create a class within a class of 'small men' who, like the 'big white men', could also own a wife. They were never able to extend this to the entire slave population, however, as this would have meant the destruction of the system itself.

Mrs Carmichael cites the case, in 1832, of a driver on her estate who owned 20 acres of grounds. He was, however, a rather important person and so unable to labour with his own hands. The work was therefore done by his wife, his son and hired labourers.[53] The ownership of a wife and wife's labour was clearly the prerogative of wealthier slaves. It is possible that the fear of this type of domination kept some creole women from forming stable monogamous units.

So far as children were concerned, it was found that few women had more than two children and apparently many had none. This shows that the large numbers of children required by the planters were seldom forthcoming. Of 6,138 children identified, 61.6 per cent lived with mothers only, 32.6 per cent lived with both parents,

51. Higman, 'The Slave Family and Household in the British West Indies', p. 2.
52. Mathurin, 'Reluctant Matriarchs', p. 4.
53. Carmichael, *Domestic Manners and Social Condition*, vol. 2, pp. 230–1.

while 5.7 per cent lived in units where one member was a parent more often the mother.[54] The use of prolonged lactation as a means of spacing births was identified as a general characteristic of the region, but instances for Trinidad were not identified.

It is possible that Higman himself began to realise the trap into which he had fallen. By setting out to disprove a series of biased and largely irrelevant premises, he had in fact lost a great opportunity to explore what the material was really saying about man–woman relationships in the Caribbean. In 1975, for example, still accepting moralistic definitions and assumptions, he gave the following as examples of the extent of 'instability':

> At Newton, of the twenty women listed as having husbands in 1796 only three were identified as having had former husbands or as being the mothers of children by more than one man. In one, or perhaps two, of these cases the former mate seems to have been dead, with a space of about five years between the children and the two fathers. The only clear case of instability seems to be that of Bella, a field slave aged 40 years, who had children by three separate men within a space of eight years.[55]

By 1979, however, a change in Higman's position was evident. In his study on Trinidad, perhaps because he was confronted with data that could less easily be made to 'fit' as the Jamaica data had, he concluded: 'Thus many women had children by men with whom they lived, a condition directly related to the slave system *but not necessarily evidence of "instability"*'.[56]

In relation to the Trinidadian situation, Higman in the end concluded that a smaller proportion of slaves lived in 'families' in Trinidad than in Jamaica and that more of them lived in mother–child units and fewer lived in extended family units. This he ascribed to the relatively larger urban and African-born population. The apparent contradiction here was that, although the African-born were more likely to form nuclear families, they were less likely to be found in domestic units in general. One possible explanation for this contradictory situation was touched on by Craton when he found that although African-born slaves were held in some contempt by Creole slaves, they were given the 'élite' and skilled positions on Worthy Park estate. Bearing in mind Higman's pre-

54. Derived from figures in Higman, 'African and Creole Slave Family Patterns', p. 60.
55. Higman, 'The Slave Family and Household in the British West Indies', p. 282.
56. Higman, 'African and Creole Slave Family Patterns', p. 60, emphasis added.

vious statement on the relationship between family headship and social and economic status, these could have been the determining factors for those Africans who succeeded in establishing nuclear units.[57]

In the light of the above discussion, therefore, a number of important conclusions can be reached. First, if we take a truly historical rather than a static ahistorical approach the changing character of relationships between women and men can be discerned. In addition, by not taking 'the slave family' out of its historical and socio-economic context, the factors that helped change and shape it in its various manifestations can be identified. For example, by the nineteenth century the reduced availability of slaves from Africa and the difficulty of importing food for them was encouraging a form of nuclear family and subsistence food production. But for both the planters and the slaves if they desired it, the true conjugal family (on the European model) was never fully possible because the planters were unwilling to give up their ultimate control over the lives and labour of the slaves. They were also unwilling to allow all men to accumulate the income, benefits, or property necessary to facilitate 'stable' economically viable households with dependent subordinate wives. By creating a small 'élite' of wealthier privileged male slaves who could afford to 'own' wives and to profit from their labour, the planters may have created a model. But that it was simply that, a model and not in many instances (only for 22.2 per cent of the slave population) a reality, is clear even from Barry Higman's own data.

As a closing note, it should be added that the existence of female-headed households does not imply the existence of female dominance, as numerous women scholars have pointed out.[58] It did possibly mean a greater degree of independence for women but within the situation of slavery this was certainly constrained. To attempt to disprove female dominance disproving the existence of female-headed households is, in many ways, a sophistical intention.

Conclusion

In this chapter on the experience of African women during slavery I

57. Ibid., pp. 52, 54; Craton, *Searching for the Invisible Man*, p. 142.
58. Mathurin, 'Reluctant Matriarchs'; Susan Craig, 'Millstones or Milestones', *Latin American Research Review*, 14: 3 (1979).

have attempted to present a basis on which the appropriation of and attitudes towards women's labour in the twentieth century can be analysed. By tracing historically the changes and developments in the Caribbean, particularly in the Trinidadian slave economy, it has been possible to identify the means by which women's productive capabilities were manipulated to serve the interests of the planter class. This, it was found, was determined not solely by individual planters, but by planters, slaves and the colonial state acting together within the framework of the expanding international capitalist system.

During most of the eighteenth century, for example, when the purchase of slaves directly from Africa was possible and profitable, little attention was paid to women as producers of the labour force. Similarly, when food was readily available, mainly from the British North American colonies, slave masters retained the responsibility for feeding their slaves, preferring to exact the maximum labour from both their male and their female slaves. At the turn of the century, however, when these circumstances had begun to change, attempts were made to alter the production relations on the plantations to accommodate the new situation and to maintain profitability. The two most important ways in which this was done were, first, by shifting responsibility for food production and the production of the labour force onto the slaves (by allocating subsistence plots or 'provision grounds') and, secondly, by encouraging selective aspects of the European conjugal family and its accompanying domestic ideology.

Within the circumstances of slavery, however, and in the interests of continued profitability, the economic basis for the conjugal family could by definition never be extended to all slaves. This would have seriously challenged the economic viability of the slave system. Even in the last days of the slave system, when the comparative advantages of slave and 'free' labour were being debated, the majority of planters stuck to slave labour because it guaranteed, as no other system could, the most complete control over labour. Instead, an élite of wealthier male slaves in skilled jobs or positions of authority was created. For these slaves it because possible to 'own' and control wives and to be heads of households.

7

Historical Evolution in the Sexual Division of Labour in Nigeria

SIMI AFONJA

Introduction

Development planners are currently having to decide whether development programmes should become more gender-specific or even female oriented. Until now they have supposedly been 'gender-neutral', but there is a growing recognition of a need to accord women their rightful place in the development process. Before this can be achieved, however, it is necessary to acquire a sound understanding of each society's sexual division of labour and of the roles women have played throughout its history.

In this chapter I analyse the historical evolution of the sexual division of labour in one particular country, Nigeria. While my basic theoretical framework is derived from historical change in Europe, I have introduced some new elements specifically suited to looking at the historical evolution of African countries. Before looking at Nigeria in detail, however, some general comments will help to clarify my approach to this complex task.

Anyone attempting to trace the history of sexual divisions in a third world country is faced with two major tasks – to analyse the place of women in the development process (which in many third world economies actually *worsened* their position in a way not anticipated by development theorists) and to relate this analysis to some framework of social change in the country as a whole.

The approach taken here builds on the framework shared by Marx and other nineteenth-century historians who envisaged European history as a sequence of 'stages' of development. These were seen as different socio-economic formations succeeding one another historically. For example, feudalism gave way to capitalism in Europe as the dynamic new system penetrated and replaced the old. Analytically, as well as chronologically, the new capitalist socio-economic formation was seen as distinct from the old feudal system.

This view of history as a series of distinct successive socio-economic systems or 'modes of production' does have its attractions, especially in that it allows the historian to isolate the most important factors in a complex process of change and to order them historically. For an African country such as Nigeria, however, there are problems associated with adopting the framework wholesale. For a start, pre-capitalist societies in Africa did not all resemble the feudal systems of pre-capitalist Europe; capitalism has not simply or smoothly replaced the pre-capitalist societies, but has continued to incorporate elements of the old systems within the new capitalist economies of Africa, and, therefore, not only do the developing capitalist economies of Africa differ from their European predecessors, but they also differ from each other. Such problems will inevitably affect interpretations of how the sexual division of labour has unfolded in an African economy such as Nigeria.

Pre-capitalist societies in Africa were different from those of feudal Europe in that, mainly because of the important role the African kinship system played in distributing economic resources, they did not (as Europe did) produce a class of landless peasants. Even centralised states which exacted taxes and tributes from the village community (such as the Hausa–Fulani) are believed to have used these resources more for conspicuous consumption than for capital accumulation (as in Europe). This meant that a capitalist system of production could not have developed in Africa in the same way as it did in Europe. As some French anthropologists argue, there is a need to formulate a 'specifically African' mode of production.

Nascent capitalist economies in Africa differ in their socio-economic formations because capitalism has only incompletely penetrated the previous systems. Capitalism now coexists with aspects of the pre-capitalist African economies and, in much the same way as the older economic systems differed from each other, so too does the course of capitalist development differ in the new capitalist economies. It is therefore unsatisfactory in the African context to envisage replacing a uniformly 'feudal' mode of production with a uniformly 'capitalist' one, or to analyse class development in a country like Nigeria simply in terms of a 'peasantry' of subsistence farmers gradually being replaced by an industrial 'proletariat' of waged workers.

This is especially true in relation to women, for whom no neat path from 'peasant' to 'wage-labourer' can be traced. In discussing the sexual division of labour it is particularly pertinent to bear in mind the persistence of elements of an old form of economic organisation, for the household typically retains forms of pre-capitalist relations.

The impact of capitalism on the sexual division of labour differed according to the type of economy in existence at the time of its introduction. In Nigeria (which contains a number of different social and economic formations) there are still differences in the way in which capitalism is developing and affecting the sexual division of labour. This is because different groups within the society have been shaped by different economic histories. Thus, although a 'mode of production' may be clear analytically, in its chronological history it invariably coexists with aspects of a previous mode. And, because of the importance of *non*-economic factors in organising the sexual division of labour in pre-capitalist economies, this has a particular bearing on the analysis of women's economic position.

Economic changes in women's roles do not necessarily affect how they are seen in their societies. Considerable hangovers from previous ways of regarding them can exist even when developments in the economy make them inappropriate. This persistent 'mismatch' of perceptions is not purely a mistake, for it can reflect the continuing influence of religious or political ways of organising the pre-capitalist economy.

One question European feminists have asked about the sexual division of labour in Europe has been the effect of the separation of 'home' and 'work' brought about by capitalism. Many feminists have even traced the onset of women's subordinate position to the split between these 'private' and 'public' domains. In Europe, women's subordination and increasing 'privatisation' within domesticity seem to go together.

In Africa, capitalism has not separated the producers from the productive resources in the way it did with the propertyless wage workers of Europe. The split between 'home' and 'work', 'private' and 'public', or 'reproduction' and 'production' cannot be used in the same way to explain women's growing subordination. Nigerian women have not been 'privatised', or confined within a separate private domestic sphere, as they were in Europe. The historical evolution of the sexual division of labour in Africa requires a quite different explanation.

Nigerian Socio-Economic Formations

The rather disparate experiences of women from different regions of the world have been problematic enough for the making of theory. The whole exercise becomes even more cumbersome where there are divergent patterns within one national boundary as we find in Nigeria. Not only had state formation progressed at various rates, but there were also remarkable variations in the mode of subsistence and in the accompanying relations of production. This variation cannot of course be isolated from that in social and political organisation. If, however, the Marxist tradition of classifying according to the mode of production is adopted, then two categories of the African mode emerge. The one is clearly recognised as the lineage mode and the other as a mere semblance of the European feudal mode. The lineage mode is more widespread and is common where the segmentary lineage principle is central to social and political organisation. The Yoruba, who are structured into semi-autonomous kingdoms, would fall into this category; so too would the Ibo and Ibibio, who have no political centralisation, and the ethnic groups of the north not engulfed into the Hausa–Fulani kingdoms – the latter being politically centralised and with a somewhat feudal structure.

The African Mode of Production

The lineage mode of production is characteristically a subsistence mode in which land, the main instrument of agricultural production, is valued and in which the labour of the women and of the young men is controlled by the adult men of the lineage. Although it is tempting to impute some element of exploitation into this relation of production, Terray[1] reminds us that before the capitalist penetration of these societies, mercantile relations were absent within the self-subsisting unit and the society's major goal was to

1. Emmanuel Terray, *Marxism and Primitive Societies*, New York, Monthly Review Press, 1972.

produce and reproduce the material conditions of existence, the community members and the structural organisation. This is not to deny the long history of internal and long-distance trade by the various groups classified into the lineage mode. But appraisals of the impact of such trade on internal economic and social relations show that the items of trade were important for their use value rather than for capital formation. Men had more control of the more profitable long-distance trade, but the inequalities apparent in this were tempered by an ideology which held that men and women's trading activities sustained the household socially and economically. The division of labour in this mode of production can therefore be described as a complementary one in which men and women's efforts and resources were devoted to production and reproduction at the level of subsistence.

The Yoruba, for instance, subsisted on agricultural production with trade and craft production as subsidiary economic activities. Although the picture of female farming is rather hazy, there is enough evidence to suggest that there was a clear-cut division of labour in farming. Most Yorubas were farmers and the household was the primary unit of production, consumption and distribution. In farming the women performed the lighter duties of planting, weeding, harvesting and carrying the harvest. The heavier tasks were carried out by the men who also controlled the major decision-making processes – when to plant, when to weed, when to harvest the product. There was a clear-cut distinction between the control of the more socially valued crops such as yams, and the crops planted in the women's vegetable gardens for household consumption and for social exchanges. Such crops provided women with a means of social exchange within her own and her husband's lineage. Recent reappraisals of Yoruba women's role in farming show that they contributed to agricultural production either on their father's or husband's farm.[2] Recent ethnographic studies of Ondo, Abeokuta and Oyo reveal that the woman's primary eco-

2. A.U. Patel and Q.B.O. Anthonio, 'Farmers Wives in Agricultural Development: the Nigerian Case', paper presented to Fifteenth International Congress of Agricultural Economists, August 1973; Adeniyi Oshuntogun, 'Rural Women in Agricultural Development: a Nigerian Case Study', and T.C. Adeyokunnu, 'Agricultural Development, Education and Rural Women in Nigeria', in A. Ogunseye *et al.* (eds), *Women and Development in Relation to Changing Family Structure*, Lagos, Ford Foundation, 1976; Simi Afonja, 'Land Control, a Critical Factor in Yoruba Gender Stratification', in Claire Robertson and Iris Berger (eds), *Women and Class Hierarchies: African Perspectives*, New York, Holmes & Meier, 1984.

nomic role was work on the family farm. Her release from this into other sectors depended on the status of the household, the security on the farms during periods of war and the availability of slave labour for farm work. The actual amount of time women spent on the farms during the period in question is unfortunately not recorded in the Yoruba ethnographies.

A clear-cut division of labour by sex was also apparent in the subsidiary economic activities of the Yoruba. According to Johnson, the men controlled the long-distance trade, while the women dominated internal trading activities.[3] Vertical loom cloth weaving, bead making and dyeing were also female domains. Men were known for woodwork, iron casting, smithery, horizontal weaving and carving. They did not interfere with each other's areas; the learning process and the sale and disbursement of the proceeds were handled independently.

Complementarity in the sexual division of labour is perhaps even more obvious among the Ibo and Ibibio than among the other non-politically centralised groups. The major difference between the Yoruba and the latter is that the women sometimes did more farm work than their men and less craft production.[4] In the traditional division of labour in Ibo society, women owned their own crops (cassava, cocoa, yams, kernels, vegetables) and men the more valuable crops such as yams and palm products. Although both sexes accumulated some surplus from their independent produce, van Allen suggests that this was not used for continued capital investment, but for social gain. The surplus was returned to the community in the form of fees, feasts for rituals for title taking, weddings and other ceremonies. The division of crops did not preclude female effort on the husband's farm, the primary source of the family's subsistence. But because of the importance of their own crops to their roles in reproduction, Ibo women spent more time in farming activities than the men.[5]

In a similar way to the Yoruba, internal trade was the domain of women while men controlled external trade. The rules governing the sexual division of labour in agriculture and trade were so

3. Samuel Johnson, *The History of the Yorubas*, Lagos, Church Missionary Society, 1921.

4. Nina Mba, *Nigerian Women Mobilized: Women's Political Activity in Southern Nigeria, 1900–1965*, Berkeley, Calif., Institute of International Studies, 1982.

5. Judith van Allen, 'Aba Riots or Igbo Women's War? Ideology, Stratification and the Invisibility of Women', in N.J. Hafkin and Edna G. Bay (eds), *African Women in Changing Perspectives*, Stanford, Calif., Stanford University Press, 1976.

rigid that women developed mechanisms of sanction against those who trespassed the traditionally-defined women's realm. The women for instance picked palmnuts and pressed the fruits. The husband owned the oil, but the kernels, a source of oil for local consumption were an accepted source of livelihood for the woman. When men invaded these areas of internal trade, they generated considerable resentment among the women. There is evidence, however, that the heavy involvement of women in farm work is not evenly distributed in Igboland. Mba shows that, compared to women in other areas, Ika–Igbo women and women from Onitsha and Oguta do little farm work. There is no reason adduced for this, but similar variations are observable in the Yoruba areas where (because of the high level of urbanisations in some parts) the urban women do relatively less work than the rural ones. A complementary division of labour is also visible among the non-Muslim ethnic groups of Northern Nigeria. Tiv women, for instance, weeded the fields, kept the mounds, and repaired and harvested the crops, while the Tiv men did the heavy work. Among the Kofyar of Jos Plateau, men and women worked side by side, with the heavier and lengthier jobs such as transplanting millet being carried out by men. Netting suggests that they lacked a rigid sexual division of labour except in craft production and magico-religious activities, reflecting the relatively unspecialised nature of subsistence production and the economic independence of the households.[6]

Women in most of the minority groups described by Meek[7] took some part in farming. The level of participation varied, however, with the scale of agricultural development. Among the higher agriculturists, farm work was principally carried out by men. Women devoted more time to the preparation of raw materials. Among the lower agriculturists, such as the Birom, the Munshi and Dadiya, women performed the major part of the field work and men took to hunting, fishing and industrial pursuits. Bolewa women expected to spend three or four days of each week on their husband's farm and the remainder on their own farm.

While additional ethnographic information would be needed to develop a more detailed picture of the sexual division of labour in the lineage mode, it can be suggested that this mode of production

6. Mba, *Nigerian Women Mobilized*; R. McC. Netting, *Hill Farmers in Nigeria: Cultural Ecology of the Kofyar of the Jos Plateau*, University of Washington, 1968.

7. C.K. Meek, *The Northern Tribes of Nigeria*, London, Oxford University Press, 1925.

required female participation in farm work. Although it is relatively more egalitarian than other modes, the lineage mode of production nevertheless imposes a double burden on women, a burden legitimised by cultural ideologies and reproduced within the capitalist mode of production. In addition, the lineage rules of inheritance deny women the right of land ownership. They could not inherit land from their husbands as this was closely guarded by the lineage and passed only to members of the kingroup. This has of course to be related to the entire kinship structure and the rules of exogamy.[8] It is relevant, however, to note that production relations in the lineage mode were governed by ideological rather than economic considerations. Although the observer may perceive this as entailing some element of exploitation, the subjects were largely unaware of the exploitative relations and would have justified them as social obligations associated with marriage.

The emphasis so far has been on Nigerian societies in which the segmentary lineage principle formed the basis of social and political organisation. The sexual division of labour in these differs from that of the more hierarchially-organised Hausa–Fulani kingdoms. In the latter, the differences between urban and rural areas, and between the work and resources of men and women are more clear cut. The city states were noted for trade, craft production and artisan services, whereas the rural areas concentrated on agricultural production. Women's participation in farm work is a highly controversial issue mainly because there is very little ethnographic information about the period before the Islamic conquest. Available information on the nineteenth century, however, shows that secluded free-born women did not do any farm work.[9] Farm labour was provided by the *gandu* (the man and his son), slave labour and, more recently, wage labour. Hausa women were not therefore part of the peasantry. Seclusion, which had penetrated the rural areas, confined women to 'house trade', namely selling products such as processed foods, cooked foods, grains, groundnut oil, salt, milk and various craftwork, which were sources of independent cash.[10] The cash nexus was so embedded in the household that members paid for items purchased from the women and the women taxed their men if they

8. Jack Goody, *Production and Reproduction: a Comparative Study of the Domestic Domain*, Cambridge, Cambridge University Press, 1976.

9. Ester Boserup, *Women's Role in Economic Development*, London, George Allen & Unwin, 1970.

10. Polly Hill, *Rural Hausa*, Cambridge, Cambridge University Press, 1972.

sold any of their agricultural products. The house trade, however, helped women to concentrate their efforts within the household sphere where responsibilities for production and reproduction overlapped.

The socio-political structure did not therefore encourage the complementary relations described for the lineage mode of production. The women's seclusion still meant that they were controlled by men despite their economic independence. That such a hierarchial socio-economic structure could engender so much female autonomy negates the expected relationship between structural complexity and female subordination. The Hausa–Fulani structure can be described as one of inequality between the sexes, but one which allows a high degree of autonomy to each sex. This is not without implications for the new sexual division of labour, as shown below.

The New Sexual Division of Labour

The structures described above were not impervious to change. Important economic and non-economic factors have, in one way or another, reshaped the sexual division of labour since the sixteenth century. Marxists give primacy to economic factors and therefore focus on the various stages of capitalist penetration of the third world. But additional factors, such as the Islamic conquest, Christianity, inter-ethnic wars and the institution of slavery, sometimes preceded the different forms of capitalist penetration. The inter-ethnic wars, for instance, robbed many communities of their active young men and left some women with the burden of agricultural production. The wars also paralysed external economic activities (namely those taking place outside the boundaries of the towns and villages) and encouraged the intensification of economic activities within the household.[11]

Wife seclusion is a phenomenon of religious change which reduced female input into farm work. But the availability of slave labour and of a high water table, the ubiquity of the donkey as a beast of burden and the general ease of access to land and good grain storage are all believed to have reduced women's input into farm work.[12]

11. I. Olomola, 'Pre-Colonial Patterns of Inter-State Relations in Eastern Yorubaland', PhD dissertation, University of Ife, Nigeria, 1977.
12. Richard Longhurst, 'Rural Development Planning and the Sexual Division of

Mercantile capitalism preceded commodity export and industrial capitalism in Nigeria. It was initiated after the abolition of the slave trade and it set the stage for the incorporation of Nigeria into the capitalist world. The items of trade were initially consumer goods from Europe, which were exchanged in a limited way for local agricultural products. The rise in demand for old and new crops such as cocoa, groundnuts, palm oil and rubber hastened the transformation of the social structure.

Mercantile capitalism created initial changes in the sexual division of labour through increased male participation in trade. In the pre-capitalist mode men were restricted to long-distance trade because of the risks of the long journeys. They were also the major participants in the slave trade. But the capital and expertise acquired in these commercial activities put them in a better position than the women. Men continued to dominate bulk buying and acted as middlemen between the Europeans on the coast and the retailers in the hinterland. Men opened retail shops in increasing numbers as it became obvious that the new mode of subsistence was profitable. The invasion of this traditional female sphere among the Ibo was a major cause of the 'women's war' early this century.[13] Similar changes occurred in Yoruba society but one should not underestimate the increase in women's trading activities, particularly their involvement in bulk purchases of agricultural and imported products. Among the Hausa–Fulani, seclusion gave men an additional advantage over women because they were restricted to retail trade, unlike southern women. The individualism generated by trade appears to have intensified the competitiveness in Hausa–Fulani households and introduced market relations into southern households. Shenton and Freund argue that the new relations of production put strains on the cohesiveness of Hausa–Fulani households and limited their size.[14]

One of the most important effects of mercantile capitalism is the increased involvement of rural women in agricultural production. The increase in the number of men traders meant that men aban-

---

Labour: a Case Study of a Moslem Hausa Village in Northern Nigeria', mimeo, 1980.

13. C. Ifeka-Moller, 'Female Militancy and Colonialist Revolt: the Women's War of 1929', in S. Ardener (ed.), *Perceiving Women*, New York, Halsted Press, 1977.

14. Bob Shenton and Bill Freund, 'The Incorporation of Colonial Northern Nigeria into the World Capitalist Economy', *Review of African Political Economy* 13 (1978), pp. 8–20.

doned the farms and women were left in charge of food production. The commercial value of food items sold by women also encouraged greater participation in farming. But their labour was usually supplemented by that of their children and by wage labour. There are in fact indications that Hausa women are now taking a more active part in agriculture, thus becoming part of the peasantry.

Export commodity production represents another stage of capitalist penetration, which intensified competition between household members and the exploitation of women's labour. That the capitalist system needs the reproductive and productive labour of women is clearly illustrated by the example of cocoa in Yorubaland.

Cocoa dominated economic activities in the forest zone from the late nineteenth century to the 1960s. The success of the crop and the increasing demand from Europe encouraged farmers to turn more land over to cocoa production. Labour was the most problematic of the factors of production, and to offset this the Yoruba farmer depended on family labour particularly at the peak of cocoa production. Wage labour was available, but the labour requirements were so high that family members participated when their labour was needed. The greatest asset to the new set of capitalists is that this is unpaid family labour. At the cocoa farming villages near Ile–Ife (Ladin–Lakoro and Iyanfoworogi), women do the planting, harvesting and spraying the pods, while men clear the bush and do the weeding. In Ladin–Lakoro, women devote as much time as the men to farm work in the peak season. They spend 41.9 per cent (as against the men's 48.7 per cent) of their time on farm operations.[15] But this only attracted a token annual cash gift in return for services rendered throughout the year. Although women's input dropped considerably during the slack season, they spent their time on housework and petty trading to procure an independent source of income. Less time, however, is devoted to food crop production now that these items are readily available at the market.

An important aspect of changes in the sexual division of labour is the perception of men and women of women's labour input. Despite their increased input into farm work, neither the women themselves nor their family members describe them as farmers. Men assume that their wives are 'helping on the farm' but are predomi-

---

15. O.I. Aina, 'Ralative Time Allocation between Women's Multiple Roles: a Case Study of Women in Cocoa Production', PhD dissertation, University of Ife, Nigeria, 1984.

nantly traders. The ideology of marital relations in the lineage mode of production is thus employed for the proletarianisation of women.

Palm oil production among the Ibo and Ibibio brought about similar changes in the sexual division of labour. In addition, men invaded traditionally-defined female spheres such as palm oil processing and the sale of kernels. The hand press, which was introduced to increase productivity, reduced female participation in palm oil production and eroded their means of capital formation. According to Usoro,[16] total man hours increased from 600 to 1,050 hours and those of women and children declined from 1,450 to 992 hours. Yet the total input of women into farmwork increased because a considerable number went into food-crop production. Cassava, for instance, acquired a new value as a noticeable source of independent income for women. Commodity export undoubtedly created a peasantry which included women, but it also introduced a stratified structure among the peasantry. Since women were proletarianised and landless, they fell on the lower rung of the hierarchy. This lack of access to land and capital and the heavy burden of reproduction hindered their mobility out of that class.

Industrial capitalism is the most developed mode of capitalist penetration. In most third world countries it takes the form of mining or manufacturing capital and requires the proletarianisation of local men and women. In this mode of production, there is a high degree of correspondence between the labour process and relations of surplus appropriation since the owners of the means of production, expatriate investors, also control the surplus. The most important consequences for the sexual division of labour are an outcome of the proletarianisation process which, in Africa, entailed some coercion. Forcing men into wage work took them away from their villages and from agricultural production and its complementary relations in the lineage mode. Where this occurred, women's involvement in agriculture increased. Contrary to the expectation of Marx and Engels, women's work is not privatised. Rather, the proletarianisation of men increased women's input into production outside the home and their responsibilities within the household. The household composition changes in size and in structure of authority. Household surveys show an increase in the number of female heads of household even in patrilineal societies.

16. Eno J. Usoro, *The Nigerian Palm Oil Industry*, Ibadan, Ibadan University Press, 1974.

Industrial capitalism sometimes leads to the proletarianisation of women, though not to the abandoning of all traditionally-defined social obligations. In fact, women's access to cash as wage earners imposes more responsibilities on them, particularly when their husbands have no regular source of income. These changes are observable among the ethnic groups of the Jos Plateau where the tin mines and the construction industry are major employers of labour. At the initial stages of capitalist penetration the natives were reluctant to join the labour force and labour, like anywhere in Africa, was transient and migratory. Birom men did not join the labour force, but their women were conscripted as unskilled labour. At the moment their heavy concentration in construction is a conspicuous feature of modern economic production in the Jos Plateau, one that sets this region apart from other regions of the north.[17] The women were, however, an industrial reserve army needed for the survival of capitalism. Their wages were low, the jobs long, tedious and insecure. In an area devoid of export crops, these industries were alternatives to food crop production for the growing market. Although their low wages were generally spent on their own and their children's maintenance, wage work for women did alter the distribution of power in the household. The regular wage for women gave them some economic power and sometimes made them household heads even within a patrilineal structure.

Conclusion

The changes in the sexual division of labour summarised above are largely associated with mercantile capitalism, export commodity production and industrial capitalism. Although each has been discussed as a separate category and backed up by specific examples, they should be regarded as part of a process in which each one succeeds the other without destroying all the elements of the former. The sexual division of labour associated with mercantile capitalism exists alongside that of export commodity production and industrial capitalism. Aspects of the pre-capitalist mode also persist in the capitalist era, exerting a major impact on emerging new structures. The new division of labour is therefore a complex

17. A.B. Zack-Williams, 'Female Urban Employment: the Case of the Construction Workers in Jos', mimeo, 1982.

structure created by economic and non-economic factors which interact in different ways in different socio-political structures. Common to all the economic formations is the dominance of women in the sphere of reproduction and their increased participation in production, whether in the market place, agriculture or industry. As the work of men and women changes, there is a tendency for the men to move into the sectors that give them greater access to critical resources, while the women stay in or move to the less profitable areas abandoned by men.

Another common feature is the peasantisation and/or proletarianisation of women without alterations in the tasks of reproduction and without incorporating men into that sphere. Recent appraisals of women's input into farming in Nigeria show that women constitute more than 50 per cent of the labour utilised for agricultural production. This peasantisation process is also becoming increasingly apparent in the Hausa-Fulani states, although at a slower rate than in the south.

As I mentioned earlier, it is important to take non-economic factors into account when analysing changes in the sexual division of labour. Kinship ideology, for instance, continues to incite the use of unremunerated female labour and to prevent male participation in household chores. Religion similarly reinforces these trends and allows them to persist in the capitalist era. Christianity, Islam and the traditional religions all possess this common feature. Marital patterns and the kinship structure are also important factors (as Goody points out in his comparative analysis of production and reproduction),[18] as is the scale of agricultural development. There are thus distinct patterns of women's input into farm work, with marked variations between the Hausa–Fulani states (where a higher techonology is utilised) and the southern regions (which rely predominantly on shifting cultivation). None of them, however, have written women into the patrilineal rules of succession and all of them practice exogamy.

The range of factors influencing the sexual division of labour and the variations in pre-capitalist structures make it difficult to chart the general course of the historical evolution of the sexual division of labour in Nigeria. The exercise requires a great deal of information on changes in each region since the fifteenth century. But, as shown in the case of the Hausa-Fulani states, the picture is blurred

---

18. Goody, *Production and Reproduction*.

for the period before the nineteenth century. There is also a dearth of information on non-agricultural groups, such as the fishing communities. None the less, it is evident that the sexual division of labour in the African modes continues to be reproduced in subsequent modes and that, consequently, the complementarity of roles is changing to a competitive structure without the privatisation of women.

8

Sexual Divisions: Women's Work in Late Nineteenth-Century England

JANE LEWIS

It is hard to think of jobs that are not gendered. Furthermore, jobs have always been gendered, even though the boundaries between what is accepted as a male or female job have changed considerably. As Margaret Stacey has perceived, there have been two quite unrelated theories about the division of labour: 'one that it all began with Adam Smith and the other that it all began with Adam and Eve. The first has to do with production and the social control of workers and the second with reproduction and the social control of women. The problem is that the two accounts, both men's accounts, have never been reconciled'.[1] The task of explaining sexual divisions has only recently been taken up and, as indicated below, the explanation has been welded not altogether successfully onto existing theories. This chapter suggests that it is necessary to take a step back and first re-conceptualise women's work in both the private and public spheres as part of the larger gender order. In the sections that follow, working-class women's work in the early twentieth century is taken as a case study to show the way in which gendered jobs are part of the construction of masculinity and femininity. Only when this is understood can we begin to attempt to integrate an analysis of sexual divisions into specific consideration of the labour market and the changes in the labour process.

1. M. Stacey, 'The Division of Labour Revisited, or Overcoming the Two Adams', in P. Abrams et al. (eds), Development and Diversity: British Sociology 1950–1980, London, Allen & Unwin, 1981, p. 14.

The Sexual Division of Labour: What has to be Explained

Major economic theories of human behaviour in recent years have paid attention to the sexual division of labour and have stressed the importance of relating women's market work to their familial roles, emphasising the importance of sex roles within the family as determinants of the division of labour in market work. In so doing they have tended to privilege paid work. Thus, neoclassicists have taken the domestic division of labour for granted and concentrated on the way in which it explains sexual segregation and low pay in market work, while marxists have been bogged down in the question of whether domestic labour is productive work.[2] Both these major theories have tried to incorporate analyses of sexual divisions into their existing theoretical frameworks, but with varying degrees of success.

The 'new home economics' of neoclassical theory recognised that adult married woman in particular allocate their time in more complex ways than men – in the unpaid non-market work of caring and household labour, as well as in leisure and waged work. It has been argued that because marriage is voluntary, the theory of preferences may readily be applied: wives will hire husbands as breadwinners, and husbands wives as childbearers, minders and housekeepers. The division of labour in the family is assumed to be a natural corollary of women's reproductive role. Because of their childbearing and childrearing activities (which again are assumed to be naturally linked) married women are held to be imperfect substitutes for men in market work. Women's expectations of marriage and children are held to make them less willing to invest in education and more prone to labour market behaviour that is unstable from the employers' point of view. The sexual division of labour is thus naturally complementary and maximises the gains of both partners.

Marxists have also argued that the sexual division of labour may well maximise family welfare, but while neoclassicists argue that the division of labour is a matter of rational choice, marxists see it as one of the few strategies available to the working class in its struggle

---

2. For the neoclassical position see Theodore W. Schultz, *Economics of the Family: Marriage, Children and Human Capital*, Chicago, University of Chicago Press, 1974. On the domestic labour debate see Eva Kaluzinski, 'Wiping the Floor with Theory', *Feminist Review* (1980). On theories of women's work generally see Alice Amsden, *The Economics of Women and Work*, Harmondsworth, Penguin, 1980.

with capital.[3] Marxists also emphasise the inherent conflict between married women's two roles at home and in waged work and point to the dramatic recent increase in the divorce rate and in the number of single parent families as evidence of increasing tension between the two roles.[4] In the recent literature which attempts to understand the labour market under late capitalism, radical dual labour market theorists suggest that labour markets are divided into primary and secondary sectors, with restricted mobility between the two, by a process of deskilling.[5] Men are thus the passive beneficiaries of capitalist strategy, dominating the primary job sector where employment is relatively stable, higher paid and tied to career ladders, while women are confined to the secondary sector of temporary and poorly paid work.

Both major bodies of theory tend to treat work in the family and work in the labour market dichotomously, despite the recognition of important links between them. More often than not women's position in the family is invoked to explain their position in the labour market. This is because work is not thought of as part of the gender order. Rather, the sexual division of work is made to fit already existing frameworks of explanation. Thus, neoclassicists emphasise the importance of choice and argue essentially that women's position reflects the nature of the choices that women make. Radical dual labour market theorists blame capital but are, in the end, like neoclassicists, forced back on female biology to explain why women find themselves in a subordinate position.

Radical feminists have got over this problem by invoking patriarchy to explain the sexual division of labour, arguing that men as capitalists, as husbands and as trade unionists control women, keeping their wages low and enforcing their responsibility for domestic work.[6] This theory of patriarchy tends to position women as passive victims, and thus oversimplifies the construction and maintenance of the sexual division of work as part of the gender order.

3. Jane Humphries, 'Class Struggle and Persistence of the Working Class Family', *Cambridge Journal of Economics* 1 (1977).

4. Veronica Beechey, 'Some Notes on Female Wage Labour in Capitalist Production', *Capital and Class* 3 (1977).

5. R.D. Barron and G.M. Norris, 'Sexual Divisions and the Dual Labour Market', in D. Leonard Barker and Sheila Allen (eds), *Dependency and Exploitation in Work and Marriage*, London, Longman, 1976.

6. Heidi Hartman, 'The Unhappy Marriage of Marxism and Feminism: Towards a More Progressive Union', *Capital and Class* 8 (1979).

I argue here that first of all it is necessary to make the analysis of work part of the analysis of the wider gender order. It is then necessary to consider the way in which separate male and female work identities have been constructed. This is a complicated process, involving consideration of male behaviour as capitalists, trade unionists and husbands and of women's behaviour as wives, mothers and paid workers. It can best be understood by attempting to reconstruct male and female work experience. Only then can the process by which sexual divisions in the workplace have persisted be understood.

Work and the Gender Order

Ray Pahl has recently perceived the need to draw together the study of production, reproduction and consumption in an effort to reconceptualise the idea of 'work' as opposed to employment.[7] He sets out to do this by focusing on the household rather than on the individual, and he thereby immediately captures the importance of gendered labour.

In fact single and married women in different social classes have combined different mixes of paid and unpaid work at different times. In the mid-nineteenth century, married and single working-class women worked outside the home in occupations segregated from men, albeit that the definition of what was a male and what was a female job changed significantly over time. Married working class women increasingly withdrew from the labour market in the late nineteenth and early twentieth centuries. They retained primary responsibility for home and family, but also often engaged in casual paid employment, much of which escaped the notice of the census enumerators. Both married and single middle class women were much more firmly excluded from paid employment, their work in the public sphere being largely confined to unpaid voluntary philanthropic effort. It is of course only since the Second World War that married women's work has increased so dramatically. These experiences must be located within a broader gender order in which the law denied women access to property and political rights, and the marriage contract often resulted in an unequal division of

7. Ray Pahl, *The Division of Labour*, Oxford, Blackwell, 1984.

resources and a particular division of roles and responsibilities.

Broadly speaking, there has been a shift over time whereby women have increasingly entered the public sphere of paid work, but have nonetheless retained primary responsibility for domestic work. This is not to say that there has been no change in the domestic division of labour. Recent research has questioned early linear models of development from segregated sex roles to the modern symmetrical family, and has revealed on the one hand evidence of a deeply based home culture in particular regions by the early twentieth century, with men sharing domestic tasks and caring, and on the other hand evidence of the persistence of profoundly separate and antagonistic male and female worlds to this day.[8] It is generally true that even when domestic work has become more equally shared, it still remains primarily women's responsibility.

Just as it is important to understand the ways in which women have combined different mixes of paid and unpaid work at different times, it is also important to recognise the way in which much of the work women do has moved in and out of the private sphere. The preparation of midday meals for schoolchildren, for example, has always been done by women, sometimes in the home and sometimes by working part-time for the local education authorities, according to the dictates of government policy. It is easy to find other examples of human service work, such as caring for the elderly, that have moved between the family and the informal and formal labour markets.

The proper framework for analysis is, therefore, not the particular dichotomies of paid and unpaid work, family and labour market, but a theory of women's work that incorporates an understanding of the gender order. It is crucial to see the gendering of work in relation not just to change in the labour process and employers' and trade unionists' attitudes, but to individual household strategies and the decision making process between husband and wife, and to the politico-legal process which structures access to resources, training and education by gender as well as by class.

8. Michael Young and Peter Willmott, *The Symmetrical Family*, New York, Pantheon, 1973; Gareth Stedman Jones, 'Working-Class Culture and Working-Class Politics in London, 1870–1900', *Journal of Social History* 7 (1974); Elizabeth Roberts, *A Woman's Place*. Oxford, Blackwell, 1984; Trevor Lummis, 'The Historical Dimension for Fatherhood: A Case Study', in L. McKee and M. O'Brien (eds), *The Father Figure*, London, Tavistock, 1982; Annie Whitehead, 'Sexual Antagonism in Herefordshire', in Barker and Allen, *Dependency and Exploitation*.

The Construction of Working-Class Male and Female Work Identities

There is clear evidence for the recent past that men and women have had firm ideas as to what constitutes men's and women's work and the male and female rate for the job. A female printing worker was reported in the early 1900s as saying 'I know my place and I'm not going to take men's work from them'. Professor F.Y. Edgeworth, the neoclassical economist, regarded this as proof of the existence of 'natural monopolies' of custom regarding male and female work practices.[9] Ramsay MacDonald, author of the classic *Women in the Printing Trades* (1904), commented that suggestions to the effect that women might undertake tasks commonly performed by men were not only rejected but treated as though something 'indelicate' had been proposed.[10] Similarly these women have traditionally earned somewhere between one half and two thirds of men's average wages.

The idea of a woman's job and a woman's rate of pay may also be applied to women's unpaid work. It will be argued here that the gendering of jobs is part of the larger construction of masculinity and femininity and may best be understood by the study of male and female work experience over time. Julia Matthaei has argued that the sex typing of jobs derives from a belief in natural difference which is shared by workers and employers; if women (or men) cross these 'natural' boundaries they risk becoming stigmatised.[11] I, too, wish to stress that ideas about what tasks are appropriate for women and what women are capable of have been shared by the majority of men and women over time; but whereas Matthaei concentrates on how sex typing has been *eroded*, I shall focus on some of the elements by which sex typing is *constructed*.

Sandra Wallman has pointed out that work controls the identity as much as the economy of the worker. The control of work entails not only control over the allocation and disposition of resources; it also implies control over the values ascribed to each of them.[12] The

9. J. Ramsay MacDonald, *Women in the Printing Trades*, London, P.S. King, 1904, p. viii.
10. Ibid., pp. 65–6.
11. Julia A. Matthaei, *An Economic History of Women in America*, Brighton, Harvester, 1982.
12. Sandra Wallman (ed.), *Social Anthropology of Work*, ASA Monograph 19, New York, Academic Press, 1979.

division between male and female workers must be located within a structure of male domination by which women's work is valued less. Because this was in turn part of the structure of femininity and masculinity, it was accepted. The concept of the family wage which emerged in the late nineteenth century was fundamental in determining the mix of activities undertaken by women, because acceptance of the family wage ensured that women took primary responsibility for husband and family and that their paid work was regarded both by society and by themselves as of secondary importance. The family wage became an ideal, held sacred by both working- and middle-class men and women for a variety of reasons, as will be seen below.

The Family Wage Ideal

In the late nineteenth century social investigators promoted the idea of the family wage because they felt that a firm division of labour between husband and wife was the best way of securing social stability and the moral integrity of the nation. Henry Higgs compared various household budgets in the 1890s and commented on the importance of the wife's housekeeping skills and unpaid labour, which could actually 'turn the balance of comfort in favour of one workman whose wages are much below those of another'.[13] He believed that the services of a working man's wife were more valuable economically when they were employed at home than in the labour market. Dr William Ogle explained to the Royal Statistical Society that men were stimulated to labour only in the hope of maintaining themselves and their families.[14] Helen Bosanquet, a pillar of the Charity Organisation Society, similarly argued that the 'stable family' of male breadwinner and female and child dependants was 'the only known way of ensuring with any approach to success that one generation will exert itself in the interests and for the sake of another'.[15] Furthermore, social welfare legislation from the period of the Liberal Welfare Reforms of the early twentieth century to the mid 1970s was constructed on the assumption that the family economy followed the male breadwinner model. Simi-

13. Henry Higgs, 'Workmen's budgets', *Journal of the Royal Statistical Society* 56 (1893).
14. William Ogle, 'On Marriage Rates and Marriage Ages with Special Reference to the Growth of Population', *Journal of the Royal Statistical Society* 53 (1890).
15. Helen Bosanquet, *The Family*, London, Macmillan, 1906, pp. 199 and 222.

larly, in the classic 1950s f... ...land
geois family form is seen as ...tion of Talcott Parsons, th...
way in which it mediates the ...tegic importance because ...
individual, particularly the child... of the larger society fo...

The argument of male trade un... wage was usually expressed in terms ... in favour of the fam... posed to male wage rates. But the behavi... threat female worke... suggests that opposition was based on ...f male trade unionists undercutting, and that their particular op... than just fear of women's work was grounded partly in the belief ...tion to married and unnatural. A male chainworker commented t... it was improper on the Factory Acts in 1876: 'I should advocate the... [women's] Commission time should be so limited as neither to interfere with thuir own health and morals or with our wages'.[17] An 1889 Select Committee heard another plea from a male trade unionist for the restriction of married women's work on the grounds that 'when the married women turn into the domestic workshops they become competitors against their own husbands and it requires a man and his wife to earn what the man alone would earn if she was not in the shop', and, he added for good measure, 'during the time she is in the shop her domestic duties are being neglected'.[18] This set of dual concerns (which should both be seen as real) was repeated by Tom Mann, the socialist organiser of semi and unskilled workers, before the Royal Commission on Labour in the early 1890s. He said that he was 'very loth to see mothers of families working in factories at all', adding that 'their employment has nearly always a prejudicial effect on the wages of the male worker'.[19]

By the late nineteenth century the ideal of the family wage was firmly accepted. Broadhurst's famous speech to the TUC Annual Conference in 1877, in which he urged male trade unionists 'as men and husbands to use their utmost efforts to bring about a condition of things where their wives should be in their proper sphere at home instead of being dragged into competition for livelihood against the

16. Talcott Parsons and R.F. Bales, *Family Socialization and Interaction Process*, New York, Free Press, 1955.

17. PP., Report of the Commissioners Appointed to Inquire into the Working of the Factory and Workshop Acts with a view to their consolidation and amendment. C.1443, 1876, XXIX, 1 p. cxvi.

18. PP., Third Report of the Select Committee of the House of Lords on the Sweating System. 165, 1889, xiii, 1, Q.18010.

19. PP., Minutes of Evidence taken before the Royal Commission on Labour. C.7063, 1893–4, 39, Q.4447

and strong men of the worl... w... as much a statement about ...culinity as about trade uni...s ...ampaign for a higher family ...age Even in Lancashire, wh... In ...ackburn, Preston and Burnley ...as ...any as one third of ...inted ...continued to work after marriage, th... Cotton Factory T...ed women's role as paid worker: 'How Sweet it is when t... sit upon the hearth once more/To whistle sing an... ...verse/With the sweetest queen in universe/In hon... way'.[21] By the 1890s, the wives of skilled men did not usuall... ork, for the ability to keep a wife had become a measure of ...king class male respectability.

Ellen Ross has pointed out that the marital relationship between working-class men and women did not enjoin romantic love or verbal or sexual intimacy, but required financial obligations, services and activities that were gender specific.[22] The importance of the economic support provided by husbands is neatly illustrated by working-class women's attitudes towards marriage breakdown. A woman poor law guardian reported the testimony of one woman, who was living in a common law relationship while her first husband remained in the workhouse, to the effect that her husband 'was no husband for her and the one that worked for her she respected'.[23] Social investigators of the early twentieth century showed clearly that the centre of working-class women's worlds was their children and that their activities were dictated by the chief purpose of providing for them. Any woman who was forced to resort to full-time work by virtue of the illness or neglect or absence of her husband was pitied by her neighbours.[24]

There was, then, a material basis for women's ideas as to their place and to their acceptance of the family wage. Domestic labour in the late nineteenth and early twentieth centuries was extremely arduous, childbirth painful and pregnancy frequent. The average woman of the 1890s could expect to spend many years in pregnancy and lactation. Doubtless women took emotional satisfaction from

20. Quoted in B. Drake, *Women in Trade Unions*, London, Labour Research Dept, 1920, p. 17.

21. Quoted in Jill Liddington and Jill Norris, *One Hand Tied Behind Us: the Rise of the Women's Suffrage Movement*, London, Virago, 1978, p. 111.

22. Ellen Ross, 'Fierce Questions and Taunts: Married Life in Working-Class London 1870–1914', *Feminist Studies* 8 (1982).

23. PP., Minutes of Evidence to the Royal Commission on Divorce and Matrimonial Causes, Vol II, Cd. 6480, 1912–13, XVIII, Q.20120.

24. Roberts, *A Woman's Place*.

caring and providing for their families, and Elizabeth Roberts has argued that working-class women saw their lives as purposeful because the welfare of their families depended on their budgeting and managing skills. In the closely knit working-class communities before 1914 the talents of skillful housewives were readily acknowledged.[25] Similarly, Joanna Bornat has argued that women played important roles organising and mediating relations between home and workplace, particularly using female networks to find jobs for young family members.[26] Brenner and Ramas have recently argued that there was in fact little room for negotiation of the fundamental sexual division of labour between husbands and wives.[27] Harsh material realities dictated the fundamental sexual division of labour.

Nevertheless, it is striking that the public statements by working women's groups stressed not so much material hardship when women were also forced to shoulder the burden of paid employment, but rather the idea that the working woman's proper role was as a helpmeet to her husband. Women in the labour movement also tended to favour the idea of a family wage, agreeing that the withdrawal of female labour would benefit male wages and enable women to better order and manage their homes. Most working women's groups agreed that the respectable woman's place was in the home, emphasising women's contribution as wives and mothers and the importance of the 'woman spirit'. The woman who worked for pay outside the home had less opportunity 'to give thought and companionship to her husband'.[28] The Women's Labour League gave priority to campaigning for the Labour Party's Right to Work Bill, introduced into the House of Commons every year between 1906 and 1908, which they believed would provide a charter of the 'Right to Leisure and Home Comfort' for working men's wives. Mary MacArthur, the leading woman trade unionist, was always anxious to acknowledge women's primary commitment to home and family and, as Deborah Thom has pointed out, a crucial role was played by women trade unionists in maintaining the sexual

25. Ibid.

26. Joanna Bornat, 'History and Work: A New Context for Trade Union History', *Radical America* 12 (Sept–Oct 1978).

27. J. Brenner and M. Ramas, 'Rethinking Women's Oppression', *New Left Review* 44 (1984).

28. R. McDonald *et al. Wage-earning Mothers*, London, Women's Labour League.

division of labour in the workplace after the first world war.[29] Women workers were open in their desire to work only until marriage. As one woman who lost her job in 1921 recalled: 'it didn't bother me, I knew I was engaged to be married and in those days as soon as you were going to be married you left your job . . . that is the only thing we girls had to look forward to, getting married and going on our own, getting our bottom drawer together and things like that'.[30] Similarly, Joy Parry has found in the predominantly female workforce of a Canadian textile town that young women workers experienced their deepest satisfaction in being caring daughters and prudently preparing for married life.[31]

Mothers First and Workers Second: the Social Reality of the Sexual Division of Labour

Large numbers of working-class families did not achieve a family wage during the late nineteenth and early twentieth centuries, something that middle class legislators failed to confront. Booth's 1889 survey of London showed that 30 per cent of the population were unable to rely on a man's wage alone and in 1921 Bowley estimated that only 41 per cent of working class families could depend on a man's wage.[32] Among those families who were not in receipt of a family wage, women had to resort to numerous strategies to make ends meet. Women themselves perceived a hierarchy of respectability in what was permissible for them to do; paid work outside the home did not rank highly. When paid work was undertaken, some jobs were more acceptable than others. For men, too, as trade unionists, employers and policymakers, some jobs were more acceptable than others, on grounds that had more to do with respectability – itself part of the construction of masculinity – than logic.

Women seeking to make ends meet often resorted to neighbours and kin, borrowing in times of need. Mrs Pember Reeves found that

29. Deborah Thom, 'The Ideology of Women's Work, 1914–25, with Special Reference to the NEWW and Other Trade Unions', PhD dissertation, Thames Polytechnic, 1982.
30. Quoted in Roberts, *A Woman's Place*.
31. Parry, Joy. 'This was a Woman's Town: Range and Limits in the Local Construction of Gender', Unpublished paper, 1985.
32. Land, *Family Wage*.

housewives in Lambeth in 1913 were reluctant to move for fear of foregoing the help they knew to be available in times of need, for neighbourliness implied reciprocity.[33] Less respectable, but very common, was the resort to credit – running up bills at the corner shop, pawning and, worst of all, moneylending. Large numbers of married women sought casual employment of some kind or other. In line with the ideal of woman's place, the most respectable of these were home based. Large numbers of women engaged in what Shelley Pennington has called 'extended homework' – washing, charring, babysitting and lodging – house keeping.[34] As Leonore Davidoff has commented, the work of lodging-house keeping is impossible to categorise as work of production or consumption.[35] Women both sought, and were considered most appropriate for, human service work in the informal sector (something that is perpetuated by the large number of part-time women workers – 40 per cent of the female workforce – in service occupations today), or for manufacturing work that was carried out in the home.

In this respect, women engaged in a wide variety of tasks at home – making matchboxes, shirts, artificial flowers, umbrellas, brushes, carding buttons, furpulling, bending safety pins and covering tennis balls. Much of this work was sweated. All homeworkers supplied their own heat, light and materials; shirtmakers had also to hire their sewing machines. Usually women made very small wages in such work. A woman finishing four pairs of trousers a day in the 1880s made 6d. Yet this sum was enough to feed a family for almost two days before the First World War, and women's casual earnings were crucial to their families' welfare before the war. Some of the trades that women took up, such as washing in London's East End, were chosen because their peak availability coincided with troughs in male employment in the gas and building trades.

It is important to consider to what extent women's direct contribution to the family economy affected relations between husband and wife within the family. John Holley's work on two nineteenth-century Scottish factory communities found both multiple earner

33. M.S. Pember Reeves, *Round about a Pound a Week*, London, G.Bell, 1913.
34. Shelley Pennington, 'Women as Homeworkers: An Analysis of the Homework Labour Force in England from 1850 to the Present Day', PhD dissertation, University of Essex, 1980.
35. Leonore Davidoff, 'The Separation of Home and Work? Landladies and Lodgers in 19th and 20th century England', in Sandra Burman (ed.), *Fit Work for Women*. London, Croom Helm, 1979.

and family wage economies existing side by side, the former charac-
terising the families of poorly paid, unskilled male breadwinners.[36]
Holley assumes that this type of family economy was 'in many
ways more democratic', but it is not altogether clear that this
was so. Patricia Malcolmson has suggested that the power of the
London women laundresses was directly related to the extent to
which they were the mainstay of their family economies.[37] Women
doing casual or homework were profoundly isolated, with no
possibility of the workplace friendships or activities enjoyed by
their men. Their motives for working were entirely familial, as Tilly
and Scott have noted, and were directed towards securing the
welfare of their families.[38] It is true that they might have taken great
satisfaction in keeping their families together, but equally their
efforts may have been overshadowed by the struggle to manage the
double day, a much more arduous task in the early twentieth
century, and possibly the threat of male verbal or physical abuse if
the task was not perceived to have been performed properly.[39]
Where women worked for wages in factories, as in the case Holley
describes, some accommodation had to be reached between the
family's need for extra income and male and female ideas about
women's proper place. Nancy Osterud found in her analysis of
Leicester hosiery workers that men supported women's work so long
as they confined themselves to the traditional female task of seaming.[40]
Thus sexual divisions in the workplace were underpinned by more
general ideas of women's place. Men as workers and as husbands
always saw women as wives and mothers first and workers second,
and male domination characterised both the family and the workplace. Even women who essentially became their family's breadwinner, whether through misfortune or neglect on the part of their
men, often felt the need to maintain the husband's authority. One

36. John Holley, 'The Two-Family Economy of Industrialism: Factory Workers
in Victorian Scotland', *Journal of Family History* (Spring 1981).
37. Patricia Malcolmson, 'Laundresses and the Laundry Trade in Victorian England', *Victoria Studies* 24 (1981).
38. Louise Tilly and Joan Scott, *Women, Work and the Family*, New York, Holt
Rinehart, 1978.
39. See the clash in views between Pat Ayers and Jan Lambertz, 'Marriage
relations and domestic violence in working class Liverpool, 1919–1939' and Elizabeth Roberts, 'Women's strategies 1890–1940', in J. Lewis (ed.), *Labour and Love*,
Oxford, Blackwell, 1986.
40. Nancy Grey Osterud, 'Women's Work in 19th Century Leicester: a case
study in the sexual division of labour', Paper given at the 4th Berkshire Conference,
Mt Holyoke, Mass., 1978.

Nottingham woman, whose husband earned only ten shillings a week as a framework knitter in the 1900s, gave him money so that he could continue to give the children their pocket money.[41]

Working-class women had strong ideas about what kind of work was appropriate and respectable. Homework was taken not just because it was the easiest to combine with childcare and domestic duties, but also because it enabled women to stay at home. The more noxious occupations, like furpulling, were not considered respectable, but button carding was clean work that could be confined to a bedroom, enabling the appearance of respectability to be maintained. Women working outside the home had a strongly developed sense of 'rough' versus 'respectable' work. Domestic service, for all its drawbacks, was respectable feminine work, considered an ideal preparation for marriage. Within the factory finishing or warehouse work was considered superior because it was light and clean and enjoyed high status, despite its low wages. Such ideas about feminine occupations were encouraged by middle-class investigators. Sidney Webb recognised that competition for respectable jobs drove down wage rates, but nevertheless felt: 'As they climb laboriously up into a more and more rarified air of respectability the codes of etiquette become more rigid and exacting and many harmless diversions and pleasures have to be sacrificed to their totem. But it is a thing to advance in them and its influence for good is incalculable.'[42]

Men, whether as husbands, trade unionists, employers or policy-makers, had clear ideas of women's place. As we have seen, male workers always linked the risk to women's health and morals to their fears that women would undercut male wages. Even when male workers in a particular trade 'lost' skill or were not strongly organised, they still demonstrated their capacity to exclude women from skilled processes. For example, after the big lockout of 1895 employers in the boot and shoe trade were able to convert to mass production methods in integrated factories using largely semi-skilled labour, but male and female processes remained distinct and the National Union of Boot and Shoe Operatives, while admitting women from the 1880s, failed to press for piecework statements for women fitters and machinists until 1907.[43] Male mule spinners in

41. Thea Thompson, *Edwardian Childhoods*. London, Chapman Hall, 1911.

42. Quoted in M. Mostyn Bird, *Women at Work*. London, Chapman Hall, 1911, pp. 16–17.

43. Alan Fox, *A History of the National Union of Boot and Shoe Operatives*,

cashire successfully resisted attempts to introduce women (who were quite able to handle the smaller spinning mules), largely because the men provided the employers with an efficient system of labour control.[44] Similarly, in the printing trade, male workers were able to turn their political skill against women workers and exclude them from the typographical associations.[45] In the weaving sheds overlookers were able to exclude women by their position as supervisors and by reserving the work of turning the looms for themselves. This relationship often involved the exercise of both economic and sexual power.[46] In the tailoring trade the position was somewhat different. Male tailors excluded women as early as 1834, but themselves became an increasingly endangered species as the market for ready-made clothing expanded. As the process of making a garment became increasingly subdivided, the demand for women's labour to stitch seams and finish the ready-made goods increased, but men continued to preserve their control over the bespoke trade. Thus technological change in the tailoring trade (together with the male tailoring unions) served to strengthen and deepen the sexual division of labour rather than to threaten it.[47]

Nor did employers act rationally and employ huge numbers of cheap adult female workers. They accepted the stereotypical ideas of women's capacities, often without any direct experience of employing women. Sidney Webb noted in 1891 that because women were rarely fully trained and rarely performed tasks such as tuning their own machines, employers tended to accept the popular idea that they were indeed of inferior value as a workforce.[48] The argument came full circle when employers declared that women were not worth training because of their tendency to leave on marriage. Employers were also often loath to employ male and female labour in the same process. As late as the 1930s, a large-scale employer of women refused to consider 'the indiscriminate mixing

1874–1957. Oxford, Blackwell, 1958.

44. William Lzonick, 'Industrial Relations and Technological Change: the Case of the Self Acting Mule', *Cambridge Journal of Economics* 3 (1979).

45. Cynthia Cockburn, *Brothers: Male Dominance and Technological Change*, London, Pluto, 1983.

46. Jan Lambertz, 'Sexual Harrassment in the 19th Century English Cotton Industry', *History Workshop Journal* 19 (1985).

47. Felicity Hunt, 'Women in the 19th Century Bookbinding and Printing Trades 1790–1914', MA dissertation, University of Essex, 1979.

48. Sidney Webb, 'The Alleged Differences in the Wages Paid to Men and to Women for Similar Work', *Economic Journal* 1 (1891).

of men and women together'.[49] Where large all-female workforces were employed, such as in Courtauld's silk mills, effort were often made to teach young women workers the principles of mothercraft and a respect for domestic ideals.[50]

Government policymakers also had clear ideas about what was suitable and unsuitable work for women. Proponents of protective legislation in the nineteenth century had morality as their predominant concern. Women in the mines and women chainmakers operating the 'oliver' – the heavy sledgehammer used to cut cold iron – were perceived as 'indecent'.[51] During the early twentieth century extraordinary pressure was also exerted in Parliament by MPs of all political persuasions to restrict the employment of barmaids. Ramsay MacDonald declared that he opposed their work on exactly the same moral grounds as he opposed women's work in the mines.[52] Women were considered to be a moralising and civilising influence, but their mission was felt to be impossible in the rough atmosphere of a bar. Heavy work, or work in unsuitable surroundings was felt to be at odds with women's role as mothers and guardians of the home. As government policy in respect to social insurance developed during the early twentieth century, it was used as an instrument to push women into the pre-eminently respectable and suitable occupation of domestic service.[53]

Conclusion

The sexual division of labour should be seen as a part of the larger gender order. Women's work is doubly gendered, first being confined to 'feminine' tasks, whether paid or unpaid, and second being subordinated to men's work both at home and in the workplace. In terms of unpaid labour women may have gained satisfaction from

49. P. Sargant Florence, 'The Theory of Women's Wages', *Economic Journal* 41 (1931).

50. Judy Lown, 'Not so much a Factory, More a Form of Patriarchy: Gender and Class during Industrialization', in Eva Gamarnikow (ed.) *Gender and Work*, London, Heinemann, 1983.

51. PP., Third Report of the House of Lords on Sweating. 165, Qs 18477 and 18510; and Fifth Report of the Select Committee of the House of Lords on the Sweating System 169, 1890, XVII, 257, p. xxxi.

52. House of Commons, Debates, 195, 2/11/08, col. 876.

53. J. Lewis, 'Dealing with Dependency: State Practices and Social Realities 1870–1945', in J. Lewis, *Women's Welfare, Women's Rights*, London, Croom Helm, 1983.

their pivotal position in securing their families' welfare, and support from female networks of neighbours and kin, but they remained emotionally and financially dependent on men. Their paid work, especially that of married women, tended to occupy an intermediate zone between home and workplace that has persisted since the Second World War in the form of part-time human service work. Such work was devalued not least because of the way in which it straddled public and private domains. Only in the closed middle-class female communities of women educators or hospital matrons, described in detail recently by Martha Vicinus,[54] did women manage to create a world dominated by female values and to achieve control over their work.

It has been argued here that the nature and conditions of women's work were not determined solely by autonomous changes in the structure of the economy, but rather should be considered as part of the construction of masculinity and femininity. Ideas of morality and respectability which carried different meanings for men and women as well as for people of different social classes played a crucial part in the construction of masculinity and femininity. Writing of women's work in agriculture in the eighteenth and early nineteenth centuries, Keith Snell has concluded that changes in the structure of the economy are sufficient to explain the changes in women's work.[55] But these do not adequately explain the more fundamental issue of the existence and persistence of sexual divisions of labour in agriculture.

It has not been part of this chapter to look at changes in the sexual division of work. These can only be explained by the complicated changes in the relationship between women and men, as workers, trade unionists, employers and the state, and in relation to the changing nature and structure of jobs, which is in turn dependent on the scale and technique of production. Sexual segregation has persisted and continues to be underpinned by ideas of masculinity and femininity, although these too are subject to change. One of the most important issues which remains to be investigated by historians is the demise of the idea that working-class male respectability depended on a non-working wife. It was during the Second World War that the idea emerged that women could combine part-time

54. Martha Vicinus, *Independent Women*, London, Virago, 1985.
55. K.D.M. Snell, 'Agricultural seasonal unemployment: the standard of living and women's work in the South and East, 1690–1868', *Economic History Review* 34 (1981).

work, marriage and motherhood without their home responsibilities being undermined. Women have, however, retained responsibility for home and family.

9

Hidden Work: Outwork in Dutch Industrialisation[1]

SELMA LEYDESDORFF

Industrialisation came late in the Netherlands. In the period in which other countries of Western Europe were industrialising, say 1760 to 1850, Dutch society had already left behind its Golden Age of the seventeenth century, and all the wealth and rich cultural and intellectual life which we associate with that most familiar period of Dutch history. From the middle of the eighteenth century the Netherlands suffered a cultural and economic decline which, especially after the French occupation (1795 to 1814), produced a general economic stagnation. Capital was invested in trade and foreign enterprises, not in Dutch industry.[2] The result was terrible impoverishment: at times during the nineteenth century as much as two thirds of the population were more or less dependent on poor relief.[3]

It should be noted that industrialisation not only created factory production but also generated a new type of home industry. This differed from the earlier putting-out system by virtue of the strong connections which existed between factory production and home-based activities. This phenomenon is not mentioned in the Dutch

1. This chapter is based on my book: *Verborgen arbeid – vergeten arbeid, een verkenning in de gescheidenis van de vrouwenarbeid rond negentienhonderd*, Amsterdam, Assen, 1977. The book has not been translated, and is based on research into Dutch sources and archives.

2. I.J. Brugmans, 'The Economic History of the Netherlands in the 19th and 20th centuries, *Acta Historiae Neerlandica* 2 (1976), pp. 260–298; J.A. de Jonge, 'Industrial Growth in the Netherlands, 1850–1914', *Acta Historiae Neerlandica* 5 (1971), pp. 1107–1212.

3. J. de Bosch Kemper, *Geschiedkundig onderzoek naar de armoede in ons varderland, hare oorzaken en de middelen, die tot hare vermindering zouden kunnen worden aangewend*, Haarlem, 1860; H. Roland Holst, *Kapitaal en arbeid in Nederland*, Vol. I, 1902, p. 41.

historical literature but my research shows that part of Dutch industrialisation depended on this revival of home-based industrial activity. Women played an important role in modern home industries and this chapter examines the significance of this role and how others viewed its implications for life both inside and outside the home.[4]

The period after 1850, especially after 1870, saw the rise of factory production in Holland, of artisanal and large scale industry. Industrial centres had been developing since the seventeenth century and the process of capital accumulation had begun.[5] In the seventeenth century there was already a considerable cloth industry around Leiden, which employed large numbers of women and children because of the low wages they commanded. Yet the accumulated trading capital was not transformed into industrial capital, so Holland remained until the end of the nineteenth century, in fact until 1945, a predominantly agrarian society with some centres of industry.[6] In what are called the 'old industries' in the east and the south and around Amsterdam, there was some factory production of commodities such as candles, pies, pottery and sometimes cigars, but this was localised and small scale and it remained the exception. Women's employment could be found in these 'old industries' but such Dutch statistics as exist for the nineteenth century and even the twentieth give little information about the numbers of wage workers among women, and what there is is often unreliable.

Research into the process of Dutch industrialisation has tended to concentrate on those industries which employed few women workers. Attention has been centred on new industries where a possible breakthrough might have been expected. Research results indicated that industrial development was gradual and that the various sectors grew slowly. It was not possible to identify a leading sector.[7] The problem with this sort of generalised study is that it cannot reveal the division of labour between men and women. For this we have to rely on eye witness accounts from that period and these state that

4. A general view on the development of women's work is given in W.N. Schilstra, *Vrouwenarbeid in landbouw en industrie in Nederland in de tweede helft van de negentiende eeuw*, Amsterdam, 1940.
5. J.G. van Dillen, *Van rijkdom en regenten: handboek tot de economische en sociale geschiedenis van Nederland tijdens de Republiek*, The Hague, 1970.
6. I.J. Brugmans, *Paardenkracht en mensenmacht. Social-economische geschiedenis van Nederland 1795–1940*, The Hague, 1960.
7. J.A. de Jonge *De industrialisatie van Nederland tussen 1850 en 1914*, Amsterdam, 1968.

the number of women involved in the rising industries was small.

It has generally been assumed that the process of industrialisation followed a similar path in all Western European countries. Dutch historians have in the past been influenced by the English model, in which a first phase of industrialisation in cotton was followed by a period of rest which was in turn followed by the development of heavy industry and banking. This model is not applicable to Holland. Around 1870 observers witnessed a development which had had a lasting influence on Dutch historiography. From that time on Holland was seen as slowly falling under the spell of capitalism.[8] In particular the rising labour movement became concerned about an assumed rise in female and child labour and campaigned against it. The exploitation of women and children was viewed as a by-product of this new phase of capitalist development. The old home industries, traditional employers of women and children, were ignored because they were believed to be a declining sector.

Italy also had some centres of industrial development which did not amount to industrialisation. Hans Medick has used the word 'protoindustrial' to describe the situation in which isolated industries exist in a predominantly agrarian and artisanal society with some regional capital accumulation.[9] This term could usefully be applied to Dutch development. A characteristic feature of a protoindustrial society is the large number of women and children helping with their husband's and father's work.

The process of Dutch industrialisation has been little researched beyond this point. New industries mainly produced semi-manufactured articles and consumer goods. The Netherlands had few reserves at its disposal to build up any form of heavy industry. The lack of capital resources was exacerbated by the persistence of colonialism which, together with a drain of capital to foreign investments, created a situation in which the greater part of the working class was un or under-employed, and lacked any kind of industrial schooling and discipline. The 'classic' description of the

8. See Holst, *Kapital*. It created an automatic relation between industrialisation and the organisation in socialist trade unions. This automatism has been challenged by J. Giele in 'Arbeidersbestaan. Levenshouding en maatschappijbeeld van de arbeidende klasse in Nederland in het midden van de negentiende eeuw', in *Jaarboek voor de geschiedenis van Socialisme en Arbeidersbeweging in Nederland 1976*, Nijmegen, 1976, pp. 21–92.

9. See also H. Medick on the issue on protoindustrialisation in *Quaderni Storici* 59; 2 (Aug. 1985); P. Kriedtke, H. Medick and J. Schlumbohm, *Industrialization before Industrialization*, Cambridge, 1981.

process of industrialisation, so often abstracted from the English experience, thus neglects the very specific situation of Holland and other countries that were late to industrialise. In that 'classic' model of industrialisation women replace men as inexpensive labour, or at very least present a perpetual threat to the bargaining position of men in the labour market. We are reminded of Frederick Engels on the position of the working class in England.[10] His account is full of men who stay reluctantly at home while their wives go out to work in the factory and he describes eloquently how humiliating this is for the men. What is known about industrialisation in the Netherlands from contemporary statistical or other sources seems, however, to present a contrasting picture.

In Holland, women never took men's place. The few contemporary accounts of early industrial society are concerned with old-fashioned industries such as brickmaking, which involved family labour. Working conditions were no better than those in England. One woman reported to a committee of inquiry: 'I left the factory eight days before the birth of my child and went back fourteen days after'.[11] This occupation involved heavy physical labour. If it were at all possible, a woman would try to secure longer leave for her confinement. One employer when questioned by a committee answered as follows:

'They get no money but they do get some time off.'

Question: 'So you don't regard giving birth as an illness. You said that they were paid for other sicknesses?'

Answer: 'Yes but that isn't the same thing . . . these are matters that they themselves are responsible for.'

Question: 'So for three or four weeks they don't earn anything?'

Answer: 'Three weeks? I recently had one return after two days, even the next morning.'

Question: 'Do you allow this?'

Answer: 'I have said to them: you are animals.'

Question: 'But you didn't send them away?'

Answer: 'No, because they wouldn't have anything to eat.'[12]

We have no idea of the degree to which women helped their husbands and children their fathers in workshops, either before or

---

10. F. Engels, *The Condition of the Working Class in England*, London, 1969.

11. *Enquete betreffende de werking en uitbreiding der wet van 19 September 1874 (Staatsblad No. 130) naar den toestand in fabrieken en werkplaatsen*, Sneek 1887, p. 219.

12. *Ibid.*, p. 196.

during industrialisation. We can only guess that it happened quite often. For several technical reasons industrial accounts and tax indexes are problematic sources. The only fact we can learn from them is that the number of registered female workers in factories remained low even into the twentieth century. Moreover, with the rise of modern industry their numbers actually decreased. Changes in the percentage of women in the total labour-force can be seen in the following figures:

1849	31.0 %
1859	18.2 %
1889	18.3 %
1899	16.7 %
1909	18.2 %
1920	18.2 %.[13]

In the census of 1849 women, as such, are mentioned for the first time. Censuses also took place in 1859, 1889, 1899 and 1909 but they do not give as accurate an account of the female working population and figures remain incomplete. Moreover, it was not until 1909 that any mention was made of women who helped their husbands in their work. Statistics suggest that female participation in the labour market was low.They should, however, be treated with suspicion, as they fail to take account of this widespread home industry. In addition, we can safely assume that women's employment is underestimated throughout, since the compilation is based on tax returns, only larger enterprises being liable for the tax concerned, and spinning and weaving firms being exempt altogether.

The doubts raised by this series can be confirmed by evidence from other sources. In brickmaking, for instance, the official figure for women workers in the whole country in 1889 was 656. But only 25 years later, after a decline in the brick industry and after a period of legal regulation of women's work which led several observers to claim that in industries such as brickmaking woman's work had decreased, factory inspectors for a single province (Gelderland) found 1,062 women working in brick factories. This is nearly twice the earlier 'national' figure. As brick-production was not especially important in Gelderland, the real national total must have been

13. The difference between 1849 and 1859 cannot be attributed to a decline in the number of women workers, but arises from a different method of counting. Because of a decline in women employed as domestic servants, the number went down during the 20th century.

considerably higher.[14] Or take the case of the women who worked at stringing herring for smoking. The official returns in 1909 give the total for the entire country as 20. But in the same year in just three provincial centres (Bunschoten, Huizen and Monnickendam) the factory inspector for women's work found a total of 252. The same holds true for diamond workers.[15] In 1909 there were officially 996 women workers in this trade, yet the union had 1,300 female members.[16]

In 1913 research was carried out into the question of why women worked. The conclusion reached was that the participation of women in industry, trade and retailing had decreased during the preceding century. The percentage of women working in domestic service was said to have fallen relative to other kinds of employment.[17] Despite statistics showing an *absolute* and not a *relative* increase in female employment in domestic service, this decrease can be mainly attributed to the expansion of the total workforce. In 1889 domestic servants formed 44.5 per cent of the female labourforce, and in 1909, 37 per cent.[18]

An analysis of women's employment in the Netherlands must go beyond the explanation that mechanised industry replaced small workshop manufacture, because this is not the case. On the contrary, there is reason to believe that the decrease in registered female employment in manufacturing led to a slight increase in registered female work in agriculture. But this may simply reflect the fact that in 1909, for the first time, women who helped their husbands in the fields were counted separately in the statistics. This might lead to the conclusion that there was no real increase in women's work in agriculture, which tends to be confirmed by an official report stating that the growing social welfare benefits for agricultural labourers rendered women's work in the fields less necessary.

If married women went out to work it was from grim necessity. In the year 1908/9, 5,256 married women were asked why they went out to work: 23.6 per cent said it was because their husbands didn't earn enough; 19.6 per cent were widowed, divorced or

14. A. Polak, *Nogmaals vrouwenarbeid in de steenfabrikage*, The Hague, 1910, p. 4.
15. Ibid.
16. *Social Jaarboek voor Nederland*, Vol. 2, Leiden, 1918, p. 257.
17. See J. Berg van Eysinga-Elias and C. Wichman, *De vrouw in Nederland voor honderd jaar*, Zaltbommel 1913, p. 64.
18. *Ibid*. See also C. Wichmann, *Het vraagstuk van den bedrijfs der vrouwen in Nederland*, Zaltbommel 1913.

deserted and had children to support. In 10.5 per cent of cases the husband was unemployed. Only 8 per cent gave positive reasons for working. These included a wish to save and a desire for social advancement; 6.3 per cent said that they would work only until they had children. In all other cases the reason was necessity of one kind or another.[19] Men and women were allocated different work within a given industry and we can talk about a sexual division of labour not only within one industry but between industries as well. But it is striking that in the development of the 'new industries' married women were never prominent as factory workers. The proportion of married women among all workers in the Netherlands was 9.7 per cent in 1880 and 10.6 per cent in 1909. Insofar as expansion of women's employment did take place in factories it involved unmarried women.

There are several reasons for this. First, during this whole period there was widespread male unemployment which probably kept men's wages sufficiently low for women's labour to be unattractive to capitalists. The new-style industries required skilled workers, and demanded qualifications that were easier for men to acquire. New factories were often built at a considerable distance from the workers' living quarters, and travelling to and from work proved more of a problem for women. There was also powerful and widespread opposition to women's work from Christian organisations, trade unions and other institutions, all of which denounced women's factory employment, in particular, as wicked and immoral. The influence of such attitudes, and especially of the argument that married women should stay at home and look after their children, was so strong that the Christian trade unions opposed all women's work, and others opposed married women's employment.[20] This was the time when a Christian offensive for civilisation and against modernity laid the basis for Christian parties with massive working-class support. The offensive was above all directed towards questions of morality, including the role of the housewife and spouse and issues of motherhood and childcare. Recent research

19. *Onderzoek naar de fabriksarbeid van gehuwde vrouwen in Nederland.* The Hague, 1911, p. 142.
20. This process can be compared with that which Barbara Leslie Epstein describes in *The Politics of Domesticity. Women, Evangelism and Temperance in Nineteenth Century America*, Middletown, 1981. There is a contrast between the bourgeois civilisation offensive in most Western countries and the one which took place in Holland. A characteristic feature of the latter was the hold which the Christian parties had over the working class. This led to a segmented society dominated by

on this campaign demonstrates the effectiveness of the propaganda among mothers in working-class families. The outcome was a standardised family in which the mother stayed at home, esteemed or criticised solely on the basis of how well she fulfilled the role of parent and homemaker.[21] But in spite of the opposition to married women's employment, men's wages were seldom sufficient or regular enough support to a family, and some contribution from his wife or children was usually needed.

There were only a few occupations in which women worked. In 1889 an inventory was made.[22] Women were effectively excluded from all but the least appreciated and lowest paid jobs. For example, contemporaries generally assumed that women who helped their husbands could also make cigars independently. During preparations for the 1898 exhibition, to which reference will later be made, the organisers looked for a woman cigar maker, but, though they visited dozens of cigar-making businesses it apparently proved impossible to find a woman capable of completing the whole process. There were no women at all in the prestige professions. Not until 1879 did the first female doctor begin to practise in Amsterdam, and she had only been admitted to the university after a long struggle.[23] Feminist observers connected this phenomenon with the debate about protective legislation of women's work and specifically with a law regulating women's work passed in 1889.[24] To understand their position we must first look at this law of 1889,

organisations which were based on belief systems and attracted much support. In the international literature this concept of *Verzuiling* is also referred to as polarisation. In such a society, the idea of women as cornerstone of the family politics played a crucial role. See S. Stuurman, 'Kirche und Arbeiterschaft', in W. Dunk and H. Lademacher, (eds), *Auf dem Weg zum modernen Parteienstaat Zur Entstehung: Organisation und Struktur politischer Parteien in Deutschland und den Niederlanden*, Melsungen 1986.

21. The role of the women plays a crucial part in S. Stuurman, *Verzuiling. Kapitalisme en Patriarchaat. Aspecten van de ontwikkeling van de moderne staat in Nederland*, Nijmegen, 1983. He must be credited for his evaluation of the impact of this specifically Dutch political phenomenon on family life and the position of women. He also elaborates on the working class. For the role of education see P. de Rooy, 'Het zwaarste beroep. Succes en falen van het huishoudonderwijs in Nederland 1875–1940', *Sociologisch Tijdschrift* 12.2 Oct. 1985, pp. 207–48.

22. M. Jungius, *Excerpt uit de uitkomst der beroepstelling in het Koninkrijk der Nederlanden op 31 december 1889, aangevende het aantal gehuwde en ongehuwde vrouwen (benevens het algemeen totaal) werkzaam als hoofd of ondergeschikte in eenig beroep of bedrijf*, Amsterdam, 1889.

23. W.H. Posthumus van der Goot and A. de Waal, *Van moeder op dochter*, Utrecht/Antwerpen, 1948 gives an account of all such data.

24. For State regulations on women's position in society at that time see J.

and the controversy surrounding it.

The first protective legislation was a law of 1874 forbidding the employment in factories of children under the age of twelve, and discussions immediately began on extending legislation to cover, among other things, workshop employment and the employment of women. The law of 1874 also regulated the employment of children between the ages of twelve and fifteen, and was the result of an official inquiry that had made it clear that children were working under miserable conditions.[25] The inquiry itself was initiated because more and more boys from the working classes, when tested for military service, were considered small and unhealthy. But it was immediately clear even in 1874 that one law was not enough.[26] The labour-power of children had to be replaced, and this could have had harsh consequences for weaker workers. To keep production expenses low, certain workers in the factories had to be further exploited. Moreover, someone had to look after the children. All these factors and apparent conflicts provoked new discussion on the regulation of factory work especially where it involved women. Limitation of maximum hours for women seemed to offer a solution to several problems simultaneously.

It is necessary to remember, however, that the new law came into being at a time when the ruling class was divided over the degree to which the State should interfere with freedom of enterprise and individual freedom. This is important because the new regulations were widely evaded in home industry and small workshops. Entering small workshops or private houses was, in the opinion of some contemporaries, an unwarrantable interruption of private life. Despite this, in 1889 reformers succeeded in regulating women's work. Women were not actually put out of work as a result of this law, but it did discourage the setting up of new factory employment for women. Feminists and part of the radical party had feared that legal regulation would cause a massive discharge of women, and make it impossible for women to work outside the home.[27] Regulation had

---

Lycklama a Nijenholt, *Rechtstoestand der vrouw in Nederland 1898–1923*, Haarlem, 1923.

25. *Rapport der commissie belast met het onderzoek naar den toestand der kinderen in fabrieken arbeidende*, Leiden, 1867.

26. C.W. de Vries, 'Van de kinderwet van Houten tot de arbeidswet 1889', *Sociaal Jaarboek voor Nederland*, Vol. 3 Leiden, 1921–2.

27. J. Outshoorn, *Vrouwenemancipatie en socialisme. Een onderzoek naar de houding van de SDAP t.o.v. het 'vrouwenvraagstuk' tussen 1894 en 1919*, Nijmegen, 1973.

been supported by socialists. The vehement debate preceding the passage of the law led to a public inquiry about the condition of women in the factories.[28] The results were published and were shocking. They are an excellent source for historical research into the living conditions of late-nineteenth-century Holland. They offer numerous examples of the prevailing prejudices against the employment of women. There were supposed to be easily sexually aroused and there was strong objection to the fact that they saw the factory men after working hours. Complaints that they also did so during work time were fewer. That was considered unavoidable, but it was thought that woman who went to work in a factory could not be decent. The health of women factory workers was particularly poor. In Amsterdam West, female workers in the candle-factories were nicknamed 'wax wicks' because they were as white as the candles they made. Another persistent concern was that women in the factories were unable to breast-feed their babies, many of whom died from the substitute diet of sweetened rice pudding. Infant mortality among the children of female factory workers was twice the average. Long hours of standing resulted in menstrual disturbances. Women and children often worked in the most cramped places where there was least ventilation.[29] The payment of wages was often arbitrary and dependent on the whims of employers. In the sewing workshops talking was forbidden. In other places women worked with toxic substances which caused foetal deformations. Some mention is made of infanticide. Records of miscarriages are frequent especially with women in the peat-cutting industry who had to work standing in water and who frequently fell down. Use of alcohol was widespread.

But in practice the law of 1889 was never really observed,[30] because there was not enough provision for enforcement. The first exceptions were made very quickly by Parliament. One of the earliest exemptions was for women in the brick industries, because their work was seen as indispensable to the work of the men.[31] Brickmaking was highly labour-intensive, seasonal work with a

28. This inquiry is mentioned in n. 11 above.
29. Detailed data can be found in *Onderzoek* 1911, *passim.*, or in *Verborgen arbeid*, p. 66.
30. A. Polak, *Vrouwenwerk in Nederland. Beschouwingen over enige zijden der vrouwenbeweging*, 1902.
31. See A. Polak, *Nogmaals vrouwenarbeid in de steenfabrifcage*, The Hague, 1910.

strict sexual division of labour which made it impossible for women to work shorter hours than men. Men shaped the bricks and carried them to the kilns; women filled and emptied the kilns and dried the bricks. There was a lot of night work, since it was cheaper to keep the kilns going continuously. Bricks were only made during the summer, at brickworks by the big rivers, using river clay. Returns on capital invested in brickworks had to come from only a few months' production, an illustration of how investment in fixed capital can lead to forced labour. Men could only get brickmaking work if they brought their women and children with them.

A further exception to the restrictions was made in 1896 for women working in butter and cheese factories.[32] As with brick-making, the exceptions concerned the continuous and seasonal nature of the work, which made it difficult or impossible to regulate. Women could not work fewer hours at their part of the work, because men's work depended on it.

Prevailing sentiment opposed women's employment as the various commissions of inquiry of the late nineteenth century made clear. The 'real' task of women was to keep a home, and all other work was 'unnatural'. To fight this and create more job opportunities for women, the feminist movement organised a National Exhibition on Women's Work which opened in 1898.[33] The Exhibition set out to fight the moral prohibition on women's employment. It was designed to show that women's work was not unnatural but normal, and that women could be found in all sorts of occupations. As part of the exhibition women were shown actually engaged in their work, where this was possible; in other cases there were photographs. A great deal of work went into setting up the exhibition and especially into gathering the information on which it was based. Investigators went out all over the country to find out about women's activities, not only in different kinds of paid work but also in literature, music, education, etc. Women wrote hundreds of letters containing information about their work and about themselves, and these provide a good sense of the prevailing ideology with regard to women's work and its strongly moralising tone.

This ideology forced women into home industry rather than factory work. The gist of the moral message was first of all that there was no way in which a factory worker could be a respectable

32. Lycklama a Nijenholt, *Rechtoestand.*
33. *Verborgen arbeid*, pp. 37–56.

woman. She was portrayed as coming from the poorest level of the working class, and was looked on as virtually a prostitute. Because of this prejudice women appear to have worked in factories only when they had no alternative: 'you'd be better with any other job', one women said to an inquiry of 1867. 'A servant with any sense of her capabilities will never become a factory-worker, and least of all a coffee-sorter'.[34]

Women in factories were treated differently from their male colleagues. They were not expected to stay long, and had no chance of promotion. The fact that the women saw themselves primarily in terms of motherhood prevented the organising of factory-women. (In fact, partly for this reason and partly because of the sexism of the trade-unions, the unionisation of women made little progress.) One exception was the seamstresses of Amsterdam, but their organisation can be explained by their experience with mass production and by their distinctive cultural background: nearly half were Jewish.[35] Jewish women had to learn a job, and normally organized themselves. By contrast, non-Jewish women often kept their work a secret, which made home industry particularly attractive, because it was so much less visible. This pressure was especially strong in the south, where the powerful Catholic clergy preached against women's work in factories. Yet there is a discrepancy between the official policy of the clergy and the actual situation. Evidence from diaries shows that this was also the case in later periods. Officially the clergy were opposed to all female labour, yet in practice they helped to find girls jobs in factories. It would have been impossible for their families to manage without their earnings. Moreover strict prohibition on the work of unmarried women would have brought them into direct conflict with factory owners who required girls since they could be underpaid for the most gruelling tasks without problem.

Women's earnings were always seen as complementary to men's. This was even true of teachers, who were supposed to be the most independent women.[36] Looking after children remained the mothers'

---

34. Enquiry 1887, vol. I, p. 56.
35. This stems from my present research on the Jewish proletariat of Amsterdam. See S. Leyesdorff, 'In search of the picture – Jewish proletarians in Amsterdam between two wars', *Dutch Jewish History*, Jerusalem, 1984, pp. 315–35.
36. Most of this kind of information stems from the archives of the Exhibition, kept in the International Archief voor de Vrouwenbeweging. Keizersgracht 10, Amsterdam.

responsibility, even if they went out to work as is suggested by the testimony of a woman whose husband was unemployed, making it necessary for her to work in a factory. The problem was that sometimes she had to stay on late at night, and did not always know her work schedule in advance. The questions indicate that the investigators assumed her total responsibility for the care of husband and children, over and above her paying job, even though he was a healthy adult out of work.

'Did you know you would have to work all night?'
'No.'
'Were your husband and children waiting at home?'
'The factory sent a message that we had to work on.'
'Who saw to that?'
'A lady.'
'Is your food brought to the factory?'
'Not always.'
'And your children?'
'Sometimes the woman next door feeds them, when she doesn't she sends someone to buy some bread.'
'So your husband is at home and with the children?'
'Yes.'
'He is not sick but strong and healthy?'
'Strong and healthy.'[37]

Management often proposed piece-rates as a solution. Their reasoning was that in this way a woman could go home whenever she wanted. A woman could theoretically decide to earn less and leave. In practice, however, piece-work seldom meant what are now called flexible working hours. Outwork or home-industry seemed a better solution; it was seen as the best way of avoiding the common complaints of female factory workers: swollen legs, ankles and feet, varicose veins, sores on the legs, menstrual complaints and back troubles. Outwork was seen as healthy and desirable – the only way to combine work and childcare. It offered a chance of lowering infant mortality by making breastfeeding possible.

Some of these ideas were aired during the exhibition of 1898. In letters and documents mainly written by non-working-class feminists, the fact that many women kept their involvement in home industry a secret was disapproved; but at the same time an open form of home industry was seen as the solution for working

37. Enquiry 1887, p. 220.

mothers. The ladies of the exhibition were aware of the fact that certain industries, such as the clothing industry, paid starvation wages to home-workers and a special booth was devoted to it at the exhibition. It represented the first stirrings of awareness in bourgeois feminist circles that something was wrong with home industry. This changed the direction of the exhibition, for it moved the discourse beyond the issue of providing more jobs for women into the question of the exploitation of women. The lady organisers, who otherwise lived lives very remote from the disasters of the world, could no longer close their eyes to the fact that the lace they wore 'was made by the blood of their sisters', as socialists might have said. The fact that such change appeared at all was mainly due to the influence of socialist women on the planning committee of the exhibition. From the first Worker Protection Law of 1874 the socialist movement had agitated against the illusion of a law regulating home industry when in fact enforcement was largely impossible. They were not in favour of women's work and certainly not married women's work, but their main focus of attention was on protection.[38] They were deeply concerned about workers' protection. They were aware that home industry created a special set of problems. Nevertheless in conformity with the ideas of Marx, they expected home industry to disappear with the modernisation of society, and more precisely with full industrialisation. They thus favoured a whole new concept of the way in which industry should be organised, and they stressed development along modern, rational lines. Although in the 1880s their main concern had been to abolish home industry, it became increasingly clear to them that the real solution lay in a totally different way of organising industry. The belief now gained currency that modern industrial technology and methods properly pursued might end the exploitation of women in factories. New forms of exploitation inherent in the glorification of motherhood were not of course discussed. Between 1870 and 1930 the idea of a new society replaced the daily fight for better conditions.

Reorganisation of industry, however, created an invisible home industry. For example food, now manufactured on a large scale, had to be wrapped. The boxes were made by home industry. Large-scale industry also changed the pattern of distribution and this had a great influence on home industry. There were streets where all the

38. Outshoorn, *Vrouwenemancipatie*.

women cleaned vegetables for the expanding vegetable processing factories. Vegetables were prepared in muddy holes under the most unhygienic conditions. Some mention is made of the extreme exploitation of young children who were supposed to be being looked after while their mothers were working.[39] Also new was the very large-scale clothing industry which again involved a great deal of homeworking. Umbrellas were also manufactured in the home, so it becomes clear that the jobs handed out to workers at home were frequently those parts of the production process which required intensive monotonous application.[40]

The factory inspectors, although they were few in number and quite powerless were the ones who noted the rise of new home industries. Very soon after the law of 1889 came into force they noted that whole factories had stopped operating and were giving the work to women in their own homes. The factory had changed into an office. From there the goods were transported to and from the women at home. One inspector wrote:

> Sometimes last winter we would arrive at a building whose sign announced it as a machine-knitting factory. On saying that we'd come to visit the work-place we'd be told that it had not existed for some years. It was clear that the work was being given out to be finished at home, by women who had machines in their houses. The work was paid for by the piece but the workers had to pay for the machine, and buy it on the installment system. In the past the machines were provided by the owner, but under the new system the women had to pay for the machines month by month. If they stopped working the employer took the machine and they lost the money they had paid on it.[41]

Employers kept wages so low that it took years to pay for the machines, and they had an agreement not to give work to women with machines from other factories. The women were trapped: they could not even change employers so as to obtain better wages. Another inspector mentioned the fact that strong young women in certain factories could go home early. This was, however, not the wish of the women themselves but of their employers. Girls and women should not be too tired to do piece-work at home for a lower wage in the evening.[42]

39. *Onderzoek naar de toestanden in de Nederlands huisindustrie*, vol. I, The Hague, 1911–14, p. 121.
40. *Factory Inspection*, 1901, pp. 982–3.
41. Ibid., 1895–6, p. 26.
42. Various factory inspection reports 1891–1905.

Some of the worst conditions were found in pea-sorting, and some detailed information has survived about this activity.[43] Market gardening had become an increasingly important activity after the 1880s with more capital, larger-scale enterprises and more widely dispersed markets. At first the outlets were mainly retail, though later processes such as canning also became important. The shelling and sorting of peas became women's work. It could not be done by machine because selection was a question not only of size but also of colour. The peas were given out by the shopkeepers to women who would take them home and work through them, often with help from their children. In the provincial market town of Middelburg, 500 pea-sorting families were found, including 135 children under ten, 107 between ten and twelve, and 142 between twelve and sixteen. In this town alone, the shopkeepers paid out 100,000 guilders a year for pea-sorting. Virtually all the women engaged in this activity were married or divorced. It was a heavy job: women themselves carried the bags of sorted peas which weighed 80 kilos. The work was checked by the shop-assistant who took a handful of peas to make sure there were no bits of pod or dirt bulking out the weight; deductions in pay would be made if anything was found. If a woman was on good terms with the assistant, she might get the best pods, with big regular peas, which meant less work and so more money than small peas, but in general wages were low, and hours extremely long.[44]

It is easy to multiply examples of exploitation, for instance shrimp-cleaning at night, which had to be done quickly against spoilage. One teacher in Harderwijk complained about the rotten shrimp smell in his classroom, because the children were so dirty.[45] Worse, the children fell asleep at school, exhausted from having to stay up at night working. Parents commonly used violence to force them to work, such as beating them or splashing them with ice-cold water.[46] The socialists campaigned against the wage lowering caused by home industry and against its inhumane conditions.

In 1906 the socialists decided to mount an exhibition on home industry similar to the one on women's work. It opened in 1909. As with the earlier exhibition, there was much media attention, and again people could read daily about the horrors of exploitation.[47]

43. Ibid., 1903–4, vol. II, pp. 60–70.
44. Ibid., 1903–4, vol. VI, pp. 14–18.
45. *Onderzoek 1911–1914*, vol. II, p. 4.
46. *Factory Inspection 1901*, pp. 198–9.

Most important for our purposes is the fact that at the opening conference the *new* home industry was analysed for the first time.[48] It was clear that the incidence of home industry had increased, despite expectation to the contrary. The government inquiry of 1911–1913 into home industry was a result of this exhibition. In the course of that inquiry 18,000 families were visited, and the whole range of home employment covered. Here is an extract from the report on onion-peeling: 'When the worker comes home, he or she puts the onions into water in every vase and basin he/she has. Then a few at a time are taken out of the water and the women and children sit peeling them.[49] An unusual form of exploitation was found in the house of one woman who had children come, sometimes from quite a distance, and peel onions for her, paying them 1 or 2 cents, which they could spend on sweets in her shop. In the clothing industry one woman, a linen seamstress, told the investigators in tears that she could not work because of pains in her hand and nervous collapse. Her husband had left her six years earlier, and she did not earn more than five guilders a week for herself and her invalid daughter.

At first the inquiry was carried out by volunteers: when the government took over the work it interviewed another 7,000 families. But still the exact number of home industrial workers in this period remains unclear. In the published statistics we find only the women who worked full time in home industry; the seamstresses who added to their wages at night, the children who went to school in the daytime after a night of labour, the husbands who helped their tired wives, do not appear.

Home industry was now analysed as a new system, distinct from the old putting-out system. It was mainly women's work, whereas the old-putting-out system had largely employed men. Men worked mainly in the footwear and tobacco industries and their work shows some resemblance with the 'putting-out' system. Investigators discovered 2,293 of these men in a few villages in the south of Holland. Women worked mainly in vegetable processing. It was estimated that there were at least 509 of them in the three villages investigated: 535 married and 712 unmarried women worked as shrimp peelers;

47. H.J. Tasman, 'De oorzaken der huisindustrie', *Report of the Congress on Home Industry 1909* (unpublished).

48. *De Werkmansbode*, 16.3, 1912.

49. See for detailed information the material mentioned in n. 39 above.

785 married and 36 unmarried women, along with more than a thousand children under nineteen worked as pea-sorters. At least 290 women stitched shoes at home in those same villages about which we have the data for men. Yet these figures are not definitive. The investigators worked unsystematically, visiting some villages and ignoring others. The figures represented the minimum and all stated that the estimate was too low.

It was now wage-earning women, dependent on employers, and exploited in new ways, who produced semi-manufactured articles. But the difference between the old and new home industries consisted largely in the role played in industrial development, not in the actual lived poverty. This was due to the quick development of capitalism in Holland. The old home industry had to become rationalized to survive the competition. Mechanisation was attractive to employers, though there were cases where it was cheaper not to mechanise where wages were low and the work labour-intensive. The division of labour into mechanised and non-mechanised sectors was the result. It was in these largely unmechanised new home industries that women, unschooled and married, now found jobs. They belonged to the most exploited of their class, for the work was seasonal, monotonous and low-paid. Speeding up various parts of the production process had an enormous impact on home industry, as the production of a product became more and more interconnected with other parts. For instance, if the cigar industry increased production, more paper boxes were needed. These were made by home industry. In Marxist terms this is the socialization of production, but it is important to note that it was no balanced process. As it turned out, sex and sex-role stereotypes were major factors. Lace-making, for instance, was seen as unskilled labour, and became one of the worst jobs for women. With the mechanisation of the textile industry more lace was needed. Today anyone who has seen a lace-maker at work has to admit that it is a hard job, requiring much skill and training, but that was not how it was defined at that time. The same is true of the umbrella industry: skilled work, but considered unskilled and paid accordingly; seasonal, and therefore women's work.

Home industry gave new profits to the employers, because it was easier to exploit the workers there. Wages were minimal, and people worked in isolation. This made demands for higher wages difficult to organise.

The relation between variable capital outlays and surplus value was easy to control because variable capital could be maintained at a very low level. Fixed capital requirements were also low because of savings on overheads, water, light and fuel, and there was no empty factory to eat up the profits in the slack season. All this, of course, was only possible at a time when people could be exploited because they had no other option. It was not surprising, therefore, to find a growth in the home industries again in the 1930s, and a similar upsurge seem to be happening at the present time.

Conclusion

In contrast to conventional interpretations of Dutch industrialisation, this chapter has endeavoured to stress the important role of women. With the onset of industrialisation a new type of work developed whose character was largely shaped by the sexual division of labour. This was the production in the home on a mass scale of semi-manufactured articles and food, mainly products that could not be profitably made by machine. Examples are box-making, pea-sorting (now for the big stores on a large scale and no longer just for the village shop), stitching uppers for shoes, and so on. With the socialisation of the relations of production (that is, the process by which industries and different forms of production become more closely integrated), new industry in the home actually increased during the first decades of industrialisation. With its increase, a new army of women and children wage-labourers was created that formed an exploitable labour reserve. Women could not go to the factory, and in their homes they were too cut off from each other to fight low wages, long working hours, and the frequent requirement that they buy from the shops of their employers. This situation remained until it became cheaper in some industries to replace exploited women by machines; though the existence of this female labour-army actually militated against the use of new machines for some time.

A feminist perspective changes our picture of industrialisation, as might also a children's perspective. Until quite recently we thought that industrialisation meant a steady replacing of workshops by factories. Now we know that a new kind of workshop emerged – the home – a place where once the door is closed any control becomes impossible. These workplaces are an integral part of industrial development and very important in the accumulation of capital. Once this is perceived it can no longer be said that married women did not work in Holland and took no part in the development of the Dutch economy.

10

Women in the Economy of the United States from the American Revolution to 1920

S. JAY KLEINBERG

Although the numbers of women in the paid labour force have been quite small until recent times, women have always worked, that is to say, women have always carried out productive tasks which have helped to sustain themselves and their families. The nature of that work, its location and, indeed, the definition of work itself have changed with the coming of industrialisation to the United States and the commercialisation of agriculture. These changes are complex, but by examining women's roles in the economy we learn much about the true nature of that economy, the relationship between the family as a production and consumption unit and the larger economy, and, of course, about the social construction and definition of women's roles as they varied by the stage of economic development, class, race, and ethnicity.[1]

1. There are many overviews of women in the economy of the United States and general histories of women. Readers are referred to Alice Kessler-Harris, *Out to Work. A History of Wage-earning Women in the United States*, Oxford, Oxford University Press, 1982; Barbara Mayer Wertheimer, *We Were There. The Story of Working Women in America*, New York, Pantheon Books, 1975; Elizabeth Faulkner Baker, *Technology and Woman's Work*, New York, Columbia University Press, 1964; Milton Cantor and Bruce Laurie (eds), *Class, Sex and the Woman Worker* Westport, Conn., Greenwood Press, 1977; Julie A. Matthaei, *An Economic History of Women in America. Women's Work, the Sexual Division of Labor, and the Development of Capitalism*, New York, Schocken, 1982; Leslie Woodcock Tentler, *Wage-Earning Women. Industrial Work and Family Life in the United States, 1900–1930*, New York, Oxford University Press, 1979; W. Elliot Brownlee and Mary M. Brownlee, *Women in the American Economy. A Documentary History, 1675 to 1929*, New Haven, Conn., Yale University Press, 1976. For general histories see: Gerda Lerner, *The Majority Finds its Past. Placing Women in History*, New York, Oxford University Press, 1979; Mary P. Ryan, *Womanhood in America from*

The key transitions examined in this chapter are the development of wage labour in the United States, the growth of women's labour force participation, and the gender restrictions placed upon their employment. Nevertheless, it is important not to limit our consideration of women's work solely to paid employment or labour force participation for several reasons. In the first place before the Industrial Revolution home and work places tended to be coterminous and blended into each other. Even where production was market oriented it usually took place within the household environment. This could mean that all members of the family participated in the productive enterprises of the household, although most tasks were allocated by gender.

There is evidence from the colonial period (before the American Revolution in 1776) that some widows assumed their husband's businesses, running taverns, small shops, printing presses and farms. Occasionally single or married women undertook such enterprises either in their own right or acting as agents for relatives at sea or away on business. Such women, however, were a rarity. Married women could not ordinarily sign contracts and had no legal right to their own earnings. Because of the legal limitations on their activities, the unwillingness of authorities to grant land to women, the high birth rates, and the paucity of opportunities for wage-earning, women who had to support themselves were at a serious disadvantage in colonial society. Jobs for single women were overwhelmingly concentrated in the service and household sectors as domestic help on farms and in homes, spinning weaving, and sewing. The proportion of women in the urban labour force (at a time when the overwhelming majority of the population were rural dwellers and farmers) has been estimated at between 5 and 10 per cent.[2]

Colonial Times to the Present, New York, New Viewpoints, 1975; Anne Firor Scott, *The Southern Lady. From Pedestal to Politics, 1830–1930*, Chicago, University of Chicago Press, 1970; Dorothy Sterling (ed.), *We Are Your Sisters. Black Women in the Ninenteenth Century*, New York, W.W. Norton, 1984; Glenda Riley, *Inventing the American Women. A Perspective on Women's History, 1607–1877*, and *1865 to the Present*, Arlington Heights, Ill., Harlan Davidson Inc., 1986.

2. For analyses of women's lives in the colonial and early national period see Nancy F. Cott, *The Bonds of Womanhood. Woman's Sphere in New England, 1780–1835*, New Haven, Conn., Yale University Press, 1977; Joan Hoff Wilson, 'The Illusion of Change. Women and the American Revolution', in Jean E. Friedman and William G. Shade (eds), *Our American Sisters. Women in American Life and Thought*, 3rd edn., Lexington, Mass., D.C. Heath & Company, 1982; Mary Beth Norton, *Liberty's Daughters. The Revolutionary Experiences of American Women, 1750–1800*, Boston, Mass., Little, Brown & Co, 1980; Julia Cherry Spruill, *Women's*

Secondly, it is important to look at productive activities within the household because that is where most of the family's needs were met, and where many women earned money although not part of the waged sector of the economy. Both married and single women engaged in household manufacturing, knitting and sewing garments, making hats, and helping to grow, process, and store the family's food, making soap, dipping candles, and helping in the cobbling of shoes. Particularly where the land was poor, as was the case in much of New England, these activities could be market oriented so that women who lived within their parents' or husbands' households could contribute cash to them.[3] This behaviour was to have important consequences as it both delayed the age of marriage and made a pool of workers available to early industrialists in the region. As was the case for rural women throughout the nineteenth century and those migrating west to the unsettled frontier regions, the money earned by women selling eggs, butter, produce, and home-made goods helped to sustain their families although these women combined such manufacturing with their other household duties and would not have considered themselves to be a part of the labour force.[4]

Yet many of the women who were productive members of the economy could not claim the benefits of their labours either for themselves or for their families. White indentured servants and blacks forcibly imported from Africa and enslaved all worked long hard hours with no recompense. Female indentured servants had a more limited range of occupations than males, received less training than did their male conterparts, and, if convicted of crimes, endured harsher sentences for similar misdemeanors.[5] One 'Susan C' was condemned by the General Court in Connecticut in 1645 for her

---

Life and Work in the Southern Colonies, Chapel Hill, NC, University of North Carolina Press, 1933; Linda Kerber, *Women of the Republic*, Chapel Hill, NC, University of North Carolina Press, 1980; Linda Grant DePauw, *Founding Mothers. Women in America in the Revolutionary Era*, Boston, Mass., Houghton, Mifflin, 1975.

3. Rolla M. Tyron, *Household Manufactures in the United States, 1640–1860*, Chicago, University of Chicago Press, 1917.

4. Joan Jensen, *With These Hands. Women Working on the Land*, Old Westbury, The Feminist Press; New York, McGraw-Hill Book Company, 1981; Jim Potter, 'The Growth of Population in America, 1700–1860', in D.V. Glass, and D.E.C. Eversley (eds), *Population in History*, Chicago, Aldine Publishing, 1965, pp. 648–9.

5. Rosalyn Baxandall, Linda Gordon and Susan Reverby, *America's Working Women. A Documentary History – 1600 to the Present*, New York, Vintage Books, 1976, p. 26.

rebellious carriage towards her mistress. For this she was sent to the house of correction, kept on hard labour and a coarse diet, and brought forth at lecture day to be publicly corrected on a weekly basis. But Susan C and her contemporaries, although treated harshly, received a small sum and a dress or other freedom dues at the end of their period of indenture. Their indentures were of limited duration and the actions of masters and mistresses towards them were subject to judicial oversight. Indentured servants thus had some redress against harsh treatment or violation of their terms of indenture.[6]

By contrast, African women and their descendants were deemed to be slaves, rarely obtained their freedom, and were subjected to much harsher conditions of servitude. Ironically, indentured servants who conceived children were punished, but slave women's childbearing abilities were valued because colonial authorities regarded the children of slave women as slaves belonging to the master rather than as children of their own parents. This increased the value of slave women to their owners, a fact which was reflected in the higher prices paid for them. Indentured women servants commanded prices about half those paid for men, however, because convention limited the tasks they performed. Slave women toiled in the fields doing much the same work as the men, while indentured women had the narrower range of activities generally engaged in by white women, alongside whom they frequently laboured. Enslaved women also performed the domestic jobs of all women, washing, cooking, sewing, nursing, and looking after children in addition to field work. They thus endured heavy agricultural work loads in addition to the domestic tasks which were the lot of all women in this era.[7]

Early Industrialisation and Women's Work

Industrialisation replaced the household manufactures with those

6. Marcus Jernegan, *The Laboring and Dependent Classes in Colonial America: 1607–1783*, New York, Frederick Ungar, 1971; Lucy Maynard Salmon, *Domestic Service*, New York, Macmillan Company, 1911.

7. John Blassingame, *The Slave Community. Plantation Life in the Ante-bellum South*, New York, Oxford University Press, 1972; Eugene Genovese, *Roll Jordan Roll. The World the Slaves Made*, New York, Pantheon Books, 1974; Herbert Gutman, *The Black Family in Slavery and Freedom*, New York, Pantheon Books, 1976.

made in factories, leading to a sharp differentiation between work, which came to mean paid wage labour and took place outside the home, and consumption, the purchase of goods, which became the main activity of the household and the housewife. As such, industrialisation transformed women's economic contributions as it became more difficult for them to combine productive activities with their domestic responsibilities. According to Joan Scott and Louise Tilly, women's labour contributions merged imperceptibly with their household chores in preindustrial societies, but as work moved outside the home into factories, married women's earning activities remained overwhelmingly domestic in nature: they took in paying lodgers, ran boarding houses, sewed, did various forms of piece work, or, under certain circumstances, worked in other women's kitchens. In many cases census takers and other surveyors ignored married women's income-producing activities because they took place within the home. Since industrial time schedules were less flexible than those of the small-scale farm, artisan workshop, or small store, and large production units demanded constant attendance and attention from their workers, they inhibited married women's earlier pattern of combining family responsibilities with the production of goods.[8]

The family remained the basic labour unit on family farms through the nineteenth century, although this was not the case for plantations where slave labour was utilised and where women as well as men worked in the fields but not necessarily with members of their own families. Even in industrial settings the family played an important role in the recruitment of labour as members of kinship networks helped each other find employment and taught each other the skills needed for these jobs. But though boys might enjoy formal apprenticeships which taught them a range of skilled jobs, girls rarely received anything more than a limited introduction to a specific set of tasks. This mirrored their situation in preindustrial settings; both as indentured servants and domestic help, they learned the housewifely arts but seldom other crafts.[9] Throughout

8. Louise Tilly and Joan Scott, *Women, Work and Family*, New York, Holt, Reinhart & Winston, 1978.

9. Lois Green Carr and Lorena S. Walsh, 'The Planter's Wife. The Experience of White Women in Seventeenth-Century Maryland', *William and Mary Quarterly* 34 (October 1977), pp. 543–71, suggest that female indentured servants did some field work if they were in poorer families, but hoped to avoid it if at all possible. Also see Wertheimer, *We Were There*, Part I.

the industrial period, women's occupations have been 'dead-end' in nature, requiring the mastery of one or two skills, usually performed over and over again, with little opportunity for advancement.

Young women, rather than men, formed the basis of the first industrial labor force in the United States. As early as 1791 Secretary of the Treasury Alexander Hamilton suggested that manufacturing would give employment to what he termed 'idle' women and children. He argued in his 'Report on Manufactures' that factory work would provide the farmer with a new source of profit and support 'from the increased industry of his wife and daughters' while women and children would be 'rendered more useful, and the latter more early useful, by manufacturing establishments, than they would otherwise be.'[10]

Young men who felt thwarted by New England's stony soil sought their fortunes at sea, in commerce, or by moving farther west to more fertile territories, while their sisters found opportunities in the textile mills which proliferated at the beginning of the nineteenth century. The first yarn spinning and carding factory opened in Rhode Island in 1789 utilising water-powered machinery. The early mills received impetus from the embargo placed upon British imports in 1807 and the War of 1812 between Britain and the United States, which closed the American market to imports. By the end of that war there were some 140 cotton manufacturers operating 130,000 spindles. In 1816 a Congressional committee found that two-thirds of the nation's 100,000 industrial workers were women; a decade later, women comprised 90 per cent of all textile workers in the New England region.[11]

The organisation of the labour force in the early New England textile mills was unique. Most of the workers were young, single women, living apart from their families in company boarding-houses usually overseen by widows. Almost all the workers during the first phase of industrialisation were native-born whites from rural areas who alternated mill work with other forms of employ-

---

10. Alexander Hamilton, 'Report on Manufactures', Reprinted in Carter Goodrich, *The Government and the Economy 1783–1861*, Indianapolis, Bobbs-Merrill, 1967, pp. 187–95.
11. This review of the development of the textile industry is drawn from Baker, *Technology*, pp. 8–9. Also see Caroline F. Ware, *The Early New England Cotton Manufacture. A Study in Industrial Beginnings*, New York, Russell & Russell, 1966. Reprint of 1931 edn.

ment, including school teaching (which paid more poorly than tending the looms and spindles in the factory). They regarded work as an interlude rather than a life sentence. Lucy Larcom, one of the early workers and later a poet, declared in her poem, 'An Idyl of Work':

> Not always to be here among the looms—
> Scarcely a girl she knew expected that;
> Means to one end, their labor was – to put
> Gold nest-eggs in the bank, or to redeem
> A mortgaged homestead, or pay the way
> Through classic years at some academy;
> More commonly to lay a dowry by
> For future housekeeping.[12]

Indeed, most of the first generation of mill workers were young (85 per cent at one mill were under twenty-five years old) and married after their years in the mill. Their families might have used their contributions to augment income derived from farming, but one major study of the social background of women workers in the Lowell, Massachusetts mills between 1830 and 1850 has noted that they came from homes of average affluence, impelled not by poverty but for the wide variety of reasons suggested by Larcom's poem, including a desire for independence, a chance to enjoy urban amenities unavailable in the rural districts where most of them originated, or to earn money for their own purposes.[13]

Initially, working conditions and wages compared favourably with those available elsewhere in domestic service, sewing, and teaching. But as mill owners strived to increase their profits, they pushed their labour force to work harder, to tend more machines, and to submit to various forms of company discipline designed to augment the managers' control over their employees and the production processes. Management also segregated women and men into different jobs, reserving the higher paying supervisory posi-

12. Lucy Larcom, *An Idyl of Work*, Boston, Mass., J.R. Osgood & Co., 1875, p. 34. Also see her *A New England Girlhood*, Boston, Mass., Houghton Mifflin, 1889. For an account of a factory worker and her subsequent life see Claudia L. Bushman, *A Good Poor Man's Wife. Being a Chronicle of Harriet Hanson Robinson and her Family in Nineteenth Century New England*, Hanover and London, University Press of New England, 1981.

13. Thomas Dublin, *Women at Work. The Transformation of Work and Community in Lowell, Massachusetts, 1826–1860*, New York, Columbia University Press, 1979.

tions for men, while relegating women to the lower paying machine tending tasks. The wages offered to men reflected the market rates for similar jobs outside the mills, but those for women did not need to be as high since women's alternative activities, including hat making and shoe binding, paid poorly or were within the domestic setting and not recompensed individually or directly. Their wages had only to be high enough to attract women away from such poorly remunerated occupations. As a result they remained much lower than those received by men, while women's chances for occupational advancement were severely restricted.[14]

Durings the 1820s, '30s, and 40s, women operatives protested over a variety of issues, including lowered piece rates, increased fees at their boarding houses, and changes in their hours of labour. Organisations such as the Lowell Female Reform Association, led by Sarah Bagley, campaigned for the ten-hour-day in the 1840s, but with little success. The speed up and stretch out in the textile mills (working at a faster rate, tending more looms) made the work less appealing to the rural women who had flocked to the mills when they first opened, while low wages and the relatively short time women spent in the mills made it difficult to sustain strikes. Overall working conditions deteriorated as owners sought to increase profit margins by cutting labour costs. Production in the mills expanded greatly after the end of the depression of 1837–43 and the imposition of a protectionist tariff in 1844, but the native-born white women no longer succumbed to the blandishments of the mills' recruiting agents. At the same time the failure of the potato crop in Ireland resulted in a mass exodus to the United States. This led mill owners to recruit Irish women, who received lower wages because they were placed in those departments of the mills which paid less and because it took them longer to advance from those tasks to better paying ones. By the middle of the nineteenth century this situation had been replicated in other textile and manufacturing centres as Irish women came to dominate the industrial labour force, but were still under-represented in those work rooms which paid most highly.[15]

Discrimination in the types of jobs employers were willing to give workers, then, was based on sex and ethnicity. It could also be based on race, which restricted the types of work available to black

14. Howard Gitelman, 'The Waltham System and the Coming of the Irish', *Labor History* 8 (1967), pp. 231–2.
15. Dublin, *Women at Work*, pp. 148–53.

women and thus lowered their wages. No black women worked alongside whites in ante-bellum factories, either in the free north or in the slave south. Though the south was primarily an agricultural region, it did have some factories devoted to processing farm products, but whereas 65 per cent of New England's industrial labour force were white women in 1840, only 10 per cent of the southern factory workers were. Southern factories relied heavily upon the labour of slaves, offering employment which was segregated on the basis of sex and race. In some districts only whites worked in the cotton factories while tobacco factories relied solely on blacks. In others, slaves also worked in the cotton mills. Most slave women, however, worked as agricultural labourers, doing much the same jobs as men, at the same pace. Though a few enslaved women were permitted to develop special skills, for example, in weaving, spinning, dyeing, midwifery, or nursing, the vast majority toiled in the fields picking cotton or tobacco, chopping wood, hoeing corn, even splitting rails. Women also peformed the domestic work on the plantations, both in their own quarters and in the Big House.[16]

Both before and after emancipation, most free black women who worked for wages did so as domestic servants, washerwomen, or seamstresses, receiving even lower wages than did white women for the same work. Domestic service dominated the employment prospects of all women outside the manufacturing towns of the northeast, but black women were even more likely than native-born white or immigrant women to be concentrated among the ranks of domestic servants. An 1838 Pennsylvania Abolitionist Society survey found that of 18,000 free blacks some 5,000 were live-in servants. In New York City at mid-century about 25 per cent of all Irish women and 50 per cent of all black women worked as domestic servants. Analyses of women's labour force participation suggests that German women were less likely to be employed than their native-born white, Irish, or black sisters. The proportion of German immigrant women who worked as domestic servants was lower overall than for Irish women, but could vary depending upon the employment opportunities offered. A study of black and white women in Petersburg, Virginia before the Civil War found that free married black

16. Jacqueline Jones, 'My Mother was Much of A Woman. Black Women, Work, and the Family under Slavery', *Feminist Studies* 8 (Summer 1982); Suzanne Lebsock, *The Free Women of Petersburg: Status and Culture in a Southern Town, 1784–1860*, New York, Norton, 1984; Sterling, *We Are Your Sisters*, pp. 13–17.

women were more likely than whites to be in the labour force, a pattern which continued after the Civil War as well and will be discussed below.[17]

Domestic service changed during the nineteenth century as native-born white women eschewed it and increasingly it became the province of impoverished immigrant and black women. While farm women may have laboured alongside their hired female help, urban women relegated the least pleasant tasks to them. Much of the productive work of the household had been superceded by industrial production, but standards of housekeeping rose during the nineteenth century leaving a great deal of work still to be done at home. Even in the south, about half the families in urban areas might have no household help. Few households had more than one servant, so she became an overburdened maid of all work. Despite the decrease in the amount of productive labour undertaken within the home there were still many onerous chores: wood or coal had to be brought indoors, fires had to be made up, water carried and heated on the stove, household and human wastes removed, and clothing and bed linen washed and ironed. Affluent women reserved the more enjoyable aspects of housework and childcare for themselves, leaving their slaves or servants to do the arduous jobs. The overall effect was to increase the distance between the doers of housework and those who benefited from others' labour.[18]

At the opposite end of the occupational spectrum from domestic service women wrote, taught, or pioneered in other professions in the middle of the nineteenth century. Many of these women had received some education at the academies and colleges for women which opened their doors to women in the 1830s and 1840s. Some, such as the abolitionist Lucy Stone and many of the first generation

17. Sharon Harley, 'Northern Black Female Workers', in Sharon Harley and Rosalyn Terborg-Penn (eds), *The Afro-American Woman. Struggles and Images*, Port Washington, National University Publications, 1978. Carol Groneman, 'She Earns as a Child; She Pays as a Man', in Cantor and Laurie, *Class, Sex and the Woman Worker*; Carl Degler, *At Odds. Women and the Family in America from the Revolution to the Present*, New York, Oxford University Press, 1980, p. 384; Lebsock, *Free Women of Petersburg*, p. 187. For an account of Irish women's experience in the United States see Hasia R. Diner, *Erin's Daughters in America. Irish Immigrant Women in the Nineteenth Century*, Baltimore, Md., Johns Hopkins University Press, 1983.

18. Lebsock, *Free Women of Petersburg*; Faye Dudden, *Serving Women. Household Service in Nineteenth Century America*, Middleton, Wesleyan University Press, 1983. On the development of housework in the 19th century, see S.J. Kleinberg, 'Technology and Women's Work', *Labor History* 17 (1976).

of mill workers, had worked in order to obtain more education than their parents were willing to provide for them or could afford. Stone alternated between attendance at Oberlin College and teaching school herself in order to earn money to pay her own educational expenses. Her father provided money for her brothers' education, but made her pay for her own schoolbooks even as a small child. Despite such obstacles the proportion of women receiving an education increased, although few black women received more than rudimentary schooling until after the Civil War. As the number of schools proliferated, so too did the number of women teachers, whom boards of education consistently paid about one third to one-half less than they paid men. The proportion of women teachers rose from 25 per cent in 1860 to 60 per cent in 1880.[19]

Many of the literary women of these decades, such as Sarah Hale, editor of *Godey's Lady's Magazine*, Harriet Beecher Stowe, author of the anti-slavery novel *Uncle Tom's Cabin*, her sister Catherine Beecher, who wrote domestic management treatises, and novelists Caroline Lee Hentz and Catherine Sedgwick, emphasised female moral superiority and virtue. Described by modern historians as domestic feminists, they celebrated the home and women's nurturant place within it at the time when the factory production of goods undermined the household manufacturing functions. Though the extent to which their exultation of domesticity can be regarded as feminist remains problematic, they greatly influenced their generation and helped to promulgate the notion of the home as women's special sphere in a way which their forebears would not have recognised.[20] This helped to lay the foundation for the Social Housekeeping movement which in turn legitimised women's reformist activities and their new careers as social workers and home economists at the turn of the century.

Other women responded to the increased formalisation of American society, in particular the need to obtain educational

19. Leslie Wheeler (ed.), *Loving Warriors. Selected Letters of Lucy Stone and Henry B. Blackwell, 1853 to 1893*, New York, Dial Press, 1981; Kessler-Harris, *Out to Work*, p. 57. Nancy Hoffman, *Women's True Profession. Voices from the History of Teaching*, Old Westbury, Feminist Press, 1981.

20. Barbara Epstein, *The Politics of Domesticity. Women, Evangelism and Temperance in Nineteenth Century America*, Middletown, Wesleyan University Press, 1981; Kathryn Kish Sklar, *Catherine Beecher. A Study in American Domesticity*, New York, Norton, 1973; Mary Kelley, *Private Lives, Public Stage. Literary Domesticity in Nineteenth Century America*, New York, Oxford University Press, 1984; Mary Ryan, *The Empire of the Mother: American Writing About Domesticity, 1820 to 1860*, New York, Institute for Historical Research, 1982.

credentials in order to undertake certain jobs, by attempting to obtain those credentials even when it contravened prescribed roles for women. Thus, the professionalisation of medicine, with the development of medical schools and licensing examinations, led Elizabeth Blackwell to apply to medical school after medical school until the students at Geneva College voted in 1847 to admit her. Blackwell refused to march in her own graduation procession, thinking this unladylike behaviour, but she went on to do advanced work at St Bartholomew's Hospital, London, and to found a medical school to train women as physicians in New York.[21] Male physicians relegated women to the sidelines of medicine, although women continued to nurse their own families, friends, and neighbours.

The nursing profession got its start in the United States during the Civil War as women volunteered to care for the sick and wounded since there were not enough male nurses. Women nurses occasionally encountered hostility from army surgeons, one of whom wrote to the *American Medical Times* that they were a useless annoyance, by nature, education and strength totally unfit for nursing wounded men. Dr Blackwell nevertheless established a training programme for nurses in 1861, but the army, hostile to women doctors, denied her the position of Superintendent of Army Nurses, which went instead to Dorothea Dix. Nurses' training schools had become common by the end of the nineteenth century, but hospital nurses were poorly paid, continuing the tradition begun in the Civil War when they received $12 a month, if they were paid at all. Doctors also turned childbirth into obstetrics performed by usually male doctors rather than midwifery (carried out by nurses or untrained, but not necessarily unskilled midwives).[22] As a result female medical practitioners remained a rarity (as physicians), underpaid (as nurses), or untrained (as midwives) until well into the twentieth century.

Women also encountered hostility in their efforts to become lawyers or ministers. Although a few colonial women, notably Mistress Margaret Brent in Maryland, had functioned in a lawyer-like capacity, women were prohibited from practising law in the

21. Wheeler, *Loving Warriors*, pp. 87–8; Mary Roth Walsh, *Doctors Wanted: No Women Need Apply. Sexual Barriers in the Medical Profession, 1835–1975*, New Haven, Conn., Yale University Press, 1977.
22. Baxandall *et al.*, *America's Working Women* p. 76; Wertheimer, *We Were There*, pp. 133–7.

United States until 1869 when Arabella Mansfield was admitted to the bar in Iowa, but other states refused to follow Iowa's example. Law schools admitted very few women until the 1890s. A few denominations had accepted women evangelical preachers in the eighteenth century and some women, such as Mother Anne Lee and Mary Baker Eddy, founded their own religious communities or churches, the Shakers (in the 1780s) and Christian Science (in the 1870s), respectively. The first woman to receive a divinity degree was Antoinette Blackwell in 1850, but few theological colleges followed Oberlin's lead and women ministers remained few in numbers until quite recently.[23]

The traditional historical benchmarks in American history, wars and elections, for example, may not have had the same significance for women as they did for men. To take but one example, many economic historians have discussed the Civil War in terms of its impact upon economic growth, but for women's roles in the economy what is most interesting about the Civil War is not that it increased female labour force participation, as historians have suggested that the First and Second World Wars did, but that it actually decreased it, while opening a few areas of employment to a limited number of women.[24] The number of black women workers declined dramatically after the emancipation of the slaves, from virtually all adult females to about half, as black women sought to shed their dual role as field hands and domestic workers.[25] An 1866 census of former slave women in Montgomery County, Virginia shows that about half those with children listed occupations compared with about three-quarters of those who were single or married but childless. This highlights the problem that mothers had in combining childcare and work of any sort as well as the desire of these

23. Barbara J. Harris, *Beyond her Sphere. Women and the Professions in American History*, Westport, Conn., Greenwood Press, 1978.
24. For one example of this approach see Ralph Andreano (ed.), *The Economic Impact of the American Civil War*, Cambridge, Mass., Schenkman Publishing Co., 1968. On women in the Civil War see Elizabeth Massey, *Bonnet Brigades. American Women and the Civil War*, New York, Alfred A. Knopf, 1966. For the suggestion that war may have only a short term impact on women's lives see D'Ann Campbell's insightful study *Women at War with America. Private Lives in a Patriotic Era*, Cambridge, Mass., Harvard University Press, 1984.
25. Paula Giddings, *When and Where I Enter. The Impact of Black Women on Race and Sex in America*, New York, Morrow, 1984, pp. 63–5; Stanley Lebergott, *The Americans. An Economic Record*, New York, Norton, 1984, p. 250; Roger Ransom and Richard Sutch, *One Kind of Freedom*, Cambridge, Cambridge University Press, 1977, pp. 232–4.

women to devote themselves to their own families. Their withdrawal from field work led to a temporary labour crisis for plantation owners which was largely resolved through the institutions of sharecropping and tenant farming where many women farmed with their husbands less from choice than from either compulsion or necessity. Landowners sometimes refused to let land to families unless the wife worked in the field, thus forcing the women to work if the family were to farm at all. Though many of these women would not have been counted as farmers (which was also true of white women who worked farms with their husbands), their labour helped to maintain the family standard of living, and they frequently took in sewing or washing besides.[26]

As with most black women, both the white and the black women engaged in the western migration which populated the United States, combined productive labour with childcare and a wide range of responsibilities *en route* and once they had arrived at their new homes. Their preparations for the journey might include weaving the cloth top for the wagon which would be the family home for the long trek westward. They prepared the food, clothing and medicines. Girls and boys acted as outriders, herding the livestock that their parents took with them to their new homes.[27] Once in the new territory, farm women helped to build as well as manage their homes. Though men's and women's tasks were separate, women frequently did much of the field work at least in the early stages of settlement or when the men took paying jobs. The daughter of a railway foreman, Irma Ingram grew up in the all-black farming community of Dearfield, Colorado. Her mother and her older brother worked the land while her father brought in a cash income. Her mother would put food on to cook before she went into the field, attending to it between milking cows and working in the

26. Catherine Clinton, *The Other Civil War. American Women in the Nineteenth Century*, New York, Hill & Wang, 1984, pp. 88–9; Sterling, *We are your Sisters*, pp. 322–6; Dolores E. Janiewski, *Sisterhood Denied. Race, Gender and Class in a New South Community*, Philadelphia, Temple University Press, 1985, pp. 12–13.

27. For the westward migration experience see Glenda Riley, *Frontierswoman. The Iowa Experience*, Ames, Iowa, Iowa State University Press, 1981, which contains an extensive critique of the stereotyped way historians have viewed pioneer women. Also Sandra L. Myers, *Westering Women and the Frontier Experience 1800–1915*, Albuquerque, University of New Mexico Press, 1982; Julie Roy Jeffrey, *Frontier Women. The Trans-Mississippi West, 1840–1880*, New York, Hill & Wang, 1979; Lillian Schlissel, *Women's Diaries of the Westward Journey*, New York, Shocken Books, 1982; Christine Fischer (ed.), *Let Them Speak for Themselves. Women in the American West, 1849–1900*, Hamden, Conn., Archon Books, 1977.

fields. Though most women migrated west with their families, some single women and female heads of households homesteaded in their own right, something not possible until the Homestead Act of 1862.[28] Other single women moved to the frontier in search of work. Increased mechanisation and specialisation of agriculture lessened women's contributions to the family farm economy, but this tended to be a more significant factor in the twentieth century. As the consumer goods became available from mail order catalogues rural women, too, became consumers rather than producers.[29]

The westward migration displaced large numbers of Native Americans and Hispanics, both because the United States government violated its agreements with the original inhabitants of the land and because settled agriculture and the practices of the new settlers disrupted the environment. The sexual division of labour among Native American peoples differed from that of the European immigrants in a number of ways. Women were the principal agriculturalists in many of the tribes, a practice the American government tried to break down early in the nineteenth century. The Commissioner of Indian Affairs ignored the agricultural role of Cherokee women in the 1830s when he described their society as a hunting society because the men hunted. He instructed that the men be taught to farm while the women were to learn spinning and weaving. Land occupied by Native Americans became 'public domain' as the federal government extended its control westwards, invalidating many Hispanic land claims and pushing Native Americans onto inhospitable marginal land. In many Hispanic communities women tried to hold the family farm together as the men sought jobs which would help their families pay the taxes imposed by the new government. The women and men of these groups all suffered the disruption of their ways of life, but together endeavoured to create a viable existence despite the presence of the newcomers.[30]

28. Jensen, *With these Hands*, pp. 93–177; John Mack Faragher, *Women and Men on the Overland Trail*, New Haven, Conn., Yale University Press, 1979 contradicts the notion that pioneering life created sexual equality.

29. On agricultural mechanisation, see Glenda Riley, 'Farm Women's Roles in the Agricultural Development of South Dakota', *South Dakota History* 13 (Spring/Summer 1983), pp. 83–121 and Corlann G. Bush, 'The Barn is his, the House is mine. Agricultural Technology and Sex Roles', in George H. Daniels and Mark H. Rose (eds), *Energy and Transport. Historical Perspectives on Policy Issues*, Beverly Hills, Sage Publications, 1982.

30. Glenda Riley, *Women and Indians on the Frontier, 1825–1914*, Albuquerque, University of New Mexico Press, 1984; Jensen, *With these Hands*, Part I; Patricia Albers and Beatrice Medicine, *The Hidden Half. Studies of Plains Indian Women*,

Women's Employment, 1880–1920

About 10 per cent of all white women had paying jobs in 1860 and almost all black women worked, though the vast majority were enslaved and received no compensation for their labours. By 1880 about 16 per cent of all women were in the labour force. Although the proportion of black women in the labour force fell sharply immediately after the Civil War, it rose sharply after 1870, and their labour force participation rates remained much higher than those of either native- or foreign-born white women until well into the twentieth century. In 1900 the employment figures for all women had risen to 21 per cent and climbed to 25 per cent in 1910. The labour force participation rates for black women were 40 per cent in 1890, rising to 44 per cent by 1920. The comparable figures for native-born white women were 15 and 23 per cent, while for foreign-born white women they were 20 and 19 per cent. The percentage increase was greatest among native-born white women, which, as we shall see below, reflects the increase in what would now be termed white-collar and professional jobs.[31]

The proportion of gainfully employed women in 1920 fell to 23 per cent, which has led some authorities to maintain that the peak 1910 figures represented an overcount. Other historians have examined the instructions to the census enumerators and found that those given in 1910 encouraged the inclusion of women, opining that 'the occupation, if any, followed by a child, of any age, or by a woman, is just as important, for census purposes, as the occupation followed by a man. Therefore it must never be taken for granted, without inquiry that a woman or child has no occupation'. By contrast, the 1920 census, which recorded a decline in the number of women in the labour force, told census takers to record no occupation for the woman 'who works only occasionally or only a short time each day at outdoor farm or garden work, or in caring for livestock or poultry . . .'[32] These instructions highlight the importance of the

Washington, DC, University Press of America, 1983; Elaine Goodale Eastman, *Sister to the Sioux. The Memoirs of Elaine Goodale Eastman*, Lincoln, University of Nebraska Press, 1978; Mario T. Garcia, 'The Chicana in American History. The Mexican Women of El Paso, 1880–1920: A Case Study', *Pacific Historical Review* 49 (May 1980), pp. 315–38.

31. United States Bureau of the Census, *Statistics of Women at Work*, Washington, DC, Government Printing Office, 1907; Joseph Hill, *Women in Gainful Occupations, 1870–1920*, Census Monograph IX, Washington, DC, Government Printing Office, 1929.

quality of data collection for historians and other researchers and suggest that official statistics may not always reflect the actual activities of women.

One important characteristic of women's employment in the industrial era was the concentration of female workers in a few main occupations. In 1870, four-fifths of all women worked in agriculture or as domestic servants; by 1900 this proportion had dropped to 58 per cent and by 1920 it had fallen to 47 per cent.[33] Although a small number of women could be found in most job categories including a few in heavy industry, the vast majority at the turn of the century still worked as domestic servants, dressmakers, operatives in textile, apparel, and knitting mills or factories, teachers, secretaries, or nurses. These occupations were overwhelmingly staffed by women. Valerie Kincaid Oppenheimer has analysed the segregation of the male and female labour markets in the twentieth century and found that men and women have separate job markets and rarely compete directly against each other for work. This trend was strong at the turn of the century and, if anything, grew stronger until the middle of the twentieth century, although it was temporarily reversed during the world wars when the needs of the wartime economy led government and employers to accept women in what had previously been men's jobs and which returned to being men's jobs after the emergency ended.[34]

The First World War brought women into unconventional jobs only when labour shortages made it apparent to government and industry alike that unless female workers were used the nation could not pursue the war effort. A few black women penetrated the colour line into industrial work, but the war did little to break down stereotypes. Thus Mexican American women found few jobs outside agricultural labour; Native American women spent the war on isolated reservations; and Asian women's employment remained concentrated in the most marginal jobs. After the war women were pushed from the new jobs in the automobile and aircraft industries but not from traditional ones in food processing, garment, textile,

---

32. Valerie Kincaid Oppenheimer, *The Female Labor Force in the United States. Demographic and Economic Factors Governing its Growth and Changing Composition* Berkeley, University of California Press, 1970. pp. 68–69.

33. Hill, *Women in Gainful Occupations, passim.*

34. Campbell makes this point most emphatically. See also Karen Anderson, *Wartime Women*, London, Greenwood Press, 1981 and Susan Hartmann, *The Home Front and Beyond. American Women in the 1940s*, Boston, Mass., Twayne Publishers, 1982.

and office work. Employment opportunities for minority women contracted quickly, negating the few gains they had made during the war.[35]

Women's labour force participation, as measured by the census, was highest in urban areas, but there was great variation even among cities in the proportion of women with jobs. Cities dominated by heavy industry had fewer female workers and these tended to be concentrated in domestic service occupations. Those at the other end of the employment spectrum specialising in textile, shoe, or clothing manufacturing, had much higher proportions of women workers and comparatively few domestic servants. Pittsburgh, Pennsylvania exemplified the first type of city. In 1900, when 27 per cent of all women in the larger American cities worked, the proportion in Pittsburgh was 22 per cent. This contrasts sharply with Lowell and Fall River, Massachusetts, where 45 per cent of all women had jobs. About half the women workers in Pittsburgh and other centres of heavy industry toiled in private households at the turn of the century, while between three-fifths and three-quarters of the women in the cotton mill towns worked in the mills and less than 10 per cent were private household workers. Nationally, about 40 per cent of all women workers had domestic service jobs at this time.[36]

Female employment patterns in northern cities presented a sharp contrast to those in the south, where the proportion of women in the labour force was high and so were the numbers concentrated in the domestic service sector of the economy. About half of all women workers in southern cities were black, but they comprised between three-quarters and four-fifths of all servants in these cities in 1900. The black woman's employment cycle differed from that of her white counterpart in one significant way: she was more likely to stay in the labour force after marriage. In 1900 less than 4 per cent of all married white women held jobs, rising to about 7 per cent in 1920, while more than one-quarter of their black counterparts were employed in 1900 and nearly one-third were in 1920. These are national figures; those for urban areas only would be somewhat

35. Maurine Greenwald, *Women, War and Work. The Impact of World War I on Women Workers in the United States*, Westport, Conn., Greenwood Press, 1980; William J. Breen, 'Black Women and the Great War: Mobilization and Reform in the South', *Journal of Southern History* 44 (August, 1978), pp. 421–40.

36. For an expanded analysis of this point see S.J. Kleinberg *The Shadow of the Mills. Working Class Women and the Family Economy, Pittsburgh 1870–1907*, Pittsburgh, University of Pittsburgh Press, 1989.

Retrieving Women's History

higher.[37]

Factory and manufaturing employments were next in importance to domestic service as occupations for women throughout the latter decades of the nineteenth and early years of the twentieth centuries. In 1880 one-fourth of the female labour force was in manufacturing and mechanical industries, the proportion increasing slightly at the turn of the century, then falling to 22 per cent by 1920. This employment was limited to white women in the north, although some black women worked in the tobacco factories in the south. Most industrial women workers laboured in the textile, clothing, cigar, tobacco and food industries. These categories accounted for four-fifths of all women industrial workers in 1880, a proportion which declined to about three-quarters at the turn of the century, and to two-thirds by 1920. Some women also worked in steam laundries, the metal and glass trades, making paper boxes and in other scattered industries.[38] As was suggested above for the textile industry, an increased use of machinery affected the way these jobs were done as well as shifting their location from inside the home into the factory. Jobs were divided into their component parts, making it possible to substitute unskilled or semiskilled workers using machines for skilled labour. The pace of production increased as piece rates forced workers to speed up output in order to maintain their incomes.[39]

Of the numerous examples of the way in which mechanisation changed the manufacturing process one or two must suffice here. The invention of the sewing machine in 1846 made it possible for garments to be assembled more quickly, for heavier materials to be sewn, and for less skilled workers to enter the garment industry. Factory production meant closer supervision of workers by their employers. The shoe and clothing industries demonstrate different facets of these long-term shifts. The introduction of the sewing machine into the shoe industry revolutionised shoe production. Before mid-century the family had been the basic work unit; fathers

37. See David Katzman, *Seven Days a Week. Women and Domestic Service in Industrializing America*, New York, Oxford University Press, 1976; on black servants see Elizabeth Pleck, 'A Mother's Wages. Income Earning among Married Italian and Black Women, 1896–1911', in Nancy Cott and Elizabeth Pleck (eds), *A Heritage of Her Own*, New York, Simon & Schuster, 1979.
38. Elizabeth Butler, *Women and the Trades. Pittsburgh 1907–1908*, New York, Russell Sage Foundation, 1909.
39. Edith Abbott, *Women in Industry*, New York, Appleton & Company, 1910; Baker, *Technology and Woman's Work*.

and sons attached the sole and heel to the uppers while mothers and daughters sewed the uppers and did fancy stitching. The use of machinery (in this case the sewing machine) moved production from workrooms which were part of the shoemaking families' homes to the factory, where single women and single and married men worked. Workers now had to arrive at a specified time, to keep pace with the production process, and to work regular hours. There was no place for married women in the new industry which made them financially dependent upon their husbands and their children and contributed to the growing assumption that a married woman's place was in the home although the rest of the world had moved into workplaces outside it.[40]

The factory production of clothing also displaced married women, though not to the same extent as in the shoe industry. While the majority of clothing workers at the turn of the century were single, many married immigrant women also sewed, though the numbers are hard to judge because census takers rarely recorded their efforts. Rising productivity undercut already low wage levels, displacing workers and increasing the competition for work. First men's, then women's clothing moved into the factory and later the sweatshop. Where seamstresses had previously made entire garments, they now did one repetitive task, sewing buttonholes, seams, or hems all day long. They were squeezed mercilessly by contractors whose profit margins depended upon keeping labour costs to a minimum. Some manufacturers charged their employees for the needles and thread they used; others assessed them for the electricity which powered their sewing machines. Fines for lateness or supposedly shoddy work were also common. By the turn of the century working conditions in the garment industry had become a national scandal, culminating in the Triangle Shirtwaist Factory fire in New York City in 1911 in which 146 women burned to death because the owners had locked the exit doors.[41]

Women workers did not accept these conditions passively, although they found it harder to organise themselves into trade unions than did men because they tended to stay in the labour force for a brief

40. Wertheimer, *We Were There*, ch. 6; Alan Dawley, *Class and Community: The Industrial Revolution in Lynn* Cambridge, Mass., Harvard University Press, 1976.
41. Ava Baron, and Susan E. Klepp, '''If I didn't have my Sewing Machine . . .'', Women and Sewing Machine Technology', in Joan Jensen and Sue Davidson, *A Needle, a Bobbin, a Strike. Women Needleworkers in America*, Philadelphia, Temple University Press, 1984.

period and so were a younger, less experienced group of workers; in addition, women encountered hostility from both their employers and their male co-workers when they attempted to unionise. Women workers were rarely able to move up the occupational hierarchies, so their wages were invariably lower than men's, making it much more difficult for them to sustain themselves if they went on strike. Moreover, women workers tended to be drawn from the poorest segments of society; their families usually depended upon their financial contributions and could ill afford to have them interrupted by a daughter going on strike or being blacklisted for her trade union activities. Despite these impediments and hostility from many male co-workers and trade unionists, women did form a number of unions and organisations to improve their lot. About 3 per cent of all industrial women workers belonged to unions in 1900, a figure which rose to nearly 7 per cent by 1920, a time when about 20 per cent of the entire male labour force were union members.[42]

Sewing women petitioned the federal government during the Civil War to change the system of distributing work on army uniforms so that government subcontractors could not victimise them. The seamstresses and sympathetic philanthropists and newspaper editors formed the Working Women's Protective Union in New York City, and similar organisations appeared in other large cities. The WWPU provided legal services to working women whose employers refused to pay their wages and acted as an employment bureau, but it did not function as a trade union directly agitating for higher wages or better working conditions. In contrast, the collar laundry workers of Troy, New York, formed a union which fought successfully for higher wages with support from the male iron-moulders' union. When the employers attempted to lock the women out for belonging to a union, they formed their own collar-making and laundering cooperative. The invention of the paper shirt collar and a boycott by manufacturers led to the demise of the cooperative and the laundry workers' union.[43]

42. Alice Kessler-Harris, 'Where are the Organized Women Workers?', in Cott and Pleck, *A Heritage of Her Own*, pp. 343–466; James J. Kenneally, *Women and American Trade Unions*, Montreal, Eden Press Women's Publications, 1981.

43. Nancy Schrom Dye, *As Equals and as Sisters. Feminism, the Labor Movement, and the Women's Trade Union League of New York*, Columbia, University of Missouri Press, 1980; Carole Turbin, 'And we are nothing but Women. Irish Working Women in Troy', in Carole Ruth Berkin and Mary Beth Norton (eds), *Women of America. A History*, Boston, Mass., Houghton Mifflin, 1979. pp. 202–19.

The late nineteenth and early twentieth centuries were a period of great collective activity for women in industrial occupations. Women printers, shoemakers, cotton and woollen mill operatives, book-binders, cigarmakers, and seamstresses formed unions on their own or tried to join existing male unions either as separate branches or in male locales. While it is not possible to recount the diversity of women's unionising efforts, the efforts of women in the garment industry, the most organised sector of the female labour force, demonstrate both the difficulties women encountered in their attempts to improve their employment situation and their successes. The decades between 1890 and the First World War witnessed vigorous activism by women in the needle trades seeking higher wages, improved working conditions, and an end to the subcontracting process. Manufacturers gave work to the lowest bidder, who then hired workers to do the work as cheaply as possible, his profit depending directly upon keeping labour costs to a minimum. These women, many of them recent immigrants from Southern and Eastern Europe, participated in more than 6,000 strikes between 1881 and 1926, with particular success in the New York and Chicago garment industries. Women shirtwaist-makers led a series of strikes which revitalised the International Ladies' Garment Workers' Union. In 1909, 20,000 women garment workers went out on strike against the New York City clothing makers over the opposition of the male union leadership. But in other cases women tried to join unions only to find that the leadership rejected their applications or set dues so high as to prohibit their paying them.[44]

It is obvious that employers would not welcome working women's efforts to obtain higher wages, shorter working hours, and better working conditions. Women represented an inexpensive source of labour, which employers regarded as more docile and manageable than men. Most employers did not take the view held by at least some economists that higher wages would increase the overall demand for products; they were more concerned with shaving their labour costs in order to increase short-term profits. It is less clear why male trade unionists were at best ambivalent and frequently downright hostile

44. See 'The Great Uprisings: 1900–1920', in Jensen and Davidson, *A Needle*; Kessler-Harris, 'Where are the Organized Women Workers?' On the ILGWU see Louis Levine, *Women's Garment Workers. A History of the International Ladies Garment Workers Union*, New York, B.W. Huebsch Inc, 1924; and Melvin Dubofsky, *When Workers Organize. New York City in the Progressive Era* Amherst, University of Massachusetts Press, 1968. Philip S. Foner, *Women and Trade Unions to the First World War*, New York, Free Press, 1979.

to women's efforts to improve their situation. Despite what we know today about labour market segmentation between the sexes, many male workers believed that women represented a threat to their jobs, that employers would introduce machinery which could be operated by less skilled workers (women, immigrants, blacks), that their skills would be debased, and, ultimately, their jobs would be lost and the entire working class would suffer. They also accepted prevailing notions about appropriate economic and social roles for women, believing that females should depend upon males and stay in the home.[45]

Most male trade unionists inhabited a world in which, despite the factory production of many goods, there was still a lot of work to be done in the home in order to maintain a comfortable environment. By the beginning of the twentieth century many middle-class women had acquired various forms of household technology which decreased the amount of work performed in their homes. This, coupled with the declining birth rate and the continued employment of domestic servants, resulted in leisure time which many middle-class women and their daughters devoted to worthy causes and social activities. But except at the very upper reaches labouring households had not yet acquired indoor plumbing, gas cooking stoves, or electricity, all of which had become standard in middle-class homes, certainly by the First World War. The household duties of working-class women actually increased in order to meet the rising standards of cleanliness and to combat the dirt and grime of industrial cities. Family service replaced production as the domestic task of all women in these years, but working-class women performed the work themselves where middle-class women had technological and human assistants. Many working-class women took boarders into their homes in order to make ends meet at the direct expense of any leisure time they might have had, since only the best paid labouring men could actually support their families on a single income.[46]

45. On the mindset of male industrial workers see, in particular, David Montgomery, *Worker Control in Industrial America*, New York, Cambridge University Press, 1979; Herbert Gutman, *Work, Culture and Society in Industrializing America. Essays in American Working-Class and Social History*, New York, Random House, 1977; and Francis G. Couvares, *The Remaking of Pittsburgh. Class and Culture in an Industrializing City, 1899–1919*, Albany, NY, State University of New York Press, 1984.

46. Kleinberg, 'Technology and Women's Work' and 'Escalating Standards. Women, Housework and Household Technology in the Twentieth Century', in

At this time most trade unionists were skilled workers who opposed or were indifferent to the organisation of the unskilled, who believed immigrant workers were a threat to their jobs, and who believed women worked for pin money. They came from the most affluent segment of the working class, their wives and daughters were unlikely to be in the labour force or to take in boarders. They believed that 'female labour should be limited so as not to injure the motherhood and family life of a nation'. Increasingly they advocated a family wage and a world view in which the man was the breadwinner while the woman stayed at home to tend the domestic fires. Most women workers were both unskilled and immigrants, thus embodying those groups most distrusted by the more affluent workers. In both 1893 and 1914, the American Federation of Labor's annual conventions passed resolutions opposing the presence of women in the labour force. Male trade unionists in the AFL agitated for higher wages for men so that they could support their families without the assistance of additional wage earners, in other words to enhance their privileged position within the work place by eliminating potential competition from other workers. They chose to protect their own jobs, perceiving women workers as a threat to their wage standards and job security. Married women were seen as a particular threat because, by definition, they had husbands who could support them. Social reformers also supported the concept of the family wage, believing that this would ensure greater stability within working-class families. The ultimate result of this family wage ideology was to prohibit the employment of married women, which was exactly what many state and local governments did during the Great Depression.[47]

Despite the obstacles placed in their way, some women did succeed in joining or forming unions in this era. Women formed the majority of members in the International Ladies Garment Workers Union although they were poorly represented in the union hierarchy. Other women turned to the Women's Trade Union League,

Frank J. Coppa and Richard Harmond (eds), *Twentieth Century Technology*, Dubuque, Iowa, Kendall Hunt, 1983; Ruth Schwartz Cowan, *More Work for Mother. The Ironies of Household Technology from the Open Hearth to the Microwave*, New York, Basic Books Inc, 1983.

47. Martha May, 'Bread before Roses. American Workingmen, Labor Unions and the Family Wage', in Ruth Milkman (ed.), *Women, Work and Protest. A Century of US Women's Labour History*, London, Routledge & Kegan Paul, 1985; also Ruth Milkman, 'Women's Work and the Economic Crisis', in Cott and Pleck, *A Heritage of her Own*, pp. 507–41.

formed in 1903 as an alliance between working women and middle-class reformers. The WTUL hoped to promote cross class cooperation at the same time as agitating for better working conditions and assisting women on strike. Like other reformist groups it supported protective legislation for women, motivated by the appalling conditions under which many women worked and their apparent inability to improve those conditions by collective bargaining.[48] Many members of the WTUL believed that the power of the state should be used to protect women, as a group, because they were weaker than men and the sorts of work they did harmed their health and fertility. In 1908 the United States Supreme Court accepted the premise that women's weaknesses deserved legislative protection when it upheld the validity of an Oregon law limiting the number of hours which women could work because their 'physical stature and the performance of maternal functions' placed them at a disadvantage.[49]

By 1917 most states regulated the hours women could work, but some industries were exempt, and the laws did not apply to agricultural or domestic workers. Protective legislation, moreover, could be used to 'protect' women out of certain jobs altogether. The Iron-Moulders wanted New York State to outlaw female employment in foundries as hazardous to women's health. Women printers found the provisions against night work barred them from lucrative jobs. In some cases men's hours of labour were also reduced and working conditions improved, but in others employers simply refused to hire women rather than be bothered with the restrictions placed on women workers.[50] Protective legislation can be seen, therefore, as a two-edged sword: it might be used to improve working conditions for all or to prevent women from working altogether.

Women White Collar Workers

At the same time that women were trying to organise to protect

48. Robin Miller Jacoby, 'The Women's Trade Union League and American Feminism', *Feminist Studies* 3 (1976), pp. 126–40.

49. Kessler-Harris, *Out to Work*, ch. 7; Judith A. Baer, *The Chains of Protection. The Judicial Response to Women's Labor Legislation*, Westport, Conn., Greenwood Press, 1973,

50. Elizabeth Faulker Baker, *Protective Labor Legislation with Special Reference*

themselves in the factories the changing nature of the economy opened up jobs to them in the white collar and service sectors, where working conditions were less hazardous. The number of women professional workers (teachers, nurses, librarians, and social workers, in particular) and white collar workers (secretaries, stenographers, bookkeepers, retail sales clerks, and telephone operators) all increased dramatically as professional, trade, and business activity expanded in the late nineteenth and early twentieth centuries. The proportion of women working as teachers and trained nurses went up from 7 per cent in 1880 to 12 per cent in 1920. The white collar trades gained even more; in 1880 about 3 per cent of all women workers wore white blouses to work; by 1920, fully 27 per cent of all women in the labour force were in this category. The number of women in clerical occupations alone rose from 7,040 in 1880 to 1,421,925 in 1920, a two-hundred fold increase.[51].

Both professional and white collar workers tended to have more education than women factory or domestic workers. This certainly was the case for the few women scientists who fought against great odds to gain admission to graduate schools. The number of nursing schools expanded rapidly at the beginning of the twentieth century. Normal schools for training teachers also increased at this time, raising the level of education available to women. Professional social workers and librarians also needed college educations. Many white collar workers in this era received at least one or two years of high school, typically in the commercial rather than the academic department of the high schools which were opening up in all urban and many rural areas.[52]

Young women who wanted more education than the minimum demanded by state laws (typically to about 12 or 14 in northern states, but few southern states had mandatory school attendance laws until later in the twentieth century) could only stay on at school if their families were willing to forego the income or services these daughters might provide. Poorer families living on the edge of

to *Women in the State of New York*, New York, AMS Press, 1969. Reprint of 1925 edition.

51. Hill, *Women in Gainful Occupations, passim.*

52. Margaret Rossiter, *Women Scientists in America. Struggles and Strategies to 1940*, Baltimore, Md., Johns Hopkins University Press, 1982; Dee Garrison, *Apostles of Culture. Public Librarians and American History*, New York, The Free Press, 1979; Mabel Newcomer, *A Century of Higher Education for Women*, New York, Harper & Row, 1959; Redding S. Sugg, *Mother Teachers. The Feminization of American Education*, Charlottesville, University of Virginia Press, 1978.

subsistence at the turn of the century could rarely afford the luxury of additional schooling for their children. Most of those going to high school and college were therefore from middle-class or skilled working-class families. This impeded the progress of immigrant and lower echelon working-class daughters into the new jobs that were opening up as stores, offices, and educational and welfare institutions proliferated. Employer prejudice also restricted the entry of these women. Most sales jobs went to native-born white women or those of Irish or German parentage in 1900. These women also dominated the teaching profession; although some black women managed to get positions in the segregated schools of the south they found it more difficult to obtain work in the supposedly integrated schools of the north. In the post-bellum decades growing numbers of black women obtained secondary and higher education; the number of black women schoolteachers rose from a handful immediately after the Civil War to 13,524 in 1900 and 22,547 in 1920. Black women found it particularly difficult to gain entry either to medical or nursing schools. There were a few hundred black nurses, mostly graduates of black hospital training programmes. White hospitals would not hire them, nor would the army or the Red Cross, but they did find employment in black hospitals and as private duty nurses.[53]

Almost all female professional workers at the beginning of the twentieth century could be found in the rapidly expanding occupations of teaching, nursing, librarians, and social workers, but where men and women overlapped, as they did in libraries, schools, and welfare departments, few women supervised men or had places at the top of their occupational hierarchies. Thus women teachers predominated in elementary schools, but there were many fewer in the secondary schools where most administrative positions were held by men, and fewer still in colleges and universities. The exception to this came in girls' schools and women's colleges, where the faculties and administrations were more likely to have women on them, highlighting the importance of all-female institutions in providing role models for girls and opportunities for women. Simi-

53. See Sterling, *We Are Your Sisters*, Parts III and IV and Susan Reverby, 'Neither for the Drawing Room nor for the Kitchen', Nancy Tomes, 'Little World of our own', Barbara, Melosh, 'More than the Physicians Hand and Hine', Mabel K. Darline, 'Staupers and the Integration of Black Nurses into the Armed Forces', all in Judith Walzer Leavitt, (ed.), *Women and Health in America*, Madison, Wis., University of Wisconsin Press, 1984.

larly, most librarians were female, but few worked in the major academic libraries or research collections. Virtually all social workers in 1890 were women, but as the number of trained social workers increased, so, too, did the proportion of men, especially in administrative and policy making positions.[54] All this suggests that even though the absolute number of women professionals increased, they remained segregated by type of occupation or relegated to the lower echelons where their employment overlapped with men's. Women professionals also found it extremely difficult to keep their jobs if they married. Most school boards fired teachers once they married and scarcely any would permit pregnant teachers to work. Women professionals therefore either gave up their jobs if they wished to have a family life, or they resigned themselves to remaining single if they wished to continue in their chosen careers.[55]

Women moving into the burgeoning white collar jobs – telephone operators, office workers, sales assistants and so on – endured a high level of control over their behaviour on the job. Department store employees frequently worked a ten to twelve hour day, six days a week, but were not permitted to sit down. Since they were expected to be decorative as well as functional dress codes were instituted. Women in these occupations also found few opportunities for promotion and wages were kept low by competition for jobs which were thought to be more respectable than factory work. Efficiency experts subdivided these jobs into their component parts, routinising them in the expectation that output would increase. In some offices, one group of women did nothing but file letters or documents all day long, while another group typed them or took dictation. Employers not only expected women to do these jobs efficiently, they also demanded that they have pleasing personalities and be cheerful while perfoming their repetitive tasks.[56]

Conclusion

Over the course of the nineteenth century, the location of women's work changed from inside the home, where it was performed with

54. Roy Lubove, *The Professional Altruist. The Emergence of Social Work as a Career, 1880–1930*, Cambridge, Mass., Harvard University Press, 1965.
55. Wertheimer, *We Were There*, ch. 13
56. Margery W. Davies, *Woman's Place is at the Typewriter. Office Work and Office Workers 1870–1930*, Philadelphia, Temple University Press, 1982.

family members to external locations, where it involved working in large groups of strangers. Both before and after this transition the work done by women was primarily defined not by individual interests or aptitude but by gender, the social conception of women's roles and their presumed nature. Women who tried to deviate from their gender roles encountered extreme hostility. Those who wanted or needed to combine wage earning with caring for a family found themselves relegated to the most marginal, poorly remunerated activities. Women competed against each other for a small number of jobs; they had difficulty getting the training or education which would have permitted them to diversify their occupations. The supply of available female workers throughout this era exceeded the demand for them, lowering wages for all women. Despite these obstacles the number of women in the labour force increased steadily, testifying to women's desire to work. The proportion of married women in the labour force remained much lower than that of single women, but it, too, increased during these years. Not all women workers were enthusiastic members of the labour force; many worked because of dire family poverty. Women of colour and those from recent immigrant groups inhabited the most marginal sectors of the labour force, meeting even more prejudice and having a much more limited range of occupations open to them. As production moved outside the household, the home and the women within it became identified with domesticity to the exclusion of other activities or interests. This in turn has been used to define and limit the activities of women to the home or to the most peripheral areas of the labour force.

Part III

Women, the State and Politics

Introduction to Part III

Prescriptive writings on women's role and status are a feature of many early legal codes and religious documents, although the relationship between women, families and the community or state has varied dramatically in tribal, feudal, pre-industrial and industrial societies. One of the most difficult areas in the study of gender relations is to understand why this is the case and why, in most, but not all societies women seem to be defined as the 'other', as outsiders against whom legal and religious codes must be written, whose behaviour must be controlled, and whose status must be defined.

While political writings on the relationship between the family and the state can be dated back to Plato, the first written rejoinder by a woman which has been preserved seems to be that of Christine de Pisan who lived in France in the late fourteenth century and who defended women against the growing misogyny of her time. There are some scholars who see this as the origins of feminism and trace subsequent activism on behalf of women to these beginnings, but feminism and public roles for women were not limited to Europe. There was a small feminist movement in Brazil in the nineteenth century as well as a rather larger one in the United States. Women in other countries at this time also began protesting against their limited rights. Women established charitable foundations in mid-sixteenth Istanbul, while many women who later pursued more diverse, non-domestic roles for women began their public careers by performing good works, for example by organising philanthropic ventures. In some countries this behaviour had a radicalising impact upon its practitioners, leading them to desire broader roles for women. In others, where such impulses might be channelled through religious orders, there was little carry over from philanthropy to other activities, although women's monastic communities have, at times, wielded economic power.

The extent to which women participated in the activities of state or community has varied greatly although it seems to be the case until

217

modern times that the more settled and state-directed a society becomes, the closer the control over women's public endeavours and, correspondingly, the less political power they exercise. But even here there are exceptions. Occasionally queens in Africa or Europe had great political power, but this came to them as individuals rather than as women. The women of pre-colonial Dahomey participated in public life on a regular basis to an extent matched in few cultures. Although these unusual instances could be replicated in many regions of the world to show similar, sporadic examples of powerful women, the overall situation of women until recently has been one of legal inequality and marginal political participation.

The essays in this section examine political history, considering women's political rights and participation in the political process in a variety of geo-cultural regions. In the first essay, Deniz Kandiyoti looks at the crucial shifts regarding the 'woman question' which took place during the process of transition from the Ottoman Empire to the modern Turkish Republic. She argues that the emancipation of women occupied a strategic place in the redefinition away from an Islamic state, as 'conservatives' and 'modernists' made the woman question into a symbolic battle-ground for their respective visions of a new society.

Marietta Stepaniants gives an overview of the formal political status of women in the Soviet Union, charting attempts to move from the view of the old Russian proverb that, 'A hen is not a bird; a woman is not a person' towards a genuine civic equality, and describing some of the obstacles which have been encountered in the process. As Lenin pointed out, 'equality before the law is not necessarily equality in fact.' Ida Blom makes the same point as she traces the slow development of women's political participation in Norway from the nineteenth century until the 1970s. She argues that much of the credit for the subsequent increase in women's involvement – which meant that in 1986 40 per cent of the country's government ministers, including the Prime Minister, were women – should lie with the new women's movement. The feminist movement recognised that more than formal equality was required to enable women to participate effectively; for example, the unequal work-load between men and women in the family as well as in society must be adjusted.

In Uruguay, as described by Villamil and Sapriza, women attained the vote, after a long struggle, in 1932. But this signalled the collapse of the independent feminist movement, and here too, despite the removal of legal obstacles to women's participation in state politics, social factors have continued to restrict their involvement.

218

11

From Empire to Nation State: Transformations of the Woman Question in Turkey

DENIZ KANDIYOTI

Among the countries of the Middle East and Europe Turkey stands out as a Republic that has addressed the question of women's emancipation early, explicitly and extensively through legislative reforms initiated by Mustafa Kemal Ataturk, the founder of the modern Turkish state. The Turkish civil code adopted in 1926 outlawed polygamy, gave equal rights of divorce to both partners and rights of child custody to both parents. Women's enfranchisement soon followed and women were granted the vote in local elections in 1930 and at the national level in 1934.

The meaning, place and political necessity of these reforms has been the subject of a great deal of comment and controversy.[1] The almost exclusive focus on Kemalist reforms has tended, however, to obscure the fact that the 'woman question' has been central to the different ideological and political reactions to the dissolution of the empire in the latter half of the nineteenth century and the beginning of the twentieth. Since the eighteenth century the Ottoman empire had been increasingly unable to hold its own against either Western economic/military supremacy or the rise of nationalist, secessionist movements in its provinces. This weakening of Ottoman power

1. First generation Kemalist women writers have stressed the inevitability of these reforms in the context of Republican ideology. See for instance Inan Afet, *Turk Tarihi Boyunca Turk Kadininin Hak ve Gorevleri*, Anakara, Turk Tarih Kurumu, 1969. More recently, the strategic importance of women's emancipation both in dissociating the Republic from the theocratic remnants of the Ottoman state and in establishing proofs of democratisation *vis-à-vis* the West have received increased attention. See Tekeli Sirin, *Kadinlar ve Siyasal Toplumsal Hayat*, Istanbul, Birikim Yayinlari, 1982.

ushered in a period of search and redefinition in the nineteenth century which lasted until the First World War and culminated in the birth of the Turkish Republic in 1923.[2] It is particularly over this period that the 'crisis' of Ottoman culture and of the Ottoman family system appeared on the political agenda. As a result women made an irreversible entry into political discourse as symbolic pawns in a complex ideological battleground. The aim of this chapter is to trace the development and transformations of the woman question in the period leading up to the Republic in an attempt to show how the treatment of this question closely paralleled successive realignments within the Ottoman/Turkish polity and reflected its changing political priorities.

By the time of the Second Constitutional Period in 1908 the relative merits of the Islamist, Ottomanist and Turkist solutions to the impasse of the Ottoman state had become a matter of public debate. The various (overwhelmingly male) advocates of the woman question also represented distinct ideological positions on a way out of the floundering empire. The dilemma posed by Westernisation and the need for 'progress' on the one hand, and the maintenance of Ottoman cultural integrity on the other, strongly coloured the debate on the status of women and infused the general polemic with high levels of emotionality. Very schematically, the Islamists saw the reasons for decay in the corruption and abandonment of Islamic law and institutions and advocated a return to the unadulterated application of the Sharia. Their political solution revolved around a pan-Islamic empire consolidated around the institution of the Caliphate. Although the adoption of Western technology was deemed acceptable in the military and economic spheres, Western culture must on no account be allowed to contaminate the values of Islam. Not surprisingly, the position of women came to represent the touchstone of such contamination and any attempts to discuss issues such as polygyny, veiling and unilateral male repudiation in divorce could be denounced as morally corrupt or irreligious.[3] This

---

2. For accounts of this process, see N. Berkes, *The Development of Secularism in Turkey*, Toronto, McGill University Press, 1964; S.J. Shaw and E.K. Shaw, *History of the Ottoman Empire and Modern Turkey*, vol. II, Cambridge, Cambridge University Press, 1977; B. Lewis, *The Emergence of Modern Turkey*, London, Oxford University Press, 1961; T. Timur, *Turk Devrimi: Tarihi Anlami ve Felsefi Temeli*, Ankara, Sevinc Matbaasi, 1968; I. Ortayli, *Imparatorlugun En Uzun Yuzyili*, Istanbul, Hil Yayin, 1983.

3. In this respect Caporal draws attention to the fact that unlike the Arab Middle East and Muslim Russia, where vigorous modernist Islamic currents could be seen,

contrasted sharply with the views of Westernists, who maintained that the superiority of the West resided not only in its technology but in its rationalistic, positivistic outlook, freed from the shackles of obscurantism and stifling superstition which stand in the way of progress. To varying degrees they held Islam responsible both for obscurantism and for what they saw as the debased position of women (which some went so far as pinpointing as the major symptom of Ottoman backwardness).[4] The Ottomanists had been trying to redress the balance between Westernism and traditionalism ever since the *Tanzimat* reforms by achieving an 'Ottoman' synthesis.[5] The most prominent figure among the Young Ottomans to address the woman question was the writer Namik Kemal, whose progressive approach could be said to emanate from a modernist Islamic perspective.[6]

Neither loyalty to Islam (actively mobilised during the reign of Abdulhamit II, 1876–1909) nor to the Ottoman cause had proved effective in stemming the tide of nationalism sweeping both the Christian and Arab provinces. By the turn of the century an Anatolian based, predominantly Turkish nation was becoming an established fact. The current of Turkism which lay the foundations of Kemalist nationalism played a key ideological role in ensuring the transition from an empire based on the multi-ethnic *millet* system to a nation state. It is within this current that we see the principal stirrings of feminism in Turkey – which have left their mark on all subsequent treatments of the woman question. The specific form and content of the discussion on women's emancipation under Ataturk's republic is thus directly traceable to the birth and development of Turkish nationalism. This point will be illustrated with particular reference to Ziya Gokalp, who is considered the main ideologue of Turkism and who has developed a clear and detailed position on the status of women. Whereas all earlier forms of

Ottoman Islam has remained more consistently conservative. See B. Caporal, *Kemalizmde ve Kemalizm Sonrasinda Turk Kadini*, Ankara, Turkiye Is Bankasi Kultur Yayinlari, 1982, p. 736.

4. Dr Abdullah Cevdet, the poet Tevfik Fikret, Celal Nuri (the author of *Dur Women*) and Salahattin Asim were among the most vocal proponents of this position.

5. S. Mardin, *The Genesis of Young Ottoman Though*, Princeton, NJ, Princeton University Press, 1962.

6. Namik Kemal was particularly critical of the more oppressive and unjust aspects of marriage and family life such as the unilateral repudiation of women, concubinage and matches without consent. The writer Sinasi also made the arranged marriage system a subject for satire in his *Sair Evlenmesi* ('The Poet's Wedding') in 1859.

feminist discourse emanated from an 'enlightened' Islamic perspective, the necessity for women's equality now became grounded in a new morality dictated by the Turkish nation. In what follows, what could be considered as the key moments in the transformation of the woman question in the Ottoman empire culminating in the birth of Turkish nationalism will be critically reviewed and analysed.

Westernisation and Secularisation: The Ottoman Reforms and their Aftermath

The decline of the Ottomans signalled by two centuries of military defeat and territorial retreat called for more radical reforms than had earlier attempts at modernisation which had been confined to the adoption of Western military technology, training and organisation. The *Tanzimat* period (1839–76) set the scene for extensive reforms in the fields of administration, legislation and education. These reforms have had far reaching consequences in that they were instrumental in the rise of a new class of Ottoman bureaucrats, relatively secure in their position within a secularised bureaucratic hierarchy, and weakened the overall political influence of the clergy (*ulema*) as well as its monopoly over the educational system. These reforms have been the subject of conflicting interpretations, denounced by some as total capitulation to the West and assessed by others as the foundation of all later developments in the creation of a secular state. There is little doubt that the Ottoman empire had suffered serious peripheralisation *vis-à-vis* European powers since the sixteenth century, so that the Tanzimat reforms can be seen as being primarily aimed at creating a central bureaucracy which could become an instrument of the smooth integration of the Ottoman state into the world economy.[7] Already the trend of capitalising upon Ottoman military misadventures to wrest trade concessions and force the lifting of tarriff barriers was well established.[8] Indeed, the official document that ushered in the Tanzimat, the Gulhane

7. H. Inan, 'Osmanli Tarihi ve Dunya Sistemi: Bir Degerlendirme', *Toplum Bilim* 23 (Autumn 1983), pp. 9–39.

8. For instance, Mahmut II's attempt to consolidate Ottoman central authority over the provinces brought him into conflict with Mehmet Ali, the powerful governor of Egypt, whome he was finally able to subjugate with Britain's naval and military support. The price of such support was the commercial treaty of 1838 which opened the vast Ottoman market to British manufacturers by lifting trade restrictions and tariff barriers.

Hatt-i Humayunu (Imperial Rescript of Gulhane) had as its net effect the extension of legal assurances to non-Muslim and non-Turkish mercantile groups affiliated to European commercial interests. The new role that the Tanzimat bureaucracy had to adopt meant that it had to articulate itself to the needs of what it saw as 'modernisation' and to the expectations of Western powers in a manner that alienated the groups and classes which were excluded from the new 'modernised' structures (such as craftsmen, artisans, the urban lower middle class, petty civil servants and not least the *ulema*) and in fact stood to lose from them. These classes were to become the focus of a resistance which often took Islamic forms. Thus the Tanzimat reforms were to create deep cleavages in Ottoman society which were reflected both at the institutional level and that of culture more generally.

An interesting case in point is the dual legal system which emerged in a series of attempts at both renovation and compromise. Despite the importation of numerous European laws in the Tanzimat period as well as Abdulhamit II's autocratic rule (1876–1909), the personal status code affecting women directly had been untouched by new legislation. The preparation of the Ottoman civic code (the *Mecelle*) by a commission headed by Cevdet Pasa represented a compromise between the adoption of a European code (an idea favoured by some) and the Sharia, by attempting a modern Ottoman code based on the Sharia. However, a religious opposition headed by the Sheyh-ul-Islam subsequently persuaded Abdulhamit to disband the commission which had only completed the legislation concerning debts and contracts thereby blocking any further changes in the fields of family and inheritance laws. It is significant, if understandable, that the traditionalists were claiming the sphere of personal status as their own. This created a dual juridical system whereby secular courts (mahkeme-i nizamiye) functioned under the aegis of the Ministry of Justice while religious courts (mahkeme-i ser'iyye) remained under the jurisdiction of the Sheyh-ul Islam. It was not until 1917 that family law would again be put on the agenda and the monopoly of religious authorities in this sphere challenged.

Nonetheless the Tanzimat introduced some modest legislative advances concerning women with the promulgation of the 1856 Land Law (Arazi Kanunu) granting equal rights of inheritance to daughters, and the ratification of a treaty abolishing slavery and concubinage. There were also some innovations in the field of women's education with midwifery courses offered at the Medical

School by European midwives since 1842, the beginning of secondary schooling for girls since 1858, of girls vocational schools in 1869 and of women's teacher training colleges in 1870. In her review of these advances Taskiran comments on the pressures resulting from the strict segregation of the sexes.[9] For instance, she mentions that because of the scarcity of trained female teachers all courses except for needlework had to be taught by elderly male teachers. In his opening speech to the teacher training school, the progressive Saffet Pasa, then Minister of Education, justified the need for such an institution by pointing out that, beyond the ages of nine or ten, girls could no longer be taught by male teachers. He also argued that segregation and veiling could not be an impediment to girls' education.

The *Tanzimat* period did not necessarily stand out as a period of substantial change in matters regarding women but rather as a period of intellectual ferment when ideas about Ottoman society, the family and the position of women started to be debated in a variety of forums and media, from the newspaper column to the novel. The cultural cleavages between a Western-looking bureaucratic élite and popular classes committed to and protected by Ottoman communitarian conservatism were reflected in key literary productions of the time in which the Westernisation of upper-class males and the position of women in society represented privileged and recurrent themes. Mardin's[10] analysis of the post-Tanzimat novel suggests that whereas writers such as Ahmed Mithat Efendi echoed the popular unease with Westernisation through satirical treatment of the superficial, Western-struck male, there was a discernible consensus among the élite with regard to women's emancipation which was discussed in universalistic 'civilizational' terms. This, however, was an issue which apparently had the potential to create important cleavages among men of different social extraction. To the lower classes, any change in the position of women had been and remained anathema and a sign of moral decay. Nor was the élite necessarily consistent: retrenchment into conservatism *vis-à-vis* women always remained just below the surface. For instance, as late as 1917 and at a juncture when the empire was

9. T. Taskiran, *Cumhuriyetin 50. Yilinda Turk Kadin Haklari*, Ankara, Basbakanlik Basimvei, 1973.
10. S. Mardin, 'Superwesternization in Urban Life in the Ottoman Empire in the last Quarter of the 19th Century,' in P.P. Benedict and E. Tumertekin (eds), *Turkey: Geographical and Social Perspectives*, Leiden, Brill, 1974.

in grave peril the Committee for Union and Progress halted all progressive leanings and constituted a committee to discuss the suitable length for women's skirts. Enver Pasa removed one of his commanders in the Dardanelles whose daughters he had seen sunning themselves on the Bosphorus.[11] This and similar observations lead Seni to conclude that the divisions between the traditionalists and modernists may have been more apparent than real:

> If the modernists distinguish themselves from the conservative current in terms of the real measures adopted for the emancipation of women, they do not escape the moralism and puritanism of their opponents. It would seem that the control of women also crystallizes a part of their Ottoman identity since when they feel that identity, the Ottoman Empire, to be under threat they backtrack on their position and regress to more conservative attitudes.[12]

There is thus a clear continuity in her view between the imperial edicts of the sixteenth century making women's attire and movements the object of direct legislation and later more modernist interventions on women's behalf including the Kemalist reforms: they all emanate from an Ottoman state tradition that recognises no sources of legitimacy outside itself. While it is easy to concur that women's bodies have been and are still today used as vehicles for the symbolic representation of political intent, it is more difficult to overlook or dismiss the very real transformations that Ottoman society underwent in the transition to the Republic and their independent impact on the position of women. Nor do these transformations stand in any mechanical or easily understandable relationship to the woman question. On the contrary, the attempts to absorb new positions into existing views of the world or ideologies often created complex, convoluted bodies of discourse.

There is little doubt that the *Tanzimat* élite was deeply influenced by the ideals of the French Enlightenment and that some of this influence was reflected in writings on the position of women. Not surprisingly however the most strenuous efforts of early feminists were directed towards making their demands compatible with the dictates of Islam. Thus most of the 'feminist' writing of the time emanated from an 'enlightened' Islamic perspective and attempted

11. Falih Rifki, Atay *Baris Villari*, quoted in Mardin, ibid. pp. 433–4.
12. N. Seni, 'Ville ottomane et representation du corps feminin', *Les Temps Modernes*, no. 456–7, (July–August 1984), p. 89.

to demonstrate that Islam need not be an impediment to progress for women. Even Fatma Aliye Hanim, the most noteworthy woman writer of her time who distinguished herself through a lively polemic on polygyny with the conservative Mahmut Esat Efendi, clearly inscribed herself within such a perspective. Nor was it an accident that the longest lived woman's weekly of this time, *The Ladies Gazette*, declared itself to be serving three principles: being a good mother, a good wife and a good Muslim.

In contrast to the nationalist stance of later periods, Islam was the only available body of discourse in which the woman question could be debated. Ozankaya's discussion of the work of Semseddin Sami, one of the most enlightened *Tanzimat* thinkers, illustrates the limitations of even the best meaning attempts at tackling the woman question.[13] Sami is ultimately unable openly to criticize Islamic rules regarding divorce, polygyny and wife-beating even though one can quite easily sense his unease with them throughout his text titled *Women*. What starts out as a plea for women's rights increasingly reads like an apologia of Islam. At any rate, universal human rights, rationalism and positivism notwithstanding even the most progressive proposals regarding women had a strong instrumentalist flavour about them. Traditional marriages and repudiation were denounced as the source of 'social ills' weakening and corroding the social fabric, the ignorance of women meant that they were inadequate as educators and mothers and finally the gulf between the sexes created by the traditional family system was a source of alienation and unhappiness for both. Yet I disagree with Tekeli's[14] contention that these concerns represented an emulation of Western, particularly Victorian ideals of monogamy and female domesticity by a rising bourgeois ruling class. I think there are specific and very significant reasons for *men* being the most outspoken critics of the Ottoman family system and, on occasion, the most fervent advocates of romantic love or at least marriages based on mutual compatibility.[15] The traditional Ottoman family based on deference

13. O. Ozankaya, 'Reflections of Semseddin Sami on Women in the Period before the Advent of Secularism', in T. Erder (ed.), *Family in Turkish Society*, Ankara, Turkish Social Science Association, 1985.

14. Tekeli, *Kadinlar ve Siyasal Toplumsal Hayat*, p. 179.

15. There is a vast literature by male writers of the time on the evils of traditional marriages and the unhappiness and alienation resulting from them. For an impassioned defence of romantic love, see Omer Seyfettin, *Ask Dalgasi*, Istanbul 1964. Seyfettin writes (p. 52): 'Here in our surroundings, the surroundings of the Turks, love is strictly forbidden. It is as forbidden as an infernal machine, a bomb, a box of

to the paterfamilias and seniority, arranged marriages, and spatial and social segregation of the sexes, were not conducive to rapport and closeness between spouses, much less to romantic love. It should not surprise us that it was 'modern' men who could openly reflect upon the oppressiveness of traditional family structure although women were more visibly the victims of it. Male writers frequently used women's plight as a means of expressing their own restiveness and dissatisfaction with patriarchal family structure which may indeed enslave women but also went a long way towards delaying and curtailing their own social adulthood in many matters crucial to their lives. It is no wonder that they denounced social convention as oppressive and stultifying. Women on the other hand may have been more timid or at least cautious in this respect. It is revealing that the author Omer Seyfettin accuses women themselves of standing in the way of more companionate relations between the sexes.[16] This is hardly surprising in a society which offered women no shelter outside the traditional family and a tenuous one inside it; where the options, however undesirable, of spinsterhood, 'genteel' female occupations and female religious orders were totally unavailable. (Duben[17] also notes the high rate of remarriage among widows in contrast to the Mediterranean and Russian patterns of the time, so that at no stage were women visible as the managers of their own property.) At least initially, women may have had a great deal to lose and very little tangible gain in following the steps of their more emancipated brothers. The 'passive' attitude of women on this issue was to last well into the Republic and to continue to draw fire from progressive men.

Beneath *Tanzimat* liberalism were powerful undercurrents that had a strong material basis. The *Tanzimat* reforms had failed to stem the tide of nationalism in the Christian Balkan provinces and had essentially strengthened the hand of local Christian merchants who were the preferred trading partners of European powers in Ottoman lands. In Berkes's terms, the more Westernisation proceeded the more Turks felt excluded from it.[18] After an abortive attempt at constitutional monarchy (1876–8) followed by an Islam-

dynamite. . . .'

16. Omer Seyfettin, *Gizli Mabet*, 1926; *Bahar ve Kelebekler*, 1963.

17. A. Duben, 'Nineteenth- and Twentieth-Century Ottoman-Turkish Family and Household Structure', in Erder (ed.), *Family in Turkish Society*, p. 117.

18. N. Berkes, *Baticilik, Ulusculuk ve Toplumsal Devrimler*, Istanbul, Yon Yayinlari, 1965.

ist backlash under the rule of Abdulhamid II (1876–1909), the Second Constitutional Period ushered in by the Young Turks' Revolution was to set the scene for a political change of gear which provided the foundations for the Kemalist revolution. The Committee for Union and Progress (CUP), the architects of the 1908 revolution, did not delay in seeing that the Ottoman nationalism which united Muslim and non-Muslim subjects in the overthrow of Abdulhamid's despotic rule in a bid for 'freedom' could not check the secessionist movements in the ethnically heterogenous provinces. Toprak suggests that Turkish nationalism which was born from the liberal currents of the 1908 revolution also represented a reaction against liberalism, especially against economic liberalism which had cost the Muslim artisan so dear. 'The nationalism which the Second Constitutional Period put on the agenda, aided by the extraordinary circumstances of World War I, produced a yearning for the creation of a Muslim-Turkish "middle class", which after the loss of the war was to constitute the cadres of the National Struggle in Anatolia.'[19]

The search for alternatives to liberalism produced a major shift in thinking about society and economy in the direction of corporatism which in the case of the Second Constitutional Period represented a blend of solidarism emanating from French corporatist thought and Ottoman guild traditions.[20] Throughout the war years the CUP consistently struggled to create a middle class consisting of Turkish-Muslim entrepreneurs, persistently stressing the ethnic dimension of the problem and favouring Muslim over non-Muslim. The effects of this national mobilisation on women have not received the attention they deserve except in connection with the war effort, a point to which I return later. It seems probable, however, that women were not totally unaffected by the new societal priorities. A suggestive though inconclusive example may be found in the effects of a law imposing Turkish as the language of correspondence to foreign firms operating in the Ottoman empire in 1916. These firms had previously employed foreigners and now had the choice of either folding up or recruiting local employees. Meanwhile vocational evening classes, especially in the fields of commerce and banking, were instituted by CUP clubs in an obvious attempt to

19. Z. Toprak, *Turkiyede Milli Iktisat (1908–1918)*, Ankara, Yurt Yayinlari, 1982, p. 21.
20. Z. Toprak, 'Turkiyede Korporatizmin Dogusu', *Toplum ve Bilim* 12 (Winter 1980), pp. 41–9.

create skilled cadres that were competent in these fields. Special business classes for women were also started. Especially at a juncture where male labour was getting scarcer because of the war, the Advanced School for Commerce had opened a section for women in the Women's University (Inas Darulfununu) which was so popular that a second section had to be opened.[21] Undoubtedly this type of vocational training must have been instrumental in creating new employment opportunities for women. However, the real social upheaval that propelled women into the workforce in greater numbers was the First World War itself.

The Effect of the Wars

The overthrow of Abdulhamit's absolutist rule and the greater freedom promised by the 1908 revolution raised hopes among women that they would also benefit from the new principles of liberty and equality. But these hopes soon turned to disillusionment and bitterness. A woman's periodical, on the occasion of the fifth anniversary of the Constitution proclaimed that it was 'Men's National Celebration Day'.[22] Nonetheless the Second Constitutional Period saw an increase in the numbers of women availing themselves of educational opportunities, increases in the number of women's associations and periodicals, and especially a tendency for women themselves to participate more actively in the women's struggle in comparison to the earlier period where the majority of the advocates of the woman question were in fact male. Many writers on this question tend to put these developments down to the effect of the wars.[23]

Already during the Balkan War middle-class women were involved in social welfare activities, bringing relief to war orphans and the wounded. The women's branch of the Red Crescent had for instance started training Turkish nurses. It was during the First World War, however, that the massive loss of male labour to the front created a demand for female labour, not unlike the case of the other warring nations. The growth of female employment did not

21. Z. Toprak, *Turkiyede Milli Iktisat*, p. 83.
22. Taskiran, *Cumhuriyetin 50*, p. 38.
23. Tekelis, *Kadinlar ve Siyasal Toplumsal Hayat*, p. 198; N. Abadan-Unat, 'Social Change and Turkish Women', in N. Abadan-Unat (ed.), *Women in Turkish Society*, Leiden, Brill, 1981, p. 8.

remain confined to white-collar jobs in post-offices, banks, municipal services and hospitals but involved attempts at wider mobilisation throughout the Anatolian provinces. A law passed in 1915 by the Ottoman Ministry of Trade instituted a form of mandatory employment which rapidly swelled the number of women workers.[24] Women volunteers were organised into workers' platoons to help the army with support services. In the agrarian sector, the Fourth Army formed Women Workers' Brigades. The Islamic Association for the Employment of Ottoman Women, founded in 1916, was instrumental in employing women workers under conditions ensuring them an 'honest' living. But if the war effort created interest in women as workers there was no less interest in an intensification of their role as mothers and reproducers of the nation. It is interesting and significant that the empire's first pro-natalist policies also had the employees of the Islamic Association for the Employment of Ottoman Women as their target for whom mandatory marriage by the age of twenty-one for women and twenty-five for men was introduced. The Association used newspaper columns for matchmaking, provided girls with a trousseau and staged well-appointed wedding ceremonies. Those who passed the marriage age limit or did not accept the matrimonial candidates proposed by the Association had 15 per cent of their salary withheld and were excluded from membership. Conversely, marriage was rewarded by a 20 per cent salary increase and similar increases for the birth of each child.[25] Thus women's service to the nation as workers and breeders was made explicitly coextensive. Nonetheless, concessions had to be made to the necessities of female employment. In 1915 for instance an imperial decree allowed the discarding of the veil during office hours. It is clear, however, that this increased female presence in the labour force was viewed with considerable ambivalence. The conditions of women's work tended scrupulously to respect the segregation of the sexes. (It is well to remember that the segregation of the sexes on means of public transport was still in effect until the end of the First World War and that man and wife could not sit together on a boat or train.) Despite the fact that women were employed in

24. A new stocking factory set up in Urfa employed 1000 women. In the Izmir, Sivas, Ankara and Konya provinces 4780 women were employed in carpet production. In Aydin 11,000 and in Kutahya, Eskisehir and Karahisar 1550 were employed in textile manufacture as well as in Diyarbakir where they had replaced men at 1000 looms.
25. Toprak, *Turkiyede Milli Iktisat*, pp. 317–18, also appendix p. 412.

public offices, they were apparently often forced by the police to return home if their skirts were shorter than the officially prescribed length.[26] There is little doubt that this period must have been full of confusion and contradictions, leading to mildly comical incidents. In September 1917 the following announcement was posted on Istanbul walls by the police: 'In the last few months shameful fashions have been seen in the streets of the Capital. All Muslim women are called upon to lengthen their skirts, refrain from wearing corsets and wear a thick *charshaf*. A maximum of two days is allowed to abide by the orders of this proclamation.' This announcement was the subject of such indignation and furor that higher level administrators were forced to rebuke their over-zealous subordinates and retract the order. The new announcement read: 'The General directorate regrets that old and retrograde women were able to induce a subaltern employee to publicize an announcement ordering Muslim women to go back to old fashions. We announce that the previous orders are null and void.'[27]

Clearly, despite women's entry into the work-force in unprecedented numbers and strenuous advocacy for their rights, changes in mores were slow to come. The fact that Prime Minister Fuat Pasa sat at the same table as his wife at a hotel pâtisserie created a sensation and was the subject of much comment and controversy. Meanwhile the intelligentsia continued to bemoan enforced segregation and the impossibility of civilised communication between the sexes. The rights demanded by feminists of the time (voiced in publications such as *Mahasin*, which started appearing in 1908, *Woman*, again published in 1908 in Salonica and *Women's World* from 1913) were relatively modest by later standards. They were: the right to education, to go out in the streets and to places of entertainment, and a limited right to work with freedom from police harassment. Greater equality within the conjugal union was a largely taboo subject despite the ongoing polemic on the evils of polygyny. The parliamentary debate in 1911 on clause 201 of the penal code regarding penalties for adultery is quite revealing in this respect. Some parliamentarians protested that the law introduced a clear double standard, giving tacit permission to male infidelity

26. E. Yener, 'Eski Ankara Kiyafetleri ve Eski Giyinis Tarzlari', *Dil Tarih ve Cografya Fak Dergisi* XIII. 3 (1955), quoted in Abadan-Unat, *Women in Turkish Society*, p. 8.
27. J. Melia, *Mustafa Kemal ou la Renovation de la Turquie*, Paris, 1929, quoted in Caporal, *Kemalizmde ve Kemalizm Sonrasinda Turk Kadini*, pp. 127–48.

provided that the bounds of decorum are respected while punishing women severely. Others strongly supported what they considered to be male superiority and prerogatives. Women themselves felt compelled to defend monogamous and more companionate marriages in the name of 'social hygiene' rather than on grounds of greater equality and basic human rights.[28]

The compromises apparent in the 1917 family code are quite indicative of the different pressures at work in Ottoman society. This law aimed at completing the task left unfinished by the *Mecelle* (the Ottoman civic code referred to previously) by legislating aspects of personal status which had been totally abandoned to the rulings of religious authorities. It was an eclectic concoction of the Hanefite, Malakite and Shaafi schools of jurisprudence (*fiq'h*) and is the first written family code in the Muslim world. The contractual aspect of the marriage was to apply to all religious groups in the empire, it being understood that this could be followed by the appropriate religious ceremonies. The clear intent of giving women more security within the conjugal union was evidenced by the presence at the ceremony of a specially empowered state employee above and beyond the two witnesses required by the Sharia, a clear step in the direction of secularization. Marriages without consent were decreed illegal and divorce was made more difficult by the introduction of a conciliation procedure. Not only was polygyny not abolished, however, but it was actually legalized even though its practice was made more difficult by stipulating the consent of the first wife.

Interestingly, the commission headed by the Minister of Justice Seyyit Bey wavered on the question of polygyny and finally accepted it not only in view of the clear Koranic licence in this respect but also on demographic grounds since numerous wars had created an imbalance in the sex ratio. (There is some historical evidence that polygynous marriage was in some instances a response to the 'excess' female population in high out-migration areas of certain Anatolian provinces.[29]) Needless to say such a law failed to satisfy either those who wanted to see fundamental changes in a family

---

28. This in itself is not surprising and the arguments are frequently reminiscent of the earlier Western feminists such as Mary Wollstonecraft in her *Vindication of the Rights of Women* (1785).

29. J. McCarthy, 'Age, Family and Migration in Nineteenth-Century Black Sea Provinces of the Ottoman Empire', *International Journal of Middle East Studies*, 10 (1979), pp. 309–23.

system considered to be 'in crisis' or those who saw the changes as clear-cut infractions of Koranic law. Minorities were also discontented with what they saw as a curtailment of the prerogatives of their own religious authorities and, in 1919, complained to the forces then occupying Istanbul and obtained a repeal of the clauses regarding Christian marriages. This law nonetheless remained in force until 1926 in Turkey and much later in the Ottoman periphery (until 1953 in Syria and Jordan for instance). It represents an interesting exercise illustrative of the muddled attempts of Ottoman legislators to introduce progressive change. These attempts were to encounter great opposition and resistance throughout this period and extend to Kemal Ataturk's own National Assemblies regardless of women's often praised contributions to the War of National Liberation.

The end of the First World War brought about the dismemberment of the defeated empire and the control of Anatolian provinces by occupying Western powers. The landing of Greek forces in Izmir in May 1919 and the occupation of Istanbul by the British in March 1920 unleashed a wave of popular protest in which women were not merely participants but public speakers in open-air meetings where they made impassioned calls for the defence of the motherland.[30] Many women joined Mustafa Kemal's forces of resistance in Anatolia, including the famous novelist Halide Edib Adivar who chronicles the events of the time in her memoirs (published as *The Turkish Ordeal*) as well as novels such as *Atesten Gomlek* (The Shirt of Flame). Associations for Patriotic Defence started springing up in the Anatolian provinces. Women did not join these directly but set up their own parallel organizations. The Anatolian Women's Association for Patriotic Defence was founded in Sivas in November 1919. Studies on some branches of the Association suggest that the active members were the wives, daughters and sisters of provincial notables and higher level state employees who were the main supporters of the nationalist struggle as well as some teachers and educational administrators. In other words, these were the women of the nascent local middle class which the Second Constitutional Period did so much to nurture. During the War of National Liberation there was a large-scale mobilisation of the whole nation in which Anatolian peasant women played a key and visible role glorified in public monuments as well as patriotic literature. Yet the

30. Taskiran *Cumhuriyetin 50*, 68–73.

coalition of nationalist forces which united behind Mustafa Kemal included men of religion who were going to remain inflexible on the woman question to the last and constitute a focus of active and vocal resistance throughout the first and second National Assemblies. In fact in 1924, soon after the declaration of the Republic, there were some regressive steps in legislation in the field of civil law.[31] The commission in charge of formulating a new draft law cancelled some of the advantages gained through the 1917 code by endorsing polygyny, eliminating the need for consent by the first wife and lowering the legal marriage age for girls to nine years old. This proposal, subsequently rejected, was part of the playing out of the opposition between religious and Kemalist forces in the national assemblies, an opposition which was finally resolved by the abolition of the Caliphate and the abrogation of the Sharia in favour of secular codes and laws. There is no doubt that the woman question became one of the pawns in the Kemalist struggle to dismantle the theocratic remnants of the Ottoman state, a struggle in which male combatants engaged each other while women remained surprisingly passive onlookers.[32] In fact, some progressive men were using newspaper columns to take women to task over their acquiescent posture. Necmettin Sadak wrote in the daily *Aksam*:

> Finally an important issue concerning Turkish womanhood has arisen. The National Assembly has started debating the Family Law proposal. This proposal which allows the marriage of nine year old girls, condones four wives for men, does not limit men's rights to divorce but also grants it to women, thereby weakening the foundations of the family even further, has passed through the Sharia and Justice commissions without a murmur from women. Almost all newspapers have cried out against this law. However, our women who engage in demonstrations with or without justification and at every possible occasion, did not act. We have witnessed this silence with surprise as well as some despair. Where were our young ladies filling sections of University classes, where those founding political parties in the pursuit of chimera? The Turkish Republic is insulting you with its own laws, why are you not crying out?[33]

The process of mobilization and the co-opting of women into the ideological struggles of the Republic can therefore be seen to be

---

31. For a detailed discussion see N. Berkes, *Turkiyede Cagdaslasma*, Istanbul, Dogu-Bati Yayinlari, 1978, pp. 519–20.

32. Taskiran, *Cumhuriyetin 50*, pp. 106–9.

33. Necmettin Sadak, 'Hanimlarimiz ve Aile Hukiki Kararnamesi', *Aksam* 21 (January 1924), quoted ibid., p. 109.

significantly different from early feminist movements in the West. In this latter, the women's struggle took place against a background where legislation was lagging considerably behind the socio-economic realities of advancing industrialism and a growing labour movement. In Turkey it was an ideological lever operating on a substantially unchanged economic base, at least so far as women's economic and familial options were concerned. Yet the specific forms that feminist discourse took continued to be indicative of the search for a new legitimacy in the transition to the Republic. From this perspective the transformations of the woman question can be better understood with reference to Republican state ideology than to any other single factor. In what follows I suggest that the main legitimizing discourse for the woman question in Turkey has been that of Turkish nationalism which has its roots in Turkism.

Turkish Nationalism: A New Paradigm for the Woman Question

As can be seen from what has been said so far, the woman question remained for a long time caught in the dilemma between Westernism and Islam without a third term to moderate the debate. This, in a sense, paralleled the state of affairs in other avenues of Ottoman life. The Turkist reaction represented an attempt at recuperation of a national identity which could be grounded in a national 'culture' rather than solely in Islam. This was in many ways a most difficult enterprise. As Berkes[34] points out, the Turks were the last to achieve a sense of nationality in the whole Ottoman formation. In the Ottoman context, Turkish nationalism could even be perceived as divisive in a situation where other ethnic minorities were restive, and it certainly found no favour among the Islamists for whom the notion of a Turkish nation constituted a threat to the Islamic *umma* (collectivity of believers). Turkish nationalism initially took the form of a populist reaction to Westernism not unlike, and certainly heavily influenced by, the Narodnik movement in Russia. The Turkish populists turned to nationalism in line with the ideals of the Muslim intelligentsia in Russia and with considerable influence from Turkish-Russian emigrés, but in time cleavages developed between pan-Turkist nationalism which had a strongly ir-

34. M. Berkes, *Baticilik, Ulusculuk ve Toplumsal Devrimler.*

redentist flavour and non-irrendentist Turkish nationalism which gave birth to Kemalist ideology.[35] The leading ideologue in this transition has undoubtedly been Ziya Gokalp (1876–1924), author of *The Principles of Turkism*. Parla in his extensive analysis of Gokalp's work characterises him as, 'the major formulator of Turkish nationalism who amidst the persistent lost causes of Ottomanism and Islamic communalism acquiesced in the dictates of history and advocated a non-expansionist, nonirredentist Turkism to ease the public conscience in the transition from empire to nation.'[36] Furthermore Parla suggests that 'his system fixed the parameters within which mainstream political discourse and action has been conducted in Turkey'.[37] This is also true of his influence on the treatment of the woman question throughout the period of Republican reforms. Gokalp who was greatly influenced by Durkheim's sociology substituted his notion of society with that of 'nation', emphasising the national-cultural rather than Islamic sources of morality. His work represents strenuous attempts at defining the nature of the collectivity called 'nation'. He settles on the idea of a collectivity based on common language and culture and representing the highest form of social solidarity. Gokalp took great pains at distinguishing the concepts of culture and civilisation from one another. In his view Islamic and Western civilisational influences need not be incompatible with Turkish national culture although admittedly his brand of Islam, ethical Sufism, is highly secular, and his preferred Western sources are drawn from European corporatism. Gokalp's search for authentic and national-cultural patterns led him to an eclectic examination of myth, legend, archeological and anthropological evidence on pre-Islamic Turkic patterns which he felt were still alive in popular culture despite the superimposition of various civilisational influences, including that of Islam. In his *Principles of Turkism* Gokalp spells out the programmatic implications of Turkism and its application to the fields of language, aesthetics, morality, law, religion, economy, and philosophy. His views on 'moral Turkism' especially on family and sexual morality represent a significant departure from earlier approaches to the woman question. He suggested that family morality based on old Turkish cultural values

35. J. Landau, *Pan-Turkism in Turkey: A Study in Irredentism*, London, Hurst & Co., 1981.
36. T. Parla. 'The Social and Political Thought of Ziya Gokalp 1876–1924', unpublished Ph.D. dissertation, New York, Columbia University, 1980, p. 2.
37. Ibid., p. 11.

included norms such as communal property in land, democracy in the 'parental' family as opposed to the autocracy of the patriarchal family, the equality of men and women and monogamy in marriage. He traces some of the origins of what he labels 'Turkish feminism' (defined exactly in these words) to the fact that Shamanistic religion and rituals were based on the sacred power vested in women in contrast to Toyonism, a male religion. This made men and women ritualistically equal, an equality which was seen to permeate every sphere of life including the political. The patrilineal and matrilineal principles were equally important, children belonged to both parents, women could control their own independent property and, interestingly, were excellent warriors (amazons, to use Gokalp's own term). This amounted to a pre-Islamic 'golden age' for women which was made much of by subsequent feminist women writers. So far as Gokalp was concerned the Turks had lost their old morality:

> Under the influence of Greek and Persian civilization women have been enslaved and lost their legal status. When the ideal of Turkish culture was born was it not essential to remember and revitalize the beautiful rules of old Turkish lore? Hence it is for this reason that as soon as the current of Turkism was born in our country the ideal of feminism was born with it. The reason why Turkists are both populist and feminist is not simply because these ideals are valued in this century; the fact that democracy and feminism were the two main principles of ancient Turkish life is a major factor in this respect.[38]

This position was not greeted with a total lack of skepticism. Mehmet Izzet for instance suggested that Gokalp's ideas might have been greatly influenced by pragmatic considerations: 'At a time when Islamic law was being abolished, improvements in women's position sought and changes in family life along the Western model were being introduced, interpreting this movement as a return to ancient Turkish law and national identity would ensure greater goodwill and sympathy.'[39] Berkes [40] also comments rather wryly on the fact that by some happy coincidence the elements of Turkish culture which Gokalp took such pains to distinguish from Western civilization matched this latter with uncanny ease. Indeed, in terms

38. Z. Gokalp, *Turkculugun Esaslari*, Istanbul, Inkilap ve Ake Kitabevleri Koll. Sti, 1978, p. 148.
39. Mehmet Izzet quoted in M. Eroz, *Turk Ailesi*, Istanbul, Milli Egitim Basimevi, 1977, p. 13.
40. M. Berkes, *Baticilik Ulusculuk . . .*

of the position of women, what might have been rather unpalatable in the form of Western influence gained a new legitimacy when it was recuperated by nationalist discourse.

We find some of the best literary examples of the search for the 'new' Turkish woman in the work of novelist Halide Edib Adivar who explicitly acknowledges the influence of Gokalp. One of her early novels *Yeni Turan* (The New Turan), a utopian tale first published in 1912, depicts through her heroine, Kaya, a model of the liberated Turkish woman. She is a political activist in the nationalist cause and a useful and active member of the community. Even though she is unveiled her garments are modest and her bearing so serious and austere as to leave no one in doubt concerning her virtue. There is no inkling of Westernism in either her appearance or ideas which are the expression of a return to the sober Turkish values which restore woman's human dignity. Not suprisingly the nationalist party in the novel is unabashedly feminist while the 'Ottomanist' party is bent upon denying women their freedom. Again we find the recurrent theme of nationalism coupled with feminism.

For Ataturk, who was to distance himself from Islam much further than Gokalp himself ever envisaged, the latter's definition of the nation was to provide a very valuable tool. In assessing Kemalist nationalism it is important to remember some of the special circumstances under which Mustafa Kemal's struggle for independence took place. Even though most of the Associations for Patriotic Defence had a clearly Islamic outlook and couched the defence of the motherland in religious terms (as a holy war against the infidel), the Istanbul government headed by the Sultan-Caliph had reached an agreement with the occupying powers to stamp out Kemalist resistance. In April 1920 the Sheyh-ul-Islam issued a *fetva* (canonical proclamation) declaring holy war against the 'Ankara rebels'. A military court condemned Ataturk and a group of his supporters to death and the defection of his forces to the Army of the Caliphate was only reversed after the outrage created by the humiliating treaty of Sevres. Henceforth *irtica* (religious reaction) was to be identified as one of the main enemies of Kemalist nationalism. Yet unlike Islam, which had very deep roots in the Ottoman-Turkish polity, Turkish nationalism was an ideal which had yet to search for its symbols and discourse. This search, already inaugurated in the work of Turkists and Ziya Gokalp in particular, was to culminate in a major onslaught on Turkish history and an extensive rewriting of it. This task was given to the Association for the Study of Turkish History, which was set up by Ataturk himself and which reported its findings to the First Turkish History Congress, held in Istanbul in 1932. These findings were to constitute the basis for 'official' Turkish history on which post-Kemalist generations were brought up. This history traced back its origins to Central Asiatic beginnings when the Turkic peoples and the Chinese were the main actors on the scene of civilisation. All the subsequent civilisations of Asia Minor and Mesopotamia were considered as so many links in the chain of Turkish civilisations. Compared to the relatively recent conversion of the Turks to Islam starting in the eighth century, this history could be traced much further back to 5000 BC. This was the new framework in which the woman question in Turkey was discussed by the first generation of Kemalist feminists. The most prominent among these, Afet Inan who was also Ataturk's adoptive daughter, devotes a long section to a consideration of Turkish women before Islam in her classic book on *The Emancipation of the Turkish Woman*,[41] in which she echoes Gokalp's convictions about women's high status and greater equality. She leaves us with little doubt that the acceptance of Islamic laws represented an important decline in the status of Turkish women, although she prefers to put this down to the social customs of Arabs and Persians rather than Islam *per se*. In purely formal terms, this type of discourse is prevalent among many third world feminisms, but the actual content of it changes according to what it is that is being recuperated by the discourse that claims to be feminist.[42] In the Turkish case it was nothing less than national identity which was deemed to have a practically built-in sexual egalitarianism component. Even though the actual realities of entrenched Ottoman-Turkish patriarchy[43] and the influence of Islam made such pronouncements seem rather remote and endowed them with a mythical quality, they continued to be part of the official discourse on women in Turkey. It may be

41. Inan Afet, *The Emancipation of the Turkish Woman*, Paris, Unesco, 1962.

42. Witness the attempts of Muslim feminists to recuperate Islam itself by invoking an Islamic 'golden age' for women which possesses many of the positive characteristics attributed to the pre-Islamic Turkish pattern, including women's equality as warriors (for the faith, in this latter case). As examples, see El Saadawi's 'Women and Islam' and Al-Hibri's 'A Study of Islamic Herstory' both in A. Al-Hibri (ed.), *Women and Islam*, Oxford, Pergamon Press, 1982.

43. Anthropological studies show that despite some regional variations in marriage practices, the patrivirilocal household was normative in Turkey. For a review of the evidence, see Duben, 'Nineteenth- and Twentieth-Century Ottoman-Turkish Family and Household Structures'.

argued that the one persistent, underlying concern which unites nationalist and Islamic discourse is an eagerness to establish that the behaviour and position of women, however defined, is congruent with the 'true' identity of the collectivity and constitutes no threat to it. Republican ideology has had an undeniably progressive impact on the status of women, however, as evidenced by the far-reaching legal reforms of the Ataturk era referred to previously. The extent to which this aspect of state ideology actually made lasting inroads in the Turkish polity is worthy of more extensive consideration, especially in view of the fact that political debates concerning the place of women (especially their modesty and appropriate modes of dress and conduct) are still very much alive. Although the terms of the current debate may seem superficially familiar (and still involve the well-worn dichotomies of Islam vs. modernisation/Westernisation), a careful and detailed analysis would have to be discussed against the background of more recent socio-economic changes and political realignments, just as I have attempted to do for the period between the nineteenth-century Ottoman reforms and the birth of the Turkish republic. However, any such analysis would have to take into account several generations of women (and men), educated and formed within Kemalist ideology, who have internalised the nationalist message.

12

Women, State and Politics:
The Soviet Experience

MARIETTA STEPANIANTS

The social revolutions of the twentieth century, two world wars, the
wide scope of national liberation movements and the scientific and
technological revolution have tremendously changed the face of the
planet. They have failed, however, to bring about the full emancipation of women.

The status of women cannot be changed until there is a clear
understanding of the causes of their social inequality. The differences in point of view concerning this problem may be reduced to a
variety of attitudes, which could be defined as biological, social and
socio-biological. These attitudes are not new, and they are no less
strong today than in the past. This was demonstrated by the papers
presented at Unesco's International Symposium of Experts on the
Changing Roles of Men and Women in Private and Public Life
(Athens, 3–6 December 1985).

According to the first stance, the unequal social status of women
is determined by their biological nature, as it is women who play the
major role in human reproduction. Hence the logical conclusion:
male and female roles are not only mutually complementary but
hierarchical, so that the former is always expected to dominate the
latter. These interrelations are allegedly age-long and inevitable, and
it is argued that any overstepping by women of the bounds of the
family circle and their participation in material production cannot
lead to the emancipation of women. On the contrary it results in a
double burden on their shoulders.

The data presented by sociological investigations, carried out in
Egypt[1] and Morocco,[2] do not in fact show that taking a job in itself

1. See N. Atif, 'Symbolic representation of maternity and its links with the

makes woman equal to man, but neither does it prove the correctness of the biological attitude. It simply reminds us that the equality of women cannot be reached without making radical changes in the economic structure, in legislation, traditional institutions, etc. In Muslim countries, in particular, the equal status of women is impossible without the prohibition of polygamy, the revision of Muslim inheritance law, or a change in the discriminatory procedure of divorce.

A rather simplified feminist attitude is shown by those experts who have tried to prove that the causes of discrimination against women are rooted mainly in the patriarchal nature of state institutions as such, which consider women to be either inferior in comparison with men, or merely supplementary. A position of this kind represents an idealist interpretation of social development and ignores the role of class struggle in the history of humanity. At the same time it underestimates the biological peculiarities of women and the vital necessity of taking into account maternity protection measures. The majority of experts at the Unesco symposium shared a sober view of the problem of the equality of men and women with due regard to both biological and social factors. There is no doubt that the physiological peculiarities of women predestined the historically established forms of the division of labour between sexes. However, at an early stage of social development, the natural division of labour did not result in economic disparity between men and women because collective forms of production and consumption levelled the significance of male and female labour. The situation radically changed with the appearance of private property. The possibility of accumulation by the few led not only to class division but also to the enslavement of women by men.[3] The removal of woman from public production, her conversion into 'the main servant' of man together with the elimination of matriarchal law meant a defeat of world-wide historic significance.[4]

Later on, the socio-economic inequality of women was maintained by law, religion, morals and so on. Thus, the Hindu Code of Manu said: 'In childhood a woman must be subject to her father; in youth, to her husband; after her husband's death, to her sons. A

---

legitimate of social structure'.

2. F. Banabdenbi, 'De la famille large vers la famille restreinte – les roles des sexes'.

3. Friedrich Engels, *Proiskhozhdenie sem'i, chastnoy sobstvennosti i gosudarstva*; Karl Marx and Friedrich Engels, *Soch*, 21.68.

4. *Sm tam zhe*, p. 60.

woman must never be free of subjugation'. In orthodox Jewish prayer, men repeat daily: 'I thank thee, O Lord, that thou has not created me a woman'. The New Testament commands: 'Wives, submit yourselves unto your husbands . . . for the husband is the head of the wife, even as Christ is the head of the Church' (Ephesians V: 23–4).

Proverbs and popular sayings echo these religious instructions: 'Daughters are the greatest misfortune' (ancient Indian saying); 'A hen is not a bird; a woman is not a person' (Russian proverb); Beat your wife thrice a day; if she escapes, beat the place where she sat', says a Turkmenian proverb.

However, side by side with the injustice of Muslim polygamy and the obligation for women to cover themselves with the *hijab*, parallel to the tragic Hindu ritual of self-immolation (*sati*) by a widow and the humiliating obligation to pay for the bridegroom, and simultaneously with the inequality of Christian women in matters of divorce and inheritance, there has existed the wisdom of the people: 'That family perishes soon, in which women suffer; that family prospers where they are happy' (ancient Indian saying).

Philosophers of the past, reflecting on the nature of the universe, on the fundamental principle of all beings, on the correlation of the material and the ideal, on belief and reason, often pondered over the secrets not only of the 'holy family', but also of the earthly one. As a result of those reflections materialist philosophers came to the conclusion that: 'men are products of circumstances and upbringing',[5] that social inequality had a material basis, in particular, 'the male domination in marriage is nothing but a consequence of his *economic* domination.'[6]

In contrast to earlier materialist philosophers, Marxism discovered the dialectics of the material and the ideal, and pointed out the narrow-mindness of those materialists who forget that though men are the product of their circumstances, 'it is men who change circumstances'.[7] Hence the Marxist conception of fundamental significance: 'The earthly family must be criticised in theory and revolutionised in practice'.[8]

5. Karl Marx, 'Theses on Feuerbach', in Karl Marx and Friedrick Engels, *Selected Works*, 3 vols, Moscow, Progress Publishers, *1969*, vol I, p. 13.
6. F. Engels, *Proiskhozhdenie sem'i, chastnoy sobstvennosti i gosudarstva. Soch*, 21.84.
7. Marx, 'Theses on Feuerbach', p. 13.
8. Ibid., p. 14.

The history of the Soviet Union, after the October socialist revolution of 1917, is the story of an unprecedented experiment to transform radically social relations. This experiment is an attempt to realise, in a creative way, the principles of Marxism.

Let us turn to facts. The first decrees of the Soviet state of 1917 and the Soviet constitution of 1918, for the first time in the history of Russia declared equal rights for men and women: equal opportunities in employment, remuneration and promotion, equal pay for equal work regardless of sex, equal opportunities in social and political activity and so on.

The proclamation of legal equality was in itself a great achievement. As we all know from experience of the past as well as of the present, however, the road from a law to its practical implementation is not simple. Lenin made this point in one of his speeches in 1920: 'equality before the law is not necessarily equality in fact.'[9] The acknowledgement of the rights of women was nevertheless of great revolutionary significance, for it enabled women to begin to overcome many objective obstacles before they were able to enjoy electoral rights: obstacles like widespread illiteracy, traditions which prohibited women from engaging in any activities outside the family circle and so on.

Great efforts were needed at state level to eliminate illiteracy, to involve women in social life and to overcome reactionary traditions in order, with every new election campaign, to increase women's participation in political life and in the process of state management. As a result impressive progress has been made in the Soviet Union today, (if compared with statistics obtainable from the most industrially-developed countries).

Women comprise 33 per cent[10] of the total number of deputies elected to the USSR Supreme Soviet, the country's highest body of state authority, 36–40 per cent of the total number of deputies to the Supreme Soviets of the constituent Republics, and almost 50 per cent (1.5 million) of those elected to local government bodies.[11]

The high representation of women in the elected bodies at federal, republican and local levels ensures their participation in the legislative process, in elaborating five-year plans, in approving the

9. V.I. Lenin, *K zhenshchinam-rabotnitsam. Poln.sobr.soch*, 40.157.

10. More than the number of women members of parliaments in all the countries of the Common Market put together.

11. TSSU SSR, *Zhenshchinï v SSSR 1986. Statisticheskie materialï*, Moscow, "Finansï i statistika", 1986, p. 5.

Federal budget, and in making decisions on vital issues of internal and foreign policy.

An important form of women's political participation in state affairs is their professional juridical work. The number of elected women judges in the country is about 4,000 (37 per cent of the total number of judges). The highest representation of women in the courts can be seen in the Republics of Latvia (53 per cent), Estonia (50 per cent), and the Russian Federation (42 per cent).[12]

The leading force in the political system of the USSR is its Communist Party. In 1920 women made up only 7.4 per cent of Party membership. Today women comprise 27.4 per cent of total CPSU membership.

In spite of the significant growth of women's participation in the social and political life of the Soviet Union, not all opportunities are taken to promote them to responsible posts in legal, administrative or Party bodies. This was pointed out at the 26th Congress of the CPSU. The situation has since improved: during the past five years the number of women elected as leaders of Party organisations at regional and city level has increased fivefold. It is quite natural therefore that women's representation at the 27th Congress of the CPSU in 1986 was much wider than in the past. They made up 27 per cent of all delegates. This is the largest number in the whole history of the USSR Communist Party. But even these figures are not satisfying. The Central Committee of the CPSU has recommended to Party organisations that they improve work among women in order to ensure even wider participation.

Young women acquire experience in political work in the ranks of the Young Communist League where they make up more than 50 per cent of its total membership of 42 million. Every third YCL leader in the regions and cities is a young woman.

Women comprise over 59.5 per cent of the membership of trade unions, the largest public organisation in the country, with a membership of more than 133 million. Women make up more than one third (35.8 per cent) of the members of the trade union central body and 51 per cent at Republican and regional level. They head a number of trade unions in different industries.

Women actively participate in the work of many public organisations, such as the Soviet Peace Committee, the Soviet Peace Fund, the Union of the Soviet Societies for Friendship and Cultural

12. *Zhenshchiní v SSSR 1986*, p. 6.

Relations with Foreign Countries and, naturally, most of all in the Soviet Women's Committee (SWC).

This Committee is a public organisation (founded in 1914) comprising representatives of all the Union and Autonomous Republics, of territories and many regions and cities of the USSR. Its members include representatives of trade unions, cooperative and youth organisations, as well as professional associations and unions of those who work in the arts. The SWC receives annually about 200,000 letters from Soviet women in which they make various proposals, and express criticism of many aspects of everyday life. This enables the Committee to be well-informed on the concerns of Soviet women. Their proposals are examined by 20 public commissions of the SWC which deal with a variety of issues. Sociologists, lawyers, economists, psychologists, medical experts and trade-union representatives take part in the work of the commissions.

The proposals made in the women's letters are summed up by the SWC commissions and submitted to the legislative bodies of the country. For example, the SWC took an active part in drafting the Fundamentals of Legislation of the Soviet Union and the Union Republics on Marriage and the Family, in drafting laws on labour and education, and the Constitution of the USSR adopted in 1977. The same is true of the Fundamentals of Housing Legislation of the USSR and the Union Republics, and the draft Guidelines for the Economic and Social Development of the USSR for 1981–5 and for the period ending in 1990.

Twenty-one women's magazines are published in the USSR with a monthly circulation of over 35 million copies. Seventeen of these magazines are published in the various Soviet languages. The most popular are *Rabotnitsa* (Woman Worker) and *Krestyanka* (Peasant Woman). Magazines have played a tremendous role in drawing women into social production and in raising their self-awareness. They give their readers wide opportunities for participation in discussions of different domestic and international problems.

As for the magazine of the Soviet Women's Committee, *Sovetskaya Zenschina* (Soviet Woman), it appears in 14 languages and is distributed in more than 140 countries.

The above mentioned figures are certainly quite impressive, but even more significant is the effort and hard work behind the statistics which have made possible the fulfilment of the aim formulated by the first Socialist State: 'to make politics available to every working woman.'[13]

The abolition of private ownership of the means of production blasted the foundation of women's economic inequality, while the legal rights they were given provided the opportunity for them to achieve equality. But in order that these opportunities should not just remain on paper, but that the proper conditions might be created to enable women to make use of them, titanic work had to be carried out not only by the women themselves, but by the country as a whole. A corresponding state policy was needed. Here are some examples of how 'people changed the circumstances' in order to create new social relations.

Post-revolutionary Russia was a country of almost general illiteracy among women. In 1908 the periodical *Vestnik Vospitaniya* (Educational News) calculated that the elimination of illiteracy among Russian women could not be achieved in less than 280 years. The situation was much more serious in the outlying regions. Between 1863 and 1914 in Kirghizia, not more than two schools were opened every year: at that rate of progress it would have taken 800 years to eradicate illiteracy there.

In Uzbekistan, out of every 100 persons, only two were literate, and of course they were not women. Hence the proverb which stated that 'there is no sense in teaching a woman: a mongrel will never become a hound'.

Measures were taken to put an end to illiteracy among women, while heeding local national and religious peculiarities. Free education did not guarantee a solution to the problem. In Turkistan, for example, the following steps were taken in order to draw Muslim women and girls into the classroom: taxes were reduced for families allowing their womanfolk to attend classes, and they were given priority in obtaining agricultural implements; special women's clubs, called red tea-houses, were arranged where women could study in the surroundings to which they were accustomed. No fewer than 20 per cent of the places in vocational schools were reserved for Muslim women. By 1926 the number of literate persons in Turkistan reached 9.17 per cent (5.85 per cent of women). These were the first achievements. In the next ten years, for every 1,000 persons, there were eleven men and five women with higher education. In 1983, women made up 60 per cent of those with higher or secondary vocational education.

---

13. V.I. Lenin, *O zadachakh zhenskogo rabochego dvizheniya v Sovetskoy respublike*, 39.204.

On the whole illiteracy among women was eradicated within 20 years. Thus the 1939 general population census showed that about 82 per cent of women aged nine to 49 were literate.

Education opened up real opportunities for women to gain vocational and professional training, and equality with men in the national economy. The right to equal pay for equal work, regardless of sex, was one of the first decrees proclaimed by the Soviet state. But this right did not by itself guarantee economic equality. The latter could be secured only by carrying out a corresponding state policy. For example, special cooperatives and artels were organised in Central Asia to liberate Muslim women from their domestic imprisonment, to draw them into social production and social affairs. Today, 93 per cent of able-bodied women in the USSR either work or study and they make up 51.1 per cent of the labour force.[14] It is significant that while 30.4 per cent of the population is made up of dependents, 31.2 per cent of men belong to this category and 29.7 per cent of women.[15] Statistics confirm the economic independence of the overwhelming majority of Soviet women.

Before the October revolution women were mainly involved in the worst-paid professions. One might say that there was a ghetto of women's labour. Nowadays women work in practically all the 290 large professional groups of social production; in 156 of them, women represent no less than 50 per cent;[16] they constitute 45 per cent of all research workers (about 28 per cent of those with Ph.D. degrees); 50 per cent of the economists and about 70 per cent of doctors and teachers.[17]

The problem of the equality of women should not be over-simplified. The law may decree equality of rights, but the latter become a reality only if the physiological nature of women is fully taken into consideration, and special attention is given to motherhood as an important social function of women.

A.M. Kollontay, a well-known champion of women's liberation, said: 'It would be a big mistake to look at the emancipation of woman from a narrow point of view – seeking *formal* equality of man and woman in labour. . . . The demand for women's participation in all the spheres of the national economy should be augmented

14. *Zhenshchini v SSSR 1986*, M. 1986, p. 7.
15. Sm.Novikova E.E. *Zhenshchina v razvitom sotsialisticheskom obshchestve*, M., 1985, p. 23.
16. *Opït KPSS v reshenii zhenskogo voprosa*, M., 1981, p. 224.
17. *Zhenshchini v SSSR 1986*, 10–14.

by the demand to organise on a very wide scale maternity and child protection, special labour protection for women.'[18]

A whole set of measures have been worked out in the USSR to create the best possible conditions to enable women harmoniously to combine their functions as workers, citizens and mothers: fully paid maternity leave (56 days before and 56 days after childbirth), retirement at the age of 55, prohibition of female labour in jobs which could be harmful to a woman's health (underground work, lifting heavy weights, long night shifts, etc.).

In order to advance further towards the liquidation of differences in average wages of women and men, it is necessary to equalise the level of their professional skills. According to sociological investigations carried out in the Soviet Union, there are still some groups of women workers with low vocational education. The fact that these workers lag behind in professional skills naturally results in low wages. Sociological inquiries in Taganrog-city in the 1960s showed that the average wage of women workers investigated was from 100 to 120 roubles, while that of men was from 160 to 170 roubles, due to their higher level of professional skill.[19]

In the last 20 years the situation has significantly changed, but it is too early yet to say that average wages of men and women have been equalised everywhere. Not only is the further improvement of women's professional skills needed, but the acceleration of technical progress in general is vitally important because, where a high level of mechanisation and automatisation is reached, the proportion of skilled workers is larger, and the difference in the average wage of men and women is practically non-existent.

One of the most complicated problems is that of establishing equality among those engaged in intellectual pursuits. A high level of education in itself is not a guarantee of equal chances in obtaining promotion, in making a career. For example, in 1984–5 women constituted 73 per cent of school teachers, while they made up 83 per cent of directors of primary schools, and only 38 per cent in secondary schools.[20]

That women fall behind men in developing their professional skills, and their relatively slow rate of promotion are both deter-

18. *Materiali I Vsesoyuznogo soveshchaniya po okhrane materinstva i mladenchestva*, Moscow, 1921, p. 28.
19. E.B. Gruzdeva, E.S. Chertikhina, *Trud i bït sovetskikh zhenshchin*, Moscow, 1983, p. 57.
20. *Zhenshchinï v SSSR*, M., 1981, p. 12.

mined to a great extent by the difficulties they face in combining intensive work with family duties. Sociological data show that engineers, for example, make their best showing after six to ten years of service. Sociologists claim that if engineers are not promoted at their prime they lose perspective, reduce the level of demands they make on themselves and begin to lag behind their younger colleagues.[21]

As is well known, however, the first years of service for most women generally coincide with the beginning of their married lives and the birth of children. Hence, they inevitably suspend their service for a rather lengthy period. The situation is aggravated by the tradition of putting the burden of housekeeping on women's shoulders. Clearly realising all the difficulties standing in the way of changing women's social status during the very difficult years of the civil war, after the Revolution, Lenin said that the real emancipation of women, their factual equality with men in the national economy and in social life could be achieved only by liberating her from the 'slavery of everyday, dull and humiliating housework.'[22]

It does not matter how just the laws are if women are not able to enjoy their constitutional rights because they do not receive assistance in bringing up their children or in their work at home – in other words, in fulfilling those functions which they willingly carry out as mothers and wives, but which become intolerable when the whole burden is placed on their shoulders. The slavery of housework is impossible to overcome by the efforts of the family alone, no matter how helpful the wife and husband are. It is a matter for the state as a whole.

It is amazing that even in 1919, a time of war, destruction and terrible economic depression and a period of extreme socio-political tension, the new Soviet state found it possible to take measures to emancipate women. 'Public dining-rooms, crèches, nurseries', said Lenin, 'are simple, prosaic, unpretentious means which can in fact liberate women. . . . These means are not new; they have been created (as well as all other material preconditions of socialism) by big capital, but under capitalist conditions, firstly they were very rare, and secondly (and this is very important), they remained mercantile enterprises . . .' [23]

21. *Sm.Sotsial'no-psikhologicheskiy portret inzhenera*, Moscow, 1974, pp. 78–80.
22. V.I. Lenin, *Velikiy pochin*, 39.23.
23. Ibid.

The revolutionary state had a programme for the emancipation of women and carried out a corresponding social policy. But for the full realisation of this programme the state needed more than goodwill; it also needed the resources and public funds which could only be created gradually along with the country's economic progress. Nowadays about 17 million children attend crèches and nurseries (the number has doubled since 1965). The state pays 80 per cent of their expenses, while the parents pay no more than 12 roubles a month.[24]

The system of prolonged day-schools is of great help to families in bringing up children. (In 1984 the number of children attending these schools reached 14 million.) Practically all schoolchildren spend their summer vacation in camps (parents cover 34 per cent of the expenses).

The growth of public funds widens the perspective for social aid to women. What does this mean? Every five-year plan envisages the introduction of new measures for the improvement of the status of women and children. In 1981–3 the state budget spent 9 billion roubles on this. The measures included more state assistance to families with children and to newly-weds (a grant of 50 roubles when the first child is born, and 100 roubles when the second or third is born); an increase in monthly allowances to single mothers; the introduction of partially paid leave to enable mothers to look after their children until they are one year old; a provision whereby women are entitled to additional leave without pay to look after their children until they are eighteen months old, and even until they are two years old; further expansion of the network of crèches and nurseries and their improvement, etc.

Thanks to a number of measures taken by the state since the October revolution much has been changed concerning the housekeeping activity of women. In comparison with the 1920s the volume of housekeeping labour has been cut by more than half. Simultaneously, leisure increased five times.[25]

There is a great deal yet to be done to improve services that can make housekeeping easier and to meet all the requirements for nurseries and kindergartens. No less important is a subjective factor connected with human psychology. The solution to the problem of the equality of women not only demands the creation of favourable

24. A. Kozlova, *Zabota o materi i rebenke*, 'Moskovskiy rabochiy', 1984, 37–8.
25. *Trud i bït sovetskikh zhenshchin*, p. 79.

political, economic and cultural conditions, but also of radical changes in social morals. Decrees were adopted to emancipate women soon after the revolution prohibiting *kalym* – a custom of buying and selling girls – banning child marriages, punishing polygamy, abolishing *Nikyah-say* – access to water resources for men only and so on.

When these new decrees were put into practice they met strong opposition from feudal elements. Muslim women who dared to take off the *hijab* which covered their faces and bodies were severely beaten. For two years (1926–8) in Turkistan alone almost 2,500 women were killed for their attempts at emancipation.[26]

It took years of work to change the old morals and old ideas preventing the liberation of women, not only through the making and implementation of the law, but also by extensive educational work, through literature, the arts, the theatre, cinema, press, radio and television.

The emancipation of women leads to changes in family roles. The traditional, patriarchal family model, where the man dominates, is giving way to the model of a family based on *partnership*.

Sociological investigations show that among families with partnership relations unhappy marriages make up only 5 per cent. It is logical therefore that even in the Middle Asian Republics of the USSR where traditional family relations are still quite strong, only 10 per cent of students supported the maintenance of the dominant status of the husband.[27] The majority of those who were questioned by sociologists in Leningrad in 1984 were in favour of sharing housekeeping responsibilities between wife and husband.[28]

The formation of a new family model is an extremely complicated process; the change of roles is psychologically difficult for both men and women. Sometimes it leads to divorce.[29]

The different social and psychological effects of women's emancipation should be studied not only by scholars, but by 'the engineers of human souls' – by writers, artists, etc. It is not accidental that during the last decade a great number of novels, films and dramas have been devoted to the problems of 'career women', to a new type

26. B.P. Pal'vanova, *Emansipatsiya musul'manki*, Moscow, 'Nauka', 1982, 27–9.
27. E.K. Vasil'eva, *Sem'ya v sotsialisticheskom obshchestve*, Moscow, Izd-vo 'Misl', 1985, p. 116.
28. *Tam zhe*, p. 141.
29. Ibid., p. 1.

of relationship between women and men both in private and in public life.

The policy of the socialist state at this stage of its development is not simply aimed at securing the socio-economic equality of women and men, at providing the equalisation of their professional levels or at creating the conditions for the liquidation of inequality in private life. It also looks for ways to overcome the possible negative aspects of women's liberation which adversely affect the birth-rate, the consolidation of family and the upbringing of children.

This is why in the Political Report of the CPSU Central Committee to the 27th Party Congress in the section dealing with the problem of improvement of socio-class relations, special attention was paid to the consolidation of the family. It stated that: 'A strong family is one of the principal pillars of society. . . . It is necessary to organise the practical work of State and public organisations so that it promotes in every way a strengthening of the family and its moral foundations.'[30] It was pointed out that the necessary prerequisite for solving many family problems is 'securing living and working conditions for women that would enable them successfully to combine their maternal duties with active involvement in labour and public activity'.[31] Accordingly in the twelfth five-year-period (1986–90) it is planned to extend the practice of allowing women (if they so prefer) to work a shorter day or week. Mothers will have paid leave until their babies are eighteen months old. The number of paid days leave granted to mothers to care for sick children will be increased. It is intended fully to satisfy the need for pre-school children's institutions within the next few years. It has been suggested that the formation of women's councils could help to solve a wide range of social problems.

The effective and complete equality of women in the socio-economical and political life of the state is not Utopian. The experience of the first socialist state convincingly proves that women's emancipation can be attained if its realisation is no longer a matter of struggle by women alone, but becomes the cause of society as a whole, a cause backed up by a consistent, planned state policy.

30. Mickail Gorbachev, *Political Report of the CPSU Central Committee to the 27th Party Congress*, Moscow, Novosty Press Agency, 1986, p. 63.
31. Ibid.

13

Women's Politics and Women in Politics in Norway since the End of the Nineteenth Century

IDA BLOM

At the general election in 1983 Norway broke a world record in that 37 per cent of the representatives elected to the national parliament were women. In May 1986 this historical achievement was repeated. In a Labour government, headed by a female prime minister, 40 per cent of the ministers appointed were women.

Until 1983 Norway was in line with the other northern European countries in this respect. The percentages of female ministers in the Danish, Norwegian, Finnish and Swedish governments were 15, 18, 22 and 26 respectively, and in their national parliaments 24, 31, 26 and 28 respectively. Women's participation in the political decision-making process in these countries is among the highest in the world.[1]

The scope of this chapter is not, however, to try to explain why this is so, but to gain insight into the complicated patterns of favourable and unfavourable conditions for women's political activity. Let us nevertheless start with a few general remarks on why northern European women are comparatively well represented in their national political institutions.

Northern European countries have, throughout history, been rather poor and have had less marked class differences than the richer countries of central and southern Europe. It seems likely that the relative absence of strong class divisions and the ethnic homogeneity have fostered an open and democratic political system with

1. See Elina Haavio-Mannila *et al.* (eds), *Det uferdige demokratiet. Kvinner i nordisk politikk*, Oslo, 1983.

few polarising problems. True, there are differences of class and culture, but these are smaller in this part of the world than in most other places and the growth of the welfare state, especially after the Second World War, has eliminated many of them.

The enormous increase in women's economic activity since the beginning of the 1960s has, in recent years, brought women more knowledge (through better education), higher motivation and greater self-reliance. Furthermore women have, since the 1960s, been able to decide how many children they want and when to have them, thanks to an efficient system of medical care and advice on contraception and abortion. Smaller families and children born at an early stage of married life have left many women with plenty of spare time at around the age of forty, thereby shortening the period when child-care made political activity problematic.[2] Even if still not practised very widely, it should also be mentioned that during the last twenty-five years husbands have taken responsibility for more of the household chores and at least no longer openly oppose women's political activity to the same degree as before. Increasing state interference in daily family life has brought problems to the political agenda that have a direct bearing on the life of the average woman. All this may explain the high degree of political participation by women in northern Europe.

In Norway this situation has been reached in two very different stages. Until recently progress was extremely slow. Major changes were not made until the 1970s, but since then they have come with an astonishing speed.

Women Organising and Fighting for the Vote.

At the end of the nineteenth century major changes started to affect economic, social and political life in Norway. About a century later than in the industrial areas of Great Britain, technological and economic development brought industrial capitalism to this mainly agrarian country. The central political institutions extended their range of activities and began to intervene more frequently in the lives of individuals and families. As power gradually shifted away from the family and the local municipality to parliament, govern-

2. Ida Blom, 'Nødvendig arbeid – skiftende definisjoner og praktiske konsekvenser', *Historisk Tidsskrift* (Norway) 7 (1985), pp. 117–41.

ment and nationwide organisations, it became important for individuals to organise themselves in order to seek power in, or at any rate to influence, the central political bodies that directed society.[3]

Men found it easier than women to adjust to these new conditions. Women still had to act primarily within the confines of the family and the local community. The distance between the home and the place of paid work increased with the emergence of factories, shops and offices, and it became more difficult than before for women to combine their work within the home with other activities. In consequence the difference in the lives of men and women was accentuated. Men were, to a much greater extent than in the agrarian society, alloted the primary responsibility for meeting the family's economic needs and for contact with society outside the family, while women were responsible for the continuance of the family line and for practical and emotional tasks within the family.

Nevertheless, like men, women began to join forces to obtain influence during the middle of the nineteenth century. In the 1840s they formed their own sections of the Missionary Society, working to spread the gospel of Christianity to other parts of the world. Later they flocked to the various types of temperance societies, and joined in organised social work through charity organisations.[4] These activities were aimed at promoting the welfare of people thought to be in some kind of spiritual or material need not at changing the conditions of the women active in the organisations. From the beginning women dominated organisations with altruistic goals, while men dominated organisations formed to promote economic, professional and political interests. Where men and women joined the same organisation, activities were mostly divided according to the same principles as in the bourgeois home: men took care of the economic and public side of affairs, women saw to the inwardly motivating and comforting chores. Recent research has shown, however, that many of the altruistic organisations maintained their activities thanks to the money raised by female members through knitting and embroidering activities.[5] In such cases

3. Where no other sources are indicated what follows is based on Ida Blom, 'The struggle for women's suffrage in Norway 1885-1913', *Scandinavian Journal of History* 8:1 (1980), pp. 3–22.

4. Ida Blom, 'Women in organizations in modern Norwegian history. Instruments of power or of protest?' *Report from the International Symposium on the Research of Women's Organizations*, Frederika-Bremer-Förbundet (Stockholm, 1978).

5. Britt Foldøy, 'Frivillig organisering blant kvinner i Stavanger fram til l. verdenskrig'. Unpublished dissertation Department of History, University of Bergen, 1982;

women constituted the economic backbone of the organisation, and there are examples of the power this gave them to obtain their own goals within such organisations. One such example is from a temperance society, where organisational reconstruction and the foundation of a nationwide organisational structure eliminated the right that female members had enjoyed to vote in the decision-making bodies within the organisation. This triggered off what might be called the strike of the knitting needles, which put an end to the prosperous bazaar activities and almost strangled the organisation economically. Within a short time these women had their right to vote within the organisation reinstated.

Organising to promote the welfare of others did bring women out of the domestic world and gradually made them aware of the necessity to obtain political influence. When the fight for the vote resulted in the formation of local suffrage organisations, there was a considerable amount of cooperation and overlapping activity between the largest of the female altruistic bodies, the Norwegian Women's Public Health Associaton, and the biggest of the suffrage associations, the National Association for Women's Suffrage, both founded in 1898.

In the mid 1880s women started organising to promote their own interests. Women teachers formed an association in Christiania (later Oslo) in the 1860s, but this was more of a social gathering of teachers than an interest group. In 1884 the Norwegian Association for the Rights of Women was started. Its somewhat vague goal was to work for women's rightful position in society. Both men and women joined the association and the first chairperson was a man. Recent research[6] shows that he precipitated the foundation of the association to avoid the question of suffrage, to limit activities to educational and professional questions and to improve the legal position of women. Gina Krog, the female instigator of the idea of collective action to promote all these interests soon brought about a split in the organisation over the suffrage question, giving rise to the Association for Women's Suffrage in 1885. Men were excluded from this organisation. The vote became the most important issue for the feminist organisations during the following decades. The Associa-

unprinted manuscript, Equal Status Council. See F.K. Prochaska, *Women and Philanthropy in 19th-Century England*, Oxford, 1980, for similar activities in England.

6. Aslaug Moxnes, *Likestilling eller særstilling? Norsk Kvinnesaksforening 1884–1913*, Oslo, 1984.

tion for Women's Suffrage did, however, decide to change its policy as universal suffrage for men was introduced during the latter part of the 1890s. Moderate members now wanted to work for a gradual enfranchisement of women, while the more radical members maintained the programme of female suffrage on equal terms with men. The radical faction broke away in 1898, forming the National Association for Women's Suffrage.

Political circumstances for achieving female suffrage have varied from country to country.[7] However, so long as only men could take part in the political decision-making process, the introduction of female suffrage must in a direct sense be seen as the result of men's political action. It is even possible to see it as the result of men's fight with other men over political power. Initially radical members of the Liberal Party supported and cooperated with women in this matter. The idea of equal rights for all individuals and of natural selection through competition, which John Stuart Mill had applied to women, fitted in well with the liberal ideology of this party. In 1891, however, female suffrage was dropped as too radical to combine with universal suffrage for men. The latter question was a necessary part of the cooperation programme agreed upon with the Social-Democrats. Although the Social-Democrats became more reliable supporters of female suffrage, they did not include it in their first national programme in 1888 and only adopted the cause more wholeheartedly after universal suffrage for men had been obtained. For some time the social democratic procession on the national day (17 May) was devoted only to female suffrage and women speakers addressed the demonstrators. By now the Conservative Party was getting interested in limited female suffrage, seeing that universal male suffrage might endanger its position. Indeed, limited female suffrage in local elections was obtained in 1901, limited national female suffrage in 1907. The limitations were so lax, however, that the women still barred from the vote were mostly female servants.[8] By 1911 universal female suffrage was obtained for local, and in 1913 for national, elections. At every stage the right to stand for election accompanied the right to vote.

Does this mean, then, that the collective action of women was of

7. Richard Evans, *The Feminists. Women's Emancipation Movements in Europe, America and Australasia 1840–1920*, London, 1979.
8. Anne Loennechen, 'Kvinners kommunalpolitiske aktivitet i Kristiania fra 1901 til 1907', unpublished thesis, Department of History, University of Bergen, 1983.

no importance to the question of female suffrage? The answer is of course, no. In 1818, parliament considered a proposal that the term 'Norwegian citizen' in the paragraph of the constitution relating to the suffrage should be supplemented by the words 'of the male sex' so as to 'show quite categorically that the female sex . . . [was] not entitled to vote'. This proposal was rejected on the grounds that 'the women of our country have not yet demanded the right to partici-pate in the management of the state', and that the proposal was therefore 'superfluous and inappropriate'. The weak ripples from the revolutionary wave in Europe in 1848, which reached Norway through the Thrane movement, demanding among many other things universal suffrage (for men) did not touch on the question of female suffrage. Thrane, the leader of the movement, rejected this as unnatural and inimical to family life. A precondition for female suffrage was thus that women should demand 'the right to partici-pate in the management of the state', which they did after 1885. Although they had to work through male supporters, it is the case that from 1885 until universal female suffrage was obtained in 1913, parliaments had to consider an address promoting female suffrage almost every year in some form or other. This activity most cer-tainly kept the question on the political agenda and forced even reluctant male parliamentarians to consider it.

Nevertheless, during the twenty-eight years of struggle, the op-ponents of female suffrage repeatedly used the argument that women themselves were not interested in the right to vote. It was claimed that women were not mature enough to exercise this right or had not expressed a desire to receive it or even that women had directly stated that they did not want to have the vote. With equal regularity these arguments were refuted by claims that the precise opposite was true: the activities of women aimed at securing the vote were cited as an indication that female suffrage should be a justifiable innovation. When it was no longer possible to ignore the concerted efforts of women for the right to vote, the anti-feminist argument shifted and it was maintained that these women repre-sented only a minority and at the very least did not represent women who lived in rural areas. Once again these arguments were refuted by pointing to occasions when women, either resident in the countryside or in very great numbers, had taken an interest in politics.

As the suffrage was gradually extended to women their use of or their failure to exercise the right to vote was employed as an argument for and against further extensions of female suffrage. Women themselves also attached great importance to demonstrating, through political activity, that they not only wanted, but also exercised their political rights.

It cannot therefore be doubted that the contribution made by women was a factor to which politically active men ascribed some weight. If some women had not clearly expressed a desire for the right to vote and taken action to secure this objective the demand for female suffrage might not have been raised at all and central arguments in its favour would have been absent. But women did much more than express their wish to obtain the vote. Organising suffrage associations was but one of the means they applied to reach their goal. As in other countries Norwegian women working for the suffrage put pressure on male politicians through various channels.

Direct addresses to party groups in parliament and to governments were sent at all critical stages in the development and sometimes just to keep the question on the agenda. Family connections were important. Though sources are naturally scant in this respect we have an example of the importance the opposition to the female suffrage gave to such influence on male politicians. In a parliamentary debate on the question in 1907, one of the conservative members complained that: 'If we now give women the right to vote in national elections in addition to the influence which they have behind the scene and which unfortunately they will always, in spite of everything, retain, the situation will become intolerable.' On a later occasion he wrote that:

> Although a majority of the members of the Storting (the Norwegian Parliament. *IB*) in 1907 were clearly aware that it was quite indefensible to give women the right to vote and to stand for election and although there was a majority against female suffrage at a Conservative party meeting the evening before the issue was to be voted on, so many weary men went over to the other side in the course of the night that a majority was obtained for female suffrage.[9]

One very important strategy was that of supporting the Liberal Party in its national policy of loosening, and eventually breaking, the political union with Sweden. This policy succeeded in 1905. Women expressed their support for it in at least two important ways.

9. Stortingsforhandlinger 1906–07, p. 3541; O. Malm, *Barneformindskelsen i Norge og dens aarsaker*, Kristiania, 1916, p. 77.

In 1896 they organised a nationwide network of women's associations. The Norwegian Women's Public Health Association worked to supply the Norwegian military forces with sanitary equipment in case of a military conflict with Sweden. As this never occurred, the organisation was changed into a support institution for the fight against tuberculosis, and soon became the largest of all the female organisations in the country. The same body cooperated with the National Association for Women's Suffrage, giving it a much broader footing than would otherwise have been possible. In 1905, when the nation was called to a referendum concerning the abrogation of the political union with Sweden, women were not allowed to take part. The two organisations then joined forces in heading a campaign to obtain as many signatures as possible from women to support the government in ending the union. This campaign was so successful that male politicians proclaimed that women had by now earned the right to vote.

Women fighting to get the vote in Norway used the strategy of acceptable behaviour whenever possible in order to gain recognition from male politicians as responsible political actors. It must not be forgotten, however, that factors which neither men nor women were able to influence directly, also played a role. One precondition for the emergence of the issue of female suffrage was the large number of unmarried women who, because they were economically active, had more contact with society outside the family than did married women.[10] Unlike their married sisters, their time was not consumed by housework. The number of women in economic activity accentuated the need for political influence as a means of securing better working conditions. From the 1880s on women started organising in trade unions, either in purely female unions or

10. According to census material about 60 per cent of all unmarried women were gainfully employed during the period 1875–1950. The percentage was then reduced, due to more young girls going to schools, universities or other educational institutions and to a reduction in the age of marriage for women. About 4 per cent of married women were gainfully employed between 1875 and 1910, after a small reduction between the wars reaching 5 per cent in 1950, 10 per cent in 1960 and 20 per cent in 1970. See Olav Ljones, *Female Labour Activity in Norway*. Samfunnsøkonomiske studier, vol. 39, Central Bureau of Statistics of Norway, Oslo, 1979, p. 27. Married women of course contributed to the family economy to a much greater extent than these figures indicate. In the urban industrial areas they worked in unregistered or badly registered jobs such as part-time employment in canning factories or washing, cooking or sewing in other people's homes (Ida Blom, 'Frauenarbeit und Familienökonomie in der städtischen Gesellschaft Norwegens von 1875 bis 1903', *Jahrbuch für Wirtschaftsgeschichte* (1984); in the agrarian areas their work

together with men. In 1901 the female trade unions combined the Social-Democratic Women's Associations in the capital in the Norwegian Labour Party's Women's Association. From 1909 this association extended its activity to become nationwide.[11]

Women in education and care-giving work also gradually formed professional organisations. The education and training that these women received made them more capable of formulating demands. The many discussions of women's lack of rights within family and society sparked off by these various organisations during the latter part of the nineteenth century led to a greater level of consciousness among women of their need to influence the development of society through activity outside the home.[12]

So women's outspoken demand for suffrage, plus the growing organisational activity among women, combined with shifting support from male politicians and the political struggle between men to drive forward the fight for women's vote. In 1913 the last battle was won. In fact the extension of the national suffrage to all women that year looked more like a festive parade than a battle. The decision was carried with unanimity in parliament. This political development was founded on thoroughgoing technological and economic changes transforming Norway from a rural to a semi-industrial country and expanding the activity of the state over local and familial units.

A Long Way from Formal to Real Equality.

With the vote, formal equality between men and women was obtained in political matters. Effective equality had not yet been reached. As Tables 13.1 and 13.2 (pp. 263–4) show, it was not until the 1970s that women had a significant number of representatives in

---

within agrarian production is only sporadically registered, though local studies confirm the economic importance of this work. See Ingeborg Fløystad, *Kvinnekår i endring. Kvinnene sitt arbeid i Arna, Hordaland, 1870–1930.* Bergen, 1986, pp. 48–94.

11. Vera Espeland Ertresvaag, 'Arbeiderkvinnenes faglige og politiske organisering 1889–1901', and Kirsten Flatøy, 'Utviklingslinjer innen Arbeiderpartiets Kvindeforbund fra 1901 til 1914', both in Ida Blom and Gro Hagemann (eds), *Kvinner selv . . . Sju bidrag til norsk kvinnehistorie,* Oslo, 1977, 2nd edn, 1980, pp. 47–94.

12. Anna Caspari Agerholt, *Den norske kvinnebevegelsens historie,* Oslo, 1937, 1973, 2nd edn, pp. 162–3, 181–3, 196–7; Ida Blom, *Barnebegrensning – synd eller sund fornuft?,* Bergen, 1980, ch. 7.

Table 13.1: Women in Norwegian municipal councils and in parliament
1901–85

Year	municipal councils		Year	parliament	
	I absolute figures	II relative figures		I absolute figures	II relative figures
1901	98	1		–	–
1907	142	1	1909	0	0
1910	210	2	1912	0	0
1913	197	2	1915	0	0
1916	192	1	1918	0	0
1919	157	1	1921	1	1
1922	149	1	1924	0	0
1925	159	1	1927	1	1
1928	189	1	1930	2	1
1931	179	1	1933	3	2
1934	234	2	1936	1	1
1937	383	3	–		
1945	512	3	1945	7	5
1947	730	5	1949	7	5
1951	890	6	1953	7	5
1955	1,056	6	1957	10	7
1959	978	6	1961	13	9
1963	904	6	1965	12	8
1967	1,291	10	1969	14	9
1971	1,985	15	1973	24	16
1975	2,088	15	1977	37	24
1979	–	23	1981	–	26
1983	–	24	1985	–	34

Sources: Torild Skard (1980), op. cit., p. 133, and *Mini-Fakta om likestiling* (1986).

municipal and national political institutions. Since 1945 all governments have contained one or two female ministers, in the 1980s
increasing to four.[13] Not until the national election in 1985 have
women accounted for more than 25 per cent of the representatives
in any of the political institutions. As mentioned at the beginning of
this chapter they then suddenly reached 37 per cent of members of
parliaments, followed by 40 per cent of ministers in the government
formed in May 1986.

13. Torild Skard, *Utvalgt til Stortinget*. Oslo, 1980, p. 133; Haavio-Mannila, p.
265, and *Minifakta om likestilling, Likestillingsrådet* (1986).

Table 13.2: Women in the Norwegian government 1945–85

	I number of ministers	II female ministers	III I as % of II
1945–65	13–15	1	7–8
1965–71	15	2	13
1971–72	15	1	7
1972–73	15	2	13
1973–76	15	3	20
1976–81	16	4	25
1981	17	4	24
1981–83	17	4	24
1983–86	18	4	22
May 1986–	18	8	40

Sources: Elina Haavio-Mannila *et al.* (1983), op. cit., p. 265.

The long path can be divided into periods with different strategic characteristics. As we have seen, women used a range of organisations to press for female suffrage. Without representation in parliament they directed pressure towards local political organisations, towards male members of parliament and towards the government.

When the vote was obtained, women chose two different strategies. The Association for Women's Suffrage recommended that women set up special female lists at elections, and even suggested that they form a special 'Women's Party'. This strategy was tried in the capital for the first three municipal elections, but with little success. At the third election a man was sent up as the representative for the Women's Party. The party programme was outright conservative and might almost be characterised as anti-parliamentarian. The other strategy advocated by the National Association for Women's Suffrage and by Liberal and Labour women alike, was to work within the parties cooperating with men and learning the art of political activity.[14] This also led to disappointment, as may be seen from Tables 13.1 and 13.2.

Around the time of the First World War women in the bourgeois parties followed the strategy that had all along guided the Socialist women: they formed their own associations within the party they felt at home in. Thus the Conservative Women's Club was born in the capital in 1910, the Liberal women followed the next year. In

14. Loennechen.

other towns the same happened throughout the following years, and in 1925 and 1928 respectively national women's organisations within the two largest bourgeois parties were formed. A closer look at how this strategy worked within one of the parties will highlight important problems for women in political activity.

'It Takes Two to Make a Happy Life'

This was the sentiment expressed by one of the male leaders of the Liberal Party on the twenty-fifth anniversary of the Liberal Party's Women's Association in 1953. The reference to conjugal happiness within the party was accompanied by the hope that liberal men and women would continue to cooperate in building a good society. Another important liberal male politician paid homage to the women for their 'self sacrificing, unselfish, quiet and loyal work', performed within a tight economic frame that they had agreed to stretch to the utmost. He, too, clearly, had the image of the ideal wife in mind. He did regret that the party had not sent one single woman to parliament, but found this to be the great task for the women to accomplish in years to come.[15]

Looking back it is interesting to note that the Liberal Party was formed in the same year that the Norwegian Association for the Rights of Women started its activities. Both organisations were the result of developments bringing new groups into political activity. The Liberal party was the result of an alliance between peasants and the liberal opposition against the conservatives, while the Norwegian Association for the Rights of Women recruited women from the same social groups as the liberal opposition. The Liberal Party consolidated a victory which lasted for some time. The Norwegian Association for the Rights of Women signalled the start of a long fight.

As we have seen, some of the important Liberal male politicians joined the Norwegian Association for the Rights of Women and supported proposals for female suffrage. Family ties quite literally bound some of these men to the women active in the Norwegian Association for the Rights of Women. In one instance the wife headed the National Association for Women's Suffrage, as well as

15. Where no other sources are mentioned what follows is based on Ida Blom, 'Kvinner i Bergen Venstre', *Streiftog gjennom Bergen Venstre i 100 år 1883–1983*. Bergen Venstre, 1983, and Ida Blom, 'En liten ondskap?', in Ottar Grepstad and Jostein Nerbøvik (eds), *Venstres hundre år*. Oslo, 1984.

the Norwegian Women's Public Health organisation. The husband was one of the top figures in the Liberal Party and their daughter helped to put pressure on the party group in parliament.[16]

The party was, however, split on a number of other questions important for women, such as better education and the right to be appointed to certain offices. The dividing line between the two groups of the party was the same as the one between its moderates and its radicals, that led to a split in the late 1880s. This division also followed geographical differences: the radicals were mostly to be found in the capital and the eastern part of the country, where industrialisation and urbanisation had been felt for a longer period than in the agrarian fishing districts of the mountainous west – the stronghold of the moderates.

Family connections also seem to have been important for finding support within the party. They helped in the formulation and realisation of political goals put forward by women sympathising with the Liberal Party, including laws to ensure a safer position for children born out of wedlock, and some economic support for mothers during confinement.

Once suffrage was won the party seems to have welcomed women into the organisation. As early as 1902, when limited suffrage for municipal elections had been carried, some of the local liberal organisations changed their laws to permit women to become members. In 1902, 25 per cent of the board members in Bergen were women and for some years the Bergen branch of the party operated a quota system allocating women a fixed number of the names on the election lists. The proportion allocated to women was 10 per cent, while 'workers' were allocated 25 per cent. This local branch seems to be the first political organisation admitting a quota system in favour of women, but then the 10 per cent might also have been a guarantee against having too many of them on the lists. For some years a few women were elected to the municipal assembly of Bergen, but they never amounted to more than two or three and during some periods, especially between the wars, there were no women representatives for the Liberal Party.

Explanations as to why women did not succeed in establishing themselves as party representatives were looked for in their lack of political experience. Women also maintained that what they needed was more training. If they were more active, men in the party would

16. Agerholt, pp. 188, 192, 207.

surely listen. It was considered the women's responsibility to capture seats in committees within the party as well as in the municipal assemblies and in parliament. Few expressed this so harshly as one of the most prominent women in the party, Anna Jebsen Henriksen, who was deputy substitute to the parliament just before the war:

> If the ordinary women had not been so terribly lazy when it comes to political activity, we would not have to be ashamed of our lack of representation in parliament. Surely no one can expect women to be carried into parliament, we certainly have to walk the way on our own feet. The men have given us what have asked for – at least most of it – but we have to shoulder our own responsibilities. The initiative is ours.[17]

This was but one of many examples of how women were given the responsibility to make themselves felt within the party. In Bergen they were asked to capture more seats in the municipal assembly, but these should not be the seats already held by their male party colleagues, it was for the women to gain additional ones. As we shall see, this was an impossible job. Not even the party's own electorate gave their votes to the women on the party list. Still, the idea that women simply had to make themselves heard and capture the seats from other parties, prevailed for a long time.

Separate – But Equal?

As already mentioned in 1911 some Liberal women tried another strategy, forming special women's associations as part of the party organisation. By 1928, when the Liberal Women's National Association was founded seven or eight local associations existed. Twenty-five years later thirty-two local associations had joined in.

This way of organising may be seen as a compromise between direct membership in the main party organisation and activity as an interest group outside the party. What the Liberal women aimed at was, however, not to promote their interests as a group, but to win more women for the party. The Liberal men had no critical word for their activity. On the contrary, it was heartily welcomed.

This may partly be explained by the overall political situation in

17. Undated cutting from *Bergens Tidende*, of an article written on 40th anniversary of the local women's organisation of the Liberal Party in 1967.

the country in 1927–8. In January 1927 the two socialist parties, which had been fighting each other for some years, joined forces again. A month later the appeal to form the Liberal Women's National Association appeared in the Liberal newspaper. Before this could happen the election in the autumn of 1927 had brought the Socialists a resounding victory and, to the dismay of the bourgeois politicians, the king called for a socialist government. It was a very short-lived experience but certainly enough to frighten bourgeois liberals. In June 1928 the Liberal Women's National Association was formed. This was one of many examples, both of how women rallied to support male politics and of how class took precedence over gender in decision-making.

Like a faithful wife the Liberal Women's National Association continued to cooperate with the main party organisation. In line with traditional expectations, the local association in Bergen did its best to give the party meeting a 'really cosy and homely atmosphere'. The problems the women raised in local politics sprang out of their daily experiences. Their first proposal was to have a roof put on the fishmarket where they bought dinner for their families several times a week. Since Bergen is one of the rainiest places in Europe, this was no bad idea. It has, however, never been done. The money raised by the women did once serve to buy new curtains for the party offices, but it was also used to bring the leader of the Liberal Women's National Assembly to speak at one of their meetings. These activities were no different from what happened in the other local liberal women's associations. Some of them had no activity other than to arrange the party's social gatherings and an occasional lecture evening. This is where we must look for the 'self-sacrificing, unselfish, quiet and loyal' party women. But others worked with problems in social politics, quite often with a direct bearing on the women's world. Most of the women's associations took part in electioneering activities and some, although a minority, did try to work for more women in the party leadership, and as representatives in municipal and national institutions.

But the seemingly idyllic cooperation had its problems, though they only rarely came to the surface. A report to the Liberal Women's National Association in 1953 from one of the local associations maintained that there had been 'a drop of malice in the activity of the women. It is first and foremost addressed to the men in the party. . . . The promises inherent in the suffrage were never kept, and women felt it might be easier to win the battle when forming a group as when working as individuals.'[18] But they did not succeed very well as a group either. They tried hard to have a woman appointed to the Liberal government which was formed in 1933, addressing the party group in parliament as well as the prime minister. But in vain. The first female minister in a Norwegian government was appointed in 1945. She was a communist, and served in a coalition government. Later governments always included one or two women, but not until 1972 did a Liberal woman reach that office. She is the only one so far, but this is also due to the fact that the party split in 1972 and never regained its important position in Norwegian politics. Not until the 1970s did women in the party better their position in the municipal councils, and only three women have ever represented the party in parliament. Between 1945 and 1977 the Liberal Party had, on average, 9 per cent of the representatives in parliament. Women accounted for 2.5 per cent of these.[19] Part of the explanation must be found in the size of the party, which has shrunk considerably since the inter-war years. Small parties do not usually stake their fate with female politicians, though this is not a rule without exceptions. The smallest of all the parties in parliament, the Left Socialist Party, has had the biggest percentage of women among its representatives. There is reason to believe that the *will* to give women a chance makes an important difference.

Another weakness in the strategy of the Liberal women may be that not even those within the same political party agreed on all political initiatives. Like men in the same party, they were divided into a radical and a moderate wing. The radical women wanted the party to take action to promote information on family planning and change the draconian laws making abortion a criminal act, but the moderates openly opposed such initiatives. Some of the leading radical women later left the party and joined the Labour Party where support for these matters was better, if not wholehearted.

Other questions, however, such as the demand that half the members of the jury in cases of sexual offences be women and that schoolchildren be taught some basic facts about human reproduction, were also raised by Liberal women.

It is important to remember that all this time *some* women remained direct members of the main Liberal Party organisation

18. Undated cutting from *Bergens Tidende*, 1952, of an article written on the 25th anniversary of the local women's organisation of the Liberal Party.
19. Blom, 1984, p. 59.

and never joined the Liberal Women's Association. Some of them even criticised the existence of such a gender-specific way of enroling women in politics, maintaining that this cemented the traditional ideas about women's special qualities and special duties. The answer to this was that women needed to train themselves for political activity without being constantly subjected to the critical or patronising eyes of the male politicians.

In the 1950s and '60s the separate women's organisations in the Liberal Party as in other parties played only a minor role. Direct participation in the activity of the main party now became the line followed by most women. This strategy accorded well with what happened in other countries at the same time, where the separate organisation of women sometimes ceased completely.[20] The idea that real equality had been established between women and men was strong in this period, and only broke down when the new women's movement became active.

A New Political Strategy for Women

Until 1970 women never comprised more than 10 per cent of the representatives in municipal and national assemblies. Then, within 10 years they rose to 25 per cent and then, in 1985, to 37 per cent of the parliament.

There seems to be no doubt that the new women's movement must be given some of the credit for these results. This was where the recognition was first formed that formal equality does not necessarily mean equal results. When people who are not equal are treated in the same way, the result will be inequality. This gave rise to a discussion that spread also to the older women's organisations, of what could be done to make it possible for women to assert themselve politically. Special treatment for women was advocated as a means of adjusting the unequal work-load between men and women in the family as well as in society. Many found cooperation between women across class and party boundaries to be the way to pursue better possibilities for women in politics.

Work within the new women's movement did for some years absorb much of the political energy of women. This was where they

20. Drude Dahlerup, 'Why separate organizations for women? Women's organizations in Denmark: their relationship to politics and to feminism', in *Report from the International Symposium*.

found the sisterhood they needed, where they discussed their problems and decided strategies for change. In many ways the new women's movement and new activity in the older women's organisations took over some of the functions of the separate women's associations within the political parties, training and motivating women for political activity. Many women working within the parties now got a more clear-cut feminist approach to political problems.

Measures at top level also helped women to assert themselves better. A Council for Equality between the Sexes studied and recommended action in situations detrimental to women's public interests and an ombudsman was appointed to investigate cases in which women (and men) felt their interests were being damaged as a result of their sex. A law of equality between men and women was passed in 1978 stipulating equal and in some cases favourable treatment of women. All this stimulated public interest in the problems women had, until then, viewed as private problems and also made male politicians aware of the difficulties inherent in being a female politician. The new development also made an impact on the Liberal Party. For the first – and so far the only time – a woman was elected *leader of the Liberal Party*, and it was agreed that all election lists should contain at least 40 per cent women. To begin with they were often placed mainly at the end of the list, but a new agreement decided that men and women should be listed alternately from the top. A special committee for equality between the sexes within the party was formed to watch over the new agreements.

The Liberal Party was quick to adopt such measures and other parties soon followed, with the Labour Party sometimes preceding the Liberals in adopting reforms. The Labour Party was also the party that in 1981 gave the country the first female prime minister. She returned as head of government for a second time in May 1986.

Looking at women's politics and women in politics through the perspective of a single party gives an impression of the problems to be overcome in other parties. So far no coherent study has been made of this issue other than for the Liberal Party, but more general discussions of why equal opportunities did not bring equal results for women in politics indicate that differences between parties are not conspicuous. In party politics, as in forming powerful organisations and in rising to the top positions in any trade, women have to overcome barriers that bear very similar imprints. Let us look more closely at the barriers to women's political activity in the period

271

under discussion.

Barriers to Women's Political Activities

The first barrier to be overcome is of course the universal right to vote and to stand for election. As we have seen, this right was obtained later for women than for men, although the time-lag of fifteen years does not seem major compared to other countries. Also Norwegian women obtained this right at national level well before women in many other countries, preceded only by Finland (1905). But then Finland was at that time not a sovereign country but part of the Russian Empire. Denmark followed closely on Norway's heels, (1915), and Sweden followed suit in 1921. The right to hold office as a member of government was extended to Norwegian women in 1916, and to Danish and Swedish women in 1921 and 1925 respectively, indicating that political power at top level should no longer be considered a male prerogative. Nevertheless it was almost thirty years before the first female minister took her seat in a Norwegian government. Equal opportunities certainly should not be confounded with equal results.[21]

Freedom of speech and assembly has been considered a basic human right since the French Revolution and the acceptance of the Rights of Man in 1791.[22] Formally it applied to both sexes throughout the period under consideration, but in reality women had much more limited possibilities than men. Discussion of female suffrage demonstrated the disgust men could muster at the thought of hearing a female voice in parliament.[23] The low wrangle over women's access to the post of priesthood in the national church also provides evidence of the limitations placed on women's right to freedom of speech. Lay women were not accepted as preachers in the churches on the same conditions as lay men.[24] One professor of theology, when asked to speak in a church where a woman had been speaking some time before, replied: 'If the whole church is thor-

---

21. Ida Blom and Anne Tranberg (eds), *Nordisk lovoversikt. Viktige lover for kvinner ca. 1810–1980*, Nordisk Ministerråd, 1985.

22. Gudmund Hernes, *Makt og avmakt*. Oslo, 1976, and Blom, 1978.

23. Agerholt, pp. 224–5.

24. Reidun Klokkersund, 'Hjemmet først og fremst, men det andet ikke forsømmes ... 'Kirkas kvinnesynbelyst med utgangspunkt i debatten om kvinners adgang til presteembetet i perioden 1891–1912', Unpublished thesis, Department of History, University of Bergen, 1986, p. 236.

oughly washed and scrubbed inside, I might consider doing so.'
General standards of appropriate behaviour for females only gradually allowed women to take the floor in public and studies of
working conditions for women in parliament (as late as 1980) reveal
different reactions to speeches by female and male representatives.[25]

There should obviously be no physical or practical barriers to any
individual participating in politics. Such barriers did exist for a long
time, however, and made it impossible to combine married life and
political activity, especially given the long hours spent in meetings
when husband and children might need attention and an ideology
teaching girls and boys different responsibilities towards the family.[26] Though in agrarian areas women's work made an important
contribution to the support of the family, the husband was considered the bread-winner. This also applied to working-class families where the wife often made a substantial contribution to the
family income, either by cleaning or cooking in other people's
houses, or by other part-time work, for instance in the canning
industries. The idea of the husband as bread-winner, the wife as the
angel of the home still to some extent makes it difficult for many
women to aim for a political career.

Another side to this question may lie in the fact that it is more
difficult to become influential in an organisation if one's interests in
it are short term and, at least in politics, this again applies more to
women than to men. The problems encountered in trying to organise domestic servants is a classic example of this difficulty. Until the
Second World War domestic service was the main occupation for
unmarried Norwegian women, yet, although several attempts were
made as early as the 1880s and 1890s to organise these young
women to fight for better working conditions, it was not until 1910
that an organisation was established. Although at times very weak,
this organisation continued to exist and carried out some valuable
work in preparation for a law regulating working conditions for
maids. By the time it was passed, however, which was after the
Second World War, maids had in any case become a disappearing
group.[27]

25. Torild Skard, *Utvalgt til stortinget*, Oslo, 1980, pp. 181, 184–7.
26. Ida Blom, 'Family history and women's history – the case of Norway', in John
Rogers and Hans Norman, *The Nordic Family. Perspectives on Family Research*,
Reports from the Family History Group. No. 4, Department of History, Uppsala
University, 1985, pp. 100–20.
27. Ellen Schrumpf, 'Tjenestepikespørsmålet i Kristiania. Tjenestepikenes kår og
organisering ca. 1880–1990', unpublished thesis, University of Oslo, 1978; Irene

As long as women have seen their own economic activity only as a short intermediate occupation between childhood and wifehood, they have taken little interest in professional organisations. The cost in time, effort and money was too high compared to the short-lived benefits they might gain from organising. As most Norwegian women until the 1960s did not continue to work outside the home after marriage, their interest in staking energy and time in, for instance, a trade union or any other professional organisation, was smaller than that of men. This partly explains why few women work at the head of such organisations. That these organisations also serve as recruitment channels into party politics and thus into political decision-making institutions, helps explain the slow progress of women as representatives at the municipal as well as at the national level.[28]

A fifth deterrent to active participation in politics can be that the results of political decision-making are at the disposal of everybody, not just those who have participated in the political process. So when some women were active in suffrage organisations, their success would also give suffrage to women who had passively waited for the vote. This meant that unless women felt a strong urge to participate they would save time and effort by just waiting for others to fight for results. This of course also applies to men, but the effect is much stronger for women because of the social expectation that they should concentrate on home and family.

This expectation actually put a cross-pressure on women, which men did not feel, and this constitutes the sixth barrier. It was encountered when it came to using the vote or organising in political groups. The conflict can be clearly seen in the many attempts made by the Labour Party's Women's Association to mobilise working-class women. In 1915, for instance, the journal of that Association contained a full account of the women's section's national conference at which the question of mobilising women had been discussed accompanied by a detailed piece on the necessity of spring-cleaning, airing, washing and eradicating dust which would otherwise collect 'the bacteria that brings disease'.[29] The journal

Storvik, 'Hushjelpene i det norske bysamfunn i mellomkrigstida – med særlig vekt på; Tromsø. Hushjelphold, levekår og organisering', unpublished thesis, University of Tromsø, 1982; Linda Kvinge, 'Hushjelpene i norske byer 1930–1948', unpublished thesis, University of Bergen, 1983.

28. Helge Marie Hernes, *Staten – kvinner ingen adgang?* Oslo, 1982.

29. *Kvinden*, 1 April and 1 July 1915. See Blom in *Scandinavian Journal of History* (1980). p. 20.

went so far in giving priority to women's work within the family that it declared that if women took an interest in politics, this would support the organisational and political work of men and make women themselves better suited to bring up their children to be good socialists.

This brings us to the seventh barrier to women's political activities. Women did not identify themselves clearly with other women. Gender as a social category was for most women weaker than class. Consequently it was more important for the working-class women to see the Labour Party prosper than to win female suffrage. So long as feminist and class interests complied, there was no problem. But if a choice had to be made it mostly followed class rather than gender divisions. This was more obvious with the Labour Party than with the Liberals or Conservatives: bourgeois women more often felt their interests to be in direct opposition to men of the same social category, than did working-class women. As long as social conflicts along class divisions were an important part of politics, women only in very few cases and for a very short time, joined forces across class barriers. Sometimes they were even outright opponents, as in the matter of accepting a law forbidding women to work night shifts. This was obviously a step in the direction of better working conditions for industrial workers as such and earned the support of most working-class women, but collided head-on with the idea of equality between the sexes. This idea was so strong in the bourgeois women's movement that the liberal and conservative women fought the proposition. It was not accepted.[30] Another example is aptly illustrated by a cartoonist in one of the daily papers in 1915 observing that the rich women in England were on hungerstrike to get the vote, while the poor women in Norway voted to get food.[31] Class differences between women made it difficult for them to cooperate even in cases where they might have had common interests.

This may be seen from the difficulties in mobilising women across class boundaries. There are examples of politically active bourgeois women openly admitting that they did not think working-class women could be considered educated enough to vote. This illustrates how women might sit back and let male politicians of their

30. Gro Hagemann, 'Særvern av kvinner – arbeidervern eller diskriminering?' in Blom and Hagemann, pp. 95-121.
31. Ida Blom, 'Kvinnen – et likeverdig menneske?', *Norges kulturhistorie* 5, Oslo, 1980.

own social group fight for them. So long as the levelling out of social injustices is an important part of politics, women will keep back their own special grievances and give preference to measures that ease the living conditions of the family as such.

The eighth barrier is found in the very structure of political activities. Long meetings, often into the small hours, a fair amount of travelling, etc., are examples of practical problems. The themes dominating the political discussions are often far from the everyday life of women and need an expertise that is more common to the education of men. One of the results of this is the vertical division of responsibilities in politics. Women outnumber men in certain sectors, mainly education and social policy, where they are also often represented at top level.[32] This is, however, a disadvantage to women in that these sectors do not offer opportunities for deciding the really important issues, such as economic policy. Moreover, it may be asked whether women's access to political decision-making institutions has actually been a fight to get into institutions of shrinking importance?[33] According to one theory, political decision-making has moved away from open political institutions to the more hidden corporative channels of committee and government administration. The most important of these corporate channels are still almost completely dominated by men, recruited from the big economic organisations and the immediate surroundings of ministers.[34]

To overcome this important barrier women will have to choose other educational areas than those dominating today's female higher education. Economics and public administration are still dominated by men, although women have started taking these courses at a much greater rate over the past ten years.

All this may indicate that to get political power women must behave like men when planning their lives and in deciding which political arenas are worth fighting to get into. This would also imply changing what sociologists term the special responsible care-giving sensibility now identified with women into the technical instrumental mentality more common to men.[35] If this is the price of

32. Skard.

33. Harriet Holter, 'Om kvinneundertrykkelse, mannsundertrykkelse og hersketeknikker', in Thordis Støren and Tone Schou Wetlesen (eds), *Kvinnekunnskap*, Oslo, 1976, pp. 61–82.

34. Hernes 1982.

35. Aase Bjørg Sørensen, 'The organizational women and the Trojan-Horse effect', and Hilduer Ve, 'Women's mutual alliances. Altruism as a premise for interaction',

complete democracy we may ask whether it is worth paying, or whether women have a more important role to play as stumbling blocks to the advancement of a technically progressive but inhuman world.

More hope is to be found in a different theory which attributes the unbalanced gender representation to the fact that women have not yet been recruited in sufficient numbers to stamp their special needs and abilities on the political agenda.[36] So long as women representatives are few they will have a tendency to comply with male attitudes and strategies. So far, even if women have put important questions on the agenda that might otherwise not have been there, they have by no means given rise to a revolution in politics. To do so it also seems that a fair number of women in top positions and strong women's organisations – maybe a strong radical and visionary women's movement – is needed to back women representatives up with new perspectives and visions.

The new Norwegian Labour government with its 40 per cent of women ministers heading a parliament with 37 per cent of women representatives may therefore mark a turning point in women's history – the start of the final stride towards complete democracy.

---

both in Harriet Holter (ed.), *Patriarchy in a Welfare Society*, Oslo, 1986, pp. 88–105, 119–35.
36. Haavio-Mannila.

14

Feminism and Politics:
Women and the Vote in Uruguay

SILVIA RODRIGUEZ VILLAMIEL AND
GRACIELA SAPRIZA

Introduction

Uruguay, a former Spanish colony which gained its independence in 1830, is a small Latin-American country wedged between two powerful neighbours – Brazil and Argentina. The port city of Montevideo is the political, financial and commercial centre of what was once little more than a sparsely-populated cattle ranch. During the last quarter of the nineteenth century, however, Uruguay became more integrated into the world market and certain internal changes, including the modernisation of cattle-raising production, the appearance of the first industries, and European immigration, began to occur.

At the beginning of the twentieth century Uruguay underwent a period of economic expansion, based mainly on cattle-raising and agricultural exports, which lasted until about 1930. Whereas at the turn of the century Uruguayan society had been highly polarised, with a small upper class controlling a predominantly peasant population, by the end of this period a relatively strong middle class had emerged. In addition, the state had begun to play an important part in the economy and had done much to improve communications and transport and to extend the educational system. Advanced social legislation, secularisation of public and private life and a protective policy regarding women were other of its characteristic features.

For almost half a century Uruguay's development strategy was predominantly *socialist* (in that it practised distributive policies), *nationalist* (in that it protected national interests) and *state centered* (in that the state played the main part in promoting these plans). Despite the crises and obstacles generated by the society's conservative elements, this development pattern continued to shape Uruguayan public life throughout the first half of the twentieth century.

Women at the Turn of the Century

The process of acquiring political rights for Uruguayan women began during the first three decades of the twentieth century. Although a detailed analysis is beyond the scope of this chapter, it should be borne in mind that this, like any other historical process, needs to be set within the prevailing economic, social, political and cultural context.

At the beginning of the twentieth century the condition of Uruguayan women was mainly one of subjection and discrimination. Legally, in common with all the other countries that adopted the Napoleonic Code as a model, they were treated very much like dependents or minors who relied on their father's or husband's protection. In Uruguay, the Civil Code (approved in 1868 and modified in relation to this aspect only in 1946) held that a woman should obey her husband and that the husband had full rights over the children.

The criteria then used to judge adultery are nowadays considered surprising. It was not only moral punishment that could befall a woman whose husband caught her in the act, for he was exempted from any penal procedure in the event of her injury or even murder. Furthermore, the 1907 divorce law (considered a 'scandal' by society at the time) would always recognise adultery on the part of the woman as a cause for divorce, but where the man was the adulterer it would be cause for divorce only if committed at the couple's residence. Woman thus appeared as a modern vestal, the keeper of the home's sacred fire. It was this 'double standard' which, in many respects still exists today, that feminists were to fight.

Although female participation in the labour force was relatively important (17 per cent of the economically-active population registered in 1908 were women) it was oriented towards the less qualified and worst paid occupations. Even in those cases in which women filled jobs equal to men, the salaries they received were invariably lower than those paid to men. The majority of women in the labour force at that time had no choice in the matter; they came from the popular and working classes. Only a small minority of middle and upper-class women chose to work, but they generally gave it up when they married.

Women were excluded from secondary and higher education mainly because of prejudice and custom rather than by law. A few women were able to attain higher education through a combination of personal strength and family backing for their decision to confront the prejudices of society. Women were not, however, allowed to vote, nor were they considered citizens, which meant they were barred from holding public appointments or practising certain professions (such as that of a notary) which required citizenship.

In effect, women were generally secluded in their domestic worlds. Yet, because of various demographic changes which were taking place in the society, their prestige as 'biological reproducers' was beginning to wane. Families were becoming smaller, marriages were taking place at a later age and female sexuality was being more strongly repressed.

Women's Movements

Although at the end of the nineteenth century most women were unaware of their subordinate position and passively accepted the roles society had assigned to them, there were some women living in Uruguay at the time who felt uneasy about the conditions under which they were living and who formed groups through which to express their dissatisfaction. The members of these groups came from a range of social and cultural backgrounds and their struggles were waged on several fronts. As a result, the movements were often fragmented and laden with contradictions.

In Uruguay, as elsewhere, two different types of women's activism emerged, which were separated by class as well as economic and cultural differences. On the one hand there was that of the women workers who had been organised at a trade union level; on the other that of the feminist groups composed of highly-educated middle and upper-class women who were often teachers or engaged in some other similar profession. For various reasons these two branches of the women's movement were unfortunately unable to agree on any important issues and they began to grow apart. They either ignored or attacked each other, but somehow never managed to understand or respect each other's position. Some pioneers, such as the socialist and feminist militant, Paulina Luisi, tried to break down the barriers, but without any great success.

Working-class women have the longest history of struggle and organisation and there were several well-known and outstanding anarchist women militants among them. In 1901 some laundress and ironing women's resistance associations were formed and, in the same year, male and female cigar workers went on strike; in 1905 a seamstresses' strike was organised. Women's liberation had begun to acquire a particular relevance in anarchist circles where the whole basis of the bourgeois family and of the subjection of women within the patriarchal system was being contested.

The anarchist newspaper, *La Batalla* (The Battle), directed by a distinguished militant called Maria Collazo, frequently tried to encourage women to develop their intellects and to use their education as a means of raising the female condition. In one edition in 1917, for example, women were told that, through study, they should 'search for ways to develop their own criteria'.

During the 1920s the women's groups in the recently-founded Communist Party, which were being developed at both the trade-union and the political levels, became important. This was an interesting, enthusiastic, radical movement which resolutely defended women's rights and, no doubt because of its youth and revolutionary political zeal, was sometimes rather intolerant, having little trust in 'bourgeois' parliaments and elections. These women favoured greater participation by women in the trade unions and demanded that unions with a strong tradition of female activism (such as the shoemakers and workers in the beer factories) accept women onto their strike committees and as union leaders. They struggled against the 'lack of confidence in and prejudice against women among the male proletarian masses'; they strove hard to persuade the trade unions to introduce equal pay for equal work into their programmes; they denounced the failure to implement labour laws and generally did as much as they could to improve conditions for the working woman. Having little confidence in parliament and bourgeois laws, however, they were relatively uninvolved in the struggle for civil and political rights, believing instead that the emancipation of women would be possible only with the abolition of capitalism. Each year, on 8 March, they celebrated the International Day of Working Women. Although the movement lost its impetus over the next few decades, it is significant that the

Communist Party representative, Julia Arévalo, was one of the first women to be elected to the House of Representatives in 1942.

Feminism

The feminist movement in Uruguay was started by a teacher, Maria Abella de Ramirez, who had founded a feminist centre in La Plata (Argentina) in 1903. In 1911, at her instigation, the 'Uruguayan Section' of the Pan-American Women's Federation was launched at the Atheneum in Montevideo to struggle for the civil and political rights of women.

The National Women's Council of Uruguay was founded a few years later in 1916. Although the initiative came from Paulina Luisi, it was established by several different associations and operated by setting up specialist commissions to tackle various issues. It rapidly developed into an efficient, popular and highly motivated organisation. In 1919 the Uruguayan Alliance for the Women's Vote was created as an offshoot of one of its commissions.

Thus the two main international women's associations[1] of that time were installed in Uruguay. Local associations brought their organisation and programmes into line with the principles established by the international ones. The two associations helped one another and many of their campaigns were conducted together.

Because of the characteristics of their members (well-educated middle and upper-class women) they adopted an essentially liberal approach and, although acknowledging the problems of working women, their main emphasis was on education and civil and political equality. *Acción Femenina* stated in 1919 that, 'the purpose of the National Women's Council [was] to establish bonds of solidarity among all women and among all associations worried about the social, intellectual, moral, economic and juridical improvement of women'. The prevailing liberal approach was also reflected in its proclaimed reliance on the 'irreversible advance of progress' which, it was assumed, would bring forth all kinds of improvements for women. They also had excessive confidence in legal and juridical means of accomplishing the effective participation of women in society, without accompanying social change.

1. The International Women's Council, founded in Washington 1888, and the International Alliance for the Women's Vote, created in England and the United States in 1904.

Included among the issues for which they campaigned were: peace, women's education and free access to all professions, the abolition of 'white slavery' and legal prostitution (which implied opposing the double standard of sexual morality), women's rights over their own bodies and the protection of single mothers. With respect to women's work, they always supported the principle of equal pay for equal productivity and denounced special protective legislation because of its adverse effects on working women's interests. An important part of their mobilisation was devoted to obtaining the vote, as well as civil equality (such as the rights of married women to handle their own possessions or to have authority over their own children).

Most of these aims, which were being put forward by feminists internationally, were easily 'absorbed' by the ruling party in Uruguay, which wished to appear progressive and advanced. Although the National Women's Council had declared itself independent of any political or religious groups, some of its most prominent members were also Colorado Party militants, which was one of the main reason why feminism lasted for such a short period as an independent movement. None the less, such cooperation did mean that the National Women's Council could fulfil its goals once equality under the law had been obtained.

It is important to point out that there were some attempts to link feminist demands to the claims of working women. Paulina Luisi was particularly active in this respect and, in 1919, took an active and decisive part (together with the general secretary of the Socialist Party, Celestino Mibelli) in founding a women's trade union, the Telephone Operators' Union. Later, in 1922, she left the National Women's Council to join the Alliance for the Women's Vote. In 1923, while Paulina Luisi was its president, the Alliance decided to change its name to that of the Uruguayan Women's Alliance on the grounds that its former name referred only to 'a small part of its programme', which was now more actively concerned with the 'economic rights' of women. A letter to its members asked everyone to cooperate in helping the Uruguayan Women's Alliance launch a vast programme of social improvements. It especially asked for the participation of all those women who had a pressing need for these improvements and who 'faced life through brave, dignified and honest work'.[2]

2. Uruguayan Women's Alliance, National General File, Particulars, Box 251, Folder 6, page 27.

283

But despite its efforts this new tendency was unsuccessful and created serious disagreements among the working women, especially the communist militants who maintained that the Uruguayan Women's Alliance was a bourgeois institution and, 'as such, would do nothing for women's liberation'. They went on to say that, 'no liberating activity – no matter how intelligent it may be – can free women of their dependency in capitalist society . . . women have double duties . . . we believe that women's liberation can be fulfilled only through a change of regime'.[3] In reply, a member of the Women's Alliance writing under a pseudonym remarked that, 'Undoubtedly her revolutionary impatience does not allow her to see the Alliance's fruitful work. . . . As in every social matter, starting is a first step. Therefore it is a difference of degree. Once the vote is conquered . . . other aspirations will appear . . . [which] should accomplish the transformation of the present capitalist regime.' The letter went on to argue that the Alliance had a comprehensive programme which took economic demands into account and to explain that: 'The majority of its members are professionals or intellectuals who might not be militants of workers' parties, but because they belong to the intellectual proletariat, it should not be assumed that they are against those demands.'[4]

Despite the harshness of this polemic, however, there was a certain amount of mutual respect on both sides. The workers admitted that the feminist's liberation activity was 'intelligent' and the feminists made it clear that they supported the workers' demands.

The feminists were engaged in a wide range of activities, including public events (often held at official places such as the women's university, the teacher's institute or the main university), conferences, publications (articles in the daily press and in the magazine *Acción Femenina*, pamphlets and other occasional publications), petitions, negotiating with public authorities and participating in international feminist congresses. Sometimes well-known feminists were seen participating in wider popular movements, such as the 'street conference' organised by the Teachers' Committee for Salary Increase in 1929, or, in 1932, at a women's meeting for peace (held because of the threat of war between Bolivia and Paraguay), at which 26 women's organisations and numerous unaligned sup-

3. 'Justicia', *Tribuna Femenina*, 14 January 1924.
4. *El Siglo*, 16 January 1924.

porters formed a column three blocks long through the main street of the capital.

Women from the wealthier classes often expressed their resentment of the prejudice, subjugation and morality imposed on them by holding poetry meetings, at which the works of women poets such as Maria Eugenia Vaz Ferreira, Delmira Agustini and Juana de Ibarborou would be read. The unmarried woman entrepreneur, Irma Avegño, was well known at the time as a representative of this upper-class faction of the movement.

On balance, there seems little doubt that in the early 1930s the mobilisation and even politicisation of women in general, but particularly of the middle classes, was becoming far more widespread as a result of these feminist campaigns having become important in influencing public opinion.

Although various statesmen were sympathetic to women's issues, theirs was by no means a universally popular cause and they had to endure conservative prejudice, mockery, the distortion or misunderstanding of most of their demands and, sometimes, even violent attacks. To face such a struggle required considerable courage and a good deal of patience.

Besides, even though their demands did not involve the majority of women, their long drawn-out struggle to accomplish the principles on women's rights raised by the French Revolution was, in essence, the struggle to obtain the right to full democratic participation in society for half the Uruguayan population.

The Ideological and Political Context

We shall now briefly describe the various ideological views on women's issues held by those groups which, in one way or another, took part in the debate on women's political rights.

Batllismo[5]

Batllismo is basically reformism with strong humanitarian impulses and its leaders could be said to have considered women's issues from much the same perspective. More specifically, Batlle's own

---

5. A predominant faction of the governing Colorado Party, under the leadership of Jose Batlle y Ordonez.

attitude towards women contained two seemingly antagonistic tendencies.

On the one hand was the protective, 'gentlemanly' paternalism, politically expressed in labour law (with its special legislation protecting women), maternity protection (viewing motherhood as 'sacred') and social security (with its special retirement conditions).

On the other hand, however, it was extended to champion women to proclaim their rights, aptitudes and possibilities as human beings and pressing them to overcome the 'state of inferiority' in which they found themselves (the Catholic church was blamed for this). In that sense women's access to secondary schooling and higher education was made possible; and active campaigns were developed to obtain equal civil and political rights. It was argued that votes for women and work outside the home were neither going to bring chaos into family life nor anarchy into society. This political party was therefore sympathetic to feminist mobilisation. It must be noted that the beneficiaries of these policies were usually women of the middle and upper classes. The protective attitude was directed rather to women of the working class.

To understand *Batllista* ideas about women, it is helpful to look at the work of the philosopher Carlos Vaz Ferreira, who, through synthesising the existing tendencies and giving them some form of theoretical basis, came up with a new point of view which more or less became the official doctrine on women. Because he held an important university chair and had been widely quoted in press articles and parliamentary speeches, his standpoint became well known and generally accepted in the society as a whole.

Vaz Ferreira took as his starting point a biological fact which he considered indubitable: 'We are a species physiologically organised to the disadvantage of the female'. From here on, he established the guiding principles for the approach to these problems: the ideal was not to render men's and women's condition equal, but to correct or 'compensate' for inequalities. He called his stance 'compensation feminism' . . . 'if you wish to give me the name of feminist, which I will not reject'.[6]

Vaz Ferreira's ideas about the family and women's role within the family still hold currency in Uruguayan society today. Women must be educated and they are able to work outside the home, but always in part-time jobs, since they have their 'own burdens' at home

6. Carlos Vaz Ferreira, *Sobre Feminismo*, Montevideo, 1933, pp. 33, 111.

which cannot be transferred because they are, in essence, derived from physiology.

We should particularly note this characterisation of these 'burdens' as not transferable. Was a more equitable distribution of domestic responsibilities between men and women completely inconceivable? Was it also inconceivable that the state or other institutions could take care of some duties? Here is one of the clues explaining the survival of this ideology: its 'functionality' for the 'welfare state' and for the continuation of society itself as it was structured. Through the gratuitous services of a highly qualified housewife, who also undertook a teaching role, the quality of life for middle-class society could improve without burdening the state.

Both tendencies in *Batllista* attitudes towards women are always present. The one, which has its origins in the ideas of the Enlightenment and later in political Jacobinism (of which *Batllismo* is an offshoot), considers that society itself generates differences between its members. It thereby ascribes a social origin to the inferiority of women and encourages policies that promote women in an attempt to counteract their social disadvantage. The presence of ideologies that hold that psychological differences are the product of biological differences can be discerned, for example, in the phrase quoted by Vaz Ferreira in which he refers to women's 'own burdens'. This tendency fosters the tutoring and protective attitude towards women characteristic of the main accomplishments of *Batllismo*.

In other contexts it has been said that 'this ideology was so strong that it succeeded in obtaining, during the nineteenth century, the reconstruction of the patriarchal family through the state's intervention'.[7] Thus, in reformist ideology we find a set of egalitarian principles and interventionist and protective practices in favour of women's domestic role upholding the same policies that are designed to improve the population's living conditions.

Socialism

More radical groups, such as the socialists, had long since had a clear position on women's issues. They pointed to the double subordination (of class and gender) to which women workers were subject.

In 1907, the Socialist Party, which was still in the process of

7. Judith Astelarra, 'El Feminismo como Concepción Teórica y como Práctica Política', *Cuadernos del Círculo*, Barcelona, 1980, p. 14.

formation, proposed a series of reforms for Uruguayan society. The situation of women played an important part in its programme, including reforms of the Civil Code, civil and political equality and 'absolute' divorce. At the instigation of its leader, Emilio Frugoni, the Socialist Party undertook to study the women's issue from a Marxist point of view. Frugoni endorsed the opinion of socialists like August Bebel, who considered that the evolution of capitalism, while requiring women's incorporation into social production, at the same time also created the material preconditions for their emancipation.

In practice, while supporting the official position in several projects, the socialists frequently took *Batllismo* to task in an attempt to improve the government's performance.

The Conservative Reaction

For the first thirty years of this century conservatives tended to adopt a traditional and intolerant attitude towards women's issues. Their ideas, which were apparently never expressly articulated by a theoretician, seem to have emerged mainly as reactions to successive *Batllista* legislation. As issues such as divorce, or women's civil and political rights were being debated in parliament and in the press, the conservatives gradually revealed the full range of traditionalist opinion, which was shown to be patriarchal, politically and socially conservative and, in religious matters, closely allied to Catholicism.

The central tenet of their argument was that the family, the home and maternity constituted women's 'natural' role and that she could not escape this biological and psychological determinism. Any excursion outside the home was considered a menace to family stability and was violently resisted. They also, along with many European conservatives, feared that, coupled with 'social subversion', women's emancipation could destroy the basis on which society was built. As a result, the conservative opposition vigorously opposed any initiatives that could possibly be interpreted as a threat to family or fortune, especially divorce and the demand for women to participate alongside men in social and economic affairs.

Many upper-class liberals agreed with the conservatives' criticisms of female emancipation. Their liberalism was mainly a stance on the religious problem, or was restricted to the political sphere, but it did not imply any questioning of social organisation, nor of traditional ideas about the roles of men and women.[8]

The father's authority, women's submission to a natural 'determinism' which ties her to the home, the idea that women are essentially passive and the conviction that there is a causal relationship between feminism and social subversion are all important elements in the conservative position.

The Process of Approval

As in all American constitutions, the Uruguayan Constitution of 1830 denied citizenship to women. The vote was also denied to salaried servants, day-labourers and illiterates. In 1917, the vote was granted to all men; women had to wait a further 15 years for the same rights.

The first steps in this process were taken when, at the beginning of the century, the new reformist tendencies incorporated the claim to equal voting rights on their political platforms. The feminist movement initiated by Abella de Ramírez was perhaps the first to demand equal civil and political rights for women. Socialism did so as early as 1907, even before becoming a political party. Later *Batllismo* began to agitate in the pages of *El Día*. From this social and political conglomerate stemmed the initiatives and projects that hallmarked to different degrees the road to the sanction of the 1932 law.

The first question when studying the subject concerns the source of the initiative. To whom should we credit the passing of this law? Should we accept that all the initiative came from the public sphere 'independently of women's claims', as Baltasar Brum[9] later asserted, or should we rather consider suffrage as a banner around which women with a common programme organised themselves, simultaneously incorporating other goals?

To place the debate in context we have researched the different ideological standpoints existing on the question of women at the beginning of the twentieth century. According to these studies we do not think the discussion should be considered as an antinomy between 'conquest' or 'concession' but rather as a dialectical rela-

---

8. In 1925 there were a remarkable number of similarities between the Catholic newspaper *El Bien Público* and the liberal's *La Razón*.

9. A well-known *Batllista* politician. See Baltasar Brum, *Los Derechos Civiles y Políticos de la Mujer*, Montevideo, 1923.

tion between principles or ideologies on the one hand and concrete political opportunities on the other.

The *Batllista* reformists manipulated their electoral programme, adapting to changing needs and electoral or political opportunities. Accordingly they sometimes backed the initiative, trying to extend their constituency, while at other times they restrained it. In the same way it is plain that even if it is true that the feminist movement was capable of leading an intense campaign in defense of equal civil and political rights for women (especially after 1916), it also had its possibilities limited by its social composition and its basic postulates. While acknowledging the effective social and political mobilisation developed by feminism, feminist activities cannot be held to have been uniquely decisive in obtaining the vote. Rather it was the sum of a series of social and political factors – some contradictory – which led to the approval of the law. Likewise, it is possible to trace a chronological and ideological parallelism between women's campaigns in favour of the vote for women and the proposals of political parties.

Rather than provide a detailed description of the presentation and approval of the bill permitting women to vote, we have decided to discuss and evaluate the various party initiatives and feminist proposals and mobilisations at four significant moments in time. These moments appeared in 1914, 1917, 1925 and 1932. The proposal presented in 1914 began the debate and informed the great reformist impulse which characterised the period. The 1917 initiative, which was framed at a time of intense political mobilisation as well as of constitutional reform, carries the distinction of having been presented by the socialists. The year 1925, although of scant political significance for the *Batllista* faction, was a period of considerable ideological creativity. Finally, 1932 marked the culmination of a complex process in a difficult political climate in which a number of very different sectors were participating.

The first concrete steps towards enfranchising Uruguayan women came from a group of *Batllista* legislators in 1914, when they presented the so-called Miranda proposal to grant women the vote. The reason put forward at the time for supporting it, which was probably designed to allay fears but now looks like a rather timid defence of gender equality, was that the vote would not distract a woman from her customary and 'natural' task of looking after her home.

Contemporary reports of women's mobilisation are contradictory. On the one hand the leader of the Uruguayan Socialist Party, Frugoni, maintains that there was no 'suffragist agitation or demonstrations of any importance'.[10] On the other hand several testimonies directly contradict this image of 'feminine shyness' by purporting that women were indeed actively participating in the political parties.

The reasons for presenting the proposal in 1914 have to be sought in the last years of Batlle's second presidential period, which were characterised by intense political debate and ambitious social reforms, including the approval of the second divorce law. The publication of Batlle's *Apuntes* in 1913 had acted as a detonator to the Collegiate Executive. The proposal to grant women the vote coincided with (and probably had a part to play in causing or at least justifying) the first conservative split within the Colorado Party. If the reformist impulse was as strong as some claim, it is possible that at a time of internal strife, the Party sought to broaden its political support by appealing to 'half the population'.

It was no coincidence that the National Women's Council was created in 1916, the year of the National Constituent Assembly elections in which the political atmosphere was highly charged at the prospect of a new constitution. The socialist delegation proposed that the Assembly grant women the right to vote and substitute the term 'men' with the word 'persons' in the constitutional text.

During the session of the Constituent Assembly, the recently-created Women's Council conducted an active campaign, collecting signatures, petitioning, rallying and publicising its ideas in *Acción Femenina* and in occasional contributions to daily newspapers. The organisation and coherence of the feminist movement grew with its political participation and its ideas became widespread. 'Everywhere, in the workshops and in the salons they talked about women's votes', asserted *Acción Femenina* in November 1919. With this increase in their popularity they were now able to participate in public activities. And, in December 1917 at the women's university, they held the first public assembly in defence of women's political rights ever to have been held in Uruguay. On the anniversary of the death of Hector Miranda (who had been a supporter of feminism), the entire Council attended and the president made a speech. The following day the newspapers commented on the astonishingly

10. Emilio Frugoni, *La Mujer ante el Derecho*, Montevideo, 1932.

large numbers of women present.

Despite all the campaigns and demonstrations, the provision included in the 1917 Constitution, voted for by two thirds of each House, granted women the right to vote only on municipal or national matters.

Although the delay in sanctioning the proposal seems to suggest that the conservative opposition might have been stronger than commonly imagined, it is also possible to detect contradictory positions among those who, in principle, supported the proposal. The conservative politicians were in no doubt that the vote should be restricted to men; after all, the belief was strong (it even outlasted the law approved in 1932) that public action belonged to men and women took on the passive, domestic roles. No wonder this group regarded suffragist women as one of nature's aberrations and synonymous with social subversion.

But even within the *Batllista* ranks, however, there were those who were unconvinced of the concrete advantages of the women's vote, which, they felt 'could provide the ballot box with a great force of reaction and recession'. While holding that the conservative role traditionally assigned to women within the family and the influence of religious ideas was a matter of debate, Vaz Ferreira himself admitted years later that he too had been a victim of the prejudice 'of attributing to women far too conservative ideas or feelings'. These reservations were probably quite important, especially for *Batllismo*, if it is true that the government's main reason for extending the vote to women was the need to broaden its political base. Several factors therefore seem to have been responsible for the delay.

In several ways, 1925 is a critical year in the study of the vote proposal. It was a critical moment for the Colorado Party because the election results of February that year gave the majority in the senate to the nationalist opposition.[11] Meanwhile certain principles were undergoing a process of maturing. During 1922 and 1923, the Colorado Party Convention discussed a statute approved in 1925, which included chapters especially devoted to women.

In this context, in which new groups were being formed and the parties were redefining their positions and looking for weaknesses in the political arena, the proposal to give women equal civil and political rights was again submitted to parliament for discussion. It

---

11. The Blanco or Nacional Party, traditional opponent of the Colorado Party.

generated a heated public debate and, as the press eloquently testified, the feminists chose that moment to mobilise. *Batllismo* (which cannot on this occasion be taken as the official line) supported 'compensation feminism': 'It is not enough to equate men and women, it is necessary to give more concessions to women in order to compensate for the way in which they are still treated in our society.'[12] The conservatives, alarmed, responded with different arguments. Catholic conservatives in particular associated feminism with all the 'subversive isms' – a posture that induced them to caricaturise and distort feminist postulates. Once again the law was not passed.

Over the next few years the feminists continued to mobilise. They lobbied the departmental assembly in 1926; appeared before the committee in charge of organising the celebration for the centennial anniversary of independence in 1929; collected 4,000 signatures in support of women's votes for presentation to parliament in 1931 and also conducted a survey on professional women.

Although they had fairly widespread support and were on the whole rather favourably portrayed in the various mass media during the 1930s, there was still some opposition, especially from the more radical conservatives, of which Juana de Ibarbourou[13] is a good example. As a strong opponent of the women's vote, she reiterated the traditional position on women's roles and, despite herself finding them oppressive (as she admitted in various poems), defended the domestic bounds as the places where women should be. She regarded the vote as a cataclysm threatening the family: 'Family equilibrium will break irreversibly. The counterbalance of men struggling out of the house, while women do so inside the house. . . . What will the family's future be? God save us from the official nursing home, from the controlled home, appraised by the government as in Russia. . . . We are walking towards the Amazon's kingdom of women-men. We will not spend time at parties, fashion shops and churches, but we will waste time at the club, propaganda tours, combat journalism. All this is a terrible danger for femininity. And femininity is also called home, family, society, human race'.[14] According to her, women's votes were a 'dangerous gift' that would

12. *El Día*, 7 October 1925, speech by the representative Minelli.
13. A well-known Uruguayan poetess known in the context of Latin America as Juana de América.
14. *Mundo Uruguayo*, 22 September 1932.

carry women to a 'fated yield'. She expressed all the fears of the middle-class women who were so afraid of the changes taking place in other parts of the world.

These misunderstandings between feminists and some middle-class women, as well as between the working women and suffragists, restricted the accomplishments of feminism, which in those years were confined to mobilisation and questioning the civil and political order. To most feminists, the women's vote was considered the 'cornerstone of all reforms'. For working women, however, this triumph represented neither a release nor a threat, maybe because, as Frugoni said, it had been a long time since working women were violently forced out of their domestic bounds and it was not exactly because of voting.

The long process which so many mobilisations, proposals and polemics had set in motion, finally culminated, on 16 December 1932, in both houses approving the proposal presented by Lorenzo Batlle Pacheco and Pablo M. Minelli. What complex circumstances had made this approval possible?

With falling exports and rising unemployment, the year 1932 was a difficult one economically. It was also difficult politically, for it was a year in which the political radicalisation initiated in 1929 by the appearance of new pressure groups, such as the National Committee for Economic Vigilance and the *Vanguardias de la Patria* (groups of militarily-trained civilians), began to bear fruit. In an attempt to deal with the crisis, the progressive sectors of each of the traditional parties joined forces, thus leaving the more conservative elements in the two parties to come to agreements among themselves. For the first time the unity within the traditional parties was broken and the country split into two hostile factions. The situation was finally resolved with a conservative *coup d'état* in March 1933. Despite evidence of growing conservative opposition, however, between 1929 and 1932 the state had responded to the crisis with the so-called 'second reformist impulse', which comprised a series of measures to strengthen statism. The approval of the women's vote was the last of these measures.

Its approval at that precise political moment – in an ideological context of reform – fulfilled a very specific political need for *Batllismo*. This faction knew that it had the sympathy of numerous women's groups and this was when it really needed their electoral support. The attitude of *Batllismo* turned out to be totally coherent.

It is surprising, however, that the conservatives and supporters of the *coup d'état* also voted for the law. Although their political change of heart can partly be explained by the universal acceptance of the inevitability of the women's vote (even among its staunchest opponents), there is also a very clear local explanation for it. There is evidence to suggest that the conservative sectors were beginning to formulate a proposal of their own during this period, for which they too needed the support of the female electorate.

The very same day on which the law was voted, the newspaper, *El Pueblo*, (which supported the *coup d'état*), published a front-page appeal to Uruguayan women which went beyond simply trying to catch their votes, which all the political parties wanted to do. This was an attempt to gain their support for the impending *coup d'état*. Rather than being dedicated to promoting constitutional reform, these factions were in reality trying to destabilise the whole electoral system. One of the proposed demands for the Feminist Party was the reform of the constitution: 'Women's practical spirit . . . cannot sustain the present regime'.

Amidst all the ideological confusion that followed, which in itself had a purpose to serve, these politicians capitalised on the prestige of the feminist movement among certain sectors of public opinion by inviting all the women's organisations to participate in the founding of the new party. Some naive feminists supported the idea in the first instance and the press published a number of women's signatures backing the manifesto. But the older, more experienced and prestigious militants, such as Paulina Luisi, rejected the whole scheme, along with all the other democratic factions.

A few months later their political intentions became clear when, on 30 March, the day before the *coup d'état*, the followers of this pseudo-feminist party were asked to sign a manifesto in support of constitutional reform. The first signatures to appear were those of the wives and sisters of well-known right-wing political figures.

Conclusion

By looking at the various political mobilisations around the question of female suffrage, we have attempted to give some idea of the role played by feminists in the social and political life of Uruguay. We have tried to show how the feminists relied on *Batllista* and socialist propaganda to influence public opinion and how, despite the radicalisation of the conservative opposition, the climate of opinion changed in favour of suffrage as the 1930s approached. We have also shown how the changing political and electoral needs of the parties influenced the way in which successive legislative proposals were presented and eventually approved and how the various parties tried to use the mobilisations created by feminism to their own advantage.

As in other countries, having won the vote and accomplished their main objective, there seemed little basis for carrying on the feminist mobilisations, especially since the political differences between the various feminist militants now seemed so much more evident. In Uruguay, there was the loss of face derived from the support some had given to Terra's dictatorship and the fact that many militants had become absorbed in *Batllismo*, which weakened the feminist movement's autonomy. In any case, once legal equality had been gained, the subordination of Uruguayan women was thenceforth declared non existent.

In 1942 the first women legislators appeared – deputies Julia Arevalo and Magdalena Antonelli Moreno and senators Sofía Alvarez Vignoli de Demicheli and Isabel Pinto de Vidal. Since then there has been little participation by women in the various legislative and executive bodies. No more than three women have been actually elected to the House of Representatives and although some have had sporadic periods in office as substitutes, even counting these, they have never amounted to more than 4 per cent of the Congress members.

The reasons for this need to be looked into carefully. This feature is common to most countries in similar circumstances and the women's own disinclination to participate in politics is generally considered to be the main reason for it. Although it is true that only a minority of (usually very highly-educated) women are interested, neither the state nor the political parties make any effort to support or encourage their participation. The fact that the feminist movement – a minority group of middle-class women – did not retain its independence, but was absorbed into the ruling party was probably also a contributory factor. In addition, these essentially 'liberal' feminists tended to be satisfied with the legal acquisition of their civil and political rights.

The result was that women who participated in politics continued to be the exceptions rather than the rule. They were mainly professional women (usually lawyers) who, irrespective of which party they represented, followed a different ideology to that prevailing in the society at large. Even although the state had lifted the legal restrictions on women's participation, those imposed by society persisted through the prevailing patriarchal ideology. Political party officials and the powers that be were hardly likely to be excessively worried about obtaining the effective participation of women in politics and, as a result, the powerful posts continued to be monopolised by men.

Towards Developing a History of Women: Regional and Cultural Challenges

Introduction to Part IV

*As the history of women has become an important academic special-
ity, its practitioners have had to consider what it means to incorporate women into historical reality. In many cases, this has begun
with a documentation of women's actual presence, perhaps of famous
or exceptional women's activities, in order to show that 'we were
there, too.' But the discipline moves on from there because the past
activities of many groups of women cannot be recovered through the
standard sources and because the scope of history itself has expanded
to include economic and social analyses of previously neglected
groups in the past. Ultimately, it moves on because the history of
women is as complex as the history of men.*

*A basic consideration for all historians of women is that the new
historiography needs to be framed in ways appropriate to the real
diversity of women's geographical and cultural experience. Eth-
nocentrism needs to be guarded against as well as gender bias. It is
essential to identify concepts, methods and theories relevant to
different countries before attempting to use the data for comparative
analysis.*

*Carmen Ramos points out that the main problems for the history
of women in Latin America in the twentieth century have centred
around the way women participate in social movements. She discusses the sources available to historians of women in that region,
emphasising popular culture, iconography, and oral history. Ramos
also suggests the importance of place and the need to examine the
specific economic, ethnic, racial and cultural experiences that framed
women's lives.*

*In India and in Muslim countries many of the fundamental
questions for feminist scholars are intimately bound up with the
relationship between religious history and cultural and social movements. Chakravarti and Roy describe the relationship between the
'rehabilitation' of women in ancient Indian history and the Indian
nationalist movements, while Fatima Mernissi describes the scholarly*

investigations into women in the history of Islam which must be the focus of feminist research in Islamic societies where political legitimacy is derived from religious authority.

Zenebeworke Tadesse highlights the complexity of integrating women into African history, itself undergoing a historiographical revolution in an ideological rejoinder to colonial historiography. Her essay identifies topics for further research, locating them within the larger framework of African historiography.

These are all perspectives which grow out of the specific cultural challenges facing women's history in different regions of the world, and they engage at different points with those theoretical and methodological perspectives which transcend national borders. For example, the writers here agree that the way to preserve the specificity of women's experience is through an increased use of those less orthodox sources – iconography, folklore, oral history, letters, diaries, religious traditions and so on – which are proposed throughout this book. And there are also certain broad commonalities between women's histories worldwide: a sexual division of labour; the regulation of women's behaviour by religious or political authorities; efforts by women to define themselves and the parameters of their actions; a universal invisibility in written history, which is just now being remedied. While no one cultural view should predominate, work in one region can often provide insights for scholars in other regions to draw upon. Such a cross-fertilisation is precisely the aim of this volume.

15

The History of Women in Latin America

CARMEN RAMOS

Women's Research Today: A Critical Overview

In her review of the inaugural meeting of the United Nations' Decade of Women in Mexico City in the mid 1970s, Hanna Papaneck notes that discussions at the meeting accentuated the need for research on women to move from generalised analyses and solutions to specific ones applicable to particular societies and classes. It had become obvious, she felt, that many of the issues were closely interrelated and had to be seen within a broad perspective over time, that is from a historical viewpoint that would make it possible to recognise, from the range of women's experience, the continuities and changes in their roles and activities through history.[1]

To incorporate a valid historical perspective it is necessary to be able to identify the relationship between continuity and change in women's statuses, in their economic and social roles and in the ideological stereotypes that define them as a gender.[2] It is precisely because women's roles and activities have been ignored for so long that women's history is sometimes seen as repetitive, as if 'nothing changes' in their lives. To counteract this tendency towards over-simplification, it is important to look at changes over long periods of time, thus locating the turning points as well as the continuities

1. Hanna Papaneck, 'The Work of Women: Postscript from Mexico City', *Signs*, 1. 1 (Autumn 1975), p. 225. Papaneck also discusses the importance of differences among women and of the need to understand them in terms of 'structural factors relating political and economic variations together in a historical context'.
2. It could, though it is a gross over-simplification, be argued that the main historical role of women is to reproduce the species, yet even this biological function has been subject to historical change. See Edward Shorter, *A History of Women's Bodies*, London, Penguin, 1982.

and the permanences.[3]

Another element to be considered in relation to women's history is its specificity, the fact that the historical experience of humankind has often been considered only in terms of men's experiences in politics, military events or salaried economic activity. Needless to say, this presents a very fragmented history of humankind.[4]

Focusing on the specificity of women's historical experience could well lead to a reconsideration of the whole concept of history itself. Reproduction patterns, childrearing practices, household organisation, food preparation processes and many other 'female activities' are legitimate subjects for historical analysis; they are certainly crucial to understanding the social organisation of human groups in the past. It is especially important to find out how the historical constructions of various female identities differ over time and in different classes and regions.

In the United States and Europe the younger generation of historians looks upon women's lives, activities and ideologies as a major field of research. In Latin America, however, research along these lines is still fragmentary and often non existent. This may be partly because history has been considered a low priority in the allocation of scarce resources for women's studies and partly because attempts to mimic the pattern of European or North American studies is bound to fail. The sources and the problems are different and research perspectives and interpretations have to reflect these differences.[5] Scholars interested in studying Latin Ameri-

3. Fernand Braudel, *La Historia y las Ciencias Sociales*, Madrid, Alianza Editorial, 1974, pp. 60–106; Tamara Hareven, *Family Time and Industrial Time: on the Relationship between Family and Work in a New England Industrial Community*, New York, Cambridge University Press, 1982.

4. Mary Nash, 'Nuevas Dimensiones en la Historia de la Mujer', in *Presencia y Protagonismo, Aspectos de la Historia de la Mujer*, Barcelona Ediciones del Serbal, 1984, pp. 9–50; also the special volume on women's history of the *American Historical Review* 89. 3 (June 1984).

5. Asunción Lavrin, 'Recent Studies on Women in Latin America', *Latin American Research Review* 19. 1, pp. 181–90; June Hahner (ed.), *Women in Latin American History, their Lives and Views*, Los Angeles, Latin America Center Publications, 1980, pp. 1–17; Susan Soeiro, 'Recent Work on Latin American Women: a Review Essay', *Journal of Inter-American Studies and World Affairs* 17 (November 1975), pp. 497–516; Mari Khaster, 'Women in Latin America: the State of Research, 1975', *Latin American Research Review* 11 (Spring 1976), pp. 3–74; Otilia de Tejeira, *The Women in Latin America: Past, Present, Future*, Washington, Organization of American States Inter-American Commission of Women, 1928–1983, 1974; Ann Pescatello, 'The Female in Obero-America: an Essay on Research Bibliography and Recent Directions', *Latin American Research Review* 7 (Summer 1973), pp. 121–41.

can women have to select research topics and issues that are particularly relevant to Latin American women.

The complex mingling of men and women's labour in Latin American peasant economies, for example, and the relationship between communities and private landowners have yet to be considered from the viewpoint of women's work. Did women improve their situation when community lands became private or were they deprived of their traditional role within their community? How did women's reproductive patterns change with rapid economic changes? These questions have deep roots in the past and, although there have been a number of analyses of contemporary Latin America, it is only by remembering that the situation of women today is the product of accumulated experience that women are able to come to grips with their past and choose their future.

Although Latin American women have always been important in various aspects of production, it is only very recently that their economic contribution has been recognised. Because women are usually only counted as economically active if they are in salaried employment, the picture of their economic participation tends to be sketchy and incomplete.[6]

In all this it is important to note the need to move beyond the notion of Latin American women in general and try to identify regional differences. In analysing the historical heritage of women in countries with large indigenous populations, such as Bolivia, Colombia, Ecuador, Guatemala, Peru and Mexico, the impact on the everyday lives of the women of the area (throughout their history) of the indigenous culture and form of social organisation has to

6. The Andean case seems to be an exception in that there is a whole school of economic historians of the region who have carefully reconstructed the economic organisation of peasant economies and the relationship between white and Indian societies. See Florencia Mallon, 'Gender and Class in the Transition to Capitalism: Household and Mode of Production in Central Peru 1860–1950', paper presented at the Social Science Research Council meeting on Gender and Social Inequality in Latin America, Mexico, 1983. The question of whether traditional methods of looking at pre-capitalist social formations can be used to examine the various relations of production in which women participate is developed by Carmen Diana Deere, 'Changing Social Relations of Production and Peruvian Peasant Women's Work', in *Women in Latin America*, Riverside, Latin American Perspectives, 1979, pp. 26–46. On the impact of modernisation on women's roles, see June Nash and Helen Safa, *Sex and Class in Latin America*. 2nd edn., Amherst, Mass., J.F. Bergin Publishers, 1980, especially Nash's article, 'A Critique of Social Roles in Latin America'.

taken into account.[7] This indigenous heritage goes well beyond aspects such as clothing, food or religious practices, and has an important influence on aspects such as work organisation, reproduction practices or political attitudes.[8] In other types of Latin American countries such as Argentina, Uruguay and Chile, the European influence is much more important and the analysis of women's lives there should consider these societies as products of massive immigration, mostly from Mediterranean Europe. Their cultural heritage is mostly related to the Western European tradition; there are similarities in cultural norms, family roles, types of women's work and political organisation.

Brazil might be considered a case in itself, since there the importance of the Iberian heritage is to some extent diminished by the important black heritage, especially in the north-eastern region which was agriculturally impoverished at the end of the eighteenth century when the sugar-plantation economy quickly decayed. Here, the differences between black, mulatto and white women are important and the heritage of a sugar economy with a slave labour force has been extremely relevant to women in the area. It is in relation to these differences that Gilberto Freyre developed his interpretation of Brazilian history and social relations as a product of the complex relationship between masters and slaves. Freyre argued in the 1930s that it was the Indian and especially the black slave women in colonial Brazil who developed hygienic and erotic practices that have survived up to the present time.[9]

The southern states of Santa Catarina, São Paulo, Parana and Rio Grande do Sul were influenced by the late nineteenth century immigration of Germans, Swiss, Polish and Russian peasants, who

7. Lois Paul, 'The Mastery Work and the Mystery of Sex in a Guatemalan Village', in Michelle Rosaldo and Louis Lampere (eds), *Women, Culture and Society*, Stanford, Calif., Stanford University Press, 1974, pp. 281–99.

8. For instance, one major phenomenon, *marianism*, is presented as a Latin American woman's response to *machismo*. See Evelyn Stevens, 'Marianism, the Other Face of Machismo in Latin America', in Ann Pescatello (ed.), *Female and Male in Latin America*, Pittsburgh, University of Pittsburgh Press, 1973, pp. 90–101; Ann Pescatello (ed.), *Power and Pawn: the Female in Iberian Families, Societies and Cultures*, Westport, Conn., Greenwood Press, 1976.

9. Gilberto Freyre, *The Masters and the Slaves*, New York, Alfred Knopf, 1956 (first appeared in Spanish as *Casa Grande e Senzala*. Rio de Janeiro, Jose Olympo, 1933). For a modern critique of his view, see Charles Boxer, *Women in Overseas Iberian Expansion*, New York, Oxford University Press, 1968, pp. 345–8. On slavery in Latin America in general see Rolando Mellafe, *La Esclavitud Hispanoamericana*, Buenos Aires Editoria Universita de Buenos, Buenos Aires, 1972.

took up coffee cultivation in the case of São Paulo and cattle raising and farming in Rio Grande do Sul and Santa Catarina. Here the analysis should focus on the extent to which European work practices and family organisation survived in the new area. What was the relationship between newly emigrated women and old-time settlers? How did women emigrate and settle in the new land? What similarities are there between this region and other areas of high immigration, such as the Argentine Pampa or the North American West? How do we account for those similarities or differences?

The situation in the Caribbean is also complex. There, as in Brazil, the black heritage is important and the region's economy was orientated mostly towards export crops produced by slave labour. It is further complicated by imperialist patterns of economic and cultural colonisation having affected women in different ways. The cultural diversity of the region provides an ideal setting for cross-cultural case studies in women's history.[10]

In the Caribbean, as in other parts of Latin America, regional variations do not necessarily follow state boundaries. Similarities and differences are more closely related to economic factors than to political frontiers. The south of Brazil, for example, has close ties with Argentina, Uruguay and other cattle-raising areas like the Venezuelan *llanos* and is very much like them, both economically and socially. Similarly, as former plantation economies, Cuba, Puerto Rico, Jamaica, Santo Domingo and Haiti are part of one group, while the continental areas of north-east Brazil, southern Mexico and the Colombian coast belong to a second. The experience of women in these regions might form the basis of another set of comparisons.

Region, however, is not the only valid perspective from which to analyse women's lives within their own environment. In highly hierarchical societies such as those of Latin America, class is also an important variable.

Until recently there has been a tendency to view the experiences of women in Latin America simply in terms of whether they were integrated into the modern or the traditional sector of the economy. Their economic role in Latin American history, however, has been far more important than this implies and there is a need to identify

10. Frances Henry, 'The Status of Women in Caribbean Societies: an Overview of their Social, Economic and Sexual Roles', *Social and Economic Studies* 24 (June 1975), p. 165.

and evaluate those areas in which their contributions have been most relevant.

In addition to their contribution to agriculture, women have played an important role in producing textiles (although primarily in artisan workshops rather than in industrialised production) and in tobacco manufacture (which for a long time was an exclusively female occupation). Embroidery, lace making and sewing have been particularly important in the region as women's crafts. But these 'needleworkers', who have always been very badly paid, have also been forgotten by contemporary historians. More research is needed into this (as well as other areas of female work) and a new, more imaginative approach should be adopted in the use of sources and interpretations of historical problems.[11] Although there have been few studies so far in this relatively new field of women's history in Latin America, certain periods and topics have none the less begun to emerge as the major frameworks for research.

The Colonial Period[12]

Chronologically speaking, the colonial period (1500–1820) has been studied more than any other, both in terms of topics and countries. As one might expect, the countries with the largest indigenous populations have been better and more thoroughly studied, especially from the point of view of miscegenation and its social implications for women. Although the most usual pattern here was for indigenous women to bear the offspring (*mestizos*) of Spanish men, liaisons among various other groups were also fairly common and, despite the Spanish Crown's attempts to forbid mixed marriages, there were rapid increases in the racially-mixed populations of many areas, especially Mexico, Colombia, Peru and Venezuela – nowadays known as the *mestizo* countries of the region. While so far there have been insufficient case studies to understand fully the complex relationship between sex and ethnicity and to unravel the

11. Asunción Lavrin, 'Algunas Consideraciones Finales Sobre las Tendencias y los Temas en la Historia de las Mujeres de Latinoamérica', in Asunción Lavrin (ed.), *Las Mujeres Latinoamericanas: Perspectivas Históricas*, Mexico Fondo de Cultura Económica, 1985, pp. 317–79.
12. The pre-Colombian period is excluded on the grounds that its wide range of regional cultures merits a separate study. For basic bibliography, see Mari Knaster, *Women in Spanish America: an Annotated Bibliography from Pre-conquest to Contemporary Times*, Boston, Mass., A.K. Hall, 1977, p. 445.

various interpretations of indigenous women's roles as concubines, mistresses and wives, it is possible that their status depended more on their position in the community than on whether their liaisons were with Spanish, black or mulatto men.

Patterns were changing though during the course of the colonial period and, despite the Spanish Crown's wish to preserve rigid racial and class divisions, a multi-ethnic, multi-class Latin American society has now evolved in which women from different backgrounds coexist in many different and contradictory ways. It might be interesting to ask what it meant to be an Indian, black, mulatto or white woman in colonial Latin America and how this has now changed. Elinor Burkitt's research shows that women of all classes were subject to a single standard of behaviour and yet, 'while all women deviated from this goal, the impact of the sanction on the individual women was conditioned by her class position'.[13]

Social status was exceedingly important to men and women in colonial Latin America and class differences were quite explicitly laid out in the law. White women often had privileged positions. They had access to wealth, social status, leisure, culture and even to a certain personal freedom. In some cases they even helped to break down the more rigid social norms that organised colonial society. In studying élite colonial families it is often found that, despite the prescriptive norms confining females to the home and church, women participated widely in economic affairs, in controlling wealth and making business decisions. Female economic activity would increase if there were no men in the family and some all-female institutions, such as nunneries, exercised a considerable amount of economic power.[14]

Some of the research looks at the sexual lives of colonial women through the use of confession books, inquisition records, trials and personal correspondence. It is important here to draw a distinction between prescriptive practices and actual actions. Both civil and ecclesiastical law were quite careful to set out which sexual practices were allowed and which were forbidden in order to determine whether or not they were sinful. For modern-day historians ma-

---

13. Elinor Burkitt, 'In Dubious Sisterhood: Class and Sex in Spanish Colonial America', *Women and Class Struggle: Latin American Perspectives* 4. (1977), p. 445.

14. Edith Coutourier, 'Las Mujeres de una Familia Noble: los Condes de Regla de México 1750–1830', in Lavrin, *Las Mujeres Latinoamericanas*, pp. 153–76; Doris Ladd, *Mexican Nobility at Independence 1780–1826*, Austin, Texas University of Texas at Austin, 1976, p. 54.

terial such as inquisition records, sermons, confessional manuals, pamphlets on marital conduct and judicial archives containing records of marriage trials contain a wealth of information for research.[15] Other aspects of sexual life such as rape, homosexuality and sexual practices among different social and ethnic groups are also being analysed, especially in relation to the complex sex–class–delinquency relationship.[16]

Legal Status

Since the Latin American countries remained colonies for such a long time and had such highly-centralised bureaucratic systems, historians have been left with mountains of legal material with which to analyse the situation of women in the colonies. Although this material mostly gives the state's point of view, it is possible to make some comparisons between the law and actual practices.[17] Details of marriage difficulties, divorce, separation, adultery, female delinquency, prostitution and disputes over money are all contained in these records, especially in the periodic law collections (*Recopilaciones*) ordered by the Crown and the records of orders given to local police officials. Records of the legislation in force at the time are a good source for studying contemporary marriage laws, especially in relation to dowries and the institutions established by the Spanish Crown to provide for women without dowries.[18]

In general, studies of women in colonial times have focused on members of the élite, mainly because there are more sources for this

15. Asunción Lavrin, 'Aproximación Histórica al Tema de la Sexualidad en el México Colonial', *Encuentro* 2.1 (October–December 1984), pp. 23–40; various authors, *Familia y Sexualidad en Nueva España*. Mexico, Secretaria de Educación Pública, Fondo de Cultura Económica, 1982; Silvia Arrom, *La Mujer Ante el Divorcio Eclesiástico*, Mexico, Secretaria de Educación Pública, 1976, Sepsetentas No. 251.

16. Several articles along these lines appeared in *Las Memoria y el Olvido*, proceedings of the Second History Symposium held at Mexico's National Institute of Anthropology and History, Secretary of Public Education, Mexico, 1985; A.J.R. Russell Wood, 'Dowries Helped to Reduce Domestic Instability, Illegitimacy and Prostitution in Bahia', in Lewis Hanke (ed.), *Latin America: a Historical Reader*, Boston, Mass., Little, Brown & Co., 1974.

17. Boxer, *Women in Overseas Iberian Expansion*.

18. Muriel Hosefina, *Los Recogimientos de Mujeres*, UNAM, Mexico, 1974; Asunción Lavrin and Edith Coutourier, 'Dowries and Wills: a View of Women's Socio-economic Role in Guadalajara and Puebla 1640–1790', *Hispanic American Historical Review* 59 (May 1979), pp. 280–304.

group. Innovative techniques and new sources need to be found to study groups such as the Indians, blacks, mulattoes and members of the lower classes.

The idyllic picture of sleepy colonial times is rapidly disappearing as deeper, more complex analyses of colonial social history begin to emerge. Too little has been written on the role of women in multi-ethnic colonial societies and the study of family reconstitution, which is the next logical step in evaluating the complicated processes associated with women's marginality or mobility, is only just beginning. More needs to be known about women and miscegenation, for regional and chronological variations may create a particularly complex picture of three centuries of multi-ethnic social relations in which women played a crucial part.[19]

The Nationalist Period

The nationalist period in Latin American history (1820–1920) has received less attention than the colonial one, which is surprising considering that there is an abundant supply of easily accessible research materials for this period. In the early nineteenth century the 'notable' woman or heroine syndrome is quite evident and there are numerous biographies of these 'free' women, the so-called *independentistas*. The Hispanic American liberation wars threw some light on the lives of women associated with local heroes (*caudillos*), but the main emphasis was on glorifying pro-independence attitudes among individual women. A more meaningful approach might have tried to understand the changes independence brought to women's lives. On the one hand, we know that consumption increased, especially among the urban upper classes, yet the economic crises with which the newly-independent Latin American republics had to deal thwarted pre-independence expectations of improving the women's situation. Surprisingly, women were in a better position towards the end of the colonial period than they were at the beginning of the nineteenth century, when their expectations were being frustrated because of the economic problems with which the new republics were being faced.[20]

19. For a discussion of trends about Mexican colonial society, see Marcello Carmagnani, 'The Inertia of Clio: the Social History of Colonial Mexico', *Latin American Research Review* 21.1 (1985), pp. 7–72.

The nineteenth century was also an interesting time in relation to women's legal status. The change over from the colonial to the new liberal legislation offers an opportunity to researchers to evaluate the roles ascribed to women by the newly-formed national states and to determine just how unequal men's and women's individual rights really were. The legal codes regulating family relations provide some useful research data in the case of Mexico.[21] Similar studies could be undertaken in other countries as well.

The political struggle for independence was a long, drawn-out process which in some cases, as in Colombia and Mexico, created quite a rift between the state and the church. The political instability in most Latin American countries during this period inevitably placed a strain on many of the prominent families in the region. It would be interesting to find out more about how women in these networks dealt with the social unrest and how it effected the cohesion of their families. There is documentary evidence to show that the nineteenth-century Latin American family played an important part in capitalist consolidation in that it was through family ties that most business deals were arranged and estates enlarged.[22]

A crucial issue for nineteenth century Latin American women's history, however, is that of how new social roles were developed to replace or modify the old colonial habits and morals. Did women's attitudes towards marriage and reproduction change with the disappearance of strict laws regulating inter-ethnic relationships? Martinez Alier's pioneer work on the class and racial characteristics of marriage in Cuba in the nineteenth century, which basically studies deviant behaviour through the use of juridical archives, provides a useful insight into the mechanisms of class and colour in a booming plantation economy.[23] It would be helpful to be able to make some comparisons between her findings on Cuba, which achieved independence in the late nineteenth century, and the situation in some of the more newly-independent republics, but for this specific case studies are required.

The late nineteenth century offers an abundance of research

20. Silvia Arrom, *The Women of Mexico City 1790–1857*, Stanford, Calif., Stanford University Press, 1985, p. 216.

21. Ibid.

22. Enrique Florescano (ed.), *Origenes y Desarrollo de la Burguesia en América Latina 1700–1955*, Mexico, Editorial Nueva Imagen, 1985.

23. Verena Martinez Alier, *Marriage, Class and Colour in Nineteenth Century Cuba: a Study of Racial Attitudes and Sexual Values in a Slave Society*, Cambridge, Cambridge University Press, 1974.

topics. It marks the beginning of women's integration into salaried work, which raises some interesting questions about the division of labour in different trades and about which were and which were not considered proper for females. Elementary school teaching, for example, was considered an essentially female occupation, as it had been ever since the sixteenth century when basic instruction was given to girls by women in their own homes. As in former times, elderly women taught embroidery, singing, music, reading and other crafts, but the qualitative change brought by the nineteenth century was the integration of women into paid wage labour.

That increasing numbers of women were entering the paid work-force (mostly in the textile, tobacco and printing industries, or as nurses or secretaries) says something about the lives of urban women at the time. Some of these women participated in labour organisations (cooperatives, trade unions, or mutual-aid societies) and it would be useful to know how much their shared experiences in the factories fostered a sense of working-class consciousness and to what extent they channelled this into making specific demands to improve their lives. Although the labour newspapers often included articles on women, we still have no overall picture of the Latin American female labour movement and its international links.

The Twentieth Century

Since the twentieth century has ushered in some important changes in the female labour force, it would be useful to link these to the productive cycles of different economies. More, for example needs to be known about changes over time in the patterns of female participation in the labour market, especially in countries where, to a greater or lesser degree, women have been in the labour force for almost a century (Argentina, parts of Brazil, Uruguay, Chile, Colombia and Mexico). Their participation in social movements is also significant; from the riots of textile workers in Colombia, Mexico and Brazil in the early part of the century to the present-day social mobilisations in Central America, they have played an active role in demanding their social and political rights as citizens and as women.

Whether it has been in the Mexican revolution, in the bout of violence in Colombia (*La Violencia*), in the Cuban revolution or in present-day Nicaragua, women's participation has always had a character of its own, which is different from that of the male-dominated political parties. A study of the patterns of women's political presence during this century would yield fascinating insights into contemporary Latin American politics.

Some Ideas for Research

Many of the questions posed so far can only be answered by moving beyond the widely-held positivist notion of history as a boring list of names and dates. Only through incorporating an interdisciplinary approach are historians likely to ask the right questions of and derive meaningful contemporary answers from the historical data. Because women's history is a relatively recent addition to Latin American historiography, it is still wide open to new ideas and suggestions for research.

One of these, outlined below, is to examine women's history in Latin America from the distinct, yet related perspectives of their demographic characteristics, their values and their behaviour.

Demographic Characteristics

Since, historically speaking, women have been mainly devoted to reproduction, it is important to know about their marital and reproductive cycles and to establish regional and chronological variations among women of different classes and regions. Historians need to know about the different reproductive cycles and the various changes in the composition of the family over time if they are to make the move from 'family history' to the history of the family as an institution. They need to analyse and compare these changes, especially over time and in terms of size, race and region. They would want to know, for example, the difference in size between an average upper-class family compared to an average slave family living in colonial Bahia, or, for that matter, between similar groups living in Lima or Buenos Aires.

Such investigations would reveal the patterns of family formation throughout history and, if analysed within a historical context, could also show the social functions of a family and the roles of its different members. Looking at family patterns can also bring about a greater understanding of the different types of family structure. This is useful because it is important to understand that illegitimacy is mainly a Western concept and that phenomena such as parallel unions or children being born out of wedlock are widespread in Latin America, with the traditional nuclear family being far less common.

Values

The history of values is of particular interest in women's studies, for it is from this perspective that long-term processes such as value formation and the construction of roles assigned to men and women would be examined. Such an approach would be helpful to anyone interested in discovering changes in sexual mores or in finding out how gender is constructed, in other words about long-term trends in male and female notions of what is considered appropriate 'masculine' or 'feminine' behaviour for men and women at a given time and place and how this affects their lives.

Values are transmitted through educational processes that are not necessarily limited to formal instruction (school). Girls start being girls long before they are even sent to school. Therefore it is necessary to pay attention not only to formal schooling and to the values that are transmitted through the curriculum, but also to the role of the family, the state, the Church and, more recently, the media in the transmission of sexual values. The advantage of analysing this process historically is to evaluate the permanence and time validity of sexual mores as well as the elements that favour change. Manuals for child rearing, sermons, school programmes and magazines for women, soap operas, songs or comics are particularly valuable sources.

Behaviour

Values are not enforced only through institutions. Individuals enforce them through particular behaviour. This process is especially important in the case of women because the values that regulate their lives have often *not* been established by women, *even* if it is women, especially as mothers and educators, who enforce them and transmit them from generation to generation. Few historical works have analysed this process and certainly not for Latin America.[24]

Women have had limited space to express themselves and if we

24. Marie Françoise Levy, *De Mères en Filles: L'Education des Françaises 1850–1880*, Paris, Oalman Levy, 1984.

wish to know how women perceive their roles and how those roles shape their individual conduct we need to use one of the few sources in which some space for female expression is left: literature, oral tradition and other forms of popular culture, such as songs and comics. These sources could be useful for studying historical variations in the social conceptualisation of women because they cover behavioural aspects absent in other sources.

Creating Historical Awareness

History is not, or rather should not be, restricted to the initiated few who happen to have a key to historical knowledge, mostly because they know how to collect and preserve historical sources and data. Latin Americans, especially in government and policy-making circles, tend to have a static view of the past. As a first step in overcoming their patriarchal approach, it is necessary to promote the idea that history is continually changing, that it is present in everyday life, in houses, clothes, food, sexual mores, social life and work, all of which are the products of particular historical experiences. Studying history means learning that some things change and others, which seem to remain constant, might change at a different, slower pace.

Most of all, being historically aware is to realise that individuals, social groups and countries have an active role in history. Events do not just happen to people, rather it is people, the individual men and women, who make history, who are history. Individuals therefore also determine what is relevant and important in history. It is precisely because different themes and problems are considered historically relevant at different times that we are now concerned with women's history. This awareness of history is not yet seen in those terms by most people in Latin America. There is, instead, a common belief that history is something official, detached from persons and even irrelevant to everyday life. People thus tend to feel alienated from it. This is even more so for women because their lives and interests have traditionally been considered irrelevant. In creating historical awareness it is necessary to realise that history is not the dead past, but rather a lively present construction of knowledge about relevant topics, meaningful to everybody's life.

As opposed to other social scientists, who have to generate data from scratch, historians in Latin America have material to work on close at hand. Historical sources abound at the regional level. Parish records, municipal archives, local newspapers, magazines, family papers, personal letters and other seemingly unimportant personal memorabilia are historical sources, as are elderly people's memories. Historians have only recently recognised the usefulness of these types of sources for historical research and so far they have been put to very little use.

Besides re-evaluating possible sources, it is also important to create an awareness that everybody is a potential historian capable of interpreting his or her past, of remembering it and finding its meaning within the context of today's world. This is particularly true for women who have traditionally been concerned with the house, children, marriage, births and other events that keep the family memory alive. Women's interest in time and important events could be channelled by encouraging them to keep letters, photographs, personal objects and, most important, their personal and collective memories and oral traditions.[25]

It is women's own perception, expressed in their own voices, that we need to hear in order to re-formulate the traditional image of women as always being dependent, lacking initiative and capacity. In Latin America, women have a voice in family affairs, but it is not considered important beyond the household. What we need is to overcome the idea that home life is unimportant and that public life is more important, mostly because it is a man's domain.

In Latin America, where illiteracy is still widespread, it is not through books that we learn about women's roles; the image of women is portrayed in comics, magazines, pictures, films and on radio and television. In most of these, women are portrayed as dependent, defenceless, rather stupid creatures who are incapable of taking decisions, much less implementing them. It is necessary to

25. On the use of diaries, personal letters and oral tradition, see Harriet H. Robinson, *Loom and Spindle*, Hawaii, Pacific Press, 1976; anon., *Marthe*. Paris, Seuil, 1982; Tristan y Moscozo, Flore Celestine and Thérèse Henriette, *Peregrinaciones de una Paria*, Santiago, Ediciones Ercilla, 1941 (originally written in French between 1833 and 1834); Concepción Lombardo de Miramon, *Memorias*, Mexico, Editorial Porrua, 1980; Villaseca (ed.), *Cartas de Mariquita Sanchez*, Buenos Aires, Ediciones Peusser, 1952; Frances E. Calderón de la Barca, *Life in Mexico During a Residence of Two Years in the Country*, London, Chapman & Hall, 1843 (reprinted under title of *Life in Mexico*, New York, Doubleday, 1970); Maria Calcott Graham, *Diario de su Viaje de Residence en Chile y de su Vioje a Brasil*, Madrid, Madrid Editorial América, n.d.; Sylvie van de Casteele and Danièle Voldan, 'Les Sources Orales pour l'Histoire des Femmes', in Michele Perrot (ed.), *Une Histoire des Femmes, est-elle Possible?* Paris, Rivage, 1984, pp. 57–70.

re-evaluate their activities, both as wage earners and as wives and mothers, if we are to restore and dignify their collective image and give new generations the possibility of a choice and/or reconciliation between family and career. It is most important that we realise that it is women themselves who, given the chance, would have much to say about themselves, and both men and women, the old and the young, would do well to listen.

The awareness of the importance of women's history is a relatively recent phenomenon and in Latin America it has been mainly confined to research institutions and to organised groups of women interested in finding out about their past. Today's task is to break away from the long-held notion of history as a mere catalogue of political events and to change to a more modern, active conception of it as a collective interpretation of the past in which women have a relevant part to play.

Although this new approach to history is slowly gaining ground in Latin America and autonomous groups of women are beginning to find the enthusiasm and initiative to explore their own past, much still remains to be done. In particular, there is a need to move beyond the 'university club' and to create a stable and extensive link between scholars and wider audiences. In addition to the traditional lecture, use should be made of graphics and audio-visual aids, as well as discussion groups led by more experienced researchers. There is also much work to be done in schools, especially at the middle and pre-university levels. Textbooks need to be written, curricula altered and attitudes changed.

Because children learn their values in early childhood, the family has an important educative function, especially in initiating boys and girls into their respective roles. Since Latin American families derive many of their social values from the media and since for many of them the *fotonovela* is their only reading material, these are important areas to penetrate. Historical work could be disseminated through these means and a new perception of women's role in history promoted. The task is urgent.

16

Breaking Out of Invisibility: Rewriting the History of Women in Ancient India

UMA CHAKRAVARTI AND KUM KUM ROY

Women, like other subordinate groups in society, are among the muted or even silent voices of history. They have been excluded both as actors and as authors from featuring as they should in history and remain one of its most neglected subjects. The exercise of rewriting the past has been confined to making women invisible: their presence has been only registered negatively, mainly through a vast silence.

In some measure this utter neglect of one half of humankind is a consequence of the traditional focus of history. Until the recent past history has been the story of those who wielded power, being primarily an account of the struggles of men first to capture power and then to retain it. The powerless sections of society have thus been absent from history, particularly because the writing of history has always been a self-conscious act. This is evident from the presence of official recorders and court historians, whose function has been to record and document events *as seen by those who succeeded in history*. Those who were subordinated in real life can hardly be expected to have succeeded in worming themselves into a history which considered the realm of power to be its natural focus. Women, like other subordinated groups, have therefore been the unmourned casualties of history – at least of any meaningful kind.

It is necessary to emphasise at this point that though women have been invisible in historical writing generally, this invisibility has varied vastly over time and space according to differences in social and cultural practices. The Indian situation represents an example of the *relative* visibility of women in historical writing, particularly with regard to certain periods,[1] because of a complex set of factors whereby writers created a certain space for women in the reconstruction of the past. However, the space conceded to them existed only within clearly-defined boundaries, which we shall outline shortly.

Historical writing in India has certain unique characteristics because the distinction between mythology and history was never very rigorously maintained in early times. Consequently, despite the existence of a rich historical tradition, the formal writing of history is a recent phenomenon and one which has been strongly determined by the political vicissitudes of a nation whose historical frame was constituted by her imperial masters. Thereafter, historical writing was taken over by the subject people, who began, for the first time, to look back consciously into their past at a time when they were still under political tutelage. These twin features underlie all the historical writing of colonial India.

It has been argued that colonialism was, among other things, a psychological state.[2] In seeking a psychological advantage, the British attempted to demonstrate their moral superiority over their colonial subjects in many subtle and not so subtle ways. One of these not so subtle ways was in the area of gender relations. The higher morality of the imperial masters could be effectively established by highlighting the low status of women among the subject population. It was an issue by which the moral inferiority of the subject population could be simultaneously demonstrated. The question of women was thus crucial to colonial ideology and was one of the first areas where the British intervened. Social practices pertaining to women formed the first foci of the colonialist masters' reformist zeal, starting with the most visible socially oppressive custom, *sati* or the self-immolation of widows, which was banned in 1829. This was followed by legislative provision for the remarriage of Hindu widows and the raising of the age of consent. By any absolute standard these were progressive interventions and had the support of a section of the subject population. But the intervention has also been characterised as a case of 'white men saving brown women from

1. Uma Chakravarti and Kum Kum Roy, 'In Search of Our Past: Problems and Possibilities for a History of Women In Early India', Paper presented at the Symposium on the Social Role of Women, Indian History Congress, Srinagar, 7–9 October 1986.

2. Ashis[h] Nandy, *The Intimate Enemy*, Oxford, Oxford University Press, 1985, p. 3.

brown men.'[3] In any case such intervention set the framework for the women's question which became the focus of the cultural conflict between rulers and subjects. History therefore came to play a major role in the cultural battleground between rulers and the ruled. It was in this context that the reconstruction of the past in India has become so obsessively concerned with cultural questions in which women have an integral part.

The real site for the historiography of women in India was located within a dual process whereby the image of a subject population was being produced by the ruling masters and this was being counterposed by an indigenous élite attempting to create a different self image from the one fixed upon them. What the colonial masters had done was implicitly to contrast the image of the backward and barbaric social practices of the subject population, especially in relation to women, with an image of their own womenfolk, who in their view suffered no major discrimination. In sharply reacting to this image imposed on them the indigenous élite began a search of their past to 'construct' a new self-image by which they could define themselves. Unravelling the 'real' position of women in their ancient civilisation, although it appeared degraded at the time, thus became a necessity. In this setting the reconstruction of women in Indian history was first undertaken.

The context of colonialism and nationalism thus foregrounded the women's question in the nineteenth and twentieth centuries and the issue itself took a central place in the national movement. This was expressed at two levels. The first was in the context of action, especially in the concern devoted to bettering the status of women, and the second was in the context of writing history. The two levels were related to each other, as the reformists advocated a reform of Hindu society, the twin evils of which were identified as the low status of women and the existence of caste. In rejecting contemporary social practices for adversely affecting women, the reformists, who were faced with violent opposition from the traditionalists, had to go back to history to justify their reforms. There was thus a direct correlation between the socio-religious reform movement (which served as the ideological handmaiden of the national movement) and the first systematic writings on the position of women in

3. See for example Lata Mani, 'Production of an Official Discourse on Sati in Early Nineteenth Century Bengal', *Economic and Political Weekly* 21.17 (26 April 1986), pp. 32–40.

ancient Hindu civilisation.[4]

The parameters for the historical exploration of women's roles were set by the nationalist historians, who, in their search for the nation's past, had confined themselves to a limited set of questions regarding the status of women. These were determined by the problems of women in upper caste households, which by virtue of their high visibility had already become the focus of attention of colonialist discourse. The economic vulnerability of the widow, the practice of enforced widowhood (especially for women widowed as a consequence of child marriages), property rights for women, the right of the childless widow to adopt, the right to education and to participate in the performance of ritual and in the deliberations of public assemblies received considerable attention.[5] On the whole, the perspective on women was confined to seeing them within the family. We shall have occasion to return to this later. For the moment we wish to draw attention to the limited exploration of women's status in the past, because the work of the nationalist historians has been of the utmost importance in constructing an image of Indian womanhood through the ages, beginning with an almost idealised portrayal of women in the Vedic age.[6]

This idealised portrayal was not just the result of historical scholarship. The reservoir of India's past, especially for building a picture of Indian womanhood, was too attractive to be the preserve of historians alone. Everyone from Indologists down to lay people dipped into it and contributed to building up the popular perception of the glory of ancient Indian womanhood. What is interesting is that there is no marked difference between the methods and conclusions of the historian and those of the Sanskritist, Indologist or even lay person. Collectively they have all directly or indirectly served to provide a paradigm for post-Independence studies of women as well.[7] The influence of Altekar in particular has been overwhelming. His detailed exposition of the position of women in Hindu civilisation was the result both of reformist zeal and national-

4. Most of the preoccupation with the women's question was displayed by Hindu social reformers and one cannot discern a similar preoccupation among the Muslim community. This area needs a separate enquiry which is yet to be undertaken. In the meantime it is impossible to avoid presenting only a fragmented picture of historical processes.
5. A.S. Altekar's influential work, *The Position of Women in Hindu Civilisation*, Delhi, Motilal Banar[a]sidass, 1956 (reprint), is a classic example of these concerns.
6. Chakravarti and Roy, 'In Search of our Past'.
7. Ibid.

ist fervour. But precisely for this reason, the analytical rigour of the historian is overlaid by the desire to regenerate Indian women for nationalist goals. The undercurrent throughout much of his work appears to be that the status of women needs to be raised to ensure that they produce heroes for the nation in order to liberate it, and then to contribute towards the 'healthy development of Independent India.'[8] Altekar's work is an example of the political use that can be made of the writing of women's history. It is also an example of women being used to argue something else, and when that limited purpose had been achieved the women's question as well as the urgency to write about women in history lapsed back into the obscurity from which it had momentarily been salvaged.

Women's Place in Indian History

The body of writing on women produced by nationalist scholars contributed both to popular perception and to the writing of general textbooks on history, even though no real work was done once the political and cultural conflict between the rulers and the ruled reached its ultimate resolution with the attainment of independence. Everyone in India now grows up with this popular perception, but it is a totally inadequate and grossly distorted representation of women through time. Here also the limited exploration of the past which set the paradigm for women as existing almost exclusively within the family has deeply affected the manner in which the scattered references to women are made. These might take the form of trivialising women, for example by confining references to them to chapters on dress and ornaments;[9] or where more serious references to them are made they could often take the form of gross distortions of their presence. This kind of distortion is particularly common in the case of women who have actually wielded power. The use of pejorative terms such as 'kitchen cabinet' or 'petticoat government' is fairly common. Their casual use indicates the prejudice against women who have never been regarded as having legitimate access to power. The influence upon the administration of an emperor's wife is always considered a case of manipulation, and the emperors themselves as effete or emasculated rulers.

8. Altekar, *Position of Women*, pp. i, 3, 28 and 368.
9. R.S. Tripathi, *Ancient India*, Delhi, Motilal Banar[a]sidass, 1977, pp. 19 and 35.

One famous medieval ruler in India has gone down in history as an opium-eater, while his wife was the real power, manipulating behind the scenes.[10]

The in-built tendency to distort situations where women have wielded power has extended even to Razia Sultan. Razia's case is unique in Indian history because she was the only woman to succeed to the throne and therefore have a legitimate right to rule. Her three-years attempt to rule effectively rather than in name only ended in failure, and the throne reverted to a male kinsman after she had died fighting to retain it. Despite her singular courage Razia has yet to be given her due place in history. Her ramshackle tomb lies virtually unknown in the middle of a crowded locality in Delhi, in sharp contrast to the memorial tombs to beloved wives. A contemporary historian writing in the thirteenth century captured the tragedy of Razia when he wrote: 'Razia was a great monarch. She was wise, just and generous, a benefactor to her kingdom, a dispenser of justice, the protector of her subjects and the leader of her armies, she was endowed with all the qualities befitting a king but she was not born of the right sex and so in the estimation of men all these virtues were worthless'.[11] (We might add that they were worthless in the eyes of historians too.) It is significant that both in history books and in popular consciousness Razia has never held the same appeal as Lakshmibai, the unrivalled heroine of India. Lakshmibai is the best known example of a regent queen, still the only category of women to hold a respectable position in history books. The regent queens stepped in to wield power on behalf of their minor sons. Lakshmibai combined heroic valour and uncompromising resistance against a foreign power with spirited action to preserve the throne for her son, exactly the right combination to be approved by nationalist historians.

It will be apparent that the bulk of Indian writing on women in history, briefly outlined above, has not been concerned with the more fundamental question of women as shaping and being shaped by the forces of society. The interconnections between women, the institutions that affected them and the context in which such insti-

10. This is in contrast to the wife of another ruler who faithfully bore him fourteen children and died in childbirth. She has been immortalised both in history and through it in the popular consciousness as the woman for whom the emperor built the best known monument in India, the Taj Mahal.

11. Minhaj-us-Siraj, *Fabaqat-i-Nasiri* (trans. Elliot and Dawson), in *The History of India as told by its own Historians*, Cambridge, 1931, p. 332.

tutions arose, are not drawn. Despite the traditional focus on women within the family, any attempt at placing the familial and legal preoccupations with regard to women in the context of prevailing kinship structures is completely missing from the works of most historians. Further, even though basic institutions of Indian society, like the joint family and the caste system, have crucially affected women, there has been no attempt to discover the effect of the origin and development of such institutions on women. In addition, various forms of social organisation have existed in India according to the nature of the society at various times – tribal, pastoral or surplus-producing agrarian – and there has been no attempt to place women within that context. There has been no framework at all, except to presume in a vague sort of way the existence of a patriarchal system in the very ancient past. Since no attempt is made to correlate women's status with its context, attention is focused on isolated traits rather than on historical development. The general references to women thrown up by this examination of the past were supplemented with biographical accounts of women who were notable because of their entry into the domain of power.

In summing up this brief survey we should like to draw attention to the fact that, despite the existence of a sympathetic climate for rewriting history based on the concerns of the nationalists, (which conceded a certain space to women) nothing substantial was achieved. Women remained at best footnotes or punctuation marks in a narrative essentially concerned with the achievements and ideas of men. If anything, occasional references to them in mainstream history led only to the belief that women did not feature in history more often because they had done so little, rather than leading readers to the alternative conclusion: that history itself had neglected women.

The Use of Brahmanical and Buddhist Sources

So far we have focused on the major impulses that initiated the writing of a history that included women, albeit in a marginalised manner, and have pointed to the most common ways in which women are represented in Indian history. The question is: was such a representation and such a reconstruction an inevitable consequence of the limited concerns of the traditional historian in India? Or was it attributable to the tools employed by historians, who rely heavily on literary texts? Both factors seem important in contributing to the invisibility of women. The first we can hope to change, as historical frontiers broaden. The second is much more important, because the bias against women extends to the very sources that form the basis of historical writing. The quest to undo years of neglect, prejudice and distortion is therefore fraught with considerable difficulties. Women, like other subordinate groups, inhabit only the fringes of the consciousness of official recorders and composers of literary texts. In India the problem is further compounded by the fact that these literary sources, especially as one goes back into the ancient past, are almost invariably religious texts. Many of these texts, composed by the specialised caste of the Brahmanas, were concerned more with theoretical formulations and less with social reality. They laid down rules for the maintenance of moral and social order, and they were almost fanatically prejudiced against women. In using these sources the historian would require a high degree of caution and a higher degree of sensitivity and historical imagination; these have not been evident in the kind of history we have surveyed above. The problem of sources is therefore real, but it is their conjunction with the limited concerns of the historian that have rendered vast areas of human experience invisible and led to sterile accounts of the past. Once the frontiers are broadened to include neglected areas, however, these same sources can be made to yield more meaningful history, as we shall demonstrate below.

Brahmanical texts, which have formed the staple fodder for historians like Altekar in reconstructing the position of women, were put to a new use as social history began to be written in the 1960s in India. R.S. Sharma has made extensive use of Brahmanical texts to focus on a large range of subjects in the context of ancient India. His pioneering works on the Sudras[12] broke new ground in social history, but unfortunately Sharma has yet to turn his attention to women in any structured way. Nevertheless, he has been somewhat exceptional in using Brahmanical texts to provide systematic information and analyses on a number of crucial linkages relating to women which are commonly overlooked. For example, his search for traces of promiscuity and incestuous relationships in early Sanskrit texts has proved fruitful. While most of these references are to gods who have relationships with their mothers, sisters

12. R.S. Sharma, *Sudras in Ancient India*, Delhi, Motilal Banar[a]sidass, 1980.

or daughters, the fact that such relationships could be conceived of at all is certainly interesting,[13] and it is a feature of the texts which is not usually concentrated on in conventional studies. Further, Sharma points out how, in so-called legal texts, from the fifth/ fourth centuries BC women are referred to along with property, suggesting that theoretically at least they had no independent right to property and were under the control of the male members of their families.[14] His analysis of the eight types of marriage mentioned in the texts is also useful. These are arranged in descending order. Sharma demonstrates that this order is broadly related to the *varna* (caste) system, with the 'best' forms being prescribed for the Brahmanas. In the 'best' form, neither the daughter nor the mother had any right to select the bridegroom, nor did the bride's family receive any compensation for the loss of her labour although the bride was regarded as an object to be given away. Less exalted forms of marriage are recommended for members of lower *varnas*, where both parents have a right to select the groom and where the mother retains a certain degree of control over the *sulka* (bride-wealth). According to Sharma, the patrilineal system was less firmly established among the lower than among the higher *varnas*. Hence, different forms of marriage were adopted by different social groups with the Brahmanas trying both to create a system out of this diversity and to propagate an ideal.[15]

Sharma's use of Brahmanical textual sources to explore various dimensions of gender inequality is a significant departure from earlier efforts to project an idealised version of Indian womanhood on the basis of Sanskrit literature. The contruction and use of gender as a category remains relatively isolated, however, from his major concern with social formations in early India.

The Brahmanical sources do, however, yield insights into how gender hierarchy is related to other recognised socio-political hierarchies.[16] This is clear from a study of the ritual texts known as the *Brahmanas*. These use gender at a number of levels. Thus, objects used in the ritual are grouped in pairs, male and female, to ensure reproduction. The importance assigned to the sexes is by no

---

13. R.S. Sharma, *Perspectives in the Social and Economic History of Early India*, New Delhi, Munshiram Manoharlal, 1980, pp. 35–44.
14. Ibid., pp. 45–8.
15. Ibid., pp. 49–61.
16. Kum Kum Roy, 'The Emergence of Monarchy in North India: the 8th–9th Century as Reflected in the Brahmanical Tradition', thesis in preparation.

means the same, consistent attempts being made to place the masculine above or before the feminine. Further, the creation myths incorporated in these texts frequently refer to the Creator as Prajapati (literally the Lord of Creatures), a male god. There are occasional references to creation starting from an indeterminate being, but none at all to creation starting from a female principle. The gender hierarchy is also used as an idiom in terms of which other socio-political relationships and inequality are expressed. Thus, the *brahma*, or the first and highest category of the *varna* hierarchy is conceived of as masculine as against the *ksatra*, the second category, and the latter again is regarded as masculine as against the *vis* (the third category). Thus the use of the masculine-feminine dichotomy to stress a relationship of subordination is obvious. Such examples can be multiplied. While systematic exploration of the connections between gender hierarchy and other socio-political institutions needs to be undertaken, it is obvious that such an attempt will contribute to our understanding not only of the position of women but also of those institutions or categories characterised as masculine/feminine.

A study of specific rituals also throws light on the possible connections between gender and other forms of social differentiation. For instance, the *upanayana* (an initiation rite) and the institution of *brahmacarya* or studentship, to which it serves as an introduction, were of marginal importance in earlier Brahmanical texts, but assume considerable significance in texts pertaining to the sixth century BC and later periods.

The *upanayana*, in texts such as the *Dharma Sutras*, is conceived of as leading to the acquisition of twice-born (*dvija*) status, the *dvija* being considered eligible to study the *Veda*, sacrifice and make gifts. He alone could participate in ritual, status–conferring activities. The rite was also used as an occasion for reiterating the hierarchical nature of *varna*-based society. This is apparent from the variations in the ritual on the basis of *varna*. While all those who performed the rite acquired *dvija* status, not all *dvijas* were equal. Hierarchical ideals are also manifest through the exclusion of women and *Sudras* from access to the rite. A number of crucial statements about ideal relationships and power were communicated through the *upanayana*: those between men and women, between older and younger men, and between men belonging to various *varnas*. These are further developed in the *brahmacarya*. Hence the general concept of superordination and subordination is highlighted as the ideal teacher-student relationship, where a virtually unquestioning obedience was expected of the latter. Given this background it was likely that the system would encourage the notion that the hierarchical ordering of society was natural and inevitable. *Brahmacarya* further reinforced the *varna* hierarchy by assigning teaching solely to Brahmanas, while the Sudras were denied any access to Vedic learning. The gender hierarchy was even more explicit, *brahmacarya* being considered synonymous with celibacy.

The importance assigned to the *upanayana* and *brahmacarya*, with their implications for the hierarchical ordering of society, has to be viewed in the context of other changes in ritual of which the most significant appears to be the decline in importance of the major *svauta* sacrifices in which most sections of the community could participate, though not as equals. As these rituals declined in importance, rituals for the individual household, modelled on the *svauta* cult, were assigned greater importance. This shift appears to be linked to political changes, the most significant being the emergence of the state related to growing socio-economic disparities. The *svauta* cult was an important means of legitimating the position of the *raja* as ruler and involved the participation of the entire community. However, with growing differentiation within the community, the *svauta* cult could no longer be used for this purpose, yet the need for legitimation remained. It is in this context that the statements communicated through ritual acquire greater significance, as they seek to validate the existing and emerging hierarchies based on *varna*, gender and patrilineal kinship structure. Once these hierarchies were accepted as natural, the authority of a ruler who upheld the *varna asrama dharma* (the social order based on caste and the ordering prescribed stages in a man's life) would appear to be natural and beyond dispute.

The reliance on Brahmanical texts was only rarely broken, and when that happened (unfortunately it happened very rarely) the results were very useful in reconstructing women's experience. It then became evident that the nature of the sources could and did significantly influence the conclusions of scholars. Buddhist sources had been used as early as 1930[17] (as well as more recently)[18] for an in-depth study of women. These sources are unique because they

17. I.B. Horner, *Women under Primitive Buddhism*, Delhi, Motilal Banar[a]sidass, 1975 (reprint).
18. Uma Chakravarti, 'The Rise of Buddhism as Experienced by Women', *Manushi* 8 (1984), pp. 22–3.

are narrative in style and deal with people, places and events. They contain a great deal of material which includes specific information on women who interacted with the Buddha. Most importantly, one of the Buddhist texts, the *Therigatha*, is probably the earliest text in the world to have been composed by women. This rare document represents a major collective contribution by a group of women who succeeded in breaking through the barriers set around them. They left behind a lasting record of women's self-expression and perceptions of the world around them.

Horner's work, entitled *Women under Primitive Buddhism*, differed markedly from contemporary works based on Brahmanical sources. The shift is evident in the very scheme of chapterisation. While most works on women in early India dealt with their place within the family, as wives, mothers, daughters and widows, Horner looked at women beyond the family circle and introduced a new category, that of women workers. This was perhaps the first attempt to analyse the role of women outside the kinship network – shaking off the domestic aspect of woman and attempting to see her as an independent entity in the context of wider society. But despite this conceptual advance Horner's sketch of the woman worker is inadequate, since it contains only a few instances of labouring women while the rest of the section concentrates on a description of various courtesans. Horner compensates for this inadequacy in her section on women in the *Sangha* (the Buddhist order of monks and nuns) where she outlines their efforts to pursue non-familial goals.

These alternative sources, the Buddhist texts, have been explored more fully by analysing the material to show how the rapidly changing society in the age of the Buddha affected women. According to these the most striking feature of this society was the appearance of the institutions of private property and the family, as well as the creation of the state to punish offences against these two institutions. Adultery and theft are mentioned repeatedly as the two major offences against which the King must take vigorous action. Society was patrilineal, land was controlled and transmitted through men, and all these changes affected women deeply. It was recognised by the authors of the texts that a woman's existence was circumscribed by various institutions and she suffered a variety of disabilities. Women were subservient to and under the control of men, be they fathers, brothers, sons, or the guild. Women were excluded from the political and economic domains; they could not sit in court, nor conduct business, nor earn a living by any profession.

Further to Horner's account, recent studies of women based on Buddhist literature suggest that there three major role models or stereotypes are evident in these texts. The first and most common was the role of wife and mother. All women were expected to marry, and within marriage women were specifically associated with service. The worthiest kind of wife is the one who ministers best to her husband's needs. The second role was that of courtesan. This appears as an alternative to the stereotype of woman as wife and mother and, according to the evidence in Buddhist literature, the courtesan did not appear to suffer from social condemnation. She had a certain degree of independence and her income gave her a measure of confidence in dealing with the world of men. Unlike the married woman, the courtesan could own and dispose of property. Recent research, however, shows that the courtesan's 'freedom' was only partial and relative, as she was still subject to male control. She continued to be trapped by her sexuality and its exploitation by society. While she may have escaped the drudgery of a household she could not escape the collective control of men.

The third role in which women appear in Buddhist literature is that of the *Bhikkhuni*. It has been suggested that the *Bhikkhuni* and the courtesan have a point in common, in that they are both 'the outcome of the refusal of womankind to accept married relations on the basis of subjection imposed by the father age'.[19] As the courtesan did not entirely escape subjection, only this third alternative provided a real escape for women. Those of them who became *Bhikkhunis* saw themselves as escaping from the trapped role assigned to them and one celebrated her liberation from the drudgery of the 'pestle and mortar' by recording her feelings in verse. She exclaims:

> Oh woman well set free, how free am I
> how thoroughly free from kitchen drudgery.[20]

The emancipation won by the Bhikkhuni was perceived as *okasa* (space) or opportunity for developing and concentrating; it was only as Bhikkhunis that women in the age of the Buddha found any liberation from the confined role assigned to them by their society.

A combination of Buddhist narrative texts and Brahmanical theoretical texts has also been used to focus on women in servitude,

---

19. C.A.F. Rhys Davids, *Psalms of the Sisters*, Pali Text Society, 1907, p. xxxiii.
20. C.A.F. Rhys Davids, (trans) *Therigatha* [*Psalms of the Sisters*], p. 25.

a category completely missing from the earlier accounts of 'glorious womanhood' in early India. Altekar's account of the Vedic age had dwelt only on Aryan women and, according to him, they had participated in all social and religious occasions and therefore had absolute equality with men. Although he was aware of women who had been captured from the subjugated non-Aryan tribes and reduced to servile status, as non-Aryans they appear to be irrelevant to his concerns.[21] Their contribution to the economy at that time, like that of labouring women in general later on, did not fit in with his limited focus on women.

Uma Chakravarti[22] turns the spotlight on women outside the family, that is, on those who laboured in the homes of the wealthy and in the fields of large landowners. In tracing their history over two thousand years she shows how such women suffered a dual exploitation, both as labouring women and through sexual exploitation. Their world was effectively circumscribed by their vulnerability in both spheres. Although they recognised their exploitation[23] they could not imagine a different life for themselves. When offered a bonus, a slave girl asked only for a new pestle and mortar.[24] In doing so she was clearly limiting herself to the realm of the possible. In conclusion, Chakravarti argues that many women in ancient India were seen as outside the familiar contours of family, property and religion. There were innumerable women who had no property and whose place within the family was irrelevant to wider society, which merely viewed them as sources of cheap labour. Their situation represents an inversion of that of the women of the upper strata, who feature in the Brahmanical legal texts as objects for whom the rules were made. These texts might debate the question of the existence or non-existence of various rights of women within the family but their role as *grihinis* (housewives) was considered sacrosanct. Not so for servant women, who were merely treated as instruments of labour to be thoroughly exploited. By ignoring their contribution to society, historians have perpetuated the prejudice which has consistently devalued the work women have put into agriculture and production.

Despite the limitations of using conventional sources most schol-

21. Altekar, *Position of Women*, p. 332.
22. Uma Chakravarti, 'Women in Servitude and Bondage: The A'grihinis of Ancient India', *Teaching Politics* 11.2 (1985), pp. 61–73.
23. I.B. Horner, (trans) *Majjhima Nikaya* [*Middle Length Sayings*] vol. II, Luzac & Co., 1976, pp. 162–8.
24. V. Fausboll, (ed.), *Jataka*, vol. II. Pali Text Society, Luzac & Co., 1957, p. 428.

ars have yet to explore alternatives. Only one scholar has in recent years exercised real historical imagination and broken new ground. Drawing on a number of disciplines – anthropology, linguistics, numismatics, statistical analysis, and mythology – D.D. Kosambi has introduced a freshness and dynamism into the writing of social history. Although Kosambi has not focused on women to any significant extent, his works contain a number of incidental references to them. One of his most stimulating analyses is that of the significance of the Mother-goddess cults.[25] Using his observation of present-day cults, he makes use of elements of mythology, ritual, classical drama and popular customs to move back and forth in time, showing the link between past and present. Kosambi demonstrates that Mother-goddess cults have assimilated elements from tribal beliefs, from funerary and fertility rites and represent survivals from a non-patriarchal, non-Aryan tradition.

Kosambi explored the theme of transition from a matriarchal to a patriarchal society more fully in his imaginative reading of mythology through the legend of Urvasi and Pururavas.[26] The legend occurs repeatedly and in varying forms in Sanskrit literature. It is present for the first time in the *Rig Veda* and for the last time in the 6th century AD. In between there were changes both in the structure of the story and in its conclusion; Kosambi attributes these to the difference between the *Vedic* society and the *Gupta* period and to the myth's transition from ritual to drama. The *Vedic* myth of Urvasi had escaped the considered attention of Indologists, but Kosambi prefaces his complex reading at many levels, suggesting that differences in social structure were responsible for the changes in the legend. Kosambi situates the whole myth in the context of the supersession of matriarchy, and in his view the hero is a symbol of the transitional period when fatherhood became of prime importance – the period when the patriarchal form was acheiving ascendancy. In the course of analysis Kosambi also charts changes in production from a pre-Aryan to a patriarchal form. While the earliest version retained a core of the myth, itself a throwback to an even earlier memory of a society in which hoe agriculture was a prerogative of women, the last version of the myth in a classical Sanskrit play is set in a society in which women are relegated to a position where they, along with the servants, are

25. D.D. Kosambi, *Myth and Reality*, Popular Prakashan, pp. 82–110.
26. Ibid., pp. 42–82.

excluded even from speaking the language of the dominant élite.

The concept of using mythology as an alternative source has led also to an analysis of the various versions of another text, the *Ramayana*.[27] This is available both in the classical and in the popular tradition, and it is therefore possible to examine the relationship between classical and popular literature. The *Ramayana* has had tremendous importance in shaping feminine identity; its heroine Sita is the model for Indian womanhood. Her name is synonymous with wifely virtue, with passivity, and with chastity. Despite the fact that there are many contrasting images of women in the *Mahabharata*, another important myth, the enduring image of Indian womanhood has been that of Sita. This is partly because the *Mahabharata* was not crafted as a totality, whereas the *Ramayana* has greater continuity of plot and theme and has therefore had greater ideological force in determining the model of wifehood. An analysis of the Sita legend in a historical context reveals however that the emphasis on chastity and the assumption that ideal marriage is based on female devotion are aspects which were grafted onto an originally simple story. Over the centuries important details were added to the story and these had a crucial bearing on the shaping of feminine identity. The historical developments in the narrative were related to the social and cultural matrix within which the narrative was changing form; unravelling these elements gives an insight into the conscious process by which the feminine identity was being conditioned.

The original story was remarkable in that there was no abduction of Sita by Ravana, whereas this was the most important element in the classical version of Valmiki. In the Valmiki *Ramayana*, the image of Sita became a potent instrument for propagating the twin notions that women were the property of men and that sexual fidelity was the major virtue for women. By introducing the abduction, Sita was at one stroke transformed into a victim who, having once lived in suspicious circumstances, was forever condemned and had to prove her chastity not just once but repeatedly. While the earliest versions had reflected possible primitive marriage patterns, the Valmiki *Ramayana* clearly represented a later stage of marriage aimed at the begetting of children of undisputed paternity to inherit the father's wealth. It was this development that accounted for the

---

27. Uma Chakravarti, 'The Development of the Sita Myth: A Case Study of Women in Myth and Literature', *Samya Shakti* 1.1 (1983), pp. 68–75.

emphasis on chastity and fidelity at the core of the Sita legend.

Once the basic narrative was constructed in the classical tradition it was possible further to embellish the image of the chaste, passive and suffering woman in response to changing circumstances. But the *Ramayana* also exists as popular literature. There are thus hundreds of versions which are part of the oral tradition, these folk versions being handed down from one generation to the other over the centuries.

While the different versions of the *Ramayana* in popular and classical literature have their roots in a common pool of floating myths and legends, they each use the basic stories in a special way to serve a definite purpose. The classical stream became the dominant tradition, and although the popular tradition was not exactly lost, it was certainly obscured. It is, however, particularly useful in reconstructing the reality underlying the classical version in high culture. In the oral tradition the basic issue between Sita and Rama is dealt with sharply and directly as an issue between a man and a woman. It is significant that the reason for Sita's abandonment by Rama (even after she had proved her chastity for the first time) is not here tied up with any notion of ideal kingship or ideal society – issues which are central in the classical version. There is no attempt at shifting the burden of the allegations on gossiping citizens, showing Rama's exemplary role as a king who at the cost of personal suffering was discharging his obligations to his people. In the folk version Rama displays pure and simple male jealousy when he finds that Sita can remember the face of her abductor. The Sita of the folk version has much greater contempt for Rama after she is abandoned by him. She repudiates Rama, gives her sons a matrilineal heritage and refuses to go back to him.[28] The significance of the folk tradition lies in its giving Sita a voice which the classical tradition has denied her. In doing so women, excluded from the classical tradition (the preserve of men) have as anonymous participants in the oral tradition expressed themselves through collective creativity and rescued Sita from the passivity with which she is associated in the classical tradition. In the oral tradition at least, women have rewritten their own history.

28. 'The Sita who Refused the Fire Ordeal', *Manushi* 8, pp. 22–3.

Conclusion

The above sections gave a brief overview of various problems relating to women in history, from their invisibility in historical writing generally to the beginnings of an effort to rewrite it from the perspective of women. Though some advances have been made, the material compiled is too scattered and disparate to be able to give even a glimpse of the totality of women's experience, far less to reconstruct it in any useful way. Given the existence of a hierarchy founded on gender discrimination, issues and themes such as those explored here will hardly be able to restore to women their rightful place in history. For this the concerns of history must change. It is not enough to look at women's participation in production, or even at their exclusion from control over production, or at the political arena and stop there. What is required is a modification of theory whereby an analysis of production (which has so far focused in the main on the relations between different categories of men) is extended to include social reproduction. Social reproduction based on domestic labour involves the day to day recreation of labour power, which in contemporary societies involves cooking, servicing the domestic area, biological reproduction and the socialisation of children. This would have a far-reaching significance for reconstructing women's history, because it is the only way in which the life and experience of women in its totality can become a valid focus of history. In social reproduction the role of women cannot be made invisible or ignored; it is one area which all women, whether or not they are involved in visible production, share. Further, the process of social reproduction, like that of production, has been subject to change, and tracing these changes will provide continuity to women's history while situating women within human experience as a whole.

If the importance of the process of social reproduction is recognised certain related questions will assume importance: how and by whom is the process controlled? What changes are discernible in the process? What are the links between production and reproduction and how do these connections change? Once the sphere of domestic activity is recognised as crucial the evidence of the *Rig Veda* about the women who were captured and reduced to servitude, commonly dismissed as being *merely* about women involved in domestic activities, will acquire a new importance.

The use of gender as a category which enables us to arrive at an understanding of the relationship between women and men in any society is obvious. A historical analysis would involve a thorough study of the ways in which men and women are differentiated, the significance of such difference in terms of the definitions of power specific to each instance, the changes in the definitions of gender and their implications, as well as links between gender and social reproduction and production. Further, the use of gender in ideological discourse also needs to be examined.

It is evident that the process of evolving a historical analysis which takes sexuality, social reproduction and production into account may not be simple. Further, the usefulness or otherwise of each of these formulations needs to be tested through the analysis of specific bodies of evidence, and modifications may be required to suit the Indian context. In the ultimate analysis it is important that we are able to explain rather than explain away. This needs to be stressed, because there is an occasional tendency to treat women's history as a soft option, a tendency as detrimental as the problems of distortion and neglect noted earlier. Whatever the difficulties, the challenge needs to be taken up in order to arrive at a fresh understanding of the history of women in early India, and to evolve in the long run a more meaningful and comprehensive historical perspective in general.

17

Women in Muslim History: Traditional Perspectives and New Strategies

FATIMA MERNISSI

Contrary to widespread belief, early Muslim historians gave considerable exposure to women in their writings. They did not, as might be expected, talk about them only as the mothers and daughters of powerful men. General history books, genealogies and chronicles identified women as active participants and fully involved partners in historical events, including the crucial emergence of Islam. In religious histories describing events which took place from the Prophet's birth to his death, as well as in religious texts themselves, such as Hadith repertories (testimonies of disciples concerning the Prophet's words and deeds), or Koran *Tafsir* (explanations, commentaries), women are acknowledged and their contribution generously praised as both disciples of the Prophet during his lifetime and as authors of Hadith after his death.

In fact, more than ever before, historical argument seems to be crucial to questions concerning the rights of women in Muslim theocracies. This is because all kinds of state policies to do with women, be they in the economic sphere (the right to work outside the home), or in the legal sphere (issues concerning personal status or family law), are justified and legitimised by reference to the tradition of the Prophet, that is, to historical tradition. Progressive persons of both sexes in the Muslim world know that the only weapon they can use to fight for human rights, in general, and women's rights in particular, in those countries where religion is not separate from the state, is to base political claims on religious history.

A particularly illuminating debate taking place in the Muslim world today concerns whether or not there is a precedent for women to exercise political power in the highly controversial role of Aicha, the Prophet's third wife, who advised civil disobedience and herself led troops on to the battlefield in armed opposition to the fourth orthodox Khalife Ali Ibn Abi Talib on 4 December 656 AD (year 36 of the Muslim calendar), thereby contributing to his downfall. One of the results of the Ali-Aicha confrontation was the division of Muslims into Shiah and Sunni, the Shiah being unconditionally for Ali and, therefore, against Aicha as the symbol, among other things, of civil disobedience and of the right to contest the Khalife when he is believed to be in the wrong.[1] Even today, an outstanding Shiite ideologue, the Iranian Ali Chari'ati, holds that the ideal for Muslim women is Fatima, the Prophet's daughter, who played no noticeable political role in Islam.[2] Aicha is for Shiah the anti-model, the monstrous image of feminity. Women should content themselves, like Fatima, with being good mothers, daughters and housewives. In Egypt, Said Al Afghani devoted ten years to writing his biography of Aicha. He says in his introduction and conclusion that he did so to show that women should be barred from politics. His book, *Aicha and Politics*, is a systematic marshalling of all conservative works on women to this end.[3]

The case of Aicha illustrates how closely the claim for or against women's rights is linked to historical scholarship in the Muslim world. Women's excellence in this field has had a tremendous impact. The definitive biography of Aicha by Zahiya Moustapha Khaddoura, a Lebanese woman scholar, which was written in the 1940s and republished in the 1970s, is a stunning rehabilitation of Aicha, which gives pride to Muslim women by supporting their claim, not only to political decision-making but also to legislation and *Chari'a* (religious law) making.[4] Aicha produced more Hadiths (which are, besides the Koran, the revealed text, the source of the

1. For two concise résumés of the historical background and complex reasons for the split between Shiahs and Sunni, see Henri Corbin, 'Le Schisme et la Philosophie Prophetique', in *Histoire de la Philosophie Islamique*, Gallimard, Paris, 1986; and Mohammed Abu Zahre, 'Furuq al Medhab as Shi-i', in *Al Madshib al Islamiya*, Maktabat Al Adeab, Egypt, n.d.
2. For an analysis of Chari'ati's work and its impact on women's rights in Iran, see Adele K. Ferdow, 'Women and the Islamic Revolution', *International Journal of Middle East Studies* 15 (1983), pp. 283–98. The references to Fatima as a model are on pp. 288 ff.
3. Said Al Afghani, *Aicha wa-as-Siyasse*, Beirut, Dar Al Fikr, 1971.
4. Zahiya Moustapha Khaddoura, *Aicha the Mother of Believers*, Beirut, Dar Al Kitab Al-Arabi, 1972. The introduction is dated 1943.

Chari'a, the religious law) than Ali. According to Ibn Hajar, the author of the seventeen-volume *Fath Al Bari*, one of the most authoritative Hadith commentaries of *Boukhari Sahihs* (authentic Hadiths, since thousands were frauds)[5] claimed that Khalife Ali contributed only 29 Hadiths, while Aicha contributed 242. And, since according to this widely acclaimed fifteenth-century scholar (Ibn Hajar died in 852 of the hegira, the Muslim calendar), *Boukhari Sahihs* do not total more than 1,602 Hadiths (and not as he previously believed 4,000), Aicha alone contributed more than 15 per cent of the bases of the *Chari'a*.[6] Fatima, the daughter of the Prophet upheld by Shiah progressive ideologues like Chari'ati as the ideal for Muslim women today, did not contribute, although she was the Prophet's daughter; nor, according to the same source, did Khalife Ali's wife contribute more than one single Hadith.

Muslim historians have been forced to grant women their due in the volumes of traditional mainstream treatises. But they have also devoted a specific genre of work to women, a genre we can call (since they often used this title themselves) *Akhbar an-Nissa* (Women's News). These are biographical portraits of famous individuals which are notable for their particular attention to detail and for their inclusion of themes that the methodological rules of scholarship prohibit in more mainstream work.

Salah Ed-Din Al Mounajid identified more than 70 of these books in an article called 'What was Written on the Subject of Women',[7] which was an attempt to provide an exhaustive listing of every mention of these works by early historians. Of course, not all of them are available today due to destruction of libraries during foreign invasions but many have been printed, and many more are still in manuscript form in Persian, Turkish and Arabic libraries (just to mention a few), waiting to come alive.[8]

5. Fatima Mernissi, 'Le Prophet et les Hadithe' and 'Enquête sur un Hadith Misogyne et sur son Auteur Abu Bakre', in *Le Harem Politique*, Paris, Michel Albin, 1987, chs 2 and 3. A summary of these findings was presented to the Georgetown University Eleventh Avenue Symposium on 'Women in Arab Society, Old Boundaries, New Frontiers, 10–11 April 1986.
6. Ibn Hajar, 'Asqlani as-Sari Moqaddimat', *Fath Al Bari*, vol. I, Egypt, Matba'a Al-Mostapha al Halabi, 1962, pp. 247 ff.
7. Salah Ed-Din Al Mounajid, 'Ma Ullifa ani An-Nissa Majallat Majma', *Lugha l-Arabiya* 16 (1941), p. 216.
8. Since 1941 several of the books which were still in manuscript form have been printed, thanks to the efforts of pro-women scholars such as Salah Ed-Din Al Mounajid.

The authors of these books were not dubious, unknown begin-
ners. They included many of the most important scholars of both
general and religious history as well as famous imams, literary
figures and genealogists. The criteria for inclusion in these biographical portraits was the display of excellence in some field;
beauty was just one of these criteria. Moreover, not only queens or
aristocrats were included. Slaves made it into the 'Women's News'
frequently and even managed on occasion totally to eclipse royalty
and occupy primacy of place. A whole series of treatises on *Qiyan* –
the cultural and literary contribution of women slaves to society –
exists and begs thorough investigation.[9]

How then, with such a glowing presence in their own history, do
Muslim women come to have such a lowly image in their own
society and in the world at large? In part I of this chapter, on
medieval history, I try to answer this question and in Part II, on
strategies for enhancing the image of Muslim women, to challenge
the situation.

As Part I will show, the lowly image attributed to Muslim women
in their own society today is not due to their absence from traditional memory or in written history. In fact, there is empirical
evidence to show that the tradition of historicising women as active,
full participants in the making of culture (which we shall call
nissa'ist, the Arabic synonym for feminist, from the word *nissa*,
women) still continues today.[10] It could be said that the only
novelty in this tradition is that women are now no longer simply
objects of Muslim history. They have become subjects as well, they
write history, side by side with men. They have since the turn of the
century been actively involved in the writing of women's history.

---

9. A sample of this genre is Abu l-Faraj al-Isbahani's *Slave Women Poets* (Al Ima'
a-Chawa'ir) in the tenth century; see also Abu l-Faraj al-Isbahani, *Al Ima
a-Chawa'ir*, ed. Noury Mohammed al-Qaissi and Younes Ahmed as-Samarrai,
Beirut, Maktabat An-Hahda al'Arabiya, 1984.

10. The equivalent of the word feminism in Arabic is coined from the word *nissa*
(women). Many compositions with this word as a radical have been adopted to
express feminist ideas or claims in many Arab conferences, including one organised
in Cairo by Nawal Saadawi, president of the Arab Women's Solidarity Association,
in September 1986. But, as always happens, and this is natural in democratic
contexts, each political faction tries to add a consonant here or a vowel there to give
the word *nissa* its ideological connotation: *nisswani, nissa'i, nisswanati*. I find the
word *nissa* by itself so charged with energy that for me, it means a whole programme
of self liberation just by itself. I would not therefore add anything to it but the
adjectival ending which consists of adding a simple 'i' to *nissa*, whence *nissa'i. Nissa'i*
is for me an adjective that designates any idea, project, programme, or hope that

The clue to this mystery resides partly in the fact that the image of women in society is not derived from historical material *per se* by any simple process, but is crucially dependent on the media which can either disseminate such research or restrict its dissemination. History, the recorded memory of a culture, is never consumed directly like other products. Historical material goes through highly complicated processes, often tightly controlled and censored by those in power, before it is presented to citizens for selectively oriented consumption. In order to simplify these multi-faceted, multi-connected processes, let us first make the basic assumption that possessing good historical material showing women as full participants in society is an advantage and can of course be recuperated and harnessed to a *nissa'ist* strategy.

Contrasting the wealth of historical evidence favourable to women with their lowly status in Muslim society leads to the inescapable conclusion that the forces shaping image-making in the Muslim world discriminate against women. But we should be careful to label these forces *conservative* and not *fundamentalist*, because, despite the way Western commentators frequently confuse the two, Muslim women's passivity in political, economic and cultural spheres cannot be explained by the influence of fundamentalism alone. In most Muslim countries fundamentalists are viewed with suspicion by those in power and considered politically undesirable by the state. This confusion between the terms conservative and fundamentalist does not further the understanding of a dynamic and complex situation in general or of women's image and status in particular.

While most Muslim regimes disagree politically with fundamentalists about almost everything, they do agree with them on women

---

supports women's rights to full-fledged participation in and contribution to remaking, changing and transforming society, as well as full realisation of one's own talents, needs, potentials, dreams and virtualities. And it is in this sense that I have always lived and defined women's liberation, whatever the language – 'feminism' or *nissa'ism*. In this chapter, however, since I am describing the dynamics and the debate around women and history in the Muslim world, I use the Arabic word *nissa'ist* to identify the progressive current supporting women's rights through historical scholarship, since Arabic is the only Islamic language I know, and also because most of the historical documents to which I shall be referring are in Arabic, although their authors may be Iranians, or Turks, etc. This progressive *nissa'ist* feminist current includes men as well as women. The content of the historical work, the ideological target of the conclusions, are taken into account not the sex of the author.

and their place in society. The very deep political conservatism at the basis of fundamentalist movements is mirrored in the political nature, opinions and aspirations of most Muslim regimes. If only fundamentalists are taken into account, it is impossible to understand why the disparaging, discrediting image of Muslim women is so present in national media and why discrimination against them attains the status of a sanctified act.

I: Medieval History and the Legitimisation of Women's Rights

Medieval religious history is crucial for contemporary Muslim politics. As I mentioned earlier, those who make any kind of statement regarding the status of women are obliged to justify their pronouncements by citing precedents in religious history and tradition. State legislators, as well as fundamentalists, claim that their ideal model of the politically passive woman, barred from the public sphere and totally secluded and estranged from the society in which she lives, is derived from and legitimated by this history and tradition. A good example of this attitude is Mohammed Arafa's book, *Women's Rights in Islam*. He argues that women should not have political rights today because they never had them in the crucial period when the Prophet built the Muslim nation. The Prophet started to receive revelations in 610 when he was in his forties, emigrated to Medina in 622 (the first year of the Muslim calendar), created the first Muslim community there and died in 630. The years from 610 to 632 therefore constitute the reference, the model and the law. Mohammed Arafa states that 'during the first decades of Islam, Muslim women played no role whatsoever in public affairs, and this in spite of all the rights Islam bestowed on her, which are similar to those accorded to men. . . . Muslim history in its entirety ignores the participation of women, side by side with men, in the managing of the state affairs, at all levels'.[11]

There are many classical criteria for participation in the making of Islam. Among these, the individual must be identified as having been a disciple during the prophetic call period, while the Prophet was still alive. The person must have taken the oath of allegiance

---

11. Mohammed Arafa, *Huquq Al Mar'a fi l-Islam*, 3rd edn. Place of publication not indicated, Al Maktab Al Islami, 1980, p. 149.

(*bay'a*) directly with the Prophet to fight for Islam's survival. And the individual must have contributed after the Prophet's death as an author of Hadiths, testimonies concerning the Prophet and his words and deeds. Using these criteria, Mohammed Arafa's thesis is difficult to support. Women are in fact identified as disciples in all the classical religious history books, which are the reference and the source for Islam past and present. The following provides impressive evidence of this.

Historical Sources

(*a*) In his famous directory of disciples' biographies, *Al Icaba fi Tamyiizi As Sahaba*, Cheikh Ibn Hajar (who died in the year 852 of the Muslim calendar – 1474 AD) acknowledges 1,552 women as disciples.[12] In a special section devoted to women (*Kitab an-Nissa*), which occupies a good part of volume 5, he summarises most of what has been written on the subject and is considered in Islam to be an important scientific author. He has been described both as the 'most outstanding of celebreties' (*Cheikh al-Islam*) and as the 'imam of the learned' (*Imam Al Huffad*). He is not, however, the first to have devoted an entire volume to female disciples' biographies, describing in minute detail their contribution during the first decades of Islam. The most famous of his predecessors is Ibn Sa'ad.

(*b*) Ibn Sa'ad's work on the 'great classes' (class meaning generation), *At-Tabqat Al Kubra*, is an enormous compilation containing the events of the Prophet's life, as well as biographies of his chief companions. Volume 8, the last one, is devoted entirely to women. The importance of Ibn Sa'ad's work resides not only in its scientific rigour but also in the fact that it is among the oldest – he lived in the ninth century and died in the year 230 (852 AD). Since his death, other imams, in conformity with his approach (for example classifying the biographies in alphabetical order), have at various times tried to compile and complete the disciples' biographies and have never failed to give women their due prominence.

(*c*) Tabari (Abi Ja'far Mohammed bnu Jarir), still one of the most quoted and referred to masters of religious history, could not resist ending the thirteenth volume of his history of nations and kings (*Tarikh Al Umam wa-l-Muluk*), in which women were already

12. Cheikh Ibn Hajar, *Al Icaba fi Tamyiizi As Sahaba*, Lebanon, Maktabat al Mouthanna, 1902.

given wide coverage, by resummarising the biographies of the disciples in what he called *A-dayl* (long annexes, often books in themselves, this one having 115 pages).[13] Women are of course identified in many chapters as active participants and supporters of the Prophet in the making of early Islamic history. Tabari died in the year 310 (932 AD).

(*d*) Ibn Amir Youszef An-Namri Al-Qortobi, known as Ibn Abd Al Barr, who wrote his *Kitab Al Isti'ab* in the eleventh century AD (he died in 463 of the Muslim calendar), carried on the tradition and ended his multi-volume study with women's biographies. He is considered 'the crown of his peers' (*Taju Agranihi*). His text is presented, according to the printing tradition of religious literature, as a footnote (*bi-l-hamish*) in Ibn Hajar's *Al-Isaba* and allows the Muslim reader to compare, at a glance on the same page, his eleventh century biography with that of Ibn Hajar written four centuries later. Early Muslims religious scholars were masters in the special footnoting techniques of *hawamich* and *hawachi*, in which two (sometimes three) books on the same theme or event but from different centuries are printed on the same page. This allows researchers to check variations for each biography from one century to the other, thus making their own independent evaluations and drawing their own conclusions.[14]

(*e*) The thirteenth century (seventh of the Muslim calendar) produced one more outstanding biographer of the disciples – Ibn Al Athir. He too did not forget women. He gave his disciples' biographies the title of *Usd Al Ghaba* (literally 'The Forest Lions) and hundreds of women are identified and alphabetically classified among them in his 200-page book of women, *Kitab An-Nissa*.[15] He died in the year 631 (1253 AD).

(*f*) Ad-Dahbi produced his biographies of outstanding personalities among the nobles, *Siyar A'lam an-Nubala*, in the fourteenth century. Here of course nobility was defined in its religious sense as the grace of having contributed to Islam's triumph. Women were classified among those who had that grace and all that accompanies

13. Tabari, 'Al Mountakhab min Kitab A-Dayl al Moudayyal min Tarikh As-Sahaba wa al-Tabi'in', *Tarikh Al Umam wa-l-Muluk*, vol. XIII, Dar Al Fikr, Beirut, 1979.
14. Ibn Abd Al Barr's *Kitab al Isti'ab* appears in appendix II of Ibn Hajar's *Al-Isaba*.
15. Ibn Al Athir, 'Usd Al Ghaba fi Ma'rifat as-Sahabe', in Al Matba's *al-Wahbiya*, ed. and compiled Moustapha Wahbi, vol. V, 1920. *Kitab An-Nissa* runs from pp. 389 to 642.

it. Ad-Dahbi died in 748 (1370 AD). This study of his, according to the editor of the most recent edition, is 'among the pride of Arab heritage'. One of the reasons for this is that it gives pre-eminence to the first decades of early prophetic Islam while at the same time trying to cover all the ground from that time (seventh century) to the author's own era (fourteenth century).[16] Besides general history and early religious history books, another historical genre yields incredibly detailed information on women and their position in society in early and even later Muslim centuries. This is the *nassab*, the genealogies. *Nassab* material is fascinating for contemporary researchers because it uncovers a wealth of information on particularly important topics – kinship patterns, marriage, divorce, conjugal life, sexual mores, childbirth and parenting, and women's initiatives in all these matters. The two following examples are selected only because they have been and still are considered achievements in the genre. Thorough listing and systematic investigation of this material is one of the tasks awaiting young generations of *nissa'ist* researchers.

(g) Abi Abdallah bnu Muc'ab Az-Zubeiri's *Kitab Nassab Goraich* is definitely the most important and 'trusted proof' in Arab genealogy. It has two features which make it an especially precious document. First, it was written in the ninth century and is, therefore, one of the earliest of its kind and, second, the author 'puts a particular effort into tracing genealogies through women as well', according to Lery Provencal, who edited and commented on its first publication.[17] This world has been widely quoted by all historians and biographers of disciples, including those quoted above, such as Tabari and Ibn Abd Al Barr, the author of *Kitab Al Isti'ab*.

(h) Ibn Hazm al-Andaloussi's, *Jamharat Ansab al-Arab*, written a few centuries later in the eleventh century (Ibn Hazm died in 452 of the hegira) is notable because it both summarises all the genealogical information accumulated until his time and also included information on non Arabs.[18] Berber, Persian and Jewish genealogies (he was an expert on the Torah) are also included. His study highlights links between Arabs and non-Arabs; women are present

---

16. Ad-Dahbi, *Siyar A'lam an-Nubala*, Cairo, Dar Al Ma'arif, 1958, p. 38. See especially vol. II, in which a concentration of women's biographies is listed.

17. Abi Abdallah bnu Muc'ab Az-Zubeiri, *Kitab Nassab Goraich*, Cairo, Dar Al Ma'arif, 1950. The quotation is from Lery Provençal's introduction, p. 9.

18. Ibn Hazm al-Andaloussi, *Jamharat Ansab al-Arab*, Cairo, Dar Al Ma'arif, n.d.

and visible and their sexual and reproductive life is documented like that of men.

(*i*) No study of religious history would be complete without mentioning the most quoted basic reference work for all Muslim historians, Ibn Hisham's biography of the Prophet, *As-Sira An-Nabawiya*. Here women disciples' lives appear to us tightly enmeshed in their historical context. They are depicted as actively involved in the Prophet's preaching, battles and debates.[19] Hisham's *Sira* is an epic fresco of the first decade of Islam's difficult birth (often overlooked today) and of each disciple's crucial contribution, support and detailed deeds. Here women appear as major builders of Islam. Without the emotional and intellectual support of Khadija, the Prophet's first wife, one wonders what would have become of Islam in its particularly difficult beginnings in Mecca between 610 and 622. She was an influential and prosperous Mecca businesswoman, fifteen years his senior. She was knowledgeable about monotheism and thus convinced the Prophet, when he lived his first Koranic revelation experiences as terrifying events, that he was indeed the Prophet of a new God. According to the Prophet's own testimony in Hisham's *Sira*, it is to Khadija that he came, after his first encounter with Gabriel, the angel who contacted him on behalf of Allah in 610. He was then in his forties: 'I came back home and went to Khadija, and put my head on her thigh. She said, "Where were you, Father of Qacem?" [one of the Prophet's surnames, after one of their sons named Qacem] . . . I told her what happened [the visions and voice hearing] and she said: "Good news, my cousin, and be assured by God. I would want you to be this Nation's Prophet".'[20] Muhammad, explains Tabari, who quotes Hisham heavily, was afraid to be just a poet under the spell of his own creativity, as there were many who had such strong fits of inspiration.[21] Khadija was instrumental in convincing the troubled Prophet that his inspiration was indeed from divine origin and not simply a poetic and therefore human phenomenon. The interest of Hisham's *Sira* is that it is a fundamental text, and one of the earliest, most trusted and revered references for all later historians of the Muslim religion.

That women did not go on to the battlefields simply to give first

19. Ibn Hisham, *As-Sira An-Nabawiya*, Beirut, Dar Ihys al-Thurat al Arabi, n.d.
20. Hisham, *Sira*, vol. I, p. 254.
21. Tabari, *Tarikh*, vol. II, p. 208.

aid to the wounded, as we are repeatedly told in many contemporary conservative and fundamentalist writings, is amply confirmed in Ibn Hisham's description of one of the most disastrous battles the Prophet had to fight, the Battle of Ohod in March 625. A woman disciple who appears in all major religious history books, Nussaiba bint Ka'b, describing her role during that battle, said that when she saw the Muslims were losing: 'I took position near the Prophet and I started fighting with my sword, in a defensive move around the Prophet ... I fought until I was wounded'.[22] It is no wonder then that contemporary *nissa'ist* intellectuals of both sexes have no difficulty proving, through the historical scholarship we shall identify in the strategy section, that women's passivity, seclusion and their marginal place in Muslim society has nothing to do with Muslim tradition and is, on the contrary, a contemporary ideological production.

II: Strategies for Enhancing the Image of Muslim Women

The best way to design effective strategies is to be pragmatic and start with what one has. As we have seen, as far as historical research on women *per se* is concerned, the Muslim world has almost everything. But what we lack is regional and international coordination of scarce skills, both in terms of communication between researchers and at the level where their findings can be fed to the various media for wider dissemination. This part of the chapter makes some specific proposals to improve the situation.

Producing Historical Research

Three themes, extremely important to all those involved in women's rights, could serve as the basis for three research projects. These are (1) research on the first decades of Islam and the production of biographies of outstanding Muslim women; (2) turn-of-the-century feminist research in Muslim countries; and (3) female slavery and prostitution in Islam. I will outline each of these in some detail to show the quality of the research potential on the one hand and the problems arising from the current lack of communication and coordination on the other.

22. Hisham, *Sira*, vol. III, pp. 86, 87.

The First Decades of Islam

Any campaigner for women's rights is accused of importing Western models and ideas. The first decades of Islam, as we have seen, are very eloquent on women's contribution at that time and produce models of femininity like the active businesswoman Khadija, or the first *Chari'a*-maker Aicha, the Prophet's third wife, or women who exercised political power within Muslim civilisation. Data on women in the first decades of Islam are vital since conservative regimes and fundamentalists base their policies on women in Muslim tradition.

Sakina Chihabi's editing of the comments of Imam Ibn Assakir's special volume on women, *Tarikh Dimachq* (History of Damascus), is probably one of the best examples of this research.[23] This volume contains 196 biographies of famous Muslim women who either lived in or visited Damascus and it gave Ibn Assakir an opportunity to summarise all existing data until his time (the twelfth century AD) on some of the most active and forceful women of our civilisation. The volume on women is the last of an 80-volume history of Damascus, the editing of which Sakina Chihabi made her life's work. She carried out what is called in Arabic *tahqiq* (literally 'investigation') which means that she did extensive background research so that the modern reader could identify, by a simple glance at the reference at the bottom of the page, all names and events quoted. She explains her motives, since most of the rest of the volumes are still in manuscript form, for privileging the volume on women: 'I preferred to bring alive Imam Ibn Assakir's volume on women . . . because it highlights a dimension of our Muslim civilisation which is still totally obscure, that concerning women'.[24] She summarises the importance of the work by saying that Ibn Assakir's women make vibrant five centuries of the political, social, literary and religious life of our civilisation'.[25]

Having acknowledged the vital importance of this investigation, however, let us go on to look both at the difficulties she encountered in carrying out her work and the problems other scholars have in gaining access to her findings.

Sakina Chihabi illustrates some of the problems researchers face

23. Imam Ibn Assakir, *Tarikh Dimachq*, Damascus, 1982. Special volume on women edited by Sakina Chihabi.
24. Assakir, *Tarikh Dimachq*, p. 5.
25. Assakir, *Tarikh Dimachq*, p. 33.

when she describes in the introduction to her book the difficulty she had in gaining access to the work of a colleague working in the same area, Dr Aida Tayyibi. The manuscript documents from which Chihabi was working were in a badly-damaged condition and, although Dr Tayyibi had published her edited edition of Ali Al Hassan Al Maliqi's classical thirteenth-century manuscript, *Biographies of Famous Women in Early Islam*, three years earlier, Chihabi was completely unable to acquire a copy of it or to link up with Tayyibi herself. In the end she had to obtain a copy of the original manuscript from the Chester Beatty Library in Dublin, Ireland. Here we have two researchers working on identical themes in the same language, yet, because they are isolated from one another and are short of funding, their research suffers from this appalling duplication of energy. Chihabi's own book is a bulky 678 pages, extremely expensive[26] and poorly distributed (no publisher is indicated).

Let us look, however, at some further research potential:

Omar Kahhala's *Most Outstanding Women in Both the Arab and Muslim World* is a bulky five-volume collection of biographies on women, particularly interesting for its scope (the Muslim world) and its time span. It includes early feminists such as the Lebanese, Turkish and Egyptian women who campaigned for human rights at the turn of the century, and describes their activities.[27] The author's introduction is dated 1959, which means that the book has waited two decades to be published.

Zahiya Moustapha Khaddoura's already mentioned biography of *Aicha the Mother of Believers* is one of the best documents available on that most important model of femininity in Muslim history. The introduction to the first edition is dated 1947, but the book was only reprinted two decades later. It mentions that Dr Khaddoura presented it to obtain a diploma from the history department of Fouad First University.

Also important is Dr Aicha Abd Arrahman's biography of *Sakina Bint Al Hussein*, the little daughter of the Prophet who refused to veil and insisted on leading an active intellectual and political life. Dr Abd Arrahman was working at Qaraouiyine University, Fez

26. It costs 160 dirhams, the equivalent of 200 francs or roughly 40 US dollars, which relative to purchasing power is a prohibitive price.
27. Omar Kahhala, *Most Outstanding Women in Both the Arab and Muslim World*, Damascus, Mouassassat ar-Rissala, 1982.

(Morocco) when the book was published.[28]

This list is merely an indication of the importance of the research that already exists in Arabic on women and does not pretend to provide an exhaustive or representative survey of the available data. Similar work has probably been carried out in Iranian and Turkish. A research project could identify systematically what has been done and where, and could evaluate whether work is worth translating and publishing and, if so, what needs to be done to make this possible. The researchers identified above could easily be traced through their publishers. Setting up networks for coordination between *nissa'ist* history researchers and activists and linking these to feminist publishers and the media could help bring together all the scattered energy already at work both inside and outside the Muslim world.

Feminist Research at the Turn of the Century

Many Western feminists were surprised by Margot Badran's biography of the Egyptian feminist, Huda Shaarawi (1879-1924), for they had been convinced that Muslim women were no more than obsequious followers in the struggle for women's rights.[29] It is true, though, that even in the Muslim world, this turn-of-the-century feminist movement had been totally forgotten, its memory swept aside by the wave of conservative and fundamentalist opinion into which the media had sunk. This is one reason why it has become necessary to organise a workshop to carry out systematic investigations into what has been written and to make suggestions about how best to ensure that it becomes more accessible. The following examples give an idea of the rich accumulation of data which are already available but scattered throughout the Muslim world.

A Turkish author, Dr Bahriye Üçok, has researched and produced some valuable biographies of women who exercised political power in Muslim countries. Such data are crucial for today's debates with fundamentalists and conservatives, who state that women have no political role. *An Nissa Al-Hakimat Fi at-Tarikh* (Women who Exercised Political Power in History) is a well-researched document on some of the women who took over political power in such

28. Aicha Abd Arrahman, *Sakina Bint Al Hussein*, Beirut, Dar Al Kitab Al-Arabi, n.d.
29. Margot Badran, *Harem Years: the Memoirs of an Egyptian Feminist*, London, Virago, 1986.

far-flung places of the Muslim world as Persia, Egypt, India, Muslim Spain and the Maldive Islands.[30] Although the book was translated into Arabic and published in 1973, it is out of print and available only from libraries. This is a pity, since it is trim, concise (173 pages), well written and easily accessible even to a high-school readership. Translation of such books into Iranian, Urdu, Swahili, Malaysian, Indonesian and other Muslim languages would be useful and publication in a cheap, well-distributed series would maximise its impact.

All this early feminist research on women in various parts of the Muslim world needs to be checked out, translated and given adequate media coverage. Attention should also be paid to nationalist movements in the Muslim world because nationalists have debated the question of women's status and rights in their attempts to try to understand why Muslim societies were defeated by Western powers. But our knowledge of this subject has come mainly from men and women's contribution remains largely unknown.

There are, however, some important clues. For example, in the 1890s Zaynab Fawwaz al' Amily, an Egyptian woman writer, published a 552-page compilation of women's biographies called *Ad-Durr al Manthour fi Tabaqat Rabbat al Khodour* (Generalisations of Secluded Housewives). In her introduction she says that she undertook the work 'to contribute to her sex's enhancement, and because that is the best gift one can give women'.[31] This indicates that not only was women's historical research being undertaken at that time but that there was also a significant demand for it. The writer states that she herself was secluded and that this greatly impeded her investigations. Freedom of movement to pursue research was one of the goals she wished to achieve. Another example is that of the Turkish author, Princess Quadriya Husseyn, who wrote a volume called *Chihhirat Nissa fi l'Alam al-Islami* (The Most Famous Women in the Moslem World), although in this case the style was closer to that of a novel than to academic research.[32]

It is evident from these and other examples that women's historical research in Islam experienced an important moment at the end of

30. Bahriye Üçok, *An Nissa Al-Hakimat Fi at-Tarikh*, trans into Arabic by Ibrahim Daqouq, Baghdad, Matba'at Sa'doun, 1973.
31. Zaynab Fawwaz al' Amily, *Ad-Durr al Manthour fi Tabaqat Rabbat al Khodour*, Boulaq, Egypt, Al Matba'a Al-Kubra, 1982, 1985.
32. Princess Quadriya Husseyn, *Chihhirat Nissa fi l'Alam al-Islami*, trans into Arabic by Abd al'Aziz Amin al Khanji, Egypt, Husseyn Husseyn Publications, 1924.

the nineteenth and beginning of the twentieth century. These re-searchers were women who both analysed their own situation in the contemporary Muslim world and contested it on historical grounds. But who were they? In which countries did the movement start? What was its significance? Where is the material they produced and how can it be used today?

A systematic regional survey, mapping feminist historical re-search in the Muslim world between the late 1890s and the Second World War, could establish what data exist in at least some of the major Muslim languages – Indonesian, Arabic, Urdu, Turkish and Iranian, for example. Such a survey could cover already-published material, as well as give some indication of what manuscripts were available and in what languages, so that these could be fed into further strategies for translation and publication. Regional research teams could be set up and coordinated, perhaps initially in Turkey, Iran, the Arab States and in Urdu and Swahili-speaking countries.

Female Slavery and Prostitution in Islam

There are important data on this theme, which are usually scattered throughout the various multi-volumed studies already mentioned, especially those of Tabari, Ibn Assakir, and Hisham's *Sira*. Clarify-ing Islam's position on slavery and prostitution and establishing how it has continually been violated, could strengthen women's position. Women campaigning for their rights might find here the arguments with which to invalidate conservative and fundamentalist grounds for interpreting the *Chari'a*. One document of this kind may briefly be mentioned. In the twelfth century, that is five centuries after the Koran made a strong stand against slavery, Ibn Batalan wrote a treatise giving rich men advice on how to buy slaves, including information on how to test women for physical fitness, according, of course, to whether they were to be used for work or sexual pleasure.[33] Since slavery and prostitution go hand in hand, searching out and exposing this material will highlight the fact that the degradation of women in Muslim countries is a violation of the Koran and its principles and laws. Serious historical research could, through a study of the past, help to lift the veil on this taboo topic in today's societies, where a careful silence surrounds prosti-tution and its clients.

33. Ibn Batalan, *Rissala fi Chariy ar-raqiq*, Cairo, Dar Al Fikr al Arabi, 1954.

Dissemination Strategies

Women can learn something from the effective way in which fundamentalists use the media to disseminate information throughout Islam. Everyone has heard about fundamentalist literature on women, but very rarely are people exposed to *nissa'ist* research. This is because the fundamentalists have a comprehensive regional and international strategy, involving rapid translation into the main Islamic (Turkish, Iranian, Arabic, Urdu) and Western (English, French) languages, as well as well-organised distribution and dissemination of printed material around the world at affordable prices. If one never hears about *nissa'ist* research, which has produced first-class scholarship on Muslim women, it is because it is being produced by isolated researchers working in difficult conditions and because it has failed to find its way into the media. Moreover, much of it is expressed in rather heavy academic jargon, exists in only one of the many Islamic languages, and is often published in obscure collections, which are more often than not out of print. There are now many Muslim women trying to set up publishing houses or make films to convey different images of women. Creating links between researchers on the one hand and media skills on the other would, in itself, encourage more research and maximise its impact on society. Another vital link is between professional historians and feminist activists in need of their research findings.

Research is, by definition, an unfinished product. Producing historical data on women is just one part of the process. Feeding the research findings into the channels that need them and are likely to make good use of them is another. The problem is essentially one of coordination and the setting up of networks. Regional and international links would allow the findings of isolated researchers to flow to all those who need them and thus encourage both more research and better use of it.

Nissa'ist Publishing Initiatives

Nissa'ist publishing is thriving despite all kinds of material and political difficulties. With more financial backing, however, not only would publishers be encouraged to work together and coordinate their efforts, but they would be able to launch a more coherent publishing strategy throughout the Muslim world.[34]

Special mention should be made of the presence in the West of numerous women scholars from Islamic societies, who have often preferred to live abroad to preserve their creativity and who play a particularly important role in publishing historical research or in coordination networks, translation teams, publishing and other media activities on the Western intellectual stage. The AMEWS (Association for Middle-East Women's Studies) would be in a position to mobilise researchers interested in Muslim women's history.

Finally, a rapid translation committee needs to be set up, not only to give information about research that has been written in other languages, but also to cater for those who do not speak Arabic (the language of textual revelations and of primary scholarship on Islam) and to produce continually updated lists of new publications in Arabic to enable Urdu, Indian, Turkish and Indonesian researchers and publishers to plan for the future translation and publication of relevant material.

A sub-committee translating pertinent data on women's religious history from Arabic into English should also be set up. Since many Arab researchers are operating from Western universities, they could play a key role in translating both information and documents into English. The AMEWS is sufficiently skilled to do this. It is well known now that if an Arabic study is translated into English it becomes more accessible to other Muslim researchers working in, say, Urdu or Iranian. Translations from one Islamic language into another are more easily carried out if there already exists an English translation of the original, for it is easier to find translators from, for example, English into Urdu than from Arabic into Urdu. Identifying scholars able to translate from Arabic into English would therefore improve communications between researchers throughout the Arab region and at the same time render the data accessible to Western readers.

34. There are already *nissa'ist* groups publishing research or translations in Pakistan (Simrog Women's Resource and Publication Centre, Lahore), France (The Arab Women Solidarity Association, Doreya al Awn, Paris), Morocco (Editions le Fennec, Casablanca), the United States (AMEWS, Association for Middle East Women Studies, University of California, Davis, Ca. 95616).

18

Breaking the Silence and Broadening the Frontiers of History: Recent Studies on African Women

ZENEBEWORKE TADESSE

A glimpse at the literature on women's studies indicates the vast potential for the emergence and institutionalisation of women's history in Africa. This potential coincides with, and in part is triggered by, major shifts in African historiography, as evidenced by the current re-evaluations of earlier interpretations of major episodes and relatively new and sectorally focused themes. The constraints, however, are as daunting as the potential and again not limited to women's history but to African historiography as a whole. What follows are notes for discussion by way of a brief review of the current literature, major tendencies and gaps in existing research.

The limitations of this chapter must be stated at the outset. The vastness of the subject of inquiry notwithstanding, it covers only the major literature published in English. The absence of literature in French and other languages is compounded by the omission of local research efforts, that is, even those written in English. Such an exhaustive and analytical review of local literature should be taken as a research priority in the writing of African history. If the major commitment that informs the writing of the history of women is the need to understand and change the present, then we cannot stop at the celebration of the birth of such a history. In other words while applauding the commendable efforts that are being made to recapture the past experience of African women, we should also stop to note the conspicuous absence of the writings of African women from most published and widely circulated materials. This chapter is in fact part of a larger project entitled: 'Origins, Development and

Trends in Research on African Women' sponsored by the Association of African Women for Research.

For women who have collectively, even if differentially, experienced a complex history of exclusion, this absence should be a major concern. More disturbing than the lack of African women writers is the fact that most of the material is unavailable, even in the major local and regional libraries and bookstores. This absence should not, however, be seen as a conspiracy to exclude African women, although that tendency does exist. The major concern here is to set out the structural constraints to the emergence and development of women's history in Africa. Concretely, it boils down to identifying a wide variety of both local and international resources that would allow African women to pose relevant questions and to devise ways and means of ensuring wide internal circulation of current research findings and appropriate storage for the resources of the future.

Trends and Highlights in Recent Literature

Alarm at the exclusion of women from historical accounts has, until very recently, merely led to their insertion into pre-existing historical records, thematic concerns and periodisations. To date, local research institutes have barely begun the major tasks entailed in the reconceptualisation of gender as an object of historical inquiry and a subject of historical explanation. The trend in Africanist historiography to adopt a defensive and romantic vision of African history is understandably aggravated in the case of women's history. The portrayal of women as eternal victims and passive objects of history is matched by accounts of women's uprisings, the myth of matriarchy, biographies of powerful women, and so on. The massive amount of data produced by feminists in the recent past, coupled with a sober analytical pause, has induced a major shift in the recent historiography of women. Moving beyond dichotomies such as class/gender, heroine/victim, private/public, having to choose one or the other, historians have begun to adopt what the late Joan Kelly called the 'doubled vision of feminist theory'.[1] While her specific reference concerns the simultaneous operation of relations of class

1. Joan Kelly, 'The Doubled Vision of Feminist Theory', in Judith L. Newton, Mary P. Ryan, and Judith R. Walkowitz, (eds), *Sex and Class in Women's History*, London, Routledge & Kegan Paul, 1983.

and gender, recent findings demonstrate that once we adopt a historical vision that takes as its object not only the recounting of conventional major events but also the details of everyday life, together with a consistent account of class relations, we begin to see women at once powerful and powerless, resisting and bowing to change.

Globally, the emergence of feminist history coincides with the growth of labour history and, in the case of Africa, with what has come to be known as the African historiographical revolution. Historians of African women have much to learn from the crisis that resulted from this short-lived revolution. Briefly, Africanist historiography revealed the contradictions and inadequacies of imperial presuppositions inherent in colonial historiography. Against African inactivity in the making of history, Africanists asserted African agency, African initiative, African choice.[2]

Initiated as an ideological rejoinder to colonial historiography, Africanist historiography remained trapped in that enterprise for almost a decade. As a recent review article has noted, although these historians failed to raise even new sets of questions, much less theoretical issues, this phase set the stage for more fundamental questions. Eventually the strength of Africanist scholarship lay stress on methods of recovering African voices from the past and seriously examined the specificity of African social structures.[3] Coinciding with the feminist upsurge, this timely focus opened up analytical space for the examination of the patterns of inequality embedded in the social structures that produce and maintain these hierarchical structures.

While earlier writers focused on pre-colonial Africa to demonstrate the capacity of the African people to make their own history, the analogous question of feminist historians influenced subsequent historical studies in Africa. Were Africans the passive objects of colonial rule, unable to influence their fate or rationally to respond to new situations? The various responses to these questions and the methodologies used have opened up a multiplicity of themes and analytical possibilities for the study of women's history.

The dominance and lengthy duration of slavery and colonialism is reflected in the choice of these themes as major objects of inquiry

2. T.O. Ranger (ed.) *Emerging Themes in African History*, Nairobi, 1968.
3. Frederick Cooper, 'Africa and the World Economy', *African Studies Review* 24 (1981), p. 2.

within African historiography. Similarly, the most conventional form of periodisation is roughly that of the pre- and post-colonial eras. Until recently the bulk of pre-colonial history has focused on long-distance trade, internal slavery and the Atlantic slave trade. While historians of Africa have been conducting heated debates on the implication of these processes in overall terms,[4] others, informed by feminist concerns, have generated some of the most valuable insights into women's history by focusing on women and slavery. Were it not for male bias in history, even without feminist theory, women, who constituted the majority of African slaves, ought to have been the subject of historical research.

Early and isolated efforts[5] at documenting the impact of slavery on women has culminated in a book entitled: *Women and Slavery in Africa*.[6] Such a focus clearly demonstrates the centrality of African women in social production, the changing mechanisms of reproductive control and the intimate links between production and reproduction to the extent that focusing on one process without the other makes for an incomplete historical account. A critical and nuanced examination of slavery warns us against a homogenised approach to women's history and points to the importance of a class-based analysis. A majority they might have been, but not all women were victims of slavery. Current accounts indicate that some were owners and traders of both male and female slaves.[7] Slavery provided free women with a mechanism for recruiting labour for both domestic and agricultural tasks. Women's ties to the institution of slavery have been cited as one of the difficulties in abolishing slavery which persisted until and beyond the Second World War in some areas.[8]

Support for the feminist theory of reproduction comes from

4. For a brief but useful summary of the major assumptions of this period, see C.C. Wrigley, 'Historians in Africa, Slavery and State Formation', *African Affairs* (1971), pp. 113–24.

5. Maya-Liisa Swantz, 'Strain and Strength among Peasant Women in Tanzania', Research Paper 49, University of Dar-es-Salaam, Bureau of Resource Assessment and Land Use Planning, 1977; Marcia Wright, 'Women in Peril: A Commentary upon Life Stories of Captives in Nineteenth Century East-Central Africa', *African Social Research* (1975).

6. Claire C. Robertson and Martin A. Klein, (eds), *Women and Slavery in Africa*, Madison, Wis., University of Wisconsin Press, 1983.

7. S.O. Biobaker, 'Madame Tinubu', in Nigerian Broadcasting Corporation (ed.), *Eminent Nigerians of the Nineteenth Century*, London, Cambridge University Press, 1960.

8. See Robertson and Klein, *Women and Slavery*.

historians of slavery. African cultivators coped with the shortage of labour by controlling a large number of labourers. Here, too, we begin to see the development of kinship systems, the fundamental character of which is the institutionalisation of the exchange of women through the control of marriage. A recent detailed look at the specific impact of slavery on women points to women having functioned as objects of exchange. In other words women were given away as wives, pawned in times of famine, or used as a payment of debt. Women were also presented to ruling lineages in exchange for political exemptions or influence and used to pay fines or reward soldiers.[9] Sources allowing, much more historical work is needed to see how women slaves resisted and adapted to their harsh conditions of existence.

Another historical theme of critical importance to historians of women is the history of state and class formation, an arena of major debate in African studies as a whole, 'although these bodies of literature do not directly pose the issues related to gender and its relationship to state/class formation'.[10] The data generated from these debates, together with valuable insights from the anthropological literature on the origins of the subordination of women, raise questions and suggest lines of analysis for women's history.[11] Moving beyond previous generalities on private property, class and state formations, historical investigation of concrete situations has begun to indicate the intricate relationship between production and reproduction, the various and changing mechanisms of the appropriation of surplus and the origins of hierarchical gender relations.[12]

Unlike the pre-colonial period, the history of women during the colonial period is relatively well documented. As the historiography of Africa shifts from a defensive posture to the historical investigation of the complexities of African responses to colonial domination, so too have recent writings on women focused on the

9. See Swantz, 'Strain and Strength'; Wright, 'Women in Peril'; Margaret Strobel, 'African Women: Review Essay', *Signs* 8 (1982).

10. John Londsdale, 'States and Social Processes in Africa: A Historiographical Survey', *African Studies Review* 24 (1981).

11. Claude Meillassoux, *Maidens, Meal and Money: Capitalism and the Domestic Economy*, Cambridge, Cambridge University Press, 1981; Karn Sacko, *Sisters and Wives: The Past and Future of Sexual Equality*, Westport, Conn., Greenwood Press, 1979.

12. Marjorie Mbilinyi, 'The Social Transformation of the Shambaa Kingdom and the Changing Position of Women', Paper delivered at the Southern African Universities Social Science Conference, University of Dar-es-Salaam, 1979.

experiences of women during the colonial period. Triggered by feminist theory on the one hand and the complex problematic posed by Ester Boserup on the other, many articles, books and conference papers have traced the changes in the division of labour by sex and the subsequent transformation of gender relations that resulted from colonial domination.[13]

A number of studies on various aspects of colonial domination have broken the silence in African historiography, challenged major conventional concepts and pointed to the resourcefulness of women.[14] Recent documents point to the previous ways in which the domestic economy was reorganised as a result of colonial land and labour policies and the resulting development of capitalist relations of production. One of the fundamental and visible changes has been women's loss of access to land.[15] The massive male migration that was enforced by labour policies, the introduction of cash crops and the less subtle forced consumption of commodities increased women's work load and brought about major changes in social structure, especially in bridewealth and marriage.

To the array of sources that document the socio-historical determinants of uneven capitalist development in Africa, those concerned with women's history have begun to examine the differential impacts of colonialism on women and men. The reorganisation and hierarchisation of inter-household relations and the subsequent underestimation of women's economic contribution, juridico-political structures and survival strategies are still considered important topics for discussion.[16] These observations show that the type of capitalist development initiated during the earlier phases of colonialism undermined subsistence production both in the physical sense of relative stagnation and in the overall assessment and conceptualisation of its value. Conceptually, once cash transaction

13. See, e.g., Nancy J. Hafkin, and Edna G. Bay (eds), *Women in Africa, Studies in Social and Economic Change*, Stanford Calif., Stanford University Press, 1976; also relevant articles in the *Canadian Journal of African Studies* 6.2 (1972) and in the *African Studies Review* 18.3 (Dec. 1975).

14. Edna Bay, 'Luo Women and Economic Change during the Colonial Period', in Hafkin and Bay (eds.) ibid.

15. Achola Pal Okeyo, 'Daughters of the Lakes and Rivers: Colonization and the Land Rights of Luo Women', in Mona Etienne and Eleanor Leacock (eds), *Women and Colonization: Anthropological Perspectives*, New York, Praeger, 1980.

16. Edna G. Bay (ed.) *Women and Work in Africa*, Boulder, Col., Westview Press Inc., 1982; Margaret Jean Hay and Marcia Wright, *African Women and the Law: Historical Excursions and Incursions*, (Boston University Papers on Africa), Boston, Mass., African Studies Center, 1982.

is introduced and wage labour is formed, the concept of work comes to be equated only with work that is directly remunerated and all other types of work are classified as unproductive.

Relatively detailed studies on changing relations of production call our attention to gradual shifts in intra-household relations. Once commodity production is set in motion relatively complementary intra-household relations are replaced by a process of differential allocation and hierarchisation of tasks on the basis of gender and age. Consequently, a process of differential control and distribution of product sets in,[17] though the ideology of reciprocity disguises the growing tension between men and women over the control of the finished product.[18] An emerging interest in the conceptual clarity of households, as well as in the changes in and tremendous resilience of intra-household relations, promises to broaden our understanding of the complexities of class-formation and social change.[19]

While previous historical works tended to concentrate on the life options of rural women, more recently some highly informative studies on working class women,[20] prostitutes[21] and domestic workers[22] have begun to make an appearance. The history of women's entry into factories and predominantly male towns and the struggle to create acceptable identities for themselves, domestic service and its implications for the analysis of class and gender categories, are all new and promising fields of study. They form part of the relatively new school of African urban history. The few

17. Mona Etienne, 'Women and Men, Cloth and Colonization: The Transformation of Production-Distribution Relations among the Baule (Ivory Coast)', in Etienne and Leacock (eds), *Women and Colonization*, pp. 214–38.

18. Richard Roberts, 'Women's Work: Household Social Relations and the Maraka Textile Industry, A Social History', Paper delivered at the African Women in History Conference, University of Santa Clara, 1981.

19. Jane Guyer, 'Household and Community in African Studies', *African Studies Review* 24.2–3 (1981), pp. 87–137.

20. Deborah Bryceson, 'The Proletarianization of Women in Tanzania', BRALUP Workshop on Women's Studies and Development, University of Dar-es-Salaam, Sept. 24–9, 1979.

21. Jeanna Penvenne, '"Here Everyone Walked with Fear": The Mozambican Labour System and the Workers of Lourenco Marques 1945–1962', and Luise White, 'A Colonial State and an African Petty-Bourgeoisie: Prostitution, Property and Class-Struggle in Nairobi, 1936–1940', both in Frederick Cooper, (ed.), *Struggle for the City: Migrant Labour, Capital and State in Urban Africa*, Beverly Hills, Sage Publications, 1983.

22. Deborah Gaitskell, Judith Kimble, Moira Maconachie and Elaine Unterhalter, 'Class, Race and Gender. Domestic Workers in South Africa', *Review of African Political Economy* 27/28 (1984).

documents that have been published tend to be theoretically in-formed and have opened up a new analytical space within which we get glimpses of the transformation of ideology and culture, chang-ing boundaries of permissible behaviour for women and the signifi-cance of financial autonomy.

A growing and most intriguing field in recent writings deals with women and resistance. The web of personal relationships women weave and upon which they depend for economic survival call for close historical scrutiny. The strengths and limitations of various types of women's networks have been the subject of many recent inquiries. One relatively widely-documented uprising by women is the 'Aba riots', locally known as the 'Women's War'.[23] Recent studies have demonstrated that, shocking as this uprising was to the then colonial powers, it was by no means the only one.[24] The struggle of South African women points to the complexities of class, gender and race.[25]

In addition to helping us to see women as both products and sources of historical change, these findings force us to go deeper and ask more questions. We now know that women's struggles im-pinged on the intent of colonisers and even altered the terms of their own exploitation. More work on culture, consciousness and ideol-ogy needs to be carried out before we can fully understand the remarkable capacity and resourcefulness of women to defend their material and cultural integrity in the face of overwhelming changes in the larger economy and society. In addition to focusing on the extraordinary and ephemeral moments of collective uprising, the history of women will have to recount everyday forms and cycles of local struggle and resistance.[26] We need to know the power of social

23. Judith van Allen, 'Aba Riots or Igbo "Women's War"? Ideology, Stratification and the Invisibility of Women', in Hafkin and Bay (eds.), *Women in Africa*.

24. Cynthia Brantley, *The Giriama and Colonial Resistance in Kenya 1800–1920*, Berkeley, Los Angeles and London, University Press, 1981; Laray Denzer, 'Towards a Study of the History of West African Women's Participation in Nationalist Politics: The Early Phase 1935–1950', *Africana Research Bulletin* 6.4 (1976), pp. 65–85; Cheryl Johnson, 'Grassroots Organizing: Women in Anti-Colonial Activity in South Western Nigeria', *African Studies Review* 25.2–3 (1982).

25. Ken Luckhart and Brenda Wall, *Organize or Starve. The History of the South African Congress of Trade Unions*, London, Lawrence & Wishart, 1980; Cheryl Walker, *Women and Resistance in South Africa*, London, Onyx Press, 1982.

26. Deborah Gaitskell, 'Wailing for Purity, Prayer Unions, African Mothers and Adolescent Daughters 1912–1940', in Shula Marks and Richard Rathbone (eds), *Industrialization and Social Change in South Africa, African Class-Formation, Culture and Consciousness 1870–1930*, Harlow, Essex, Longman, 1982.

convention through an exploration of the relationship between ideology and women's lived experiences. Are women automatons of ideology? From such a perspective the issue of women and religion becomes a crucial research topic. The Christian conception of womanhood, as well as that of Islam, ought to be examined, not from the perspective of the doctrines, but of women's actual practices. For more work needs to be done on the history of households and on the institutions of marriage and divorce.[27]

The purpose of this chapter has been twofold. Primarily, it has attempted to identify topics for further research by looking at suggestive insights in selected studies of African women in history. Secondly, it has tried to locate these topics within the larger framework of African historiography. The latter has been intended to explore the breadth of available sources, the constraints with which the larger framework has grappled and, where possible, to trace changing perspectives. The difficulties involved in reconstructing African history have necessitated a consistent search for an exceptionally broad array of sources ranging from interpretation of archaeological records, folktales, songs, figurines and rituals, to oral history.[28] By so doing it has established a tradition of flushing out subtle and long-term changes from elusive evidence. Every search for a fresh and novel interpretation and the use of unconventional techniques has been faced with several interpretive problems. To be sure, writing about women in history has had, and will still have, to devise more imaginative sources.

In the meantime, writings about women in history can benefit from existing sources and methods, while avoiding the pitfalls and remaining conscious of methodological fragility. Writers on women in history will have to be open to alternative interpretations, methods and results. This is not just another branch of Africa's historiography, but a fundamental challenge to the incomplete and narrow focus of accounts which fail to use gender as a core analytical category in describing past experiences.

---

27. Krishn Man, 'The Dangers of Dependence: Christian Marriage among Elite Women in Lagos Colony 1880–1915', *Journal of African History* 24; Carol Bohmer, 'Modernization, Divorce and the Status of Women: Le Tribunal Coutumier in Bobo-dioulasso', *African Studies Review*, (1980).

28. Elizabeth Tonkin, 'Steps to the Redefinition of Oral History: Examples from Africa', *Social History* (Oct. 1982), pp. 329–35.

Notes on Contributors

Soha Abdel Kader is currently Research Associate at the Social Research Center of the American University in Cairo, where she has been working since 1971. She has studied economics, political science, sociology and anthropology and has a PhD in Mass Communications. Her most recent publication is a book on the Egyptian feminist movement entitled: *Egyptian Women in a Changing Society: 1899–1987*. She is currently working on the creation of a Regional Information Network on Arab Women (RINAW).

Simi Afonja is a reader in sociology and anthropology at the Obafemi Awolowo University, Ile-Ife, Nigeria. She holds a PhD degree from the University of Birmingham, England (1971). Her main research areas are industrial sociology and women's studies, in both of which she has published several articles. One of her latest publications, *Social Change in Nigeria*, is co-edited with Dr Ibitola Pearce. She is a member of the Executive of the International Sociological Association and one of the Directors of the Nigeria–Canadian Link Programme in Women's Studies.

Ida Blom was born in Denmark and studied languages in Switzerland, England and France, and history in Bergen, Norway. She is professor of history at the Bergen University and has lectured at a great number of European universities and at international conferences. She started out researching into decision-making processes in the formation of foreign policies and wrote her doctoral theses on the Danish-Norwegian dispute over Eastern Greenland between the wars. Later her interests moved towards social history and women's history, and she has written two books and a great number of articles in these areas. She is president of the interim board for the International Federation for Research in Women's History.

Anna Davin lives in London and is a visiting lecturer at the State University of New York. She is a free-lance writer and an editor for *History Workshop Journal*.

Ayesha Imam is a lecturer in the Department of Sociology, Ahmadu Bello University, Zaria in Nigeria, presently on study leave at the School of African and Asian Studies, University of Sussex, United Kingdom. She is also an active member of Women in Nigeria (WIN) and the Association of African Women for Research and Development (AAWORD). Her main research has been on gender ideologies and the mass media, and women's projects. She is now working on social reproduction, households and sexuality/subjectivity.

Deniz Kandiyoti is a senior lecturer in the social sciences division of Richmond College, Surrey, England. She taught in the social sciences departments of the Middle East Technical University, Ankara and Bogazici University, Istanbul, between 1969 and 1980 and is the author of numerous publications on gender and development issues, and the status of women in Turkey. Her current research interests include the relationships between gender issues and processes of state formation in the Middle East.

Notes on Contributors

S. Jay Kleinberg received her PhD from the University of Pittsburgh in 1973. She has taught at several American universities and the London School of Economics, and is now head of the American Studies Programme at the West London Institute of Higher Education. Her publications include *The Shadow of the Mills*, a study of the relationship between industrialization, urbanisation, and the working class family in Pittsburgh. Current research interests include intergenerational equity, women's role in the labour force and in the home, and the development of family relations in the United States in the late nineteenth and twentieth centuries.

Jane Lewis is a lecturer in social administration at the London School of Economics. She has published many books and articles on women's history and women and social policy and is on the editorial boards of *Gender and History* and the *Social History of Medicine*.

Selma Leydesdorff is an historian at the University of Amsterdam. Her major research interest is in oral history. Publications include *Verborgen arbeid – vergeten arbeid, een verkeening in de geschiedenis van de vrouwenarbeid rond negentienhonderd* (Amsterdam, Assen, 1977) on outworking in Dutch industrialisation. Her latest work, *We Lived As Human Beings*, a study of the Jewish proletariat in the Netherlands between the two world wars, will be published by Wayne University Press in the near future.

Fatima Mernissi is author of *Beyond the Veil: Male-Female Relations in Muslim Society*, Al Saqi Books, 1985, and *Doing Daily Battle* (translated from the French by M.J. Lakeland) Women's Press, 1988.

Michelle Perrot is professor of modern history at the University of Paris VII-Jussieu. Her writings have been seminal in the development of women's history in France. Among the most recent are *Une Histoire des femmes est-elle possible?*, Paris-Marseille, Rivages, 1984; volume IV of *l'Histoire de la Vie Privée: De la Révolution française à la Grande Guerre*, Paris, Seuil, 1987, and a special issue of *Mouvement Social*, Métiers de Femmes, 141 (Oct.–Dec. 1987). She is now working with Georges Duby of the Collège de France and a whole team of historians on a large Women's History due to appear in 1990 Éditions Laterza (Rome).

Kum Kum Ray teaches history in Satyawati co-educational college, University of Delhi. Her doctoral thesis on 'The emergence of Monarchy, 8th–4th centuries BC', currently in preparation, explores the links between the emergence of political institutions and various forms of social stratification. She has an on-going interest in studying the history of women in early India, and has presented a few research papers on this theme.

Rhoda Reddock is a research fellow at the Institute of Social and Economic Research (ISER) on the St Augustine campus of the University of the West Indies. She was formerly a lecturer in Women and Development at the Institute of Social Studies at The Hague. She is working on the history of women's labour and political movements in the Caribbean and is presently collaborating on an international reader on plantation women.

Silvia Rodríguez Villamil is a historian from Montevideo, Uruguay. Coming from the field of social history, her main research interests are now focused on women in history. She has studied early women's movements in Uruguay, and the achievement of political and civil rights, as well as state policies related to women. At present she is interested mainly in women's labour and class and gender consciousness in women activists. Like Graciela Sapriza she is a researcher at GRECMU.

Graciela Sapriza is a historian and researcher in the field of social and women's History in GRECMU (a group studying the condition of women in Uruguay). In recent years she has worked on the struggles of early women's movements in Uruguay and the public policies related to women. Her current interests include the participation of women in the trade unions and politics based on life histories.

Marietta Stepaniants has been head of the division of oriental philosophies in the Institute of Philosophy, USSR Academy of Sciences in Moscow since 1980. Her main research interest is in the history of Oriental philosophy. She is the author of seven books, the latest of which is 'The Philosophy of Sufism'. Since the 1960s she has been deeply involved in the activities of the Soviet Women's Committee and participated in various national and international conferences and seminars on the status of women.

Zenebeworke Tadesse used to work for the Economic Commission for Africa in Addis Ababa, Ethiopia. She has also been involved with AAWORD, the African Association for Women's Research and Development. Ms Tadesse currently works for CODESRIA, an African research and development association based in Dakar, Senegal.

Bibliography

Books

Abdel Kader, Soha (1979), *The Status of Research on Women in the Arab Region, 1960–1978*, Paris, Unesco
—— (1987), *Egyptian Women in a Changing Society, 1899–1986*, Boulder, Col., Lynne Rienner Publishers
Acosta-Belen (ed.) (1986), *The Puerto Rican Woman*, New York, Praeger
Albers, Patricia and Beatrice Medicine (1983), *The Hidden Half: Studies of Plains Indian Women*, Washington, DC, University Press of America
Albistur, M. and D. Armogathe (1977), *Histoire de Féminisme Français*, Paris, Editions des Femmes
Al-Hibri, A. (ed.) (1982), *Women and Islam*, Oxford, Pergamon Press
Al-Masry, Youssef (1966), *Le Drame Sexuel*, Paris
Al-Torki, Soraya (1986), *Women in Saudi Arabia: Ideology and Behavior among the Elite*, New York, Columbia University Press
Andors, Phyllis (1983), *The Unfinished Liberation of Chinese Women, 1949–1980*, Bloomington, Indiana, University of Indiana Press
Arrom, Silvia (1985), *The Women of Mexico City 1790–1857*, Stanford, Calif., Stanford University Press
Atkinson, Dorothy et al. (1977), *Women in Russia*, Stanford, Calif., Stanford University Press
Awori, T. (ed.) (1972), *La Civilisation de la Femme dans la Tradition Africaine*, Paris
Badran, Margot (1986), *Harem Years: The Memoirs of an Egyptian Feminist*, London, Virago
Bay, Edna G. (ed.) (1982), *Women and Work in Africa*, Boulder, Col., Westview Press
Beck, Lois and Nikki Keddie (eds) (1978), *Women in the Muslim World*, Cambridge, Mass., Harvard University Press
Beckwith, Karen (1986), *American Women and Political Participation*, Westwood, Conn., Greenwood Press
Beddoes, Deirdre (1983), *Discovering Women's History*, London, Routledge & Kegan Paul/Pandora
Berends, A. B. (1979), *Beroepsarbeid door Vrouwen in Nederland*, 's-Gravenhage, Staatsuitgeverig

Bisilliat, Jeanne (1987), *Women of the Third World: Work and Daily Life*, Cransbury, Associated University Presses

Bjorkman, James Warner (1986), *The Changing Division of Labor in South Asia*, Riverdale, Md., Riverdale Company

Blunden, Katherine (1982), *Le Travail et le Vertu: Femmes au Foyer: Mystification de la Révolution Industrielle*, Paris

Borthwick, Meredith (1984), *The Changing Role of Women in Bengal, 1849–1905*, Princeton, NJ, Princeton University Press

Boserup, Ester (1970), *Women's Role in Economic Development*, London, George Allen & Unwin (1983, New York, St Martin's Press)

Bousquet, G. H. (1966), *L'Ethique Sexuelle de l'Islam*, Paris, Maison Neuve et Larose

Boxer, Charles (1968), *Women in Overseas Iberian Expansion*, New York, Oxford University Press

Byrne, Pamela and Suzanne R. Ontiveros (1986), *Women in the Third World. A Historical Bibliography*, Santa Barbara, Calif., ABC-CLIO

Campbell, D'Ann (1983), *Women at War with America: Private Lives in a Patriotic Era*, Cambridge, Mass., Harvard University Press

Cantor, Milton and Bruce Laurie (eds) (1977), *Class, Sex, and the Woman Worker*, Westport, Conn., Greenwood Press

Capel, Martinez, Rosa Maria (1982), *El Trabajo y la Educación de la Mujer en España (1900–1930)*, Madrid, Ministerio de Cultura

Catasus, S. et al. (1988), *Cuban Women: Changing Roles and Population Trends*, Geneva, International Labour Office

Chaki-Sircar, Manjusri (1984), *Feminism in a Traditional Society: Women of the Manipur Valley*, Delhi, Shakti Books

Chinn, Carl (1988), *They Worked All Their Lives: Women of the Urban Poor in England, 1880–1914*, Berkeley, Calif., University of California Press

Conveney, Lal, Margaret Jackson, Sheila Jeffreys, Leslie Kay and Pat Mahony (1984), *The Sexuality Papers: Male Sexuality and the Social Control of Women*, London, Hutchinson

Cott, Nancy F. (1977), *The Bonds of Womanhood: Women's Sphere in New England, 1780–1835*, New Haven, Conn., Yale University Press

Coward, R. (1983), *Patriarchal Precedents*, London, Routledge

Cutrufelli, M. R. (1983), *Women of Africa: Roots of Oppression*, London, Zed Press

Daniels, Kay and Mary Murname (1980), *Uphill All the Way: A Documentary History of Women in Australia*, St Lucia, University of Queensland Press

Davies, Margery W. (1982), *A Woman's Place is at the Typewriter: Office Workers, 1870–1930*, Philadelphia, Temple University Press

Deere, Carmen Diana (1979), *Women in Latin America*, Riverside, Latin American Perspectives

Degler, Carl (1980), *At Odds: Women and the Family in America from the Revolution to the Present*, New York, Oxford University Press

Dodgson, Elyse (1983), *Motherland*, London, Heinemann Educational

Dubisch, Jill (1986), *Gender and Power in Rural Greece*, Princeton, NJ, Princeton University Press

Duby, Georges (1981), *Le Chevalier, la Femme et le Prêtre*, Paris, Hachette

Edmundson, Linda (1983), *Feminism in Russia, 1900–1917*, London

Ehrenreich, Barbara and Deidre English (1978), *For Her Own Good: 150 Years of the Experts' Advice to Women*, Garden City, NY, Anchor

Emecheta, Buchi (1974), *Second Class Citizens, the Bride Price and the Slave Girl*, London, Allison & Busby (reprint 1976, 1977)

Erder, T. (ed.) (1985), *Family in Turkish Society*, Ankara, Turkish Social Science Association

Etienne, Mona and Eleanor Leacock (eds) (1980), *Women and Colonization: Anthropological Perspectives*, New York, Praeger

Evans, Richard (1979), *The Feminists: Women's Emancipation Movements in Europe, America and Australasia, 1840–1920*, London, Croom Helm

Farge, A. and C. Klapisch-Zuber (1984), *Madame ou Mademoiselle?, Itinéraires de la Solitude Féminine, 19–20e Siècles*, Paris, Montalba

Fernandes, Maria Patricia (1984), *Women in the Maquiladoras*

Fernea, Elizabeth (1965), *Guests of the Sheikh*, New York, Doubleday

—— and Bezirgan (1977), *Muslim Middle Eastern Women Speak*, Austin and London, University of Texas Press

Frey, Linda and Joanne Schneider (1984), *Women in Western European History: A Select Chronological, Geographical and Topical Bibliography. The Nineteenth and Twentieth Centuries*, Westport, Conn., Greenwood Press

Gamarnikow, Eva (ed.) (1983), *Gender and Work*, London, Heinemann

Giddings, Paula (1984), *When and Where I Enter: The Impact of Black Women on Race and Sex in America*, New York, Morrow

Glickman, Rose (1984), *Russian Factory Women: Workplace and Society 1880–1914*, Berkeley, Calif., University of California Press

Gorbachev, Mikhail (1986), *Political Report of the CPSU Central Committee to the 27th Party Congress*, Moscow, Novosty Press Agency

Green, Martin (1979), *The Von Richtofen Sisters [Les Soeurs Von Richtofen: Deux Ancêtres du Féminisme dans l'Allemagne de Bismarck face à Otto Gross, Max Weber, et D. H. Lawrence]*, French translation, Paris, Le Seuil

Greenwald, Maurine (1980), *Women, War and Work: the Impact of World War I on Women Workers in the United States*, Westport, Conn., Greenwood Press

Grieve, Norma and Ailsa Burns (1986), *Australian Women: New Feminist Perspectives*, Melbourne, Oxford University Press

Guilbert, M. (1966), *Les Femmes et l'Organisation Syndicale avant 1914*, Paris, Centre Nationale de la Recherche Scientifique

——, N. Lowit and M.-H. Zylberg-Hocquart (1977), *Travail et Condition Féminine*, Paris, Editions de la Courtille

Gutman, Herbert G. (1976), *The Black Family in Slavery and Freedom: 1750–1925*, Oxford, Blackwell and New York, Pantheon Books

Hafkin, Nancy J. and Edna G. Bay (eds) (1976), *African Women in Changing Perspectives*, Stanford, Calif., Stanford University Press
—— (1976), *Women in Africa: Studies in Social and Economic Change*, Stanford, Calif., Stanford University Press
Hahner, June (ed.) (1980), *Women in Latin American History, their Lives and Views*, Los Angeles, Latin America Center Publications
Hanawalt, Barbara (ed.) (1986), *Women and Work in Preindustrial Europe*, Bloomington, Ind., University of Indiana Press
Harrison, Cynthia E. (ed.) (1979, 1985), *Women in American History. A Bibliography*, Santa Barbara, Calif., ABC-CLIO
Hause, S. (1984), *Women's Suffrage in France*, Princeton, NJ, Princeton University Press
Hay, Margaret Jean and Marcia Wright (1982), *African Women and the Law: Historical Excursions and Incursions*, Boston, Mass., African Studies Center
—— and Sharon Stichter (1984), *African Women South of the Sahara*
Heinemann, Klaus (1983), *Arbeitlose Frauen: zwischen Erwerbstatigkeit und Hausfrauenrolle*, Weinheim, Beltz Verlag
Hill, Polly (1972), *Rural Hausa*, Cambridge, Cambridge University Press
Holter, Harriet (ed.) (1986), *Patriarchy in a Welfare Society*, Oslo
Honig, Emily (1986), *Sisters and Strangers: Women in the Shanghai Cotton Mills, 1919–1949*, Stanford, Calif., Stanford University Press
Horner, I. B. (1975), *Women under Primitive Buddhism*, Delhi, Motilal Banar[a]sidass
—— (1976), *Middle Length Sayings*, vol. 2, Luzac & Co.
Horowitz Murray, Janet (1982), *Strong Minded Women*, New York, Pantheon
House, William J. (1983), *Discrimination and Segregation of Women Workers in Cyprus*, Nicosia, Department of Statistics and Research
Inikori, J. E. (ed.) (1982), *Forced Migration*, London, Hutchinson
International Archief voor de Vrouwenbeweginig (1980), *Library Catalogue*, Boston, Mass., G. K. Hall
Irfan, Mohammed (1986), *The Determinants of Female Labour Force Participation in Pakistan*, Islamabad, Pakistan Institute of Development Economics
Jayawardena, Kumari (1986), *Feminism and Nationalism in the Third World*, London, Zed Press
Jensen, Joan and Sue Davidson (1984), *A Needle, A Bobbin, A Strike: Needleworkers in America*, Philadelphia, Temple University Press
John, Angela (1980), *By the Sweat of our Brow*, London, Croom Helm
Johnson, Kay Ann (1983), *Women, the Family and Peasant Revolution in China*, Chicago, University of Chicago Press
Kahhala, Omar (1982), *Most Outstanding Women in Both the Arab and Muslim World*, Damascus, Mouassassat ar-Rissala
Kessler-Harris, Alice (1982), *Out to Work: A History of Wage-Earning Women in the United States*, Oxford, Oxford University Press

Khaddoura, Zahiya Moustapha (1972), *Aicha the Mother of Believers*, Beirut, Dar Al Kitab Al-Arabi

Kleinberg, S. J. (1989), *The Shadow of the Mills: Working Class Women and the Family Economy in Pittsburgh, 1870–1907*, Pittsburgh, University of Pittsburgh Press

Knaster, Mari (1977), *Women in Spanish America: an Annotated Bibliography from Pre-conquest to Contemporary Times*, Boston, Mass., A. K. Hall

Koontz, Claudia (1987), *Mothers in the Fatherland*, London, Jonathan Cape

Kuhn, A. and A. Wolpe (1978), *Feminism and Materialism*, London, Routledge & Kegan Paul

Kung, Lydia (1983), *Factory Women in Taiwan*, Ann Arbor, Michigan, UMI Research Press

Kuper, Adam (1982), *Wives for Cattle: Bridewealth and Marriage in South Africa*, London, Routledge & Kegan Paul

Lavrin, Asuncion, *Latin American Women: Historical Perspectives*, Westport, Conn., Greenwood Press

Levy, Marie Françoise (1984), *De Mères en Filles: l'Education des Françaises 1850–1880*, Paris, Oalman Levy

Lewis, Jane (1983), *Women's Welfare, Women's Rights*, London, Croom Helm

—— (1984), *Women in England, 1870–1950*, Brighton, Wheatsheaf Books and Bloomington, Ind., Indiana University Press

—— (ed.) (1986), *Labour and Love*, Oxford, Blackwell

Leydesdorff, Selma (1977), *Verborgen Arbeid, Vergeten Arbeid*, Amsterdam, Assen

Liddington, J. and J. Norris (1978), *One Hand Tied Behind Us: the Rise of the Women's Suffrage Movement*, London, Virago

London Feminist History Group (1983), *The Sexual Dynamics of History: Men's Power, Women's Resistance*, London, Pluto Press

Loraux, N. (1981), *Les Enfants d'Athéna*, Paris

Lougee, Carol (1976), *Le Paradis des Femmes*, Princeton, NJ, Princeton University Press

Macias, Anna (1982), *Against All Odds: The Feminist Movement in Mexico to 1940*, Westport, Conn., Greenwood Press

McKenna, Joanna (1975), *Great Women of the Ancient Middle East*, Cleveland, Ohio, Cleveland Association of Arab Americans

Maher, Vanessa (1975), *Women and Property in Morocco*, Cambridge, Cambridge University Press

Makhlouf, Carla (1979), *Changing Veils: Women and Modernization in North Yemen*, Austin, University of Texas Press

Martinez Alier, Verena (1974), *Marriage, Class and Colour in Nineteenth Century Cuba*, Cambridge, Cambridge University Press

Martin-Fugier, Anne (1983), *La Bourgeoise: Femme au Temps de Paul Bourget*, Paris, Grasset

Matthews, Basil (1953), *Crisis in the West Indian Family*, Port of Spain

Matthews, Jill Julius (1984), *Good and Mad Women: The Historical Construction of Femininity in Twentieth-Century Australia*, Sydney and London, Allen & Unwin (reprint 1985)

Mba, Nina (1982), *Nigerian Women Mobilised: Women's Political Activity in Southern Nigeria, 1900–1965*, Berkeley, Calif., University of California Press

Meillassoux, Claude (1981), *Maidens, Meal and Money: Capitalism and the Domestic Economy*, Cambridge, Cambridge University Press

Melman, Billie (1988), *Women and the Popular Imagination in the Twenties*, Basingstoke, Macmillan

Mernissi, Fatima (1985), *Beyond the Veil*, London, Al Saqi

Michaud, Stephane, *La Muse et la Madone: Visages de la Femme Rédemptrice en France et en Allemagne de Novalis à Baudelaire*, Paris, Seuil

Miller Orkin, Susan (1979), *Women in Western Political Thought*, Princeton, NJ, Princeton University Press

Mitchell, Juliet (1974), *Psychoanalysis and Feminism*, London, Allen Lane

—— and Jacqueline Rose (1982), *Feminine Sexuality: Jacques Lacan and the Ecole Freudienne*, London, Macmillan

Moreau, Thérèse (1982), *Le Sang de l'Histoire, Michelet, l'Histoire et l'Idée de la Femme au 19e Siècle*, Paris, Flammarion

Mumtaz Khawar and Farida Shaheed (1987), *Women of Pakistan*, London, Zed Press

Nandy, Ashish (1985), *The Intimate Enemy*, Oxford, Oxford University Press

Nash, June and Helen Safa (1980), *Sex and Class in Latin America*, 2nd edn, Amherst, Mass., J. F. Bergin Publishers

Oakley, Ann (1972), *Sex, Gender and Society*, New York, Harper & Row

Obbo, Christine (1980), *African Women: Their Struggle for Independence*, London, Zed Press

Ogunseye, A. et al. (eds) (1976), *Women and Development in Relation to Changing Family Structure*, Lagos, Ford Foundation

Omvedt, Gail (1981), *Effects of Agricultural Development on the Status of Women*, Mahabeleshwar, India, International Labour Office

Paulme, Denise (ed.) (1971), *Women of Tropical Africa*

Perrot, Michelle (ed.) (n.d.), *Travaux de Femmes dans la France du 19e Siècle*

—— (ed.) (1984), *Une Histoire des Femmes, est-elle Possible?*, Paris, Rivage

Pescatello, Ann (1973), *Male and Female in Latin America*, Pittsburgh, University of Pittsburgh Press

—— (1976), *Power and Pawn: the Female in Iberian Families, Societies and Cultures*, Westport, Conn., Greenwood Press

Pierson, Ruth Roach (1983), *Canadian Women and the Second World War*, Ottawa, Canadian Historical Association

Quataert, J. (1979), *Reluctant Feminists in German Social Democracy, 1885–1917*, Princeton, NJ, Princeton University Press

Riley, Denise (1983), *War in the Nursery: Theories of the Child and Mother*, London, Virago

Riley, Glenda (1984), *Women and Indians on the Frontier, 1825–1914*, Albuquerque, University of New Mexico Press

Roberts, Elizabeth (1984), *A Woman's Place*, Oxford, Blackwell

Robertson, Claire and Iris Berger (eds) (1984), *Women and Class Hierarchies: African Perspectives*, New York, Holmes and Meier

Robertson, Claire and Martin A. Klein (eds) (1983), *Women and Slavery in Africa*, Madison, Wis., University of Wisconsin Press

Robins-Mowry, D. (1983), *The Hidden Sun. Women of Modern Japan*, Boulder, Col., University of Colorado Press

Rogers, Barbara (1981), *The Domestication of Women: Discrimination in Developing Societies*, London, Tavistock Publications

Rosaldo, Michele Zimbalist and Louis Lampere (eds) (1974), *Women, Culture and Society*, Stanford, Calif., Stanford University Press

Rossanda, Rossana (1979), *Le Altre*

Rowbotham, Sheila (1973), *Hidden from History*, London, Pluto Press

Ruis, Vicki (1987), *Cannery Women, Cannery Lives: Mexican Women, Unionization and the Californian Food Processing Industry, 1930–1950*, Albuquerque, New Mexico, University of New Mexico Press

Ryan, Mary P. (1982), *The Empire of the Mother: American Writing about Domesticity, 1820–1860*, New York, Institute for Historical Research

Saadaw, Nawal (1979), *The Hidden Face of Eve*, London, Zed Press

Schubert, Friedel (1980), *Die Frau in der DDR*, Apladen, Leske und Budrich

Sharma, R. S. (1980), *Perspectives in the Social and Economic History of Early India*, New Delhi, Munshiram Manoharlal

—— (1980), *Sudras in Ancient India*, Delhi, Motilal Banarasidass

Shorter, Frederick C. and Huda Zurayk (eds) (1985), *Population Factors in Development Planning in the Middle East*, New York and Cairo, Population Council

Sicherman, Barbara, William Monter, Joan Scott and Kathryn Sklar (1981), *Recent United States Scholarship on the History of Women*, Washington, DC, American Historical Association

Sievers, Sharon, *Flowers in the Salt: The Beginnings of Feminist Consciousness in Japan*, Stanford, Calif., Stanford University Press

Silva, Manuela (1984), *The Employment of Women in Portugal*, Luxembourg

Siu, Bobby (1982), *Women of China: Imperialism and Women's Resistance, 1900–1949*, London, Zed Press

Smith, Bonnie G. (1981), *The Ladies of the Leisure Class: the Bourgeoises of Northern France in the Nineteenth Century*, Princeton, NJ, Princeton University Press

Smith, R. J. and E. L. Wiswell (1983), *The Women of Suye Mora*, Chicago, University of Chicago Press

Snitow, Ann, Christine Stansell and Sharon Thompson (eds) (1983), *Powers of Desire: the Politics of Sexuality*, New York, Monthly Review Press

374

Sowerwine, C. (1982), *Sisters or Citizens? Women and Socialism in France since 1876*, Cambridge, Cambridge University Press

Steady, F. C. (1981), *The Black Woman Cross Culturally*, New York, Schenkman

Steedman, Carolyn (1982), *The Tidy House: Little Girls Writing*, London, Virago

Sterling, Dorthy (ed.) (1984), *We Are Your Sisters: Black Women in the Nineteenth Century*, New York, W. W. Morrow

Stetson, Dorothy (1987), *Women's Rights in France*, Westport, Conn., Greenwood Press

Taylor, Eve (1983), *Eve and the New Jerusalem*, London, Virago

Tejeira, Otilia de (1974), *The Women in Latin America: Past, Present, Future*, Washington, DC, Organization of American States Inter-American Commission of Women

Tillion, Germain (1966), *Le Harem et les Cousins*, Paris

Tilly, Louise and Joan Scott (1978, 1987), *Women, Work and Family*, New York, Holt, Rinehart & Winston; London, Methuen

Transgaard, Henning (1981), *An Analysis of Danish Sex-Linked Attitudes*, Copenhagen

Trofimenkoff, Susan Mann and Alison Prentice (1977–1985), *The Neglected Majority*, Toronto, McClelland & Stewart

Tucker, Judith (1985), *Women in the Nineteenth Century in Egypt*, Cambridge, Cambridge University Press

Vicinus, Martha (1985), *Independent Women: Work and Community for Single Women*, London, Virago

Vitale, Luis (1981), *Historia y Sociologia de la Mujer Latinoamericana*, Barcelona, Fontamara

Walker, Cheryl (1982), *Women and Resistance in South Africa*, London, Onyx Press

Walkowitz, Judith (1980), *Prostitution and Victorian Society*, Cambridge, Cambridge University Press

Wallman, Sandra (ed.) (1979), *Social Anthropology of Work*, ASA Monograph 19, New York, Academic Press

Weeks, Jeffrey (1985), *Sexuality and its Discontents. Meanings, Myths and Modern Sexualities*, London, Routledge & Kegan Paul

Weiland, Daniela (1983), *Geschichte der Frauenemanzipation in Deutschland und Österreich*, Düsseldorf, Econ-Taschbuch Verlag

Weiner, A. B. (1976), *Women of Value, Men of Renown. New Perspectives in Trobriand Exchange*, Austin and London, University of Texas Press

Wikan, Unni (1980), *Life Among the Poor in Cairo*, London, Tavistock

Wilson, Amrit (1978), *Finding a Voice: Asian Women in Britain*, London, Virago

Windschuttle, Elizabeth (ed.) (1980), *Women, Class and History: Feminist Perspectives on Australia, 1788–1978*, Australia, Fontana/Collins

Young, Kate, Carol Walkowitz and Roslyn McCullagh (eds) (1981), *Of Marriage and the Market*, London, Routledge & Kegan Paul

Young, Kate (ed.) (1988), *Women and Economic Development: Local, Regional and National Planning Strategies*, Oxford and Paris, Berg/Unesco

Young, Michael and Peter Willmott (1973), *The Symmetrical Family*, New York, Pantheon

Articles

Al-Torki, Soraya (1977), 'Family organization and women's power in urban Saudi Arabian society', *Journal of Anthropological Research*, 33, pp. 277–87

Badran, Margot (1979), 'Middle East and North African women', *Trends in History: a Review of Current Periodical Literature in History*, 1 (1), pp. 123–9

Blom, Ida (1980), 'The struggle for women's suffrage in Norway 1885–1913', *Scandinavian Journal of History*, 8 (1), pp. 3–22

Bohmer, Carol (1980), 'Modernization, divorce and the status of women: le tribunal coutumier in Bobo-dioulasso', *African Studies Review*, 34 (2)

Bornat, Joanna (1978), 'History and work: a new context for trade union history', *Radical America*, 12, Sept-Oct

Breen, William J. (1978), 'Black women and the great war: mobilization and reform in the south', *Journal of Southern History*, 44, August, pp. 421–40

Brenner, J. and M. Ramas (1984), 'Rethinking women's oppression', *New Left Review*, 44

Burkett, Elinor (1977), 'In dubious sisterhood: class and sex in Spanish colonial America', *Women and Class Struggle: Latin American Perspectives*, 4

Carmagnani, Marcello (1985), 'The inertia of Clio: the social history of colonial Mexico', *Latin American Research Review*, 21 (1), pp. 7–72

Chakravarti, Uma (1983), 'The development of the Sita myth: a case study of women in myth and literature', *Samya Shakti*, 1 (1), pp. 68–75

—— (1984), 'The rise of Buddhism as experienced by women', *Manushi*, 8

—— (1985), 'Women in servitude and bondage; the a'grihinis of ancient India', *Teaching Politics*, 11 (2), pp. 61–73

Craig, Susan (1979), 'Millstones or milestones', *Latin American Research Review*, 14, 3

Davidoff, Leonore (1979), 'Class and gender in Victorian England', *Feminist Studies*, 5 (1) Spring

Davin, Anna (1978), 'Imperialism and motherhood', *History Workshop Journal*, 5, Spring

Davis, Madeline and Elizabeth Lapovsky Kennedy (1986), 'Oral history and the study of sexuality in the lesbian community: Buffalo, New York, 1940–1960', *Feminist Studies*, 12(1), Spring

Davis, N. Z. (1976), 'Women's history in transition: the European case', *Feminist Studies*, 3

Deacon, Desley (1985), 'Political arithmetic: the nineteenth-century Australian census and the construction of the dependent woman', *Signs*, 11, Autumn

Denzer, Laray (1976), 'Towards a study of the history of West African Women's participation in nationalist politics: the early phase 1935–1950', *Africana Research Bulletin*, 6 (4), pp. 65–85

El-Guindy, Fadwa (1983), 'Veiled activism', *Femmes de la Méditerranée: peuples méditerranéens*, 22–3, January-June

Emeagwali, G. T. (1980), 'Explanations in African history', *Journal of the Historical Society of Nigeria*, 10 (3), pp. 95–110

Farge, Arlette (1983), 'Dix ans d'histoire des femmes en France', *Le Débat*

Ferdow, Adele K. (1983), 'Women and the Islamic revolution', *International Journal of Middle East Studies*, 15, pp. 283–98

Gaitskell, Deborah, Judith Kimble, Moira Maconachie and Elaine Unterhalter (1984), 'Class, race and gender: domestic workers in South Africa', *Review of African Political Economy*, 27/28

Garcia, Mario T. (1980), 'The Chicana in American history: the Mexican women of El Paso, 1880–1920: a case study', *Pacific Historical Review*, 49, May, pp. 315–38

Guyer, Jane (1981), 'Household and community in African studies', *African Studies Review*, 24 (2–3), pp. 87–137

Hakim, Catherine (1980), 'Census reports as documentary evidence: the census commentaries 1801–1951', *Sociological Review*, 28

Hartman, Heidi (1979), 'The unhappy marriage of marxism and feminism: towards a more progressive union', *Capital and Class*, 8

Henry, Frances (1975), 'The status of women in Caribbean societies: an overview of their social, economic and sexual roles', *Social and Economic Studies*, 24, June

Higman, Barry (1975), 'The slave family and household in the British West Indies, 1800–1834', *Journal of Interdisciplinary History*, 6 (2)

—— (1978), 'Household structure and fertility on Jamaican slave plantations', *Population Studies*, 27

Humphries, Jane (1977), 'Class struggle and persistence of the working class family', *Cambridge Journal of Economics*, 1

Hunter, Janet (1988), 'Women in the Japanese economy of the 1920s and 1930s', London School of Economics, ST/ICERD Discussion Paper

Jacoby, Robin Miller (1976), 'The Women's Trade Union League and American Feminism', *Feminist Studies*, 3, pp. 126–40

Johnson, Cheryl (1982), 'Grassroots organising: women in anti-colonial activity in South Western Nigeria', *African Studies Review*, 25 (2–3), pp. 137–58

Jones, Jacqueline (1982), 'My mother was much of a woman: black women, work and the family under slavery', *Feminist Studies*, 8, Summer

Kaluzinski, Eva (1980), 'Wiping the floor with theory', *Feminist Review*

Kandel, Liliane (1980), 'L'Explosion de la presse féministe', *Le Débat*, 1, May

Kanner, Barbara and Olwen Hufton (1983), 'Review article', *Past and Present*, 101

Kaplan, Temma (1982), 'Female consciousness and collective action: the case of Barcelona, 1910–18', *Signs*, 7

Keddie, Nikki (1979), 'Problems in the study of Middle Eastern women', *International Journal of Middle East Studies*, 10, April, pp. 225–40

Kelly-Gadol, Joan (1976), 'The social relations of the sexes: methodological implications for women's history', *Signs*, 1 (4), Summer

Khaster, Mari (1976), 'Women in Latin America: the state of research, 1975', *Latin American Research Review*, 11, Spring, pp. 3–74

Kleinberg, S. J. (1976), 'Technology and women's work', *Labor History*, 17

Koontz, C. (1976), 'Nazi women before emancipation', *Social Science Quarterly*, 56

Lambertz, Jan (1985), 'Sexual harrassment in the nineteenth-century English cotton industry', *History Workshop Journal*, 19, Spring

Lavrin, Ascunción (n.d.), 'Recent studies on women in Latin America', *Latin American Research Review*, 19 (1), pp. 181–90

—— and Edith Coutourier (1979), 'Dowries and wills: a view of women's socio-economic role in Guadalajara and Puebla 1640–1790', *Hispanic American Historical Review*, 59, May, pp. 280–304

Leydesdorff, S. (1984), 'In search of the picture — Jewish proletarians in Amsterdam between the two wars', *Dutch Jewish History*, Jerusalem, pp. 315–35

Lonsdale, John (1981), 'States and social processes in Africa: a historio-graphical survey', *African Studies Review*, 24

McCarthy, J. (1979), 'Age, family and migration in nineteenth-century Black Sea provinces of the Ottoman empire', *International Journal of Middle East Studies*, 10, pp. 309–23

Man, Krish, 'The dangers of dependence: Christian marriage among elite women in Lagos Colony 1880–1915', *Journal of African History*, 24

Mani, Lata (1986), 'Production of an official discourse on sati in early nineteenth century Bengal', *Economic and Political Weekly*, 21 (17), 26 April

Martin, Biddy (1982), 'Feminism, Criticism and Foucault', *New German Critique*, 27

Mason, T. (1976), 'Women in Nazi Germany', *History Workshop*, 1 and 2

Mathurin, Lucille, 'Reluctant matriarchs', *Savacou*, 13

Mernissi, Fatima (1977), 'Women, saints and sanctuaries', *Signs*, 3, pp. 101–12

Papaneck, Hanna (1975), 'The work of women: postscript from Mexico City', *Signs*, 1 (1), Autumn

Passerini, Luisa (1979), 'Work ideology and consensus under Italian fascism', *History Workshop Journal*, 8, Autumn

Patterson, Orlando (1982), 'Recent studies on Caribbean slavery and the Atlantic slave trade', *Latin American Research Review*

Perrot, M. (1981), 'Sur l'Histoire des femmes en France', *Revue du Nord*, 63
—— (1984), 'Sur le Front des sexes: un combat douteux', *Vingtième Siècle*, 3, July

Pescatello, Ann (1973), 'The female in Ibero-America: an essay on research bibliography and recent directions', *Latin American Research Review*, 7, Summer, pp. 121–41

Pleck, Elizabeth H. (1972), 'The two-parent household: black family structure in late nineteenth century Boston', *Journal of Social History*, 4

Rapp, Rayna, Ellen Ross and Renate Bridenthal (1979), 'Examining family history', *Feminist Studies*, 5 (1), Spring

Riley, Denise (1981), 'The free mothers: pronatalism and working mothers in industry at the end of the last war in Britain', *History Workshop Journal*, 11, Spring

Roberts, Richard (1984), 'Women's work and women's property: household social relations in the Maraka textile industry of the nineteenth century', *Comparative Studies in Social and Economic History*, 26 (2), pp. 229–50

Ross, Ellen (1982), 'Fierce questions and taunts: married life in working-class London 1870–1914', *Feminist Studies*, 8 (3), Autumn
—— (1985), 'Not the sort that would sit on the doorstep: respectability in pre-WW1 London neighbourhoods', *International Labour and Working-Class History*, 27, Spring
—— and Rayna Rapp (1981), 'Sex and society: a research note from social history and anthropology', *Comparative Studies in Society and History*, 23 (1), January

Saleh, Saneya (1972), 'Women in Islam: their role in religious and traditional culture', *International Journal of Sociology of the Family*, 2, September, pp. 35–42

Scott, Joan (1983), 'Survey article: women in history', *Past and Present*, 101, November

Seni, N. (1984), 'Ville ottomane et représentation du corps féminin', *Les Temps Modernes*, no. 45–7, July-August

Sharma, Ursula M. (1978), 'Women and their affines: the veil as a symbol of separation', *Man: Journal of the Royal Anthropological Institute* (London), new series 13, pp. 218–33

Smith, Bonnie G. (1984), 'The contribution of women to modern historiography', *American Historical Review*, 89

Smith-Rosenberg, Carroll (1975), 'The female world of love and ritual', *Signs*, 1

Snell, K. D. M. (1981), 'Agricultural seasonal unemployment: the standard of living and women's work in the south and east, 1690–1868', *Economic History Review*, 34

Soeiro, Susan (1975), 'Recent work on Latin American women: a review essay', *Journal of Inter-American Studies and World Affairs*, 17, November, pp. 497–516

Solein, Nancy (1960), 'Household and family in the Caribbean: some definitions and concepts', *Social and Economic Studies*, 9 (1)

Strobel, Margaret (1982), 'African women: review essay', *Signs*, 8

Tonkin, Elizabeth (1982), 'Steps to the redefinition of oral history: examples from Africa', *Social History*, October, pp. 329–35

Tucker, Judith (1983), 'Problems in the historiography of women in the Middle East: the case of nineteenth century Egypt', *International Journal of Middle Eastern Studies*, 15

van Allen, Judith (1972), '"Sitting on a man": colonialism and the lost political institutions of Igbo women', *Canadian Journal of African Studies*, 6 (2), pp. 165–81

Van Dusen, Roxanne (1976), 'The study of women in the Middle East: some thoughts', *Middle East Studies Association Bulletin*, 10, pp. 1–20

Welter, Barbara (1966), 'The Cult of True Womanhood', *American Quarterly*, 18

Wright, Marcia (1975), 'Women in peril: a commentary upon life stories of captives in nineteenth century East-Central Africa', *African Social Research*

Wright, Sue (1978), 'Prattle and politics: the position of women in Doshman-Ziari', *Journal of the Anthropological Society of Oxford*, 9, pp. 98–112